W9-CMK-309

Mere Civility

MERE CIVILITY

Disagreement and the Limits of Toleration

TERESA M. BEJAN

Harvard University Press

CAMBRIDGE, MASSACHUSETTS

LONDON, ENGLAND

2017

Copyright © 2017 by the President and Fellows of Harvard College
All rights reserved
Printed in the United States of America

First printing

Library of Congress Cataloging-in-Publication Data
Names: Bejan, Teresa M., 1984– author.
Title: Mere civility : disagreement and the limits of toleration / Teresa M. Bejan.
Description: Cambridge, Massachusetts : Harvard University Press, 2017. | Based on the
author's thesis (Ph. D.— Yale University, 2013). | Includes bibliographical references and index.
Identifiers: LCCN 2016021054 | ISBN 9780674545496
Subjects: LCSH: Courtesy— Political aspects. | Toleration— Political aspects. | Discussion—
Political aspects. | Freedom of speech. | Forums (Discussion and debate)— History.
Classification: LCC BJ1533.C9 B45 2017 | DDC 177/.1— dc23
LC record available at https://lccn.loc.gov/2016021054

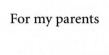

For my parents

CONTENTS

Citations and Abbreviations

The major works of Roger Williams, Thomas Hobbes, and John Locke are cited frequently in the following chapters. Full bibliographical details can be found in the references, but the following abbreviations will be used for citations in the text, followed by page number, (except where otherwise noted).

Williams

Key   Roger Williams, *A Key into the Language of America* (1643) in Vol. 1 of *The Complete Writings of Roger Williams,* ed. Perry Miller. New York: Russell & Russell, 1963.

BT   Roger Williams, *The Bloudy Tenent of Persecution for Cause of Conscience* (1644) in Vol. 3 of *The Complete Writings of Roger Williams.* New York: Russell & Russell, 1963.

YMB   Roger Williams, *The Bloody Tenent Yet More Bloody* (1652) in Vol. 4 of *The Complete Writings of Roger Williams.* New York: Russell & Russell, 1963.

GF   Roger Williams, *George Fox Digg'd Out His Burrowes* (1676) in Vol. 5 of *The Complete Writings of Roger Williams.* New York: Russell & Russell, 1963.

Hobbes

EL   Thomas Hobbes, *The Elements of Law, Natural and Politic* (1640), ed. J. C. A. Gaskin. Oxford: Oxford University Press, 2008.

DC   Thomas Hobbes, *De Cive* (1642), ed. Richard Tuck and trans. Michael Silverthorne. Cambridge, UK: Cambridge University Press, 1998.

L   Thomas Hobbes, *Leviathan* (1651), ed. Noel Malcolm. Oxford, UK: Oxford University Press, 2012. Parenthetical citations include the volume, chapter, and page numbers.

B   Thomas Hobbes, *Behemoth, or the Long Parliament* (1681), ed. S. Holmes. Chicago: University of Chicago Press, 1990.

Locke

FT and ST   John Locke, "First Tract of Government" (1660) and "Second Tract of Government" (c. 1662) in *Locke: Political Essays*, ed. M. Goldie. Cambridge, UK: Cambridge University Press, 1990.

LCT and ECT   John Locke, "A Letter Concerning Toleration" (1689) and "An Essay Concerning Toleration" (1667) in *A Letter Concerning Toleration and Other Writings*, ed. M. Goldie. Indianapolis, IN: Liberty Fund, 2010.

SL and TL   John Locke, "A Second Letter Concerning Toleration" (1690) and "A Third Letter for Toleration" (1692) in vol. 5 of *The Works of John Locke*. London: Rivington, 1824.

STCE   John Locke, "Some Thoughts Concerning Education" (1693) in *Some Thoughts Concerning Education and Of the Conduct of the Understanding*, ed. R. Grant and N. Tarcov. Indianapolis: Hackett, 1996.

Mere Civility

People who expect deference resent mere civility.

—MASON COOLEY, *City Aphorisms* (1990)

Introduction

Wars of Words

Empowered by faith, consistently, prayerfully, we need to find our way back to civility. That begins with stepping out of our comfort zones in an effort to bridge divisions . . . stretching out of our dogmas, our prescribed roles along the political spectrum. . . . Civility also requires relearning how to disagree without being disagreeable.

—BARACK OBAMA, *Remarks at the National Prayer Breakfast* (2010)

TODAY, POLITICIANS AND PUBLIC INTELLECTUALS across the political spectrum warn that we face a crisis of civility, a veritable war of words that distorts our public discourse, threatens our democracy, and penetrates the deepest reaches of our private lives.[1] Controversies over whether universities should tolerate the uncivil speech of students or professors appear as only the latest outbreak in an epidemic, the inflammatory effects of which can be felt from the halls of the Ivory Tower to the partisan swamps of Washington, in the nation's pulpits and its neighborhood streets, and in the scorched earth exchanges passing for debate in the media and online, above all. The rich metaphorical language used to describe our predicament conveys a danger deeper than poor manners. Words wound, rhetorical heat fans the flames, and vitriol corrodes the affective bonds between citizens. Incivility infects the body politic as a source of creeping social discord and decay. When wars of words rage unchecked, it suggests, can wars of swords be far behind?

Whereas a decade ago, talk of a "civility crisis" focused on the decline of civic solidarity and social capital,[2] this twenty-first-century crisis focuses instead on how individuals speak to each other and, more particularly, how they *disagree*.[3] Although its primary site is politics,[4] the sense of crisis extends well beyond the increasingly partisan and polarized tenor of democratic debate to religion, education, and areas of broader social and cultural

1

concern. Parallel controversies about hate speech and religious insult in Europe confirm that heated and hateful disagreements are not exclusively American afflictions.[5] Still, across the United States, a plethora of centers, initiatives, and scholarly programs have emerged dedicated to the study of civility as a matter of pressing domestic concern.[6] This is only fitting, as universities themselves have become ground zero in the latest crisis, with rising protests against hate speech and "microaggressions" on college campuses issuing in calls for "safe spaces" to protect students from expressions of contempt, whether subtle or overt.[7]

Wars of words, it seems, are catching. On the surface, "eliminationist" political rhetoric, religious insult, and hate speech may seem to have little in common; however, these species of incivility are closely connected. As forms of "verbal violence,"[8] they all arise in the context of disagreements we consider to be *fundamental*—to our worldviews, as well as to our personal and social identities. One does not discuss religion or politics at the dinner table because these are the commitments that people really *disagree* about, and those disagreements become heated and hateful because we define ourselves and our opponents in the controversy.[9] These questions of believing and belonging go straight to the heart of how we see the world—and each other. Whether in politics, religion, or the ideological and identitarian hothouses of academia, the fears underlying declarations of a crisis of civility are the same: that even when they do not bring us to blows, our uncivil disagreements will exacerbate our fundamental differences and push us farther and farther apart.

This fear is not without foundation. Since the 1970s, ideology and partisan identity have outstripped race as the lines along which Americans divide themselves, both socially and geographically. The retreat of academics into like-minded disciplines and of students on campus into activist enclaves reflects a similar trend of ideological "sorting" and polarization on the micro level.[10] Given the ubiquity of claims that rising incivility is to blame for this trend, however, the causal evidence is surprisingly anecdotal.[11] Recent work using survey data and content analyses of news reports has demonstrated that the *perception* of a crisis of "rude" and "nasty" politics in the United States has been on the rise since the 1980s. Still, without a clear baseline scholars are generally overhasty in drawing conclusions about the underlying realities or long-term trends.[12] As some more skeptical commentators note, periodic *cris de coeur* about a loss of civility have been a more or less permanent feature of the American political landscape since the earliest days of the Republic. As uncivil as our language may be in an election year, modern Americans are (we hope) still a long way from canings on the Senate floor or the regular riots, insurrectionary protests, and mob politics of other periods in our history.[13]

This civility-skepticism is healthy, but it also misses the point. It doesn't really matter whether incivility is, in fact, on the rise, because the "crisis" of civility is identical with the growing perception that there *is* such a crisis and that something must be done. But what? The solution seized upon by political practitioners and theorists alike has been "more civility." In societies committed to free expression, this consummately liberal virtue would seem the only plausible restraint—and a largely uncontroversial one. Not only did Obama's predecessor, George W. Bush, make the need for civility a central theme of his first inaugural address,[14] Michael Sandel dubbed civility "an overrated virtue" over twenty years ago precisely because it *is* so uncontroversial, and "democratic politics, properly conducted, [should be] filled with controversy."[15]

Endorsed by so many, in such different places and times, one might be forgiven again for thinking the current crisis much ado about very little. Calls for civility can often sound more like whining about the ordinary dirtiness of politics, while accusations of incivility have proven to be an effective, if cynical, strategy for scoring points against one's political opponents.[16] Even so, many political theorists such as Jeremy Waldron and even Sandel now insist that the harms caused by certain forms of egregiously uncivil speech are so severe that they require more than encomia to conversational virtue. Specifically, the damage done by hate speech, religious insult, and other forms of "group libel" to vulnerable groups and individuals, as well as to society at large, is significant enough that these forms of incivility should be banned outright.[17]

While the hate speech laws defended by Waldron offer the clearest example of efforts to restore and maintain civility through legislation, speech codes on college campuses provide another. As Jacob Levy has argued, private organizations like universities or churches often have compelling interests in regulating the speech of their members to which the free speech protections applicable in public spaces and institutions do not apply. While they may not be "laws" in the fullest sense of being authoritative enactments by the state, the internal rules and sanctions imposed by non-state institutions nevertheless have legal standing.[18] For instance, a student expelled from a university for violating its speech code, like a person excommunicated from a church, cannot appeal to the state for readmission. And since the 1990s, these codes have been formulated increasingly in the language of civility as a standard of conversational decorum applied to students and professors alike.[19] Thus, while they may at first seem quite different, hate speech laws and speech codes are of a piece. Both proceed on the shared assumption that standards of (un)civil speech can be articulated in the form of general rules that can, in turn, be reliably and impartially enforced.[20]

This is, of course, precisely what opponents of such legislation dispute, even many who share the goal of a "more civil" public discourse. In matters of civility, they insist, not only is unequal enforcement inevitable, but the voices most critical of the status quo will necessarily be the hardest hit. The result is a "chilling effect" on public debate, one that dooms the possibility of fundamental, yet civil, disagreement that the proponents of legislation sought to safeguard in the first place. Civility may well be a worthy goal, even an essential virtue. But under the banner of "free speech," these critics view all attempts at enforcement with profound suspicion.

In debating these questions, commentators on both sides often assume that the current crisis of civility is unprecedented, the product of technologi-cal, social, and cultural transformations unique to the modern world. One often hears that the Internet is to blame, along with other forms of mass media associated with modern, mass democracies.[21] Yet concerns about the propensity of fundamental disagreements to become heated and hateful have an ancient pedigree. In Plato's *Euthyphro*, Socrates complained that differences of opinion about "the just and the unjust, the noble and shame-ful, and good and bad" made for "quarrels," "enmity," and "anger" between the gods as well as men.[22] The word *polemic* itself derives from the Greek word for war, and Roman writers on rhetoric would regularly counsel con-versationalists to avoid the insults and violent expressions characteristic of *pugna verborum* or "the battle of words."[23] Such concerns about uncivil dis-agreement were not exclusive to the West. Issued in India in the third centu-ry BCE, the edicts of the Mauryan Emperor Asoka enjoined religious sects to exercise "control of one's speech" and to "honor" each other's doctrines for the sake of social harmony.[24]

These long-standing anxieties about uncivil disagreement rose to new prominence in Western Europe after the Reformation, when—with the help of that recent advancement in communications technology, the printing press—Protestants and Catholics began to broadcast their polemics far and wide and hurl insults at each other at an alarming rate. The ease and abundance of printed material, along with new (if sporadic) attention to popular literacy through the Protestant emphasis on *sola scriptura* and biblical translation, meant that theological controversies hitherto the province of elites became irreversibly democratized.[25] Democratization was accompanied, in turn, by increasing ideological division, insulting invective, and sectarian splintering that, from the standpoint of our contemporary crisis of civility, can look surprisingly familiar. Indeed, many of the religious labels (literally, denominations) that appear entirely uncontroversial to us today—including Protestant, Baptist, Puritan, and Quaker—actually began in this period as pejoratives capable of deeply wounding a believer's "tender conscience."[26] In sixteenth- and seventeenth-century England, this was understood specifically as a crisis of *civility*, and as this book will show, participants on all sides of the ongoing debates about religious toleration in this period would appeal to the concept in familiar ways—both as the norms of respectful behavior or "civil worship" governing social interactions and as a conversational virtue reflecting one's willingness to observe these rules, especially in disagreement with others.[27]

In the midst of this increasingly vitriolic war of words, fears that uncivil religious disagreements and so-called "persecution of the tongue" might sever forever the *vinculum societatis* ("bond of society") of true religion and Christian charity quickly spread. Much like today's so-called "civilitarians,"[28] many early modern European writers were deeply concerned about the war of words and struggled to find a solution. *Eirenic* thinkers (from the Greek word for peace) hoped that by talking to each other through persuasion, not polemic, religious opponents could be brought to acknowledge a consensus on the *fundamenta* or fundamentals of Christianity deeper than their differences. Some, like Erasmus, even endorsed legislative solutions. Chapter 1 will discuss these efforts, along with other attempts to impose a civil silence on controversial questions by banning "any discourse about Religion, for fear of falling out."[29] The Peace of Augsburg (1555) imposed a similar gag order on religious discussions on pain of death—a penalty the French legal and political philosopher Jean Bodin would note with approval.[30]

Still, in their efforts to combat uncivil disagreements other early modern thinkers proposed to cast the net more narrowly by passing laws targeting persecution of the tongue, in particular. Today, many scholars assume that laws against hate speech emerged only in the twentieth century in response to the horrors of the Holocaust and modern mass genocide. Yet Chapter 1 will show that religious insult statutes akin to modern hate speech laws were enacted after the Reformation in *both* the officially intolerant societies of the Old World and many colonies committed to toleration in the New.[31] Although scholars have consistently overlooked them, these institutional efforts to address uncivil disagreement through discussion bans, speech codes, and other forms of civilitarian legislation were an important part of early modern debates about religious toleration, both in England and her American colonies. As such, they represent a crucial—if forgotten—aspect of the political and legal context in which canonical figures in the history of political thought, such as Thomas Hobbes and John Locke, and important early defenders of toleration like Roger Williams, the founder of Rhode Island, thought and wrote.

For thinkers then, as now, determining what civility required could be complicated. Some restraint on the war of words seemed surely necessary to make the proliferating fundamental disagreements tolerable. And yet the prosecution of incivility was often difficult to distinguish from persecution—as paradigmatically "uncivil" groups like the early Quakers, American Indians, and English Catholics soon discovered.[32] How early modern thinkers like Williams, Hobbes, and Locke conceived of civility, and how they proposed to enforce it, was thus closely tied to how they envisioned a tolerant society, both in its perils and its possibilities. Recovering the theological and legal context in which they worked through these problems is thus imperative for understanding their influential theories of toleration, as well as the vastly different institutional and ethical forms they took. Moreover, this book will argue that doing so can also shed considerable light on the growing perception of a civility crisis afflicting our own tolerant society today.

Modern calls for civility, whether in politics or religion, reflect concerns about the corrosive effects of uncivil disagreement on social bonds and tender consciences very similar to those in the seventeenth century. These appeals suggest that if only we could get the *manner* right, the very practice of disagreement itself might work to harmonize our fundamental differences, thus making it possible for us to regard one another across those differences not as enemies, but friends.

In *The Harm in Hate Speech,* Jeremy Waldron puts the question thus: "Is a tolerant society just a society free from . . . persecution, or is it a society in which people cohabit and deal with one another, in spite of their . . .

differences, in an atmosphere of civility and respect?"[33] For Waldron, the answer is clear. Some speech about others and their fundamental identities and commitments is simply *so* uncivil, so intolerant, degrading, and disrespectful that it constitutes a form of *persecution* against which a tolerant society can and should act. Yet in liberal democracies like the United States the question is not so simple. This is because, as a regime, liberal democracy is distinguished by its dedication to *two-fold* toleration: (1) of diversity in its members' fundamental identities and commitments (especially in politics and religion) and (2) of the disagreements those differences inspire. Indeed, the self-conception of liberal societies as "tolerant" hinges on the fact that members are not compelled to confine their differences to a private sphere of individual skulls or intimate familiars, but are permitted, even encouraged, to express them freely in public and to compete for adherents.

Accordingly, in complaining about a "crisis" many commentators present civility as *the* essential virtue for liberal democracies that promise to protect diversity while allowing for active, often heated disagreement in the public sphere. In the United States, especially, we pride ourselves on our First Amendment freedoms not only to *differ* but to *disagree*, and our recent crisis of civility feels so critical because it brings these defining commitments into conflict. Controversies about whether to tame uncivil disagreements through legislation—whether through campaign finance reform, hate speech laws, or college speech codes—are thus usually presented as a conflict between free speech, on the one hand, and the demands of diversity and inclusion, on the other. Yet the early modern toleration debates described in this book, in which concerns about persecution of the tongue and proposals to ban it could be heard on all sides, suggest a different interpretation—namely, that underlying these controversies is a more fundamental conflict between *competing* conceptions of civility, understood as a virtuous standard of conversation and conduct that should govern the members of a tolerant society *as such*. This is clear especially in the case of campus speech codes, which attempt to articulate the standard of civility appropriate to universities as tolerant societies par excellence.

Even so, these efforts to impose and enforce civility legislatively are controversial in the United States in a way they are not in other "tolerant" liberal democracies. Waldron and others have traced America's peculiar permissiveness toward uncivil speech—exemplified in its unwillingness to adopt the hate speech and religious insult statutes embraced elsewhere— to a peculiar "First Amendment Faith" in which religious toleration and free speech go hand in hand.[34] Few societies protect speech as insistently as we do, and few societies expect that allowing people to insult one another, along with their most cherished commitments or beliefs, will make them *more* tolerant, not less. Still, even if they cannot see eye to eye on whether a tolerant society should tolerate incivility, commentators in the United States and other Western liberal democracies generally agree that uncivil speech is a threat to the tenuous balance between diversity and disagreement on which ostensibly tolerant—and civil—societies depend. Wars of words are thus both a symptom and a cause of deeper ills, a sign that once the war of swords has ended the real work of tolerance has only just begun.

While politicians and political theorists continue to present civility as the key to reconciling difference and disagreement in a tolerant society, a crucial question remains unanswered. What, exactly, *is* civility? Despite the constant handwringing over our perceived lack of it, this conversational virtue remains notoriously difficult to define. While its origins can be traced to the Latin *civilitas,* as the art of good citizenship or government, the evolving and overlapping valences of the term have become difficult to disentangle.[35] Civility is akin to politeness, and yet calling someone uncivil is far worse than calling him impolite. The former is potentially "intolerable" in the way the latter is not. Yet *civil* has too many other antonyms—not only "rude" but also "savage" and "barbaric"; "criminal" as well as "military"; "violent" but also "spiritual" and "religious"—to permit of easy definition.[36]

Perhaps unsurprisingly, the scattered (and often repetitive) genealogies of civility put forward in recent scholarly accounts generally locate the origins of the concept in early modernity. For those concerned about verbal violence or "civilizing" fundamental disagreements so that wars of words do not end at dawn with guns drawn, the sense of the civil as a synonym for peaceful or nonviolent is primary.[37] Still, most modern proponents of civility have something more in mind. Those who present it as a civic virtue or "democratic ideal" of public spirit and participation stress its neorepublican roots in the *vivere civile* of the Italian Renaissance.[38] For others, civility is an essentially eighteenth-century virtue characteristic of "bourgeois" civil society and the manners of the marketplace that make coexistence and cooperation in complex commercial societies possible and productive.[39]

In political theory, proponents of deliberative and other forms of democracy often combine both senses of civility—as public virtue and private

manners—highlighted by historians and present it as a key virtue of "dialogic citizenship."[40] Yet these ideals of civic duty and public spirit, on the
one hand, and politeness and *la doux commerce,* on the other, clearly exceed
the conversational virtue at stake in contemporary debates. When Obama
enjoins citizens to "disagree without being disagreeable," he has something
else, and something less, in mind. Definitions of civility as "the minimum
degree of courtesy required in social situations," often with negative over-
tones, hit nearer the mark. We might call this *mere* civility: a minimal conformity to norms of respectful behavior and decorum expected of all members of a tolerant society as such. Others' incivility *feels* so egregious for this
reason—it places them potentially beyond the pale of social life.[41]

Noting this exclusionary element, however, a growing cadre of critics
have begun to question whether civility in this sense should be considered a
virtue at all. While supporters stress its civic associations, these critics take
their cue from Norbert Elias and Sigmund Freud in order to highlight the
dark side of civility.[42] A synonym for *civilization,* as in Samuel Johnson's
definition of 1755: "freedom from barbarity; the state of being civilized,"
civility would seem to be irredeemably imbricated with colonialism and
empire.[43] Against this backdrop of the displacement and oppression of the
"savage" by the "civilized" in the conquest and colonization of the New,
and then the known, World, appeals to civility today take on a decidedly
more ominous cast.[44] These critics view a call for "civility" not as an ex-
hortation to virtue but a covert demand for conformity that delegitimizes
dissent while reinforcing the status quo. It functions as nothing more than
a rhetorical ploy meant to set up the speaker as a model of decorum and
silence anyone else with the temerity to disagree. In the immortal words of
Ring Lardner: "Shut up, he explained."[45]

One need not endorse the critics' suspicions as to the sinister motives
of their opponents to recognize that wanton civility-talk carries with it an
implicit threat of exclusion. Designating certain behaviors or beliefs as "uncivil" effectively banishes them beyond the pale of conversational community. Little wonder then that contemporary debates about civility in political theory and the broader public sphere are so unsatisfying. Beyond the
disaffected bloc of civility skeptics, they ping-pong endlessly between two
extremes: those who present "more civility" as a panacea for all that ails
our tolerant society and the critics who see it as something altogether more
sinister—a civilizing discourse aimed at silencing dissent and marginalizing
already marginal groups.

Its supporters might respond by pointing out that even those quickest to condemn civility are offended when their voices are drowned out by insults and interruptions from the gallery. And yet, sensitive to its exclusionary implications, these defenders are understandably hesitant to specify what they take the standard of civil behavior to be, or how much conformity will meet the minimum. For the critics, this ambiguity and imprecision simply offers further proof of the exclusionary essence of civility and its emblematic power to silence, deflect, and exclude anyone uncivil enough to question it. And so the debate ping-pongs on.

This book promises to move beyond the impasse in popular and scholarly debates about civility through an appeal to history. This approach may, at first, seem counterintuitive. And yet, just as many of the pressing problems facing modern liberal democracies recall early modern concerns about the limits of toleration in the face of evangelical sectarianism and persecution of the tongue, the concept of civility invoked in early modern attempts to refasten the social bonds severed by the Reformation represents a possible ancestor, and promising analogue, to the minimal conversational virtue at stake today.

Moreover, this early modern concept of civility has significant advantages. As the sorry state of contemporary debates demonstrates, calling for "more civility" simply as the key to peaceful and productive disagreement is not enough. Like *toleration*, civility can be defined in more or less suppressive or exclusionary ways, as something "mere" or something more. How one defines it, as well as how one believes it should be enforced, matters quite a lot. And one's answers to these questions will, in turn, determine where the limits of toleration lie. While calls for civility in the seventeenth century thus display a familiar and frustrating dynamic of exclusion, early modern authors also tended to make civility's status as a condition of inclusion *explicit* in a way that its modern proponents do not. It is therefore possible to reconstruct and reevaluate these seventeenth-century arguments in such a way as to illuminate this complex relationship between civility, disagreement, and the limits of toleration—and in doing so, to shed some much-needed light on the twenty-first-century crisis of civility confronting us today.

To this end, the book's central chapters will recover the competing conceptions of civility put forward by Roger Williams, Hobbes, and Locke and show how they informed these thinkers' influential theories of toleration in important and unexpected ways.[46] As some of the usual suspects in the ongoing, ahistorical search for "early liberals" by political theorists and intellectual historians, each of these figures remains a continuing presence in modern debates about liberalism and the limits of toleration. Yet approaching Williams, Hobbes, and Locke through the conceptual frame of civility allows us to recover aspects of their thought that commentators more concerned with the well-worn themes of liberty of conscience and the separation of church and state have neglected. Specifically, it allows us to appreciate the superior psychological insight these early modern authors possessed into the dynamics of disagreement underlying the tension between inclusion and exclusion that bedevils theorists of civility and toleration to this day.

Although they ended up in very different places, Williams, Hobbes, and Locke began alike from a shared understanding of human nature as partial and proud. They therefore recognized a certain *disagreeableness* inherent in disagreement that inevitably placed pressure on the affective bonds between individuals. The possibility of toleration thus hinged for each on what would be required, ethically and institutionally, to render religious disagreement sufficiently "civil" to overcome its negative affective dimension. While they could agree that tolerant societies neglected the war of words at their peril, however, they disagreed profoundly when it came to what civility entailed and how it should be enforced. Would the hypocritical, outward performance of "civil worship" suffice, or did true civility demand something more—a scrupulously civil silence on controversial questions, perhaps? Or a sincere respect, even affection, for others based on a recognition of the value and reasonableness of their beliefs? As for enforcement, did toleration demand the bridling of intolerant tongues through law? Or should a tolerant society tolerate its members' incivility, too?

The competing conceptions of civility that Williams, Hobbes, and Locke developed in the course of answering these questions—what I call *mere civility, civil silence,* and *civil charity,* respectively—were not superficial calls for politeness, but rather sophisticated efforts to think through what coexistence under conditions of fundamental disagreement requires. Chapter 1 lays the conceptual and institutional groundwork for their theories by detailing the efforts of eirenic writers like Erasmus and Sebastian Castellio to restore *concordia* or concord to Christendom. These thinkers encouraged Catholics and Protestants to seek harmony within their differences through *comprehension* and *colloquy,* two policies aimed at achieving consensus on the fundamentals of Christianity. In these efforts, persecution of the tongue appeared to be as pressing a danger as that of sword and stake, while toleration seemed a sure way to make the wars of words worse by bringing evangelists into closer contact and encouraging them to compete. And yet, as the *vinculum societatis* of religion gave way to increasingly fractious and fundamental disagreements, some thinkers began to surrender the hope for *concordia* and advocate for toleration and civility as sublunary institutional and ethical solutions.

Chapter 2 turns to Roger Williams, the famous Puritan exile and colonial founder, as an opponent of efforts to legislate civility, as well as a prime example of the sort of polemical, evangelical Protestant that "eirenicists" like Erasmus despised. For Williams, as for many other religious radicals, the ongoing war of words was not a form of persecution but rather the essence of toleration. His tolerant society of Rhode Island and Providence Plantations was one in which not only Protestants but also American "pagans," "Jewes," "Turkes," and even Catholic "Anti-Christians" enjoyed the freedom to worship, associate, and evangelize (or anathematize) as they wished. His conception of "meer" civility as the bond of tolerant societies thus went hand in hand with an unapologetically cacophonous and evangelical approach to toleration.

To Thomas Hobbes, Williams's mere civility and its intimate connection with evangelism were utterly anathema. As we shall see in Chapter 3, far from being indifferent, Hobbes was so concerned about the harm in hate speech that he made "contumely" a violation of a fundamental natural law. Civil disagreement was for him, strictly speaking, a contradiction in terms, because "the mere act of disagreement is offensive" (DC 26). A tolerant society would thus require a *civil silence* on controversial questions, so that individuals might differ in religion but never disagree about it. With this Hobbesian alternative of "difference without disagreement" in mind,[47] Chapter 4 turns to the most famous seventeenth-century tolerationist, John Locke. Locke has long been considered the primary architect of "liberal" toleration, understood as the separation of church and state and a regime of individual rights. Yet this reputation ignores his lasting preoccupation with incivility and religious insult as obstacles to coexistence. Chapter 4 describes how after his early flirtation with Hobbesian civil silence, Locke's *Letter Concerning Toleration* came to present civility as a form of sincere *civil charity* toward others and their beliefs. It argues that in this, Locke's positive vision of toleration as a form of *concordia* ultimately revived the eirenicists' demand for a fundamental consensus in light of which all religious disagreements could be downplayed as "indifferent" or dissolved.

Placing civility at the center of their arguments about toleration not only helps us to see familiar figures like Hobbes and Locke in a new light; it also brings much-needed analytical clarity and insight to the tension between difference and disagreement that continues to perplex political theorists today. Most appeals to civility—in the seventeenth century as in the twenty-first—attempt to reconcile this tension by privileging one element over the other. They propose either, like Hobbes, to suppress disagreement in the name of the peaceful accommodation of difference, or like Locke, they exclude persons or positions deemed "uncivil" for the sake of social concord and productive (as opposed to destructive) disagreement. This dynamic explains both civility's critics' suspicions and its proponents' coyness about where, exactly, they would draw the line. Is it possible to "civilize" disagreement without dissolving it altogether, whether through conformity or consensus?

With these alternatives in mind, the Conclusion returns to recent accounts of civility and toleration in contemporary political theory. Following Rawls, some theorists invoke civility in arguments about public reason and other constraints on democratic deliberation, while others, like Waldron and Sandel, stress the negative effects of uncivil speech on diversity and dignity for the members of tolerant societies.[48] Although modern critics of civility may be wrong to impugn the motives of its proponents, these theorists' robust understandings of civility often do create covert demands for conformity that threaten to civilize disagreement by putting an end to it entirely. Whether they construe civility as a civil silence on controversial questions or as an expression of sincere respect for others and their conscientious commitments, the "uncivil" are left only two options: a sincere conversion to the fundamentals of political liberalism or silence.

The early modern theories of toleration and civility recovered in the following chapters may confirm the critics' suspicions about the civilizational implications of civility; however, they also suggest that not all civilizing discourses are created equal. Ultimately, this book recovers these three competing conceptions of civility in order to defend one. Roger Williams emerges in this account as an unlikely hero, one whose life and works offer a particularly promising approach to confronting our own crisis of civility in the present. Compared with his more famous and urbane contemporaries, Williams remains a relatively obscure figure, distinguished mainly by his theological intolerance and evangelical zeal. He developed his conception of "meer" civility—a minimal adherence to culturally contingent rules of respectful behavior compatible with, and occasionally expressive of, contempt for others and their beliefs—in the course of his evangelical interactions with the American Indians and his fellow Puritans in New England. In this context, the possibility of common ground between the parties seemed vanishingly slim. Nonetheless, Williams argued that a "bond of civility" might be forged that could unite even these most unpromising materials into the most tolerant society the world had ever seen.

This resolutely low-but-solid early modern virtue—a commitment to mutual contempt rather than mutual admiration—is at odds with the aspirational tenor of most contemporary political theory. Mere civility, if it is indeed a virtue, is one governing relations with ex-spouses and bad neighbors as well as members of the opposing party or sect. As such, it falls far short of the lofty and attractive ideals of sincere respect, recognition, and political friendship political theorists more often have in mind. And yet as Williams's own example reveals, mere civility, like mere toleration, can actually accommodate more and deeper kinds of difference than the alternatives, while sustaining a commitment to fundamental disagreement *despite* its inherent disagreeableness. Modern readers may find Hobbesian civil silence or Lockean civil charity more congenial. Nevertheless, Williams's mere civility emerges in this account as a promising path, forgotten or not taken, not least in the way it challenges our reigning assumptions about what a tolerant society—or a civil one—should look like.

Although what follows will be highly historical, this book is not an exercise in antiquarianism. As a work of what Andrew Murphy has called "historically informed political theory," it draws on historical texts and contexts in order to bring sorely needed critical insight and perspective to the perennial crises of civility afflicting modern liberal democracies, as well as to proposed solutions.[49]

The sophisticated theories of civility and toleration developed by Williams, Hobbes, and Locke offer rich and unexpected resources within an Anglo-American liberal tradition for thinking through these questions today. Nevertheless, while John Rawls's famous statement in *Political Liberalism* that "the historical origin of political liberalism is the Reformation and its aftermath, with the long controversies over religious toleration in the sixteenth and seventeenth centuries" has long been accepted as a commonplace among political theorists, early modern concerns about incivility and the war of words have been largely ignored.[50] This is perhaps because most theorists assume that toleration emerged in the early modern period after a long gestation as a solution to a particular set of problems—namely, religious violence, persecution, and warfare between sects. Growing evidence to the contrary, modern liberals reassure themselves that we solved these problems, at least, long ago. The uncivil disagreements that plague our tolerant society must therefore be a new challenge to which the history of political thought has little, if anything, to say.

As our early modern authors understood quite well, however, a society's decision to forego uniformity in favor of tolerating religious and other fundamental differences actually *creates* a problem. As we are discovering anew in our current crisis, not only do policies of toleration afford sectarians and partisans the opportunity to disagree openly and acrimoniously on the most important questions, they also do nothing to explain how people who differ so very fundamentally should manage the mundane business of unmurderous coexistence, let alone cooperation, day-to-day. Because of this, as the following chapters make clear, the choice in the seventeenth century was never simply between *persecution*, on the one hand, and *toleration*, on the other. While contemporary political theorists remain beholden to this dichotomy, Williams, Hobbes, and Locke understood quite well that a wide variety of institutional arrangements were possible under both labels, including laws against religious insult.

The same institutional variety—and indeed, the same institutions—can be seen across the many self-proclaimed "tolerant" societies around the world today. Indeed, one major theme of this book is simply to point out how *strange*, unusual, and fragile the American faith in an essential and obvious connection between religious toleration and free expression is—geographically, historically, and theoretically. While most self-professed liberals in the United States and elsewhere take this combination for granted, at least in theory, their complacency is generally grounded on oversimple understandings of history, misinterpretations of canonical thinkers, and sloppy thinking about the relationship between religious intolerance and persecution. As Waldron and others have noted, the idiosyncratic American view that toleration demands unrestricted free expression is in marked contrast with the openness to hate speech legislation in other Western liberal democracies.[51] Yet our free speech "fundamentalism," as Stanley Fish might call it (with an imputation of unsavory evangelical zeal), not only *tolerates* incivility but positively encourages it through its indiscriminate emphasis on free expression as a fundamental right.[52] This raises a series of important questions: How and why did the peculiar institutional arrangements associated with liberal toleration in the United States develop? And more importantly, should we keep them?

My own answer to the latter question is "yes." I will return to both questions in the Epilogue and argue that America's idiosyncratic First Amendment Faith rests partly on an adaptation of the position defended by Williams, who viewed evangelical liberty—including conscientious incivility toward those one regards as damned—as an essential element of free exercise. For now, it is worth noting that the obvious salience of these early modern arguments to contemporary questions about civility and toleration makes political theorists' failure to consult them rather striking. This may be due, in part, to their tendency to treat the term *civil worship* exclusively as a synonym for another concept of longer-standing interest to historians of political thought—namely, civil religion. Although much of this work is valuable, it has obscured the more mundane "civil respects" early modern authors often had in mind.[53]

Also to blame are the infamous definitional difficulties plaguing scholarly treatments of *tolerance* and *toleration*. Although attempts to distinguish these terms systematically in English have so far floundered,[54] theorists and historians generally use the former to refer to an attitude, with positive connotations of acceptance or at least nonjudgment, while the latter refers to an individual or social practice with a more negative cast.[55] Theorists, in particular, associate toleration with a state policy meant to pacify society, with origins in early modernity. Many therefore see it as tainted by its emergence out of the medieval idea of *tolerantia*—a policy of permission without approval that Christians applied to "acknowledged evils" like sewage, prostitutes, and Jews.[56] In keeping with this, to "tolerate" something—or someone—still carries an unmistakable whiff of contempt at odds with the respect and atmosphere of inclusiveness many commentators view as the sine qua non of a tolerant society. Some theorists thus follow Thomas Paine in viewing toleration "not [as] the opposite of intoleration but the counterfeit of it"[57] or Goethe, who observed that "to tolerate is to insult."[58]

Critics of toleration argue that it is inherently repressive, further evidence of a disqualifyingly "civilizational" approach to difference at liberalism's core.[59] This critique dovetails perfectly with that offered by modern critics of civility. Many defenders of liberalism have thus felt the need to distance themselves and their tradition from the "mere" toleration of early modernity.[60] Determined to redeem toleration, they do so usually by reconceptualizing it as something more robust—as *itself* a form of respect for others as moral and political equals or of recognition for the positive value of diversity as such.[61] This growing disillusionment with mere toleration may explain why political theorists have been disinclined to consult early modernity in thinking about civility.

Further obstacles arise from the ways in which theorists make use of history—or not—in approaching contemporary questions more generally. Here, this book seeks to combat two opposite yet equally pernicious tendencies. One tendency is to dismiss the salience of early modern arguments to contemporary questions and so consign canonical theories of toleration to the antiquarian dustbin. Theorists often treat these debates as doctrinal disputes between European Christians that were resolved ultimately through a combination of battle fatigue and institutional and intellectual efforts to "Protestantize" all religions.[62] On this view, early modern theories of toleration are not only inherently suspect but also inadequate to the needs of multiethnic and multifaith societies in an increasingly globalized and wired world. Pioneered by postcolonial critics of liberalism, this debunking maneuver has become all but routine. Yet it ignores the profundity of the religious, social, and political rifts the Reformation instigated within Western Christendom. As Chapter 1 will argue, these religious differences posed an unprecedented challenge not because they were theological or belief-based, but because of the concrete demands different beliefs placed on social and political practices and the supremely disruptive, vocal, and evangelical ways in which they were expressed.

Here, one must remember that early modern sectarians were not the ecumenical mainliners of modern experience but rather righteous schismatics and enthusiastic evangelicals who were unwilling—or in conscience unable—to hold their tongues or keep their peace. Most theorists not only underestimate the heterogeneity of early Protestantism but also the diversity of "Christendom" in an age of aggressive missionizing and expansion. Scholars often treat early modern toleration debates, especially in England, as entirely domestic affairs. Yet the emergence of *civility* as a central category therein reminds us that the growing sense of difference, distance, and alienation experienced by Europeans in regarding (and often dehumanizing) their fellow Christians unfolded simultaneously with a growing awareness of the wideness, strangeness, and staggering diversity of the non-Christian inhabitants of the globe. In particular, the colonial encounter with native peoples in the Americas gave rise to pressing and immediate questions about coexistence and cooperation across vast social and cultural differences. This is true not only for Williams, who dealt directly with American "Pagans" in Rhode Island, but also for Hobbes and Locke, who drew on New World examples in theorizing toleration at a distance. As we shall see in Chapter 2, Williams's plea for toleration on behalf of Narragansett "Divell" worship is a salutary reminder that genocide was not the only option.

If much recent scholarship on the usual suspects in the history of toleration seems intent on showing how or why they do *not* speak to contemporary questions, there is an equally misguided tendency among political theorists determined to prove that they do. These scholars ransack the past and select historical figures as candidates for revival based on how far they appear to agree with modern assumptions. In doing so, they usually misrepresent their chosen historical thinkers by domesticating them past recognition. Such is the case with Martha Nussbaum's recent revival of Roger Williams as a paragon of neo-Kantian secular liberalism, or the ongoing efforts among theorists and historians of political thought to recover a "more tolerant" Hobbes.[63] By contrast, Locke—whose real sin, discussed in Chapter 4, was to ask for a form of toleration so demanding as to approach a requirement for universal Christian charity as the bond of civil societies—has become synonymous with "mere" toleration and all that is wrong with minimalist liberalism.

In contrast with this approach which wrests thinkers from their historical context and congratulates them for being ahead of their time, this book assumes that the real advantage of consulting the past lies in opening ourselves to the ways in which it challenges our own commitments and assumptions, especially about what it means to be "civil" or "tolerant" today. This requires that political theorists divert our attention from the great abstractions—justice, tolerance, respect—and pay closer attention to texts *and* contexts so as to understand the concrete practices and policies historical thinkers had in mind in arguing about these terms. This is especially crucial when the topic is toleration, in which theory and practice are deeply and irrevocably intertwined.

In adopting this approach in what follows, my own purpose is somewhere between exorcism and resurrection.[64] I certainly do not mean to suggest that the problems facing our tolerant society are exactly the same as those facing thinkers in the seventeenth century. Historicizing their arguments should serve, in part, to alienate us from these authors and ideas like civility and toleration that—when they are not summarily rejected—are too often treated as obvious and *ours*. But it can also counteract a characteristically modern myopia, our "endearing but frustrating tendency to view every development in public life as if it were happening for the first time."[65] Historical perspective may not solve our problems, but it can help us to see that certain favored solutions have been tried before—and to understand why they failed.[66]

Done well, historicizing should also humanize. Part of my purpose in this book is to reveal some of the titans in the history of political thought to be frail and finite human beings confronting the kinds of problems that partial and proud creatures like ourselves will inevitably encounter in living together with others of our kind. In the chapters that follow, we shall see these figures jumping to conclusions, making mistakes, and changing their minds. We will also see that, while our problems are not identical to theirs, neither are they unprecedented. In the seventeenth century, thinkers like Williams, Hobbes, and Locke confronted firsthand the challenges of building a tolerant society out of materials altogether less reasonable, secular, and tolerant than even they might wish. Seeing them so engaged should make them *more,* not less relevant to us. We would be foolish not to learn from them, even as we try to do our thinking for ourselves.

1

"Persecution of the Tongue"

Toleration and the Rise of Religious Insult

> Take heed of becoming persecutors: some think there is no per-
> secution but fire and sword; [but] there is the persecution of the
> tongue; there are many of these persecutors now-a-days, who, by a
> devilish chymistry, can turn gold into dung, the previous names of
> God's saints into reproach and disgrace.
>
> —THOMAS WATSON, "Concerning Persecution" (1660)

THE CRISIS OF civility afflicting our own tolerant society suggests that what we say to each other, as well as how we say it, is a matter of profound importance. But it also holds out the hope of a reasonably straightforward solution. If only we could get the manner of disagreement right, it suggests, what was *polemic* might be made *eirenic*. Civility will do the work of harmonizing our differences, so that we might regard one another, despite our fundamental disagreements, not as enemies but friends.

This vision of civility as the key to social harmony is shared by political theorists and social scientists alike.[1] In *Political Liberalism,* Rawls presents the "duty of civility" in public reasoning as essential to the "harmony and concord" of overlapping consensus in a well-ordered society in contrast with the "bitterness and resentment" of a mere modus vivendi.[2] Likewise, Jeremy Waldron's vision of a tolerant society is one of "affirmative harmony" in diversity, illustrated with an image borrowed from Pierre Bayle: "a harmonious Consort of different Voices, and Instruments of different Tones, as agreeable at least as that of a single Voice."[3] In presenting harmony as the essence of a tolerant society, both theorists are tapping into a much older social ideal—that of *concordia* or concord as the health and mutual affection of a "shared heart." At the same time, they hold out the hope of a civilitarian solution: through the "duty of civility" in public reasoning, on the one hand, and through laws against hate speech and religious insult, on the other.

But why should we think that something so superficial as *how* we speak to each other would solve the deeper problems—the private hatreds, resentments, and mutual contempt—in short, the *discord*—plaguing our own society? Indeed, why on earth would talking to each other, however civilly, about the questions and commitments that divide us most deeply bring us closer together at all? Plato, a source of many Stoic and early Christian ideas of *concordia,* certainly did not think that the "quarrels," "enmity," and "anger" arising from fundamental disagreements could be dissolved in this way. Rather, the true art of the *politikos* was the weaving together of diverse souls through the "divine bonds [of] true opinion"—that is, through education oriented towards a kind of consensus or *homonoia* (literally, "like-mindedness") on the "right opinion[s] concerning what is good, just and profitable and what is the opposite."[4] In the *Republic,* Socrates compares this agreement to "a kind of harmony" in which all citizens "sing the same song together."[5] And while Aristotle accused Plato of "turn[ing] harmony into a mere unison," he too believed that certain kinds of disagreement posed a problem for community (*koinonia*) as such—not simply in the manner of disagreement, but the *fact.*[6] For both philosophers, the affective bonds of political friendship or concord were predicated on *homonoia,* at least on matters that were truly fundamental.[7]

So where did this vision of harmonious disagreement in a tolerant society—and civility as the key—come from? Rawls and Waldron point to early modernity, each rehearsing in his different way a familiar story about the "rise" of toleration after the Reformation as a response to religious warfare and persecution. In contrast with traditional Whig narratives about the inevitable progress of liberal Enlightenment, this account depicts the triumph of toleration as the result of "battle fatigue" and a prudential response to a century of intensifying religious violence. On this view, early modern toleration was always only "a last resort for those who often still hated one another, but found it impossible to go on fighting."[8] As a form of "unmurderous" coexistence,[9] toleration was thus compatible with a significant degree of incivility. But for Rawls and Waldron this simply confirms the conviction that *true* tolerance calls for something more, something possible only after the modus vivendi of mere toleration has taken root—i.e., the shared heart of social concord.[10]

Although this narrative has been challenged persuasively by a new generation of revisionist historians,[11] it continues to hold remarkable sway across a wide range of political theorists. For critics of liberalism, the battle fatigue narrative confirms their suspicion that its early modern origins have left modern liberals ill-equipped to deal with the challenges of cooperation and coexistence facing modern multicultural societies. Similarly, for liberal proponents of legislation against hate speech or religious insult, it suggests that the unconcern with incivility characteristic of an American "First Amendment Faith" can be traced to its origins in an Anglo-American tradition intellectually and institutionally indifferent to the evils of private intolerance and the need for social harmony. For theorists like Waldron, disagreements disfigured by hateful speech are not violations of civility simply because of any physical violence that might ensue. The intrinsic dignitarian harms to individuals and to the "mutual assurance" of social concord cut deep enough.[12]

An original neglect of the war of words where it did not lead to swords, if true, might thus explain liberalism's characteristic deafness to what Waldron calls the "harm in hate speech." Yet this chapter will argue that such criticisms rest on a faulty understanding of the early modern debates to which modern liberals trace their origins. As we shall see, the distinctive challenge confronting the participants was not simply religious violence or diversity, as such—which had, after all, preceded the Reformation—but rather the threat posed to the *concordia* of Christendom by the new and highly uncivil forms of disagreement to which the Reformation gave rise. This chapter will thus trace how the ancient ideal of social harmony as *concordia* embraced by early modern Christians was fatally challenged after the Reformation by the simultaneous explosions of fundamental disagreement, partisan polemic, and conscientious incivility.

In that fateful moment, theological and technological changes worked together to raise the volume on religious dissent, dissonance, and discord higher than ever before. While proponents of persecution pursued the path of coercive uniformity, early modern eirenicists like Erasmus hoped that by taming men's tongues, persuasion might restore the common ground and bring concord to Christendom once more. This is the hope revived by Rawls, Waldron, and other contemporary proponents of civility. Their proposals for civilizing men's disagreements through legislation, moreover, replicate some of the eirenicists' favored solutions. Yet it was only when this ideal of *concordia* gave way in the face of the irremediably discordant theologies and technologies unleashed by the Reformation that the toleration of difference and disagreement became a real possibility. And even then, its "rise" was tenuous and a long time in coming.

The Tongue

In 1525, eight years after Martin Luther's Ninety-Five Theses began to turn the world of Western Christianity upside down, Desiderius Erasmus began his treatise *The Tongue* with a familiar complaint. "Nowadays," he wrote, "a backbiting tongue [does not] spare any man . . . indeed calumny is common practice."[13] Of all the forms of calumny polluting the public sphere, including "grumb[ling] against our officers and princes and bishops," one form disturbed Erasmus in particular:

> To call one's neighbour a heretic . . . a schismatic, and a debaser of the faith is common practice . . . and the men who do this most are those who boast . . . themselves in the number of those to whom Christ gave these teachings: "Love your enemies . . . and pray for them that persecute and calumniate you." . . . Good God, how far they are from this rule, when they slander the undeserving . . . with harmful tongues?[14]

To Erasmus, in the increasingly vitriolic theological and political disputes following the Reformation it seemed that religious insults were everywhere—and that this was due, in no small part, to Martin Luther's own example.

From the beginning of his campaign against corruption in the Church, Luther had argued that "scandalizing the scandalous" was integral to the godly work of spiritual and social reformation. To other, true Christians one had a duty to be charitable, but to the unregenerate one must "do the very opposite, and offend them boldly lest by their impious views they drag many with them into error."[15] In *The Murderer of Dresden* (1531), Luther announced himself "unable to pray without at the same time cursing": "If I am prompted to say 'Hallowed be thy name,' I must add 'Cursed, damned, and outraged be the name of papists and of all those who slander your name . . . thus orally, every day and in my heart without intermission." He concluded: "I am well convinced that God will hear our prayers."[16] Ever determined to practice what he preached, when Pope Leo X declared forty-one of the Ninety-Five Theses to be heretical in 1520, Luther responded by calling the pope "the Antichrist."[17] The long-standing Protestant fondness for excoriating Catholics as "papists" and "anti-Christians" (i.e., followers of the papal anti-Christ) originated here, while Catholics gave as good as they got by denouncing their theological foes as "heretics" and "schismatics."

Indeed, the curses Luther hurled at his Catholic opponents were themselves a deliberate play on the accusations of heresy and subsequent anathemas with which he and his followers were met. The proclamation of *anathema sit* ("let him be accursed") had long been the formulation by which offenders were publicly excommunicated from the Catholic Church—that is, barred from the sacrament of communion and hence "cut off" from the body of Christ. When the pope declared Luther anathema in the bull *Decet Romanum Pontificem* (1521), Leo pointedly extended the curse to Martin's followers and bestowed upon them an insulting "denomination" of their own: "Our purpose is that such men should rightfully be ranked with Martin and other accursed heretics and excommunicates . . . they shall likewise share his punishments and his name, by bearing with them the title 'Lutheran' and the punishments it incurs."[18]

Still, if Luther's singular vituperative virtuosity in the ongoing exchange of curse and countercurse was a critical factor in the rise of religious insult, another was the novel approach he shared with other Reformers to the oldest of Christian duties, evangelism. From *euangelion,* meaning "good message" in Greek, evangelism describes the act of preaching or promulgating the good news of the Gospel as the Apostles had done throughout the Hellenic world. Through the idea of the priesthood of all believers, Luther elevated evangelism as a central duty of all Christians—laymen as well as clergy. On this view, the activities of preaching and "prophesy" were essential dictates of Christian charity, for there was no surer demonstration of love for one's neighbor than to seek his salvation by rescuing him from error.[19] As the pejorative label "Protestant" conferred by their opponents suggested, Luther and his early followers did this in the first place by *protesting*—that is, speaking out and bearing witness against sins, spiritual errors, and other works of Antichrist wherever they found them. As Luther explained to one correspondent, "If you understand the gospel rightly, don't think that the matter can be done without revolt, offence and unrest. You can't turn the sword into a feather . . . the Word of God is a sword."[20] After all, as he reminded his followers, the Greek *euangel* could also mean "a shout."[21]

Many of the self-described "evangelical" Christians—both mainstream Protestants and sectarian radicals—who emerged in the ensuing years took Luther's advice to heart, often to his chagrin. In addition to anathemas, many sectarians—including, as we shall see later, the Quakers—experimented with "enthusiastic" forms of preaching and other evangelical activities that were deliberately offensive to social mores and disruptive of public order, including the so-called Adamite practice of going naked "for a sign."[22] Moreover, the words that they employed in propagating the Word were often forceful, with partisans on all sides of the ongoing theological disputes toeing the line of verbal violence. Sometimes, the violence was not simply verbal. After the bloody 1534 Anabaptist rebellion in Münster—"Anabaptist" being the insult leveled at those who followed the principle of *sola scriptura* into questioning infant baptism[23]—sectarian Protestants often fell under suspicion from their erstwhile allies for being purveyors of violence and sedition in their reforming zeal.

Of course, early Protestants who saw themselves as the inheritors of "primitive" Christianity were not the first evangelicals to make noise or to accuse their fellow Christians of spiritual corruption. Nor were they the first to separate themselves from the Church. As Paul's Epistles to the Corinthians show, "schismatics" had troubled Christianity since its earliest days as a religion. And yet, with the aid of recent advancements in communications technology (i.e., the printing press), the Reformation unleashed what Edmund Burke once called the "dissonance of dissent" inherent in Christianity on an unprecedented scale. There were, of course, other forces beyond technology at play in the forging of new denominational identities during the religious, social, and political disruptions of early modernity. Processes of early modern state formation and confessionalization played an important role, as did the grisly cycles of mutual martyrdom and persecution.[24] But when Luther took the decisive step of denominating the pope as the Antichrist in response to the bull *Exsurge Domine* (1520), it is crucial that he did so in German (i.e., in the vulgar tongue) and *in print*. That is, Luther wrote to be read—and to be read widely—in vivid language intended to speak not only to erudite elites or scholastic theologians but also directly to the common man.[25] The printing press did not create theological disagreements—although, as Brad Gregory has argued, Protestant methodology and emphasis on scriptural interpretation surely did.[26] Much like the Internet however, it popularized hitherto elite controversies, encouraged anonymity, and rewarded vulgarity and vitriol in ways that polemicists on all sides found difficult to resist.

As one of the earliest Protestant defenders of toleration, Sebastian Castellio, put it in his treatise *Concerning Heretics* (1554): "There is none who questions his own judgment, none who does not . . . envy and revile—[and] if anyone disagrees with us on a single point of religion, we . . . pursue him to the corners of the earth with the dart of tongue and pen."[27] The resulting positive feedback between polemical excess, schism, and spiraling sectarianism should be familiar to students of modern religion and politics. Increased communication led to an increasing awareness of religious differences and a proliferation of insulting labels to describe and classify them, while attempts by the authorities to stem the tide through persecution simply contributed to the hardening of sectarian identities, in turn.[28]

Against this backdrop of mutual contempt and competition, commentators in England and on the Continent would return repeatedly to Jeremiah's protests against the "arrows" of men's tongues in the Old Testament and to St. Paul's counsels against the dogmatism of small differences that led Christians to "debates, envyings, wraths, strifes, backbitings, whisperings, swellings, [and] tumults" in the New.[29] St. James's injunction to "offend not in word" and "bridle" the tongue, which "is a little member, [but] boasteth great things," seemed especially germane:

> Behold, how great a matter a little fire kindleth . . . the tongue is a fire, a world of iniquitie . . . it defileth the whole body, and setteth on fire the course of nature . . . the tongue can no man tame, it is an unruly evil, full of deadly poison. Therewith bless we God, even the Father: and therewith curse we men, which are made after the similitude of God.

James's conclusion—"For where envying and strife is, there is confusion and every evill worke"—proved particularly suited to the times.[30]

In *The Tongue*, Erasmus cited all of these passages and many classical sources besides. Echoing James, he accused Christians of carrying with them "the fire of hell in [their] tongues" while thinking themselves "splendidly scrupulous with [their] Pharasaical pretences." The resulting hypocrisy meant that "men nowadays are not double-tongued, but a hundred-tongued"—"especially those who are proud in the profession of a special form of religion."[31] Here Erasmus put his finger directly on the cycle of uncivil religious disagreement, insulting denominations, and schism that Luther's own cutting tongue had set in motion. In chastising the specialists on all sides, Catholic and Protestant, for their pride he reminded them of Paul's words to the Corinthians and warned them to "despise the warnings of so great an Apostle" at their peril. "What would you say, Paul, if you saw

Christians now suffering at the hands of Christians, colleagues suffering from colleagues, theologians from theologians . . . in short the dead suffering from the living, all snarled at, savaged, and torn apart with the madness of a rabid dog?"[32]

By the late sixteenth century, the epidemic of incivility and sectarian splintering had spread to England, where observers regarded the emergence of many new sects—and the coining of many new and imaginative "denominations" to abuse them—with considerable consternation. As we have seen already, in addition to traditional labels like heretic and schismatic, many familiar names like Protestant and Papist, Baptist and Lutheran, as well as more obscure ones like Adamite and Familist, began in this period as pejoratives—and, indeed, as in the case of Puritans, Ranters, and Quakers, often as implicit accusations of incivility against new groups. Indeed, the word *puritan* started as an insulting label for the "hotter sort of Protestant," those within the Church of England who complained forcefully that the work of Reformation had not gone far enough. In 1571, Archbishop Whitgift lectured Puritan dissenters on their evident unwillingness to "conform . . . be quiet and hold [their] peace," instead employing their "unchristian" and "unbrotherly" tongues "both publicly and privately, [to] rail on those that shew humanity towards you, and slander them by all means you can."[33]

The explosion of popular literacy and pamphleteering in the seventeenth century, along with the breakdown of censorship during the long years of social and political upheaval, simply exacerbated processes already underway.[34] In its middle decades especially, complaints about uncivil tongues could be heard on all sides. At the height of the second Civil War, William Walwyn lamented the "nicknames of 'Puritan,' 'heretics,' 'schismatics,' 'sectaries' . . . [and] 'independents,'" among others, with which he and his fellow Levellers (itself a pejorative) "were reviled and reproached."[35] And more than a decade later in 1660, Thomas Watson, a preacher and Puritan nonconformist, urged his fellow Christians to "take heed of becoming persecutors" by turning "the previous names of God's saints into reproach and disgrace." While "some think there is no persecution but fire and sword; there is the persecution of the tongue [and] there are many of these persecutors now-a-days."[36] Writing after the Restoration of the monarchy and the Episcopal Church of England, Watson likely did not have in mind his fellow Puritans alone, but also the restored bishops eager to emulate the persecutory policies of Archbishop Whitgift.

From *Homonoia* to *Concordia*

That uncivil disagreements in religion led inevitably to bloodshed and civil war seemed like a safe conclusion in the perpetually war-torn Europe of
the sixteenth and seventeenth centuries. As the French Chancellor Michel de
l'Hôpital explained to the Estates-General of Orleans in 1561, "It is folly to expect peace, quiet, and friendship among persons of various denominations":

> No sentiment is so deeply rooted in the heart of man as the religious
> sentiment, and none separates one man more deeply from another. . . .
> A Frenchman and an Englishman of the same religion are more friendly
> towards each other than two citizens of one town, but of different reli-
> gions, so far does the relationship of religions surpass that of nationality.

For l'Hôpital, the answer to rebuilding the ties of national belonging lay in
a confessional state that might realize "the old proverb: One faith, one law,
one king." One may be tempted to dispute the solution, but one can sym-
pathize with his reasoning, that in the face of "diversity and opposition of
sentiment, it is difficult for men to refrain from taking up arms . . . [thus]
war follows closely on, and accompanies discord in speech."[37]

Eirenic writers like Erasmus—so named because of their desire to restore
the "Peace of the Church"—were likewise concerned about the propensity
of Christians to go to war with each other on religious grounds.[38] But their
concerns about religious wars of words also went deeper—as, for that matter, did l'Hôpital's, as his final reference to discord suggests.[39] Persecution
of the tongue was not simply an obstacle to earthly peace (*pax*); it was also
a violation of the duty of Christian charity and hence a direct assault on
the social and spiritual harmony of *concordia*. As we saw earlier, this Latin
rendering of the Greek *homonoia* emphasized not only the like mind but
the shared heart. On this view, a peaceful society should reflect not only the
serenity and harmonious order of a musical cosmos but also the unified
whole (*universitas*) of a healthy body, the diverse members of which are
united through bonds of reciprocal affection and fellow feeling.[40]

This corporate ideal of *concordia,* in particular, was taken up by early
Christians, who envisioned the Church as a universal *corpus Christianum.*
Modeled on the body of Christ, the members of this body of Christians
were united through bonds of faith, charity, and mutual belonging maintained through the sacrament of communion.[41] In this, the like mind and
the shared heart went hand in hand. Christian doctrine (in this case, a belief

in the miracle of the Eucharist) and worship (the ritual partaking of the body and blood of Christ) supplied the *vinculum societatis,* the chain or bond holding society together.[42] As Paul explained in Romans: "For as we have many members in one body . . . so we, being many are one body in Christ, and every one members one of another."[43] Excommunication was thus a "cutting off" from that body as an exclusion from its community and its sacramental life's-blood.

This account of premodern social imaginaries is necessarily compressed; nevertheless, it is essential for understanding just how traumatic the uncivil, evangelical Christianities unleashed by the Reformation really were as an enthusiastic and seemingly irreparable *dismemberment* of the body of Christ. Erasmus chastised the squabbling schismatics for claiming to be evangelists preaching the Gospel of love while shattering the *vinculum* of mutual charity. "Christ wished the sentiments of philanthropy, or universal concord, to be fixed deeply in the hearts of his followers," he lamented; "How long shall your lives contradict your profession"?[44] Christians were supposed to love their neighbors, not libel them. Yet when sectarians "agree not in the minutest points," "the warmth of disputation advances from argument to abusive language, and from abusive language to fisticuffs; and if they do not proceed to use real swords . . . they stab one another with pens dipt in the venom of malice; they tear one another with biting libels, and dart the deadly arrows of their tongues against their opponent's reputation."[45] Any "peace" that might obtain in the midst of such unfettered polemic and verbal persecution between Christians was unworthy of the name. The eirenicists watched in despair as the flood of self-appointed evangelists enlisted the organs of the post-Reformation public sphere in publicizing their theological controversies and anathematizing their opponents, while the harmonious peace of *concordia* gave way to discord and din.

What could be done? Erasmus criticized his contemporaries' unwillingness to take action: "We have done nothing so far to control the reckless frenzy of men's tongues, and we are still doing nothing. Meanwhile, the sickness grows each day and is passing beyond cure."[46] Still, many of his contemporaries *were* taking action to restore *concordia* to the community of Christians—albeit through persecution. Proponents of religious coercion rarely described it as such, because the term *persecution* properly applied only in cases where the coerced were also the righteous. True Christians could be persecuted, but the "erroneous" consciences of heretics and schismatics could not. And indeed, there were plenty of resources within

Christian scripture and tradition to justify the use of force in "correcting" the latter.

As an embattled minority, early Christians had spread the Gospel and disciplined their congregations through preaching, admonishment, and excommunication alone. Yet with the conversion of the emperor Constantine, they began to deploy previously unavailable institutional sources of coercion for pastoral ends. Early modern Europeans concerned to take action against heresy as a source of scandal and corruption within the *corpus Christianum* thus looked to early church fathers like St. Jerome, who had counseled Christians to "cut away the rotten flesh, expel the diseased sheep from the fold, lest the whole house, the whole dough, the whole body, the whole flock, burn, perish, rot, die."[47] Here, Jerome had in mind the lasting schism caused by the Arian heresy in the fourth century: "Arius was but a little spark in Alexandria; but because the spark was not quenched forthwith, the whole world was laid waste by its flame."[48]

Still, it was St. Augustine who perfected the rationale for nonlethal force in the "correction" of heretics.[49] Although he originally opposed coercion, Augustine's dealings with the Donatists as bishop of Hippo in Northern Africa changed his mind. So denominated as followers of Donatus, bishop of Carthage, the Donatists argued that priests who had cooperated with the Roman authorities during the recent Diocletian persecutions had desecrated their office and so could not administer the sacraments. To take communion, in particular, from such a fallen officer was a source of pollution that tainted the true Christian and compromised his salvation. Not content to separate themselves from the source of pollution, the Donatists rioted, attacking priests on the altar and dragging them through the streets. Yet Augustine decried the separatists primarily for their arrogance, not their resort to violence. "In the perversity of their error," he complained, "[they] maintain rebellious hostility against the unity of Christ . . . [and] condemn the communion of the whole world on account of charges alleged against a man."[50] In doing so, Augustine insisted, they condemned only themselves; after all, the concord of the *corpus Christianum* was essential to the *salus*—a word meaning both "health" and "salvation"—of its members.[51] "No one can be righteous so long as he is separated from the unity of this body . . . in the same manner as if a limb be cut off from the body of a living man, it cannot any longer retain the spirit of life."[52]

Unlike Jerome, Augustine argued that if schismatics would not return of their own accord, Christians in positions of authority had a duty of charity to employ moderate punishments for the sake of *salus populi* and save these corrupt members from themselves.[53] No less an authority than Christ had indicated the necessity of *compelle entrare,* or compelling those outside the Church to come in.[54] Force could not compel belief, perhaps, but it could pressure apostates to come to mass in the hope that feigned conformity might, in time, become sincere faith. For this to happen, participation in the ritual of communion in which belief and affective belonging went hand in hand, was crucial.

After the Reformation, these patristic arguments would be revived in turn by Catholics and Protestants alike.[55] In justifying Geneva's decision to burn the anti-Trinitarian theologian Servetus at the stake, Calvin echoed Jerome: "Shall the whole body of Christ be mangled that one putrid member remain intact?"; "If the Son of God drove out those who on the pretext of religion sold sacrifices in the temple . . . why may not the pious magistrate use the sword committed to him to coerce perfidious apostates who profane and violate the temple of God with open contumely?" Much like his eirenic opponents, Calvin was concerned that the tongues of heretics like Servetus, if left unfettered, would cut the concord of Christendom to pieces. The civil and religious authorities thus had a duty, he insisted, to see that "impure and petulant tongues should not be allowed to lacerate the sacred name of God."[56]

For eirenicists like Castellio, Calvin's insistence on killing Servetus in order to save him appeared as nothing more than self-serving madness. Castellio's rejoinder—"to kill a man is not to defend a doctrine, but to kill a man"—is justly famous, but he attacked the corporate idea of membership used as justification for "cutting off" the diseased member as equally specious. Excommunication was one thing; execution another. "To kill a man is not to amputate a member. . . . When a man is killed as a heretic, he is not amputated from the body of Christ, but from the life of the body."[57]

Beyond Toleration: Comprehension and Colloquy

Because they opposed coercion in the cause of uniformity, political theorists and historians partial to the standard narrative have long heralded Castellio and Erasmus as harbingers of tolerant modernity and enlightened humanism.[58] But here it is important to see that their objections to persecution were more often about means than ends. Persecutory strategies of suppression and exclusion, whether through excommunication or execution, were self-defeating. "Cutting off" dissenters would not convert them; it would only convince them of their righteousness. There was, after all, no surer sign of one's status as a true Christian than suffering persecution for the cause.

The eirenicists' key insight was that while *homonoia* on all points would be impossible, it was also unnecessary—as Aristotle had pointed out, harmony presupposed the existence of different instruments, different voices, and different tones. To maintain the affective bonds of *concordia* within Christendom in the face of increasing diversity, then, one needed only to distinguish between those religious differences that were, in fact, "indifferent" (*adiaphora*) and those that were "fundamental" (*fundamenta*). The early Cynic and Stoic philosophers who had originated this distinction used it to distinguish the matters of the outside world that fell beyond one's power—above all the laws and customs or *nomoi* of Greek society—from the inward realm of virtuous self-control.[59] While earlier Christian theologians applied it to distinguish those actions that were intrinsically evil, such as blasphemy, from those that were neutral, such as (in Thomas Aquinas's example) plucking a blade of grass, Erasmus and his followers revived the Stoic emphasis on the indifference of "externals" versus the all-important inward realm in the context of Christianity.[60]

"The sum and substance of our religion," Erasmus wrote in 1523 to his patron at the court of Charles V, Jean de Carondelet, "is peace and concord. [But] this can hardly remain the case unless we define as few matters as possible and leave each individual's judgment free on many questions."[61] Surely, he argued along with Castellio, all Christians, whether Catholic or Protestant, could agree that *some* beliefs (e.g., the Trinity) and sacraments (baptism and communion) were *fundamenta*, while others, such as the outward forms and particular ceremonies of worship, were *adiaphora* lacking explicit scriptural warrant. According to this eirenic view, "the differences of the churches were so many Babels of scholastic jargon."[62] For the most part, they had to do with peculiarities of doctrine and worship that were, when surveyed impartially, really matters of indifference. It was the insistence on consensus in these things that led to acrimony and mutual persecution. In themselves, these differences were simply not worth disagreeing about, let alone breaking communion with one's fellow Christians.

Because of this, far from being proponents of toleration or "indulgence"—that is, of repealing or suspending the civil laws punishing dissent and so accepting the permanent existence of more than one Christian church—Erasmus and other eirenic thinkers favored an arrangement known as *comprehension*. Also called latitude, comprehension attempted to restore concord to the *corpus Christianum* through creedal and ritual minimalism and sacramental community. Although it has largely fallen out of liberal narratives about the rise of toleration, comprehension was, as Benjamin Kaplan has argued, "the most ambitious and charitable of all forms, requiring a genuine acceptance of beliefs different from one's own as valid and a willingness to take Holy Communion with those who maintained them."[63] As an expression of *concordia,* comprehension was motivated by a principle of inclusion that accepted religious diversity as a permanent feature of society while finding unity and community within it. It thus sought to achieve through patience and persuasion what the Augustinian strategy sought to impose through force—namely, the reintegration of wayward members into the body of Christ.

Contrary to the standard revisionist narrative then, for a long time after the Reformation *no one* considered toleration to be an adequate solution to the problem of coexistence, because the problem was not simply how to restore the peace destroyed by religious war but also the *concordia* shattered by the warring tongues of the schismatics. To tolerate this would be to surrender to endemic discord and the permanent dismemberment of the body of Christ. Much like Plato and Aristotle, the eirenicists believed that "the divine bonds" of at least *some* true opinions would be needed to refasten the *vinculum* of Christian charity. Hence toleration was a duty of Christians only insofar as it was a necessary precondition for persuasive evangelism oriented toward consensus on the "fundamentals." True evangelicals should thus not condemn others as "heretics" and "infidels" but persuade them, through argument and example, of the superior moral truth of Christianity: "Let not the Jews or Turks condemn the Christians, nor let the Christians condemn the Jews or Turks, but rather teach and win them by true religion, and let us, who are Christians, not condemn one another."[64] Instead of putting it down, Christians had a duty to take up the pen in a spirit of charity and brotherly love. For "even though in some matters we disagree, yet should we consent together and forebear one another in love, which is the bond of peace, until we arrive at the unity of faith."[65]

As we shall see again when we come to Locke and Roger Williams, the historical and genealogical importance of these evangelical arguments for early modern toleration should not be underestimated.[66] Still, as a supplement to comprehension, this "evangelical toleration" is a far cry from the positive affirmation of diversity with which we often associate *tolerance* today. As a form of forbearance in the face of an acknowledged evil, it is tolerant in the traditional sense of *tolerantia*, as a limited permission of lesser evils (including heretics and non-Christians) for the sake of avoiding greater ones.[67] For medieval writers like Aquinas, the difference between religious outsiders (Muslims and Jews) who could be tolerated and deviant insiders (heretics and schismatics) who could not had been essential.[68] In reviving and repurposing these arguments after the Reformation, even Protestant proponents of persecution were willing to endorse toleration as a provisional outsider status belonging to non-Christians. Castellio grumbled that although Calvin, a failed would-be classicist, "bans some books [by Christians]," he "permits the Koran, Aristotle, and Ovid in Geneva."[69] Recalcitrant religious insiders, however—in this case, Catholics or Protestant sectarians—must somehow be brought back into the fold.

Rather than rejoin the recalcitrant to the *corpus Christianum* by force, Erasmus and Castellio took a page from Plato. While they agreed with the persecutors that *concordia* required unity and consensus, the eirenicists argued that only the noncoercive methods of evangelical persuasion employed by the primitive Christians would be effective.[70] The tongue alone could restore what it had cut asunder. "O ambivalent organ," wrote Erasmus, "from which such a great plague of life can spring up . . . it is Eris, rouser of quarrels, but the same tongue is Grace, who wins good will. . . . It is the source of wars and civil strife, but it also parent to peace and concord."[71] As Gary Remer has shown, the key to religious compromise or *rapprochement* for Erasmus and his followers was dialogue.[72] By talking to each other, they insisted, men could be brought to recognize the fundamental consensus underlying their differences and so reaffirm the bonds of their shared faith. Erasmus made this eirenic strategy of interfaith dialogue or *colloquy* into a long-lasting and popular literary genre while also putting the theory into practice himself, albeit unsuccessfully, with no less a polemicist than Luther.[73] Others followed suit. One admirer at the court of George of Saxony, George Witzel, wrote a series of fan letters to Erasmus, begging him to lead the *via media* between the Catholic Church and the Reformers: "The Church is overwhelmed by factions; the barbaric Schools cause equal harm. . . . The former impose their particular views; the latter do not know how to abandon theirs. . . . The heretics will leave nothing alone in the Church whilst the gentlemen of the Sorbonne refuse to leave out anything."[74]

Joseph Lecler has argued that the spate of formal colloquies between Catholic and Protestant theologians convened in the ensuing decades throughout the imperial and princely courts of Europe were the brainchild of humanists like Witzel inspired by Erasmus's example.[75] Beginning with the Diet of Augsburg in 1530 and ending with the Colloquy of Poissy in 1561, the goal of these events was to bring Catholic and Protestant theologians together for decorous dialogue so as to reconcile the parties through an agreement on a mutually acceptable creed or list of *fundamenta* that would put an end to the schism once and for all.[76] The papal legate to the 1541 Diet of Regensburg, Cardinal Contarini wrote, "As I have often said to the Pope, in essentials the differences are not as great as many think." Instead he placed the blame for discord squarely on the highly uncivil way that partisans on both sides had defended their cause, including "several [that had] written in favour of the Catholic position in a way which did more harm than good."[77]

Contarini's optimism was not completely unwarranted—at Regensburg, the representatives were able to reach an agreement on the doctrine of justification, but discussion soon broke down thereafter. As colloquy after colloquy failed to produce a consensus, the possibility of restoring *concordia* to Christendom through persuasion *or* persecution seemed ever more remote. The 1561 Colloquy of Poissy represented a last-ditch effort to heal the rift between French Catholics and Calvinists. Sponsored by l'Hôpital, it was a spectacular failure. His call for the parties not to "regard as enemies those who are said to belong to the new religion, and who are Christians and baptized like themselves, but call them and seek them out . . . receive them in all gentleness . . . without bitterness or obstinacy" apparently fell on deaf ears.[78] The colloquy ended with the Catholic participants reaffirming their own profession and cutting off all others from their communion *and* the conversation: "Whoever believes differently *anathema esto* . . . henceforth such people should no longer be heard."[79]

It may be tempting to write off this lack of success in interfaith dialogue as a failure of the parties to approach the proceedings in the right spirit of Erasmian concord. But comprehensive creed-making is always a double-edged sword; even the most latitudinarian efforts to define orthodoxy will cast certain doctrines as beyond the pale. Indeed, defining one's creed so as to exclude a mutually despised Other can often serve as an effective shortcut in establishing common ground with those that one would comprehend. Attempts at Catholic-Protestant conciliation were doomed in

part due to the parallel efforts at colloquy taking place within Protestant
countries like England, which sought to reconcile sectarians to the national
church by emphasizing the dissenters' shared distance from "Popery." In
this way, Protestant attempts to define orthodoxy through creeds and cat-
echisms contributed to religious polarization as much as those of Count-
er-Reformation Catholicism after the Council of Trent.[80]

Recognizing this fact, some theologians argued that the path to concord
lay in an ever more minimal and inclusive conception of Christianity. As
Charles II canvassed opinions as to how to settle ecclesiastical matters after
the Restoration, the Presbyterian Richard Baxter extolled the virtues of a
comprehensive national church that dispensed with creed-making in favor
of an affirmation of the bare "Essentials" of "MEER Christianity":

> The [Apostle's] Creed, Lord's Prayer, and Decalogue alone [are] our
> Essentials or Fundamentals: which at least *contain all* that is necessary
> to Salvation, and hath been by all the Ancient churches taken for the
> Sum of their Religion. And whereas they still said, [*A Socinian or a
> Papist will Subscribe all this*] I answered them, So much the better, and
> so much the fitter it is to be the Matter of our Concord: But if you are
> afraid of Communion with Papists and Socinians [i.e., non-Trinitar-
> ian Christians], it must not be avoided by making a new Rule or Test
> of Faith . . . but by calling them to account whenever in Preaching or
> Writing they contradict or abuse the Truth.[81]

We shall return to these seventeenth-century efforts at latitudinarian comprehension within the Anglican Church in our discussion of Locke in Chapter 4. For now, it is simply worth noting that the failure of comprehension
and colloquy to restore *concordia* to Christendom was not simply a failure
of intolerant dogmatists or cynical diplomats to put Erasmus's theory of
colloquy into practice adequately. The failure extended to the theory itself.

The problem was, of course, that in entering the fray and trying to persuade their opponents of the indifference of their spiritual errors, neither
side was persuaded. The polemicists were understandably offended at the
suggestion that the commitments they considered to be *fundamenta* were,
in fact, *adiaphora*, while the eirenicists found themselves dragged down into
the vitriolic depths.[82] Whereas Erasmus boasted that his dialogic overture
toward Luther in *De Libero Arbitrio Diatribe sive Collatio* (1524) had been
the height of "civility," his second salvo *Hyperaspistes* (in response to Luther's characteristically contentious reply) took a much more pugnacious

tone while accusing Luther himself of *pugna verborum:* "[Like] combatants who, in the heat of a quarrel, turn whatever is at hand into a missile. . . . Who will learn anything fruitful from this sort of discussion—beyond the fact that each leaves the discussion bespattered with the other's filth?"[83] For those genuinely concerned about the concord of Christendom, the safest strategy seemed to be to channel one's vituperative zeal in a more productive—and potentially unifying—direction, for instance toward the Ottoman menace: "But now, when we strive with hate and persecutions . . . the Gospel because of us is made a reproach unto the heathen. We rather degenerate into Turks and Jews than convert them into Christians."[84]

Writing to Erasmus in 1532, Witzel concluded that the key to a successful colloquy that might "put an end to discord" once and for all lay in carefully curating the conversationalists beforehand, by including only those sincerely committed to the enterprise and "cutting off" all others: "Neither Luther, nor the sophists [i.e., the Scholastics], but only Erasmus and his peers should be heard, that is those who do not belong to any party, and wish to rescue Christianity with sincerity."[85] This all-too-human intuition that disagreements limited only to those one views as reasonable, open-minded, and sincere are more likely to be productive explains, perhaps, why Erasmian colloquy remained a popular genre of philosophic fiction long after the final anathema had been proclaimed at Poissy. These idealized dialogues were invariably elite affairs, with the participants always the souls of piety, sobriety, and erudition—and, most crucially, always open to persuasion and the unforced force of the better argument.[86] In his *Colloquium Heptaplomeres,* one of the most radical installments in the genre in its aporetic ending and the range of its participants (including a Catholic, a Lutheran, a Calvinist, a Jew, a Muslim, a Skeptic, and a natural philosopher), Jean Bodin insisted that the *concordia discors* of the proceedings derived from the fundamental similarity underlying the interlocutors' differences: all "lived not merely with sophistication of discourse and charming manners, but with such innocence and integrity that no one so much resembled himself as all resembled all."[87]

The "Rise" of Toleration

So long as the shared hearts and minds characteristic of *concordia* remained the ideal—forever tempting the orthodox to "cut off" others, if not from the body of Christ or the life of the body, at least from the conversation—*tolerantia* would face an uphill climb. Still, as the sixteenth century drew to a close, the failures of Erasmian persuasion *or* Augustinian persecution to restore concord to Christendom had begun to take their toll. The destructive effects of unceasing and relentlessly uncivil disagreements in religion were felt particularly acutely in England. Under Elizabeth, Archbishop Whitgift's solution had been to compel Puritans and other dissenters to conform and "hold their peace," but even he seemed to have surrendered the Augustinian hope that this feigned conformity would one day transform into sincere worship, let alone *homonoia*.[88]

In the intervening decades of unrest and civil war, the simultaneous explosions of popular literacy and pamphleteering only made matters worse.[89] The ideal of concord lived on, as in *Paradise Lost* ("O shame to men! Devil with devil damned firm concord holds; men only disagree").[90] Yet growing skepticism that religious divisions and animosities could be ameliorated through the "divine bonds of true opinion" any longer led Milton and others to seek out sublunary institutional and ethical solutions. Most politicians and theologians held out the hope for some kind of comprehension. Still, as English Christians began to reconcile themselves to discord, toleration became for a small number of religious radicals an increasingly desirable—if remote—possibility.

In departing from their eirenic forebears, proponents of "indulgence" faced significant difficulties.[91] Tolerating the existence of multiple churches in a society would permit, even encourage, evangelical disagreement characterized by sectarian identities, unshared premises, and stakes as high as salvation. Moreover, the irreversible democratization of religious disagreement through the advent of printing and cheap, mass media meant that neither the audience nor the participants could be restricted to an educated elite. Even those in favor of toleration feared that mutual offense would inevitably follow from open disagreement on religious questions, with perceptions of bigotry and blasphemy on all sides. Critics, on the other hand—one of whom described a policy of toleration as "the whore of Babylon's backdoor"—argued that the public permission of diversity would encourage a proliferation of uncivil disagreement and verbal persecution that would only tear society further apart.[92] (The "Whore of Babylon" was yet another popular Protestant slur against the Catholic Church drawn from the Book of Revelation.)

Toleration, its opponents argued, would lend succor to Papists while encouraging fissures in the united front of English Protestantism against the "Antichristian" menace. The civil and ecclesiastical anarchy of the 1640s and 1650s seemed to bear these fears out. In the brief window between the abolition of the infamous organ of royal censorship, the Star Chamber, in 1641 and the enactment of the Licensing Act by the Long Parliament in 1643, the English markets were flooded with polemical pamphlets featuring imaginative insults, group libels, and obscene images that made the war of words all the more colorful—and threatening.[93] Would not a policy of official indulgence simply make matters worse by providing verbal persecutors with both a pretext and an opportunity?

The conviction that uncivil tongues were among the chief obstacles to the peaceful accommodation of religious difference in seventeenth-century England was widely shared among tolerationists and their opponents alike—sometimes even in the same person. Jeremy Taylor, a minister ejected by the Long Parliament after the abolition of episcopacy, would become an avid persecutor of dissent himself after the Restoration. In 1647, however, he began his pro-toleration pamphlet *A Discourse on the Liberty of Prophesying* by complaining of the "zealous Ideots" and "exterminating spirits" who "endure none but their own sect" and condemn all others as "fooles and wicked persons."[94] The subtitle of the work, *Shewing the Unreasonableness of prescribing to other Mens Faith, and the Iniquity of persecuting differing opinions,* put the focus squarely on the heat and hatred arising from religious wars of words. With his own Puritan persecutors—and future persecutees—firmly in view, Taylor complained that "some zeales are so hot and their eyes so inflamed with their ardors, that they do not think their Adversaries look like other men."[95]

When it came to solving the problem, however, Taylor proposed a counterintuitive solution: "for Princes to give Toleration to disagreeing persons, whose opinions by faire meanes cannot be altered" and for individuals to display "a charitable and mutuall permission to others that disagree from us."[96] He was, he insisted, by no means endorsing schism—"no part of this Discourse teaches or encourages variety of Sects, and contradiction in opinions, but supposes them already in being."[97] But alas, the ship of concord and comprehension had sailed: "We are not now in those primitive daies, when there was one common sense among Christians, when if one member suffer'd, all the members suffer'd with it."[98] Nevertheless, toleration was *not* an invitation to licentiousness. Rather, it was a "tak[ing] away a license of judging . . . [and] dogmatizing whatever one please."[99] As the "charitable and mutuall permission of [those] that disagree from us," toleration demanded that "disagreeing persons" not simply abstain from physical violence but from *verbal* persecution as well.[100]

In light of the collapse of *concordia*, the chief philosophical and practical challenge facing defenders of toleration like Taylor was how to civilize the discordant disagreements to which religious diversity and evangelical competition gave rise. To modern ears, his complaints can sound eerily familiar: "The fault I find and seek to remedy is, that men are so dogmaticall and resolute in their opinions, and impatient of others disagreeing."[101] If only men "were capable of coole and tame Homillies, or would hear men of other opinions give a quiet account without invincible resolutions never to alter their perswasions" or less "hasty in calling every dislik'd opinion by the name of Heresy, and when they have resolved, that they will call it so . . . beat [the erring person] like a dog, or convince him with a gibbet."[102]

The many moralistic treatises on the "government" of unruly tongues inspired by Erasmus and appearing in English at this time sounded a similar theme.[103] Richard Allestree, also an Anglican minister, has been credited with the 1667 treatise *The Government of the Tongue,* which detailed all of the "guilts"—against God, one's neighbor, and oneself—to which "our unrestrained licentious Tongues hurry us":

> That which should be the store-house of relief and refreshment to our brethren, is become a magazine of all offensive weapons against them, spears, and arrows, and sharp swords. . . . We do not only fall by the slipperiness of our Tongues, but we deliberately discipline and train them to mischief . . . that which was intended for the instrument, the aid of human society, is become the disturber, the pest of it.[104]

As a prime example, Allestree cited the sin of calumny through which "persons of all ranks do mutually asperse, and are aspersed," a sin he, like Erasmus, saw as peculiarly rife among religious opponents. "Yea, so Epidemic is this disease grown," Allestree lamented, "that even Religion (at least those Parties and Factions which assume that name) has got a taint of it; each sect and Opinion seeking to represent his Antagonist as odious as it can."[105]

This "Epidemic" of incivility and religious insult was not simply a threat to civil peace: although as "one of the grand Incendiaries which disturbs the peace of the world, [it] has a great share in most of its quarrels . . . [which] take their rise from injurious and reproachful words."[106] Like his eirenic predecessors, Allestree viewed the early modern crisis of civility as an impardonable violation of the "Evangelical precept" of Christian charity and *concordia* as well. Incivility "breeds such strangeness, such animosities amongst Neighbors, that you cannot go to one, but you shall be entertain'd with invectives against the other; nay perhaps you shall lose both, because you are willing to side with neither."[107] In "this vindictive age" of "insulting vice," men ignored the dangers to their country *and* to their souls at their peril. Yet the "liberty of the Tongue" had gotten "such a prepossession, that men look on it as part of their birth-right, nay do not only let their tongues loose, but studiously . . . use the spur where they should the bridle."[108]

Rather than counsel Christians to turn their tongues to persuasion as Erasmus and Castellio had done, however, Allestree held out the hope that *civility* might provide a more straightforward solution. Under the unfortunate conditions of religious discord, one could attend to the manner of disagreement, even if one could not address the fact. If men could be persuaded to "at least be civil" ("tho they will not be pious") by avoiding insult or blaspheming against each other's sacred commitments, they would be "no loosers by it: for at the utmost, 'tis but keeping in a little unsavory breath."[109] Once men's tongues were tamed and "common civility" upheld in the "intimacies and endearments of friendship and . . . recreative discourses," only *then* could men of different persuasions in religion live together peacefully while also seeing to their Christian duties of mutual reformation—"converting [their] Detraction and backbiting into Admonition and fraternal correption [sic]" by exercising "friendly vigilance . . . over each others' souls."[110]

"Common Civility"

Orthodox Anglicans like Allestree and Taylor, as well as nonconformists like Watson and Baxter, could and did disagree profoundly when it came to the virtues of tolerating dissent or who, exactly, were the most egregious verbal persecutors. And yet in the course of these disagreements they all appealed to *civility* and complained about its inverse in similar—and familiar—ways: first, as the social norms of "civil worship" and the performance of respect toward one's fellow men analogous to the *adiaphorous* ceremonies of religion and, second, as a virtue reflecting one's willingness to observe these rules in conversation with others. Things became more complicated, however, when it came to what kind of standard of "common" civility these seventeenth-century English writers had in mind.

As we discovered in the Introduction, civility is—and was—a vexingly capacious concept with distinctive resonances in different linguistic and cultural contexts. Inspired by Norbert Elias, many historians have focused on early modern civility as the norms of decency and the "art of conversation" taught by the courtesy and conduct manuals popular in Western Europe. Elias credited Erasmus himself, in his *De Civilitate Morum Puerilium* (1530), for inventing the genre and reimagining classical *civilitas* to reflect new standards of "civilized" behavior and bodily propriety.[111] Yet as numerous scholars have pointed out, Castiglione's account of *"la sapienza civile"* in the *Book of the Courtier* predated Erasmus's manual by two years and subsequently ignited an international trend. These countless handbooks of *converzatione civile* were culturally particular and often contradictory. While the Italian *civiltá* and *vivere civile* emphasized urban living, republican citizenship, and civic virtue, the French discourse of *courtoisie, civilité,* and *politesse* was more status conscious, courtly, and aristocratic. The English *civilitie,* by contrast, rejected complicated forms of address and byzantine rituals of mutual compliment in favor of ideals of "gentleness" and "good breeding."[112] Anna Bryson has argued that the elite standard of behavior appropriate to the "gentle" classes captured in early modern English discourses of civility emerged as the product of a social and political order that remained unquestionably hierarchical and "enduringly aristocratic."[113] Civil worship, like divine, dealt paradigmatically with the performance of respect between unequals, usually from inferiors to superiors, including children to fathers and subjects to their sovereign.[114] The proper performance of these forms was a sign of gentility, as opposed to the "rudeness" or "clownishness" of the rustic and vulgar.

Here the eighteenth-century definition of civility as a synonym for *civilization* opposed to *savagism* and *barbarity* offered by Samuel Johnson is also key. As Bryson points out, the "civic" and "civilizational" senses of civility that many theorists and historians of political thought have sought to separate were, historically, intimately connected. Both originated in medieval Scholastic translations of Aristotle, in which the difference between *barbaroi*—non-Greeks who babbled nonsensically and lived as wild men or slaves—and *polites,* or Greeks whose *logos* or reasoned speech suited them for political life, was rendered in Latin as the distinction between *barbari* and *cives*: that is, barbarians who lived a wild and nomadic existence and citizens who lived in settled communities under law (*civitates*). After that other great revolution of early modernity, the exploration, conquest, and colonization of the New World, this sense of *civilitas* or "civilitie" as a civilized condition of "living together in good and politic order," as one English Aristotelian put it, took center stage.[115] As we shall see in Chapter 2, English observers—including Roger Williams—would use these anthropological categories in trying to make sense of the Americans to themselves and to each other, often with disastrous results.[116]

All of these discursive contexts—sixteenth-century conduct literature, eighteenth-century political and social thought, Renaissance humanism, and imperial ideology—are important for understanding how the post-Reformation concerns about persecution of the tongue discussed above came to be understood as an early modern crisis of *civility*. However, none captures fully the conversational virtue pertinent to fundamental religious disagreement invoked by English writers in the seventeenth century.[117] Allestree and others were clearly concerned about bodily propriety and *politesse*, yet their civility was not the elite standard of courtly manners or *bel parlar* demanded of gentlemen or courtiers. "Common civility" suggested a much lower standard that could be expected from all members of society—true or false Christians, perhaps even non-Christians, alike.

Here the incipient secularity of the "civil" as a conceptual sphere distinct from the "spiritual," "religious," and "ecclesiastical" comes to the fore. In complaining about the persecuting tongues of the sectarians, Allestree and others grudgingly accepted the fact of religious disunity while simultaneously universalizing concerns and conversational standards that had hitherto been the preserve of political and social elites. Not only must civility grease the wheels of gentlemanly conversation and commerce; it was also called upon to temper evangelical disagreements on all levels of society, disagreements in which one or both sides would try to convert the other and point out their damnable errors. Thus, a conversational virtue desirable under the best conditions came to be seen, under conditions of protracted diversity and discord, as absolutely indispensable. In the absence of *concordia*, civility might fill the breach by ensuring that heated disagreements between combustible individuals did not ignite.

Governing the Tongue

Those who could agree on the social importance of civility, however, often found themselves divided on the question of enforcement. For Taylor and Allestree, the work to be done was primarily ethical.[118] Others suspected that exhortations to conversational virtue would be insufficient to stem the tide of verbal persecution. Even that exemplary moralist, Erasmus, had criticized his contemporaries' unwillingness to take legal action and praised

Solon's law "forb[idding] anyone to hurl abuse against the dead . . . [because] he thought it was humane and civilized . . . not to allow quarrels to perpetuate themselves without limit."[119]

That early modern complaints about the malign effects of men's lingual liberty led to attempts to "bridle" men's tongues through law should come as no surprise. Still when it came to legislating civility in the seventeenth century, as today, there were many possibilities. One strategy, increasingly popular in the confessional states of early modern Europe, was to ban certain modes of religious speech and the dissenting groups that practiced them by linking them with political sedition. Queen Elizabeth's campaign against "prophesying"—including all *ex tempore* preaching outside of a recognized place of worship and the communal practice of "searching" the Scriptures in the private religious meetings known as conventicles—targeted evangelical and mystical sects like the Family of Love as purveyors of sedition, as well as Puritans within the Anglican establishment. In 1576, Elizabeth suspended Whitgift's predecessor as the Archbishop of Canterbury for his refusal to carry out her proposed ban on prophecy within the Church, and the 1593 Conventicle Act further sought to stamp out this practice by forbidding participation in any Puritan assembly.[120] This was the "prophesying" for which Jeremy Taylor demanded liberty in his 1647 pamphlet. "Restraint of Prophesying," he argued, "imposing upon other mens understanding, being masters of their consciences, and lording it over their faith, came in with the retinue and train of Antichrist . . . and the cooling of the first heats of Christianity."[121] And yet Taylor included a crucial caveat when it came to conventicles—a caveat he would not hesitate to exploit in justifying his own persecution of nonconformists after the Restoration—namely, that "if [sects] be publikely prohibited, they will privately convene, and then all those inconveniences and mischiefes which are Arguments against the permission of conventicles are Arguments for the public permissions of differing religions."[122]

Another strategy, perhaps inspired by the handbooks of civil conversation ubiquitous at the time, was to impose a civil silence on sectarians by banning discussion of religion altogether. Many early modern conduct manuals employed the language of post-Reformation eirenicism to argue that discussion should be limited to "indifferent matters" and avoid those that gave rise to disputes.[123] In apparent contrast with his *Colloquium Heptaplomeres,* Bodin's *Six Livres de Republique,* translated into English in 1606, argued that "once a form of religion is accepted by common consent, further disputation should on no account be admitted," and he cited many "kings of the East and of Africa" and "the Ordinances of Spain" as examples. Bodin singled out the king of Muscovy in particular for praise, who "seeing his people divided into divers sects and factions, by reasons of the divers preachings and disputations of the ministers . . . thereupon forbad them upon paine of death any more to preach or dispute of religion."[124]

Laws imposing a civil silence on religious controversy were not simply a figment of Bodin's philosophical imagination. The Peace of Augsburg (1555) forbade all discussion of religion on pain of death in certain German towns, and this strategy was also tried in England by Charles I, who in 1628 charged Archbishop Laud with enforcing a ban on all disputations about the meaning of the Thirty-Nine Articles of the Church of England, with disastrous results.[125] After the Restoration, the Earl of Newcastle encouraged Charles II to emulate his father's strategy by banning all theological disputations in the vernacular and to see that "any book that may make the least rent in church or state . . . be immediately condemned and burnt by the hangman, and the authors . . . severely punished even to death."[126]

Speech controls were not always a tool of persecution. An English visitor to the Netherlands in the 1670s, William Aglionby, noted that in its religiously diverse neighborhoods, statutes prohibiting "any discourse about Religion, for fear of falling out," were common. Still others cast the net more narrowly, targeting persecution of the tongue in particular by forbidding neighbors "in anyway to offend, injure, or speak any contemptuous words, profanity, or evil and indecent words to one another."[127] L'Hôpital had tried a similar tactic in his quest for concord and uniformity in France, enjoining his countrymen to "avoid those devilish names of parties, factions, and rebellions, those names of Lutherans, Huguenots and papists," and a royal edict forbidding people to "debate, quarrel, or reproach one another in matters of religion" or to use the names "Huguenots" and "Papists" in particular, followed in 1561.[128]

Similar injunctions against "contumelious words" like "Papist, [Hypocrite] and Pharisee" were issued by Henry VIII and his daughters during their reigns.[129] And yet in England, the most vocal supporters of early modern bans on persecution of the tongue were not absolutist opponents of the liberty of conscience but rather the primary targets of religious insult themselves—namely, dissenters. In 1626, John Yates, a critic of the rising Arminian tide within the Anglican establishment, declared, "I could wish with all my heart, that this offensive name of a Puritan, wandring at large, might have some Statute passe[d] upon it, both to define it, & punish it: for certainly Satan gains much by the free use of it."[130] While some sectarians grudgingly appropriated the denominations bestowed upon them by their opponents, others made calls to ban words like Quaker—along with insults like "pratlingstants" and "pickthankly knaves"—in England and her American colonies.[131]

When it came to persecution of the tongue, emigrant dissenters in the New World demonstrated a decidedly ecumenical concern for the "tender" consciences of others. In Maryland, a Catholic colony, the Toleration Act of 1649 not only protected the "free exercise" of religion but also included the following exhaustive provision:

> Whatsoever p[er]son or p[er]sons shall from henceforth vppon any occasion . . . in a reproachful manner or Way declare call or denominate any p[er]son or p[er]sons whatsoever . . . an heritick, Scismatick, Idolator, Puritan, Independent, Prespiterian, popish priest, Jesuite, Jesuited Papist, Lutheran, Calvenist, Anabaptist, Brownist, Antinomian, Barrowist, Roundhead, Sepa[ra]tist, or any other name or terme in a reproachfull manner relating to matter of Religion shall for every such Offence forfeit and loose the somme of tenne shillings sterling.[132]

And Maryland was not alone. The article establishing liberty of conscience in the 1682 Great Law of Pennsylvania included a provision declaring that "if any person shall abuse or deride any other for his or her different persuasion and practice in matter of religion, such shall be looked upon as a disturber of the peace, and be punished accordingly."[133]

As we shall see in Chapter 4, concerns about verbal persecution were also closely linked with the establishment of religious liberty in another colony associated with the most famous defender of toleration in the seventeenth century, John Locke. The 1669 *Fundamental Constitutions of Carolina* included an article proclaiming, "No person shall use any reproachful, reviling, or abusive language against the religion of any church or profession."[134] Although the degree of Locke's authorship of the *Constitutions* remains contested, one finds the same idea expressed in Maryland and Pennsylvania—namely, that religious insult was a form of persecution, hence banning it a logical extension of toleration.

These colonial provisions have been consistently overlooked by scholars, and yet their similarity to modern-day religious insult laws—and their contrast with the First Amendment—is striking. In this, the reigning assumption that hate speech laws are a twentieth-century invention and the now-standard "battle fatigue" narrative about early modern toleration have alike contributed to scholarly neglect. Crucially, these early modern statutes were not simply restrictions on so-called "fighting words." For example, the Maryland statute's demand for restitution pointed beyond the contingent harms of incivility in disturbing the public peace to its intrinsic harms as a violation of Christian charity, hence a sin against God and one's neighbor. Thus, despite scholars' protestations, what these statutes express is a demand for *tolerance*—as an attitude of acceptance toward difference—not just toleration.[135] As Scott Sowerby has recently shown, this mood was reflected in Old England as well by another doomed Stuart, James II.[136] Canvassing for the enactment of his own tolerationist program in 1687, the king encouraged the people of Chester "to set aside all animosities, and distinctions of parties and names . . . [as] we had as little reason to quarell with other men for being of different opinions as for being of different complexions."[137]

The fact that opposition to James's tolerationism—seen, once again, as a front for the "Whore of Babylon" and "Popery"—was one of the chief motivations for the so-called "Glorious" Revolution of 1688 should seriously complicate any residual Whig notions political theorists may have about the uncomplicated "rise" of tolerance *or* toleration in the seventeenth century. Still, whether in the service of toleration or uniformity, these early modern attempts to tame men's tongues through law reflected a widespread belief that societies neglected wars of words at their peril. In calling for civility—and accusing others of incivility—tolerationists and anti-tolerationists were thus united. Yet, then as now, agreement on the importance of civility did not necessarily entail agreement as to who or what should count as "uncivil." Indeed, disagreements on this score could and did engender their own heat.

Even as he lamented the "floods of heresy . . . poured out in city and country, which have overflown the banks, not only of religion, but of civility," Watson complained that this conversational virtue often masked hypocrisy ("the hypocrite's tongue may be silver, yet his heart stone") and neglected the all-important inward realm:

Civility doth but wash the outside, the inwards must be washed. . . . A sow may be washed, yet a sow still. . . . Civility, like a star, may shine in the eyes of the world, but it differs as much from purity as the crystal from the diamond; civility is but strewing flowers on a dead corpse.[138]

Watson's concerns about civility, especially when extolled by establishment Anglicans like Taylor also went deeper: "The civil person hath an aching tooth at religion; his heart riseth against holiness . . . [and] hath a secret antipathy against the ways of God."[139] For Watson and other self-styled evangelicals, the spirit of protest at the heart of Protestant Christianity often demanded conscientious *incivility* in the form of disruptive witness against a political, social, and spiritual order they saw as irredeemably corrupt.[140] Sectarian radicals like the Quakers thus shared Puritan suspicions that in calling for civility, Anglicans had it out for "godly zeal."[141]

Jeremy Taylor's turn from calling for toleration to facilitating the enthusiastic persecution of nonconformists after the Restoration seemed to prove the radicals right—as did increasing attempts after the Civil War to redefine heresy from a matter of doctrinal heterodoxy to the *manner* in which a religious opinion was held—or rather, held forth. For example, George Gillespie insisted that heresy was not just any "gross and dangerous error," but one "*voluntarily* held and *factiously* maintained"; Obadiah Sedgwick, too, emphasized the adverbial: "an erroneous or false opinion . . . *obstinately* maintained and *pertinaciously* adhered to."[142] Little wonder that for dissenters like Roger Williams, whom we will encounter in Chapter 2, there often seemed little distance between prosecuting incivility and persecuting righteousness.[143]

Conclusion

It is a common complaint against revisionist histories of toleration that by unsettling the categories of "toleration" and "persecution" they make it impossible to say with any certainty whether a historical situation counted as one or the other. After all, one man's persecution (e.g., fines for church attendance) is another's tolerationist alternative to boring heretics' tongues, branding them with a "B" for "Blasphemer," or burning them at the stake. Matters become all the more complicated when one takes the myriad institutions and policies proposed in early modern Europe for governing religious difference into account. As we have seen, these went well beyond a simple choice between toleration or persecution, to include more or less latitudinarian forms of comprehension and national establishment, strategic "tests" or restrictions on office holding, bans on public and private preaching, and laws against religious insult.

As a consequence, it can often seem difficult to say what, if anything, *changed* with the Reformation. But the early modern arguments canvassed in this chapter suggest that something did change, and something big.

They thus make the case for seeing the emergence of toleration as a central category in early modern political theory and practice in a new way, not as a narrow response to the "Wars of Religion" or religious violence, per se—"religious" wars had been fought before, and they continue to be fought today. Rather, toleration emerged in the early modern period as one possible response among many others to the shattering of the *vinculum societatis* and *concordia* of Christendom—one especially threatening consequence of which was the advent of competing and conscientiously uncivil, evangelical, and schismatic Protestantisms in a transforming and expanding public sphere.

Seeing the "rise" of toleration in this way suggests that one of the key differences between persecution and toleration must be the degree to which a particular institutional arrangement accommodates this form of evangelical religiosity and its sectarian logic, leading ultimately to the emergence of independent *churches* as opposed to a single, comprehensive Church. The particular arrangements we associate with liberal toleration—the separation of church and state through disestablishment and individual rights of expression and association—are from this perspective the most tolerant of all. But these policies were barely on the political spectrum in the seventeenth century, let alone in the sixteenth. And when they were put forward, as we shall see in Chapter 2, they were espoused not by the eirenicists but by "schismatic" and "enthusiastic" radicals like Williams.

Rawls, Waldron, and other political theorists are thus right to point to early modernity as the origin for the emergence of something like liberalism. But in holding onto the idea of concord—an ideal in which consensus on the *fundamenta* forms the basis of social harmony and mutual affection—they revive the hopes and fears of the eirenicists who sought to press the printing press into the service of public persuasion only to end up writing colloquies in which reasonable evangelists talked exclusively to themselves. The brilliant insight of early modern tolerationists was thus not the surrender of an absolute or final truth, as Rawls would suggest, but rather that of affective concord predicated on fundamental consensus as a social and political ideal. In this, their hope that civility might stop the centrifugal forces of sectarian disagreement gave way to another—namely, that this conversational virtue might *itself* replace the traditional *vinculum* of true religion or Baxter's "MEER Christianity" by uniting those who were of different religious "persuasions" through the practice of disagreement itself. Williams described this as "a bond of civility." It is to his distinctively evangelical approach to toleration that we now turn.

2

"Silver Alarums"

Roger Williams's Mere Civility

Whenever a toleration of others' religion and conscience is pleaded for, such as are (I hope in truth) zealous for God, readily produce plenty of scriptures written to the church . . . all commanding and pressing the putting forth of the unclean, the cutting off the obstinate, the purging . . . of heretics. As if, because briars, thorns, and thistles may not be in the garden of the church, therefore must all be plucked out of the wilderness [of the World]. Whereas he that is a briar, that is, a Jew, a Turk, a pagan, an Anti-Christian today, may be (when the word of the Lord runs freely) a member of Jesus Christ tomorrow.

—ROGER WILLIAMS, *The Bloudy Tenent of Persecution* (1644)

IN A SEARCH FOR early modern thinkers who might have something to teach us in confronting our own crisis of civility, Roger Williams may seem an odd choice. He remains a marginal figure in most histories of toleration, ahead of his time perhaps, but with little real influence in seventeenth-century England or on the shape of things to come.[1] In the United States, he is remembered mainly as the founder of Rhode Island and for coining the phrase "wall of separation" between church and state later popularized by Thomas Jefferson.[2] While American exceptionalists, popular biographers, and now political theorists have tried periodically to revive him as a forgotten "First Founder," he remains relatively obscure.[3]

Yet this fringe figure on the colonial periphery was also on the extreme, cutting edge of the early modern debates about toleration outlined in Chapter 1. His chief toleration tract, *The Bloudy Tenent of Persecution for Cause of Conscience* (1644), made a powerful case for extending toleration not only to all Protestant sects but to "the most Paganish" (i.e., American Indian), "Jewish," "Turkish" (i.e., Muslim), and "Antichristian" (i.e., Catholic) "consciences and worships," as well (BT, 3). This went well beyond the limited comprehension and indulgence endorsed by Erasmus or Castellio, not to mention Locke's infamous exclusion of Catholics, "Turks," and atheists in *A Letter Concerning Toleration* almost fifty years later. Moreover, Williams did something that these figures more beloved of political theorists and historians would never do—he put his theory into practice by founding and governing a tolerant society himself. The hypothesis to be tested in Williams's "livelie experiment" in Rhode Island—"that a most flourishing civil state may stand and best be maintained . . . with a full liberty in religious concernments"—was wholly unprecedented. Residents were not simply "indulged" in their dissent in *adiaphora* or comprehended in an inclusive national church. Rather, the 1663 royal charter of Rhode Island and Providence Plantations granted colonists the unheard of "free exercise and enjoyment of all their civil and religious rights," regardless of religious affiliation, in a society with no established church at all.[4]

Thus, one finds in Williams's colony all of the institutional hallmarks (disestablishment, equal protection, and individual rights) of liberal toleration. Yet it is Williams's exceptional biography—his banishment from Massachusetts Bay, his friendship with the Narragansett Indians, and his struggles to preserve Providence as a safe haven for dissenters in the face of considerable opposition from other colonies, hostile tribes, and indeed many of those dissenters themselves—that has caught the attention of his recent revivers. Foremost among these is Martha Nussbaum, who presents Williams as an attractive alternative to Locke as a proto-liberal, even proto-multiculturalist, theorist of toleration. It was "Williams's experience of finding integrity, dignity, and goodness outside of the parameters of orthodoxy," she argues, that led him to understand toleration not as mere sufferance or permission, but as a *respect* for difference itself.[5]

In foregrounding Williams's relationship with the American Indians as decisive in the development of his views on toleration, Nussbaum is not alone.[6] Here, she and others have seized especially on his conception of "civility" as the core of a positive vision of diversity in a tolerant society "characterized by camaraderie, cooperation, and mutual respect."[7] Similarly, James Calvin Davis has argued that Williams's civility—understood as a "social kinship . . . and basic sense of common morality" in a tolerant society that grounds the possibility of "public agreement on moral norms and values"—would prove a helpful corrective to the crisis of civility dominating American political discourse today.[8] While Nussbaum and Davis are right to place civility at the center of his thought, this chapter will show that in their eagerness to press him into the service of an unmistakably eirenic vision of toleration as concord acceptable to modern liberals, they have lost sight of what was so very unusual and challenging about Roger Williams.

In what follows, we shall see that Williams was one particularly strident voice in the early modern debates traced in Chapter 1. Like Erasmus or All-estree, he too was searching for an alternative *vinculum societatis* that might hold in the face of protracted fundamental disagreement and discord. Yet his experience of living under conditions of endemic instability among the Americans and other enthusiastic verbal persecutors like himself in the New World led Williams to develop a wholly new perspective on this prob-lem—and to offer an ingenious and unprecedented solution. This fascinat-ing vision of "meer" civility crucially informed his toleration project while offering something less respectful, less than mutual, and more uncomfort-able than the "mutual respect" claimed by his modern-day revivers. More-over, Williams's insistence on *liberating* men's tongues in and about religion and tolerating their incivility scandalized his contemporaries, who viewed wars of words and persecution of the tongue as the chief impediments to toleration. For many modern American readers, his alternative approach of tolerating incivility may seem intuitive. And yet Williams's unabashedly evangelical reasons for doing so may well give them pause.

An "Intolerant Tolerationist"

Before we consider how an unapologetic purveyor of persecution of the tongue like Williams became one of the foremost seventeenth-century spokesmen for civility and toleration, it is necessary first to see that for Roger Williams, life and work—like theory and practice—were intimately connected. Born in the cosmopolitan and commercial center of London around 1603, Williams was one of four children and the only son not to follow his father (a merchant tailor) into trade. Under circumstances that remain unclear, perhaps due to his facility with shorthand, he came to the attention of Sir Edward Coke, the famous jurist and defender of the rights of Englishmen against the Crown. Williams joined Coke's household as a secretary and subsequently owed his world-class education—first at the Charterhouse school in London, then at Cambridge—to his patron's influ-ence and largesse.[9]

The opportunities in seventeenth-century England for talented young men of little means opened up by an Oxbridge education enjoyed through the patronage of a wealthy benefactor will be a consistent theme in Chapters 3 and 4. At Cambridge, Williams became friends with John Milton, with whom he shared a passion for languages and godly zeal. In addition to his later facility with Narragansett, Williams knew Dutch, Hebrew, Greek, Latin, and French, and it seems that he and Milton may have exchanged language lessons. After his graduation in 1629 and despite his growing Puritan leanings, Williams took holy orders in the Church of England. But rather than pursue his own parish, he became a private chaplain to a Puritan gentleman, a common path for clergy inclined to "hotter" Protestantism and heterodoxy. It is significant, perhaps, that the gentleman in question was Sir William Masham, grandfather-in-law to Damaris Masham (née Cudworth), Locke's great friend and confidante. William's time at Otes, the Mashams' Essex estate, would be brief—Locke's stay in 1689 after his return from exile would be much longer—but this tenuous biographical link has proven too tantalizing for scholars determined to draw a line of influence between the two men to ignore. I will return to the issue of Williams's possible influence on Locke in later chapters. In any case, after having been at Otes for less than two years and in the face of the rising tide of anti-Puritanism led by William Laud, Charles I's ill-fated Archbishop of Canterbury, Williams left Old England for New in 1631.

Williams would later claim to have had "converse with some *Turks, Jews, Papists* and all sorts of *Protestants* and by Books to know the *Affairs* and *Religions* of all *Countries*" over the course of his lifetime (GF, lxiv).[10] The importance of knowledge about other, especially non-Christian, religions and cultures would be a consistent theme in his toleration writings. Recent efforts to put this lifelong interest and experience of other religions at the heart of his uncommon openness to diversity are thus well placed. But in stressing his ostensibly secular influences—for instance, John Barry has focused on Coke and his nemesis, Francis Bacon, while Nussbaum highlights the neo-Stoicism Williams would have encountered at Cambridge—scholars concerned to recover a cosmopolitan, or even multicultural, Roger Williams downplay the single most important influence in his life and works. This was, of course, religion—and it happens that Williams's brand of English Calvinism was in a decidedly hot, evangelical, and schismatic vein.[11]

Williams experienced his first spiritual conversion at the age of eleven, and his sense of the ineffable exactingness of true spirituality compared with the corruption of the professed Christians around him would only grow. Upon his arrival in Boston, the elders of the town church offered him the position of teacher, an honor he unceremoniously declined. In his reasons for refusal, one can hear echoes of the Donatists that so vexed Augustine: the Boston church was officially "unseparated" from the Anglican, which still reeked of its "Antichristian"—that is, Catholic—origins. While in England, members of the congregation would participate in worship and, more importantly, take communion in their parish churches. For Williams, this was to allow the community of "saints" to endanger their already tenuous hopes for salvation through spiritual association with the unregenerate. He promptly offended his fellow refugees by accusing them of spiritual uncleanness and refusing to worship with them lest he become similarly polluted.

Scholars inspired by the breadth and liberality of Williams's toleration like to portray him as a kind of enlightened proto-liberal running around the New England wilderness.[12] Yet this revisionism obscures a very important fact—namely, that Williams did not support toleration because he was open-minded or "Enlightened." It was just the opposite. In Andrew Murphy's phrase, Williams was "an intolerant tolerationist."[13] Indeed, by both modern *and* early modern standards he was a religious fanatic of exemplary intolerance, constantly alert to what he saw as others' irredeemable errors and motivated by an uncompromising determination to separate himself from them. His famous opposition to established churches was thus a product of spiritual self-interest and the fear that the godly would be sullied by being forced into communion with the unclean.

For proponents of concord through comprehension like Erasmus, Williams represented exactly the sort of unreasonable fanatic with whom colloquy would be impossible, and the drama of his life aptly illustrates the logic of schism of which eirenic writers were so critical. Shortly after his arrival, Williams removed to Salem (later famous for its witch trials), due to its reputation for superior spiritual rigor. Soon, however, Williams would find even the Salem congregation wanting. He spent the rest of his life in search of a church that would meet his exacting standards. Although he is often identified with the American Baptists, Williams's association with the nascent movement in Rhode Island was brief. By the end of his life, he worshipped in a congregation of only two, him and his wife—and he may not have been entirely sure about her.

John Cotton would later justify Williams's banishment from Massachusetts on the grounds that he had exiled himself first by excommunicating himself from their communion and separating from them.[14] His separatist scruples, however, were not the only thing that rendered Williams obnoxious to the denizens of Massachusetts Bay. He first ran afoul of the authorities in 1634 by insisting that women wear veils in public and for his opposition to oaths and the English flag as alike improper uses of religious symbols and ceremonies for "civil" ends.[15] Significantly, in this early period Williams's demand for spiritual purity extended even to civil worship, with ridiculous results. Cotton Mather would later relate an incident wherein Williams had "insisted vehemently upon the unlawfulness of calling any unregenerate man by the name of Good-man such and one."[16] After all, how many of them could *really* claim to be good men?

Williams's increasing familiarity with the local tribes among whom he ventured first as a missionary, then as a trader, rendered him even more suspect. His subsequent publication of a tract (now lost) arguing that the New English had no right to the Americans' land—and thus that the whole English colonial enterprise was a "National Sin" predicated on fraud—proved at last a bridge too far. The Massachusetts authorities took the extraordinary step of banishing Williams in the winter of 1635. Sheltered first by the Wampanoag then the Narragansett, Williams founded Providence on land he received as a gift from the Narragansett chief, Canonicus. It quickly became the favored destination for other religious and political "firebrands" who had found the rest of New England similarly unwelcoming, including the "Antinomian" (another slur) Anne Hutchinson.

While Williams's exile has cemented his reputation as a tolerationist hero—and Massachusetts's reputation as a persecuting society par excellence—it should be clear by now that the story is a bit more complicated. In fact, Massachusetts tolerated Williams's heterodoxy for years before taking the extraordinary step of banishing him. Beginning in 1631, he was called repeatedly before the assembly for "admonishment" before finally being exiled four years later. Moreover, the original sentence was for deportation back to England, but it was converted into banishment in winter de facto due to Williams's escape from house arrest. Finally, it was imposed *not* because he held heretical opinions but rather due to his well-documented unwillingness to stop preaching and publishing those opinions after he had promised repeatedly to do so.

Above all else, it was this dogged unwillingness to simply *hold his tongue* that made Williams intolerable to the citizens of Massachusetts Bay. But in this, he argued that he, not they, exemplified the true "puritan" and "protestant" spirit of evangelical Christianity. Like Luther, Williams insisted that the saints must witness against others' spiritual errors and "cal[l] [Christ's] *peo-ple* more and more out of the *Babel* of confused *Worships, Ministries,* &c. . . . [and] finishing of their Testimony against the *Beast.*"[17] He would describe himself in these early years as "a faithfull Watchman on the Walls to sound the Trumpet and give the Alarum [against] publike sins," and it is clear that he viewed his published contributions to the wars of words raging in England upon his first return to London in 1643 as an extension of this polemical, "purgative testimony" in a different medium.[18] As a combatant, he took full advantage of the breakdown of censorship to add his own fuel to the fire.

Refastening the *Vinculum*

Long viewed as a quintessentially American figure, Williams would have remained a local eccentric of little account if not for his determination to publish what he preached—and the fact that he did so in London over the course of two stays that overlapped with key stages of ecclesiastical upheaval during the Civil War and Interregnum. Back in England in 1643 to secure a patent for his fledgling colony, Williams quickly reconnected with Milton, who was beginning to make a splash himself on the pamphlet scene and who introduced Williams to a publisher. Williams's *Key into the Language of America* (1643), the first work of its kind published in English, captivated audiences eager to make sense of the *Barbari* with its detailed descriptions of American life. Indeed, the Long Parliament credited Williams's "great industry and travail in his printed Indian Labours" and *not* his views on the liberty of conscience in granting him his colonial patent. *The Bloudy Tenent,* with its radical defense of toleration, appeared only after his departure, whereupon the same Parliament ordered it burned.[19]

Thankfully, Williams was already safely on his way back to Providence, patent in hand. Nevertheless, he would have to return a second time in 1651 to seek a charter from the newly established Commonwealth. At that point his friend Milton would be serving as official propagandist and Secretary of Foreign Tongues for the republican regime.[20] In reviving Williams, it is thus crucial to remember that his arguments were addressed to an English audience in the context of the post-Reformation controversies about comprehension, toleration, and civility discussed in Chapter 1. Doing so reveals that in bringing insights born of his experience confronting radical difference on the colonial frontier to bear, Williams was also subtly changing the terms and the scope of the debate. This transformation of traditional concepts and categories is nowhere clearer than in his "obsessive" recourse to the concept of civility in making the case for toleration.[21] *The Bloudy Tenent* claimed that "if Men keep but the Bond of Civility," no matter how many "spirituall oppositions in point of Worship and Religion," there will not be "the least noyse . . . of any Civil breach, or breach of Civill peace amongst them" (BT, 74). Again, in *The Examiner Defended* (1652): "Notwithstanding several *Religions* in one *Nation,* in one *Shire,* yea in one *Family,* if men be . . . but truly *Civil,* and walk by the rules of *Humanity* and *Civility;* Families, Townes, Cities, and Commonweals (in the midst of *Spiritual* Differences) may flourish."[22]

In describing an essential "bond" of civility sufficient to unite men despite their fundamental differences, Williams was deliberately recalling the idea of the *vinculum societatis.* As the prospect of restoring *concordia* to Christendom became ever remote, he suggested that civility might fill the breach. But what exactly did he mean? In unpacking Williams's distinctive take on this term, all of the senses of *civility* outlined in Chapter 1 were in play. Like classical *civilitas,* Williams's civility was closely related to living "peaceablie" under law and government. "Civil" citizens acknowledged the authority of the magistrates to govern them "in their *bodies* and *goods,*" lived orderly and settled lives, obeyed the laws, and refrained from any "scandalous" offenses against the "Commonweale and profit" (BT, 354; YMB, 222).

Insofar as it meant simply keeping the peace, few if any of Williams's opponents would have disagreed. The Presbyterian minister George Gillespie, whose adverbial definition of heresy we encountered in Chapter 1, declared that he should "never consent to persecute" men who were "peaceable," but nevertheless questioned whether "those also who are as pestilence or a Gangrene . . . men of corrupt minds and turbulent spirits . . . also ought to be spared and let alone."[23] But Williams also used civility in the sense most relevant today, as the manner of speech and "civil worship" governing social interactions. His anti-Quaker work *George Fox Digg'd Out his Burrowes* (1676) defined it as "Courteous Speech," "Courteous Salutation," and "respective Behaviour" (GF, 308). While Davis renders this as "respectful,"[24] Williams's use of the adjective *respective* reflected the fact that the civility he had in mind was not necessarily an egalitarian virtue. Rather, particular forms of civil worship, hence the standard of civil behavior, would differ "respective" of others' rank and often dealt specifically with those "sober rules" governing interactions with one's "Superiors, the eldest and highest" (38).

Here again however, Williams's opponents would not have disagreed. Indeed, his fellow Puritans in New England had accused him of lacking precisely this conversational virtue in justifying his exile. Cotton denied that Williams's banishment from Massachusetts had been "for cause of conscience" at all, but rather due to his "disturbances to the Civill Peace"—not simply in the substance of his doctrines, as "that we have not our Land by Pattent from the King, but that the Natives are the true owners of it," but in the uncivil manner in which he had expressed them, as in his "vehement" refusal to swear an "Oath of Fidelitie."[25]

As we have seen, Williams was a devout and principled practitioner of exactly the kind of conscientiously uncivil, polemical evangelism that Anglican civilitarians like Taylor and Allestree despised. At this point, we must confront directly a difficult question that other commentators have overlooked. Why on earth would someone like Williams embrace civility, especially when his fellow evangelical Puritans and radical sectarians like the Quakers, who were justifiably suspicious that it would be used to silence and persecute dissent, did not?

"Meer" Civility

Rather than reject civility, Williams made it the linchpin of his argument for an unprecedented degree of toleration. His decision to embrace the civil/ uncivil distinction becomes even more curious when one considers that he scrupulously eschewed the other conceptual distinctions—between public and private, indifferent and fundamental—on which contemporary tolerationists like Milton and Locke relied. The former simply "take[s] away from the Magistrate that which is proper to his cognizance, as the complaints of servants, children, wives, against their parents, masters, husbands, &c.," and the latter could just as easily be marshaled for the cause of intolerance as its opposite (BT, 163–164). If something were truly *adiaphorous,* he argued, why should one be granted liberty therein?

To see why Williams embraced civility, one must first get clear on what, precisely, he had in mind in designating it as the appropriate *vinculum societatis* in a tolerant society. Here his "vehement" objection to civil oaths affords a clue. Ever the separatist, Williams rejected oaths and other "civil" ordinances, such as tithes, marriages, and burials in consecrated ground, as "spiritual" worship imposed by the state. In making this distinction, he drew on the traditional Calvinist opposition between the "civil" and the "spiritual" realms, while rendering it consistent in a way that Calvin, who was happy to enlist the civil magistrate's support in spiritual affairs (and vice versa), did not. Today, this thoroughgoing distinction between civility and spirituality is best remembered as the basis for Williams's insistence on disestablishment and an institutional "wall of Separation" between the "Garden of the Church" and the "Wilderness of the world."[26] But the distinction went deeper. *The Bloudy Tenent* explained that civility and spirituality, as such, were "essentially Distinct" and of an altogether different "sphere and nature" (BT, 254). The civil sphere was that "meerly concerning [the] *bodies* or *goods* of" citizens, while the spiritual or religious was that "concerning *Soule* and *worship*." Each had its own proper "Governments, Governors, Laws, Offences, Punishments," the "confounding of which brings all the world into Combustion."[27]

Williams's use of the modifier *meer* in distinguishing civility and spirituality throughout his works is suggestive. Although in modern usage "mere" means simply minimal, verging on insufficient, in early modern English, it could also mean "pure," "unmixed," or "absolute."[28] This was the sense employed by Richard Baxter in his arguments in favor of comprehension on the basis of the bare essentials of "meer Christianity" in Chapter 1. We can see this same sense reflected in Williams's argument that the "essential" distinction between civility and spirituality derived from their different origins. Whereas spirituality and spiritual government derived from God, the "originall and foundation" of civility was "the people" (BT, 249). Civility in this sense was part and parcel of a republican political theory that placed the origin of civil government in "the peoples choice and free consent," and consequently limited its jurisdiction to "the common-weale or safety of such a people in their bodies and goods" (354).

Here the elite understanding of civility as a virtue of "prudence" and "love of the public good" espoused by other English republicans provides a helpful contrast. Milton, for example, presented civility as something noble, high, and fine. Against the expectations of scholars like John Pocock and Michael Walzer, who treat the discourses of civility and "civic" virtue as antithetical, Milton saw them as synonyms in contrast with the self-interested pursuit of "money or vain honour" by merchants and tradesmen. In *Of Education*, he argued that "a compleate and generous Education [is] that which fits a man to perform justly, skillfully and magnanimously all the offices both private and publick of peace and war" and so redound to the "encrease of learning and civility everywhere."[29] Unlike his friend however, Williams emphasized the popular origins of the civil realm mainly to counter his contemporaries' arguments for an established church with the civil magistrate at its head. Such an authority might be appropriate to the governance of carnal matters, but it was entirely inappropriate to matters as weighty as salvation. Spiritual peace, "whether true or false," was "of a higher and farre different nature from the Peace of the place or people, being meerly and essentially *civill* and *humane*" (BT, 73).

Williams's civility was thus also "meer" in the sense of being minimal, a fact evidenced by its ubiquity. As he never tired of pointing out, successful civil societies were not the singular achievements of Christendom, as any student of "history or travel" could attest (YMB, 222). The history of the world and the experiences of adventurers like himself showed that civil peace did not require anything like Christian *concordia,* just as the recent experience of Christendom showed that a shared profession of Christianity was itself no safeguard against civil war and discord. By contrast, the many examples of "glorious and flourishing *Cities* of the world" that were ignorant of the Gospel proved that men could be good citizens without being godly and that civil peace could be maintained very well in the absence of *homonoia* on the fundamentals of Christianity (BT, 72).

It is here, in contradistinction to Christianity, that Williams's "meer" civility comes into view as a standard of behavior governing membership in the *civil* community of the commonwealth, while "godliness" was the appropriate standard for membership in the *spiritual* community of the true church. Williams has sometimes been accused of equating civility with charity or "Christian love," but this is exactly wrong.[30] In *Christenings Make Not Christians* (1645), he distinguished explicitly between civility, which is natural to men and the cause of all flourishing societies throughout human history, and those "corporall mercies"—such as the charitable obligation to feed the hungry, visit the sick, and bury the dead—required of Christians in society, "for [non-Christians] have them not."[31] Thus, against anti-tolerationists like Gillespie, who insisted that the end of civil magistracy must be "to make *bonum hominem,* as well as *bonum civem,*"[32] Williams argued that although "Spirituall" and "Civill Goodnesse or Virtue" were complementary, to confuse "impiety or ungodlinesse" with "incivility" would lead inevitably to "heapes upon heapes in the slaughter houses and shambles of Civill Warres" (BT, 162–163, 270).

To conflate civility with Christianity thus simultaneously set the bar for entry into civil society too high and that for spiritual communion far, far too low. The "meer" civility belonging to man as man could serve as the *vinculum* of tolerant societies precisely because it was so common—not a ceiling but a floor. Nevertheless, by Williams's reckoning many thousands of men failed to meet this standard, first and foremost those who would persecute others and deny them "the common aire to breath in, and a civill cohabitation upon the same common earth" simply for differing in spiritual matters.[33] These many cases in which men failed to be "but civil" served as a reminder that mere civility was itself "commendable and beautifull," though godliness was "infinitely more beautifull" still (BT, 246).

Civility and Civilization

Throughout his writings, Williams employed civility as a kind of minimal, sufficient condition qualifying one for toleration. So long as people were "but civil," religious difference would pose no threat to the body politic; there would be no need to call down the sword of persecution. But in their determination to conflate the standards of civility and spirituality and so transform what should be *mere* into something more, Massachusetts followed England's example made "the Common weale and Church . . . but one."[34] They therefore defined *civility* as we saw proponents of comprehension do in Chapter 1—that is, in opposition to those individuals or sects they wanted to *exclude*, be they Catholic "Antichristians," enthusiasts like Williams, or, increasingly, the American Indians. The claim that ordinances like civil oaths were "meerly" civil was an especially effective method for forcing religious undesirables to place *themselves* beyond the pale when they refused to swear—as Williams himself had discovered.[35]

According to Williams, the "very nature and essence" of civility was "the same in all parts of the *World,* where ever people live upon the face of the *Earth,* agreeing together in *Townes, Cities, Provinces,* [and] *Kingdomes,*" whether in "*Europe, Asia, Africa,* [or] *America*" (BT, 354, 251). His insistence on the exemplary civility of non-Christians, and of the Americans in particular, has long made Williams attractive to scholars on the lookout for historical precursors to modern multiculturalism. Yet Williams's recognition of civility as a basic human capacity expressed across cultures did not entail any particular respect for those cultures, let alone "cultural relativism," as some commentators have claimed.[36] Rather his point was that "all the *Nations* of the *Earth*" are "alike uncleane . . . untill it pleaseth the *Father* of *mercies* to call some out to the *Knowledge* and *Grace* of his Sonne, making them to see their *filthinesse* and strangenesse" (BT, 327).

Ever attuned to the filthiness and strangeness of others, Williams was often entirely conventional in his use of "*barbarisme,* which is a *wilderness* of *life* and *manners*" as an antonym for civility similar to that employed by his fellow English in describing and despoiling the Americans (YMB, 222).[37] *George Fox* contrasted civility with "the carriage of Barbarous & Unciviliz'd People" and claimed the whole of humanity was divided "into two Sorts": "first, The wild and Pagan, whome God hath permitted to run about the world as wild Beasts" and, second, "the *Civill*" who are "brought to *Cloaths,* to *Lawes* &c. from *Barbarisme*" (GF, 258). Like many contemporaries, Williams did not understand the categories of "civil" and "barbarian" in racial terms. In *Hireling Ministry,* he invoked "an eminent person" who "upon occasion of a debate touching the conversion of the Indians" noted that "we have Indians at home, Indians in Cornwall, Indians in Wales, Indians in Ireland."[38]

In light of such statements, Williams's appeals to civility look much less like a matter of Nussbaum's "mutually respectful civil peace among people who differ" and more like a civilizing discourse wherein the superiority of one's own civilization is asserted against an "uncivil" Other, who must conform or perish.[39] Yet unlike most of his contemporaries, Williams consistently refrained from equating civilization with civility. Although he viewed the New English as unquestionably superior in the former, like Las Casas and Montaigne he insisted that there was often more civility to be found among the "Unciviliz'd" than the clothed. Like their conflation of "meer" civility with true Christianity or civic virtue, Williams argued that the confusion of *civility* with *civilization* had led the English to ignore the abundant evidence of the former among the Americans, and hence to deny them the "the civill priviledges and rights (which are their due)" (YMB, 414).

Here another contrast—this time between Williams and his chief rival in American affairs, the so-called Apostle to the Indians, John Eliot—is helpful. Like Williams, Eliot had graduated from Cambridge and took holy orders in the Church of England before his own Puritan inclinations led him to Massachusetts Bay. Unlike Williams, however, Eliot did not separate from Massachusetts or the Church of England. Instead, he spearheaded state-funded missionary efforts among local tribes. Eliot's missionary work began in earnest in 1646 with the preaching of regular sermons, followed by the composition of a catechism and the translation of the New Testament into Algonquin, and he eventually established fourteen "praying towns" for American proselytes, the first at Natick in 1650.[40] Eliot claimed that although he had encountered many Americans desirous of converting to Christianity, it was "absolutely necessary to carry on civility with Religion." Before proselytes could join together in church fellowship, they needed to abandon their "wild and wandering course of life" and be brought to "co-habitation, Government, Arts, and trades" in "particular Townes and Cities."[41] They could not be trusted with that "Treasure of Christ"—a church—"whilst they live[d] so unfixed, confused, and ungoverned a life, uncivilized and unsubdued to labor and order."[42]

For Williams, Eliot's insistence on "civilizing" the Americans deliberately ignored the ample evidence of American civility. Here again he invoked the idea of civility as the *vinculum societatis*. Anyone who cared to look could see that "the very barbarians and Pagans of the world themselves are forced by their holding and hanging together . . . to use the ties and knots, and bands of a kind of civil justice against scandalous offenders against their Commonweale" (Key, 135). Not only did the Americans have government, they had *good* government, as well as marriages (albeit polygamous), industry, and, most crucially, property, "notwithstanding a sinfull opinion amongst [many] that Christians have right to Heathens lands" (180). The First Table of the Ten Commandments detailing one's duties to God may have been observed only in Christian nations, yet the ubiquity of government showed that the Second Table detailing one's duties to one's fellow men was "written in the hearts of all Mankind yea even in Pagans."[43]

The case of Richard Chasmore, a resident of Williams's colony accused by two Indian witnesses of engaging in multiple acts of bestiality with his cows, offers a good illustration. Chasmore had gone on the lam (so to speak) and was apprehended when he came back for his herd. But he was ultimately acquitted by his Pawtuxet neighbors, who dismissed the eyewitnesses as "Barbarians," just as Williams had feared.[44] Like the residents of Pawtuxet, Eliot ignored evidence of American civility because he confused civilization with the adoption of a specifically *English* way of life and manners. Eliot reported the hopes among some of his American acquaintances that in "40 years or more, some Indians would be all one English, and in an hundred years, all Indians here about, would so be" and noted "a great willingnesse to conform themselves to the civill fashions of the English."[45] For Williams, by contrast, a crucial aspect of civility was its cultural particularity: "Every Nation, every *Shire,* and every *Calling*" had its "particular *Properties* or *Idioms* of Speech" (GF, 306).

While the rules of civil worship differed from culture to culture, the existence of such rules was universal. A hallmark of civility on Williams's theory was thus an awareness of—and a conformability or accommodation to—the culturally specific norms of others. He knew from experience that negotiating this boundary would never be easy. In an early letter to Winthrop, he described his discomfort with the New English settlers' participation in the local custom of taking and exchanging trophies from the dead—such as scalps, hands, and so on. Nevertheless, Williams insisted on tolerating these customs in the traditional sense of *tolerantia*. That is, he "was willing to permit what I could not approve [lest] . . . I should have incurred suspicion of pride and wronged my betters, in the natives and others eyes." Accommodating oneself to local norms of civility in this way did not require that one also affirm them; rather, "I have alwaies showne dislike to such dismembering the dead and now the more."[46]

Nussbaum and others conclude from Williams's praise for American civility that he must have entertained a deep respect for their culture. Yet with them, as with his fellow Puritans, he was never shy in expressing his disagreement or disapproval. In keeping with his separatist principles, he "durst never [be] an eye witnesses, Spectator, or looker on" to their religion, "least [he] should have been a partaker of Satans Inventions and Worships" (Key, 212). In addition to his concerns about spiritual pollution, he stated openly that he "abhor[red] most of their customes." Williams would accuse local tribes of "all kind of whoredoms, idolatries and conjurations" and insisted that it was "notoriously knowne what conscience all Pagans make of Lying, stealing, Whoring, Murthering . . . and as for Drunckennes allso."[47] In 1666, he wrote to the King's Commissioner to the United Colonies regarding a dispute between colonists and natives over land rights and warned him not to hazard himself "amongst such a Barbarous scum, & offscouring of mankinde." He continued: "The business as circumstantiated will not be effected without bloudshed: barbarians are Barbarians."[48]

Evangelical Toleration

For those concerned to recover Williams as a multiculturalist *avant la lettre*, these statements may be hard to swallow. Needless to say, in appealing to civility he clearly had something less than Nussbaum's "camaraderie, cooperation, and mutual respect" or Davis's "public agreement on moral norms and values" in mind.[49] As the *vinculum* of tolerant societies, mere civility explicitly permitted much of what Williams's modern-day revivers want to rule out. It certainly did not forbid peremptory contradiction, dogmatic and unwanted counsels, expressions of disgust, or sharp rebukes. Although it placed some constraints on overt expressions of contempt, it nevertheless left individuals free to show their disapproval of others' most sensitive and sacred commitments in other ways.

And yet at the same time—and *for these very reasons*—mere civility served as the linchpin in Williams's argument for a radically inclusive form of toleration, one that included American "Barbarians" and Catholic "Antichristians" alike.[50] As he pointed out to Cotton and the Massachusetts elders, who could not "promise to approve" another form of worship "until wee see how *approvable* the men may be, and what Discipline it is that they would set up," one will inevitably run up against the limits of what one finds "approvable" long before one exhausts the bottomless well of human differences.[51] That was precisely the point of toleration. It must be remembered that "it is one thing to command, to *conceale,* to *councell,* to *approve Evill,* and another thing to *permit* and *suffer Evill* with *protestation* against it, or *dislike* of it, at least without *approbation* of it" (BT, 165).

For Williams, mere civility made toleration possible by allowing individuals to permit while nevertheless *protesting against* that which they could not approve. Here we come to the crux of its importance for Williams as a conversational virtue compatible with the antagonistic evangelism he practiced and preached. While his fellow evangelicals suspected that civility would rule out such conscientious protestations against the sins of others, Williams defended his conception of civility in a tolerant society on unabashedly evangelical grounds. *The Bloudy Tenent* insisted that "next to the saving of your own souls (in the lamentable shipwrack of Mankind) your taske (as Christians) is to save the Soules . . . of others" (BT, 5). In order to do this, one must "not onely be patient" and "earnestly and constantly pray for all sorts of men," whether "*Jewes, Turkes, Antichristians,* [or] *Pagans,*" "but [also] endeavour (to [one's] utmost abilitie) their participation of the same *grace* and *mercy*" in fellowship with Christ (93). All must be tolerated because all were potential converts: "[H]e that is a *Briar,* that is, a *Jew,* a *Turke,* a *Pagan,* an *Anti-christian* to day, may be (when the Word of the *Lord* runs freely) a member of *Jesus Christ* to morrow" (95).

That happy event would almost certainly never come to pass, however, while persecutors insisted on "pressing [and] putting forth of the *uncleane*" or "cutting off" heretics to the point of denying them a "Civill life and being" (BT, 94–95). Thus, one of the dangers of conflating the standards of civility and spirituality and so excluding the ungodly from civil life was that it precluded that soul-saving conversation: "If regenerate and truly repenting English thus come forth from the unregenerate and unrepenting, how would the name of the Lord Jesus be sanctified . . . and one good meanes practiced toward the convincing and saving of the soules of [others]"?[52] The true form of Christ's worships eluded even the saints; nevertheless, they could fulfill their evangelical duty by witnessing against that which was false in Christendom and "calling out" their fellow saints, who were as yet unaware of their "Captivitie." These souls "must *first* necessarily be inlightened . . . before they can be next fitted and prepared for the true Church, Worship, and Ministrie."[53] Spiritual consort with the unregenerate was an impediment to salvation; however, "civill converse and conversation" was an essential "preparatory Mercy" to their souls (BT, 117; Key, 215).

Williams's modern revivers have been quick to dismiss this argument about the duty of the godly to engage the ungodly in civil conversation about salvation as instrumental lip service to the prejudices of his opponents, rather than indicative of any genuinely conversionary commitments on his part—especially when it came to the Americans. According to Nussbaum, for example, "despite his fervent Christian beliefs, there is no record that he ever tried to convert any of [them]."[54] Yet the *Key* reveals that Williams talked to the Americans about their spiritual errors, God, the Gospel, and damnation constantly. Indeed, the Rhode Island Charter commended him and over twenty other settlers by name for "godly edifying themselves, and one another, in the holy Christian faith and worship, as they were persuaded," while also attending to the "gaining over and conversion of the poor ignorant Indian natives . . . to the sincere profession and obedience of the same."[55] According to Williams himself, his evangelical efforts and expectations ranged even further, and he boasted of his own informal "labour in *Europe,* in *America,* with *English,* with *Barbarians,* yea and also I have longed after some trading with the *Jewes* themselves."[56]

Pace Nussbaum then, a "respectful curiosity" about their customs was not the only thing that led him down into the Narragansett's "Smoakie holes"—he was also motivated to do what little he could with respect to their salvation by witnessing for truth against their errors.[57] To deny this is fundamentally to misunderstand his toleration project and the priority it placed on conversation—and disagreement—with others *about* their fundamental differences. In this, his Indian dialogues and English pamphlets were of a piece. The *Key*'s introduction told the story of Wequash of the Pequot tribe, whom Williams acquainted "with the *Condition* of all mankind, & his *Own* in particular," especially "How *Man* fell from *God*, and his present *Enmity* against *God*, and the *wrath of God* against Him until *Repentance.*" On his deathbed, Wequash supposedly assured Williams that his "words were never out of my heart to this present . . . me much pray to Jesus Christ" (Key, 86–87). Williams claimed that it was for the sake of such "occasional discourse" that he resolved to compile the *Key* in the first place. The title of the work was a purposeful allusion to the New Testament and the "power of the keys" to "open and shut the Consciences of men" (BT, 217). American language, he thought, was a key of keys, a key that might, through God's blessing, one day open "Doors of unknowne Mercies" both to the New English and to the Americans (Key, 80, 279).

Williams's frequent references to "Berean Civilitie" also attest to civility's evangelical significance as a necessary precondition for conversionary conversation.[58] This was a reference to Paul's sojourn in Berea after fleeing persecution in Thessalonica described in Acts. The Bereans "were more noble . . . they received the word with all readiness of mind, and searched the Scriptures daily, whether those things were so. Therefore many of them believed."[59] The similarity to his own sojourn among the Wampanoag and Narragansett was intentional. For Williams, the Americans, like the "noble" and "gentle" Bereans, were exemplars of "Ingenious Civility" not only for accepting the exiled evangelists but also for their willingness to listen and participate actively in their own evangelization.[60] But Williams's evangelical efforts among Barbarians were not limited to the Americans. Writing to the daughter of Sir Edward Coke, who happened to be an inveterate (and hostile) Anglican, Williams recommended Jeremy Taylor's *Liberty of Prophesying*, "one Booke of your owne Authours . . . in wch is excellently asserted, the Tolleracion of differing Religions: yea in a Respect that of the papists Themselves wch is a new Way of Soule Freedome, and yet is the old Way of Christ Jesus."[61] The recipient was not amused and accused Williams of having "a face of brass, so that you cannot blush." As for Taylor's book: "I think it and you would make a good fire."[62] So much for Berean civility.

Williams evidently took his duty to spread news of the "written word of God" in the Old World and the New and to counteract the deceiving words of false evangelists and "grievous wol[ves]" like Eliot quite seriously.[63] One of his main objections to Eliot's missionary efforts was that the self-styled Apostle's language skills were not strong enough to be certain that sound spiritual knowledge was being conveyed through his Algonquian preaching.[64] Neither a multiculturalist handbook nor a catechism, the *Key* modeled an engaged and inclusive form of evangelical toleration in which criticism and controversy flowed both ways.[65] So long as they were willing to listen, Williams was willing to talk. And talk—and talk—he did.

Consider the following dialogue included in the *Key* as a guide for discussing spiritual matters with the Americans, replete with "some proper expressions . . . which from myself many hundreds of times, great numbers of them have heard with great delight and great convictions":

> *Friend, I will aske you a Question.*
> *Speake on.*
> *What thinke you? Who made the Heavens? The Earth, the Sea? The World.*
> *Some will answer* Tattá *I cannot tell, some will answer* Manittôwock *the Gods.*
> *How many Gods bee there?*
> *Many, great many.*
> *Friend, not so. There is onely one God.*
> *You are mistaken.*
> *You are out of the way. . . . I will tell you, presently. I will tell you newes. One onely God made the Heavens, &c. . . .* Besides, they will say, *Wee never heard of this before:* and then will relate how they have it from their Fathers, that *Kautántowwit* made one man and woman of a stone, which disliking, he broke them in pieces, and made another man and woman of a Tree, which were the Fountaines of all mankind (Key, 215–218).[66]

To those who would use it, the *Key* thus demonstrated how to confer or create a common idiom with which to communicate across profound cultural difference.

It was Williams's hope that through the help of constant conversation "one Candle will light ten thousand, and [that] it may please God to bless a little Leaven to season the mighty Lump of [the American] Peoples and Territories" (Key, 80). And as ever, Williams's words could be forceful. The chapter on American religion ended with another helpful dialogue about damnation: "*Friend, when you die you perish everlastingly. You are everlastingly undone. God is angry with you. He will destroy you. For your many*

Gods. The whole world ere long be burnt" (251). At other times, he "argued with them about their Fire-God," and when he talked to them about Hell-fire, they talked back. To his assertion that *"English-men, Dutch men, and you* [Americans] *and all the world, when they die . . . that know not this God . . . goe to Hell or the Deepe [and] shall ever lament,"* his American inter-locutors responded, *"Who told you so?"* Williams's answer—*"Gods Booke or Writing"*—acknowledged that his own word was not enough. While he sought to convince his auditors of the superiority of Scripture, it was im-perative that they vent their objections freely and come to "the Word" with-out coercion (Key, 218–219).[67]

Here one is reminded of an important fact that his modern-day revivers appear all too eager to forget: Roger Williams could be obnoxious. After all, even *he* conceded that his banishment from Massachusetts had had some-thing to do with his "constant admonishing of them" in their "unclean walk-ing."[68] In contrast with Eliot's state-sponsored didacticism and coercive civ-ilization, Williams's agonistic evangelism was a messy, unconstrained, and altogether uncertain affair. Conversion required contestation, not a cate-chism. Only God could bring a person "to forsake a long continued Fathers worship, and to imbrace a new, though the best and truest" (BT, 354). The evangelized must be left to judge for themselves, "according to their Indian or American consciences, for other consciences it cannot be supposed they should have" (250). But this depended, in turn, upon a double freedom: of the saints to witness and of the evangelized to respond. And this entailed a form of toleration the likes of which the world had never seen—including for American "devil-worship." In response to the frequent sallies of Eliot's converts among them, the Narragansett "importun'd" Williams upon his second return to England in 1651 "to present their peticion [for toleration] to the high Sachims of England that they might not be forced from their Religion, and for not changing their Religion be invaded by War."[69]

For Williams, neither toleration nor civility required citizens to grant each other a respectful *laissez-faire* in matters of conscience while going to Hell in their own fashion. Like medieval *tolerantia,* his toleration was an un-apologetically negative form of permission without approval; nonetheless, its emphasis on ongoing evangelical converse and conversation among the tolerated demanded an ethic of inclusion and engagement that went well beyond sufferance or forbearance. In Williams, one thus finds a prime ex-ample of what I described in Chapter 1 as "evangelical toleration." And yet, in drawing on this traditional argument, he offered something altogether new. His American dialogues were not motivated by an eirenic orientation toward the future reunification of Christendom, a prospect of which he was wholly suspicious. Both in their manner and their substance—not to mention their participants—they flew in the face of the decorous colloquies envisioned by Erasmus, Witzel, or Bodin.[70]

Instead, Williams seems to have been motivated by a desire to accommodate the uncompromisingly active, engaged, and polemical form of schismatic evangelicalism unleashed by the Reformation—in other words, precisely the sort of uncivil evangelism that got him exiled from Massachusetts in the first place. But if this is right, why is it that another group of conscientious incivilitarians was the only one ever to test the limits of his toleration? Here, we must turn to Williams's infamous antipathy to "the People called Quakers," in which he finally found common ground with his erstwhile persecutors in Massachusetts.[71]

Tolerating Incivility

Although Williams set the bar of "meer" civility far lower than did contemporaries like Eliot or Milton, it was not so low that no one failed to meet it. Given the truly radical extent of Williams's toleration, which unlike Locke's included even Catholic "Antichristians,", his antipathy to the Quakers can come as a shock. Many scholars have been tempted to dismiss it as a mysterious and unfortunate departure from the principles they find so appealing. Williams's anti-Quaker polemic, *George Fox Digg'd Out His Burrowes*—the title of which was itself an uncivil play on the names of two leaders of the movement, George Fox and Edward Burroughs—was published in Boston in 1676. Not only was it the only work by Williams to be published in America during his lifetime; it apparently found favor in the colony of Massachusetts Bay, which had in the intervening years executed several Quaker missionaries and flogged and imprisoned many others.[72]

One can thus understand the temptation of Williams's admirers to downplay or explain away this episode of his career. But to understand his position, one must first remember that early Quakerism bears little resemblance to the pacific Society of Friends today. In the mid-seventeenth century, the Quakers were the epitome of the extreme, enthusiastic, and sectarian Protestantism birthed by Luther and associated with the New Model Army during the Civil War. It can be difficult to distinguish the facts from enemy propaganda; still, Quakers were notorious for going naked in public "for a sign," as well as interrupting others' worship by banging pots and pans or shouting down the minister. In one instance, a Quaker man reportedly took off his pants in an Anglican church and lay down on the communion table.[73] It was behavior like this that led Cotton Mather to describe the Quakers as "the vomit cast out in the by-past ages . . . lick'd up again for a new digestion."[74] When Quakers began flocking to Rhode Island in the 1650s, Williams was terrified that they would prove the critics right—that toleration was, indeed, the "Whore of Babylon's backdoor" and a recipe for disorder and civil strife.

George Fox thus began with an extensive list of complaints against them:

> All that their Religion *requires . . . to make* Converts *and* Proselites, *amounts to no more than what a* Reprobate *may easily attain unto. . . .* [Its] *Spirit . . . tends mainly . . .* [*t*]*o reduce Persons from* Civility *to* Barbarisme. *To an* Arbetrary Government, *and the Dictates and Decrees of that* sudden Spirit *that acts in them. To a sudden cutting off of* People, *yea of* Kings . . . *opposing them . . .* [and to] *as fiery* Persecutions *for matters of* Religion *and Conscience, as hath been or can be practiced by any* Hunters or Persecutors *in the world* (GF, 4–5).

According to Williams, Quaker religion set the bar of true spirituality far too low by replacing it with the inner light of the enthusiast. Their demand for "liberty of conscience" was thus a claim to antinomian impunity in every action they sincerely believed to be required. The result, he insisted, was a civil and spiritual anarchism in the midst of which no tolerant society could stand.

Given the severity of these charges, it is striking that Williams devoted most of his attention to criticizing another aspect of Quaker incivility— namely, their persistent refusal to adhere to those rules of "respective Behaviour" or civil worship embraced by Rhode Island society. He decried the Quakers for, among other things, replacing the practice of kissing hello with an "*uncouth, strange,* and *Immodest* way" of "*feeling* and *grabling*"—that is, shaking—hands (GF, 211). They made themselves "ridiculous" in their use of the familiar "Thou" and "Thee" with strangers, "which our *English Ideom* or propriety of speech useth in way of familiarity or of Anger, Scorn and Contempt" (306–307). He reported his incredulity in hearing "that the *Quakers* have commended the spirit of the *Indians,* for they have seen them come into *English Houses* and sit down by the fire, not speaking a word to any body . . . with out any respect in word or gesture to the Governour or chief of the family whosoever." In this he insisted their "spirit and carriage" was far worse than that of the Americans, who were scrupulous in their civil worship and the "use both [of] Reverent words and Gestures towards their Sachims, Wiyouhs and *Rulers*." Moreover, "if they were saluted by the English . . . they are very ready to receive your *Salutation* kindly, and return you another," and despite their customary nudity, "while they are amongst the *English*, they keep on the *English* apparell, but pull off all, as soon as they come again into their own Houses, and Company" (309–310). The Quakers, Williams noted with consternation, persistently refused to "resalute" and had been known to go naked, should the spirit move.[75]

What worried him above all else, however, was the their predilection for persecution of the tongue.[76] Despite his own long career of unapologetic evangelism, Williams claimed that he had "never met with such a Judging Censuring Reviling *spirit* as is the *spirit* of the *Quakers*"—nay, not "amongst *Jews* and *Turks, Papists* and *Protestants* and *Pagans* (with all of which I have conversed)." They had even "upbraid[ed]" and called him names such as "Blind Sot in the open Street."[77] In his public debate against several Quakers at Newport in 1673, Williams endured endless interruptions and "insulting" and "grievous Language," despite his protests "that such practices were against the sober rules of *Civility* and *Humanity*" (GF, 38–39). In the Quakers' persecuting tongues, he discerned a persecuting spirit akin to that in Massachusetts Bay: "Their Tongues are the most Cutting and bitter of any that I can hear of professing the *Protestant Reformation,* and it is certain, where the Tongue is so . . . they will be as bitter and Cutting in Hand also, where God pleaseth to permit a Sword to fall into it" (207).

Given the Quakers' long-standing commitment to liberty of conscience as founders of the most celebrated tolerant society in the New World (Pennsylvania), as well as the terrible persecution they suffered in England and Massachusetts, this accusation is wrong, at best, and at worst, in horrifically bad taste. Yet to understand the essence of civility for Williams, one must dig a little deeper. What connected the Quakers as paragons of incivility with persecution in his eyes was their attempt to "cut off" those who disagreed with them in religion from civil life and conversation. Far from being spiritual egalitarians, as they claimed, the Quakers declared both "by principle and practice, that there are no men to be respected in the World but themselves as being Gods and Christs" (GF, 306). Their conscientious incivility seemed to deny that divinely inspired saints could live together with others as "meerly" men or citizens, at all. Williams worried that, in this, they had produced a more perverse conflation than either the Massachusetts authorities or the Church of England. Rather than equating the principles of civility and godliness, the Quakers came dangerously close to confusing true Christianity with *incivility*. Williams was convinced that this equation must work to overturn all civil peace and order and so doom his lively experiment with evangelical toleration in Rhode Island.

Here the centrality of civility can be traced once again to Williams's vision of a tolerant society as a discordant whole held together by the ongoing, evangelical, often heated disagreements of its members. In this singular vision of social life as an endless argument about salvation, the Quakers' silence was as great a threat as violence or verbal persecution. "Their *dumb* and *deaf* Spirit" is "without Colour of *Common Humanity*"; moreover, their habit of falling to prayer in the middle of conversation was an abuse of "the Ordinances and Name of the *Spirit of Prayer* for a sudden *Silencing* of their Opposites" (GF, 210).[78] To top it all off, their own frequent accusations of incivility against their critics served the same purpose. Like the refusal to "resalute" or acknowledge another's greeting, these were all lesser instances of the peculiar evils of persecution and exile, "a sudden cutting off of People . . . opposing them" and an unwillingness to permit them a "Civill life and being" (GF, 5; BT, 94).

Williams's repeated use of this metaphor echoed Castellio's retort to Calvin or the anathemas that ended the Colloquy of Poissy. To "cut off" others in conversation was not to convert them but rather to destroy the essential flow of civil disagreement that was the life's blood of a tolerant society. By putting an end to disagreement such uncivil silencing, like persecution, takes "away all *civility*, and the *world* out of the *world*, and [lays] all upon heaps of *confusion*" (BT, 201). On Williams's view, the Quakers thus made the same mistake as their persecutors by failing to distinguish between the standards of mere civility and true spirituality. They refused to be hypocrites in civil *or* spiritual matters, and Williams saw this as a major problem. Take, for example, the issue of "hat honor." Even though he considered this form of civil worship a "vanity" and in doing so sinned "against [his] own persuasions and resolutions," Williams declared his intention to set the American "barbarians" a good example by continuing to "doff and don" his hat in accordance with the norms of his community. This led William Coddington, one of Williams's political rivals in Rhode Island and a convert to Quakerism, to remark sneeringly that although Williams refused to take off "his Cap at Prayer" he did not hesitate to "put it off to every Man or Boy,

that puls of[f] his Hat to him."[79] (Note that Coddington's complaint reflected a significant change from Williams's own early days as a conscientious
objector to Puritan norms of civil worship.)

Quakers like Coddington criticized the insincerity of mere civility as a
form of flattery or "complaisance," but for Williams this was precisely the
point. The virtue of civility in a tolerant society rested on the way in which
the rules of respectful behavior could be observed and maintained no matter
what one thought about others, their culture, or their most fundamental and
sacred beliefs. Experience had taught Williams that toleration in no way required respect for others or their folly; nor did it require that one keep one's
negative judgments to oneself. It did require, however, that one continue to
include and engage others in conversation, in accordance with whatever culturally contingent norms of civil worship obtained. The aim of civility was
always more conversation and more speech. One's Christian duty to instruct
and correct those in error also required that one be willing sometimes to
"leave Your Adversaries alone to Consult" and so allow them to "find an Inter-
im, to utter their Thoughts."[80] One need not be open to changing one's mind;
still, one must afford one's opponents the opportunity to speak their minds,
no matter how distasteful one found their convictions.

Williams convicted the Quakers of intolerable incivility on these grounds.
And yet it remained an open question how to respond. By distinguishing
the civil from the spiritual, he had significantly limited the scope of the
magistrate's authority. Yet by making civility a sufficient condition of toleration he seemed to open the door, at least in principle, to an expansion of
the state's role as the legitimate regulator of any and all incivility—including uncivil silence and persecution of the tongue. The civil sword existed
for the "*suppressing* of *uncivill* or injurious persons or actions," and so, it
seemed, for securing the necessary conditions for the "civil conversation" of
the commonwealth to continue (BT, 160).

Williams's famous "Ship of State" letter to the town of Providence suggested as much, with the Quakers clearly in view. It argued that liberty of
conscience could never justify the abdication of responsibilities the civil
magistrate deemed crucial:

> There goes many a Ship to Sea, with many a Hundred Souls in one
> Ship, whose Weal and Woe is common; and is a true Picture of a Com-
> mon-Wealth. . . . I never denied, that notwithstanding this Liberty
> [of conscience]. . . . If any Seamen refuse to perform their Service, or

Passengers to pay their Freight . . . if any refuse to obey the common Laws and Orders of the Ship, concerning their Common Peace and Preservation . . . if any shall preach or write, that there ought to be no Commanders nor Officers, because all are equal in CHRIST . . . I say, I never denied, but in such Cases, whatever is pretended, the Commander or commanders may judge, resist, compel, and punish such Transgressors according to their Deserts and Merits.[81]

While we are embarked, Williams argued, it is the commander of the ship who alone must determine which incivilities were tolerable and which were not.[82]

The extent to which an uncivil tongue could be dealt with in the same way as an uncivil sword would depend on the broader social and political circumstances. "Experience tells us that when the God of peace hath taken peace from the Earth one sparke of action word or Cariage is too powrefull to kindle such a fire as burnes up Families Townes [and] Cities."[83] Williams's particular worries about the Quakers thus derived from the tenuousness of order in Providence, where civil peace was continually threatened from both within and without. After surveying the Quakers' myriad incivilities in *George Fox,* he went so far as to declare that "a due and moderate restraint and punishing of these incivilities (though pretending Conscience)" is "as far from Persecution (properly so called) as that it is a Duty and Command of God" (GF, 307). However, the occasion of this remark was in stark contrast with its tenor. In a classic example of trying to combat uncivil speech with more speech, *George Fox* recounted the public debate to which Williams had challenged several leading Quakers. Even though he was old and ill, at times having to be carried into the venue on his sickbed, he spent three days in trying to convince them of their theological errors, while suffering considerable persecution of the tongue for his trouble.

Here, it is essential to remember that during the decades of protracted and heated public debate with Quakers and other sectarians in Rhode Island, Williams never called down the civil sword on his interlocutors, no matter how gross their violations of civility. Instead, he gave thanks to God for blessing him with "such Patience to weather" their rudeness and hoped to teach his adversaries by example.[84] Given that there was actual "brawling continually in Mr Williams medow," he showed remarkable restraint.[85] He knew from experience that claims to necessity and public order could be abused, and in 1675 (one year before *George Fox* was published in Boston) he would criticize the Massachusetts authorities for using the threat of war with the Americans as an excuse to censor "licentious" printing and engage in covert persecution.[86]

In tolerating the Quakers' incivility, Williams's motivations were, once again, primarily evangelical. As often as he attributed the Quakers' bad behavior to the "pretense" of religion, the time and energy he devoted to arguing points of Scripture with them—including especially Christ's "*Courtesie & Gentleness & Sociableness* with open *Sinners*"—acknowledged that their uncivil practice was the result of a genuine, spiritual error, as well as his conviction that it was his duty to save them from it (GF, 308). Accordingly, the magistrate's role was not to stifle any disagreement that might upset the peace by imposing another form of (un)civil silence, but rather to secure the conditions under which those disagreements—along with the annoyance, disapproval, and disgust they inevitably engendered—could proceed.

Evangelical Liberty

Scholars often treat Williams's antipathy to the Quakers as a late, lamentable abandonment of his tolerationist principles. But rather than an abdication of those commitments, I want to argue that his determination to tolerate the Quakers in Rhode Island, despite his personal contempt for them, should be seen as a powerful illustration of what true toleration—as the willingness to coexist with those people and views one finds most contemptible—really looks like.

Still, given his concerns about their cutting tongues, one might wonder why Williams did not insist upon a law like those found in Maryland—or, indeed, in Pennsylvania—in his own colony. He clearly believed that the civil magistrate had the authority to punish other kinds of speech, including fighting words, slander, and sedition.[87] Perhaps he feared that his own penchant for calling others "Divell"-worshippers and "Antichristians," or accusing them of "spiritual whoredom," might put him at risk of prosecution.[88] But Williams's reasons for rejecting religious insult laws also went deeper. They were the same reasons that led him to place so much value on civility in the first place—namely, his evangelical commitments to negative witness and to continued conversation with the unregenerate in the hopes of their conversion. He appealed to Luther's metaphor of the two swords throughout. The first of these was the sword of steel belonging to the magistrate. The second was "the sword of Gods Spirit, expresly said to be the

Word of God" (BT, 160). In true Lutheran fashion, Williams insisted that this sword was carried in the mouths of Christ's servants—and they needed to swing freely.

As his struggles with the Quakers show, Williams was under no illusions that more speech in this evangelical vein would discourage religious insult—or, for that matter, necessarily convert anyone. Moreover, he was well aware that evangelism was an activity that those on the receiving end often found decidedly uncivil. But for this very reason, he feared that the legal restriction of religious insult or offensive names—much like the adverbial definitions of heresy put forward by Gillespie and others—would necessarily confuse the manner of disagreement with its substance and so impede evangelical activity. "Arrogance" and "impetuosity" in the "holding forth [of] Doctrine or Practice" were inevitably in the eye of the beholder (BT, 26, 29). "When a kingdome or state, towne or family, lyes and lives in the guilt of false God, false Christ, false worship: no wonder if sore eyes be troubled at the appearance of the light, be it never so sweet . . . if persons sleepy loving to sleepe be troubled at the noise of shrill (though silver) alarums" (79–80).

The Bloudy Tenent argued that Cotton and other defenders of persecution routinely conflated the substance of beliefs with the manner in which they were expressed. There may be, in fact, a "way and manner of holding forth, (either with railing or reviling, daring or chalenging speeches, or with force of Armes, Swords, Guns, Prisons, &c.) that it may not only tend to breake, but may actually breake the civill peace" (BT, 78). Persecution represented just such a case, with any breach of peace on account of religious difference the result of "that wrong and preposterous way of suppressing, preventing, and extinguishing such doctrines or practices." Thus, "the sons of men . . . disquiet themselves in vain, and unmercifully"—and uncivilly—"disquiet others" (101–102). In the case of evangelism however, the manner of expression could not be separated from its substance. Accordingly, legislation targeting uncivil religious disagreement would preclude "all true preaching of the Gospell or glad newes," which was properly done in a "zealous," "immoveable, constant, and resolved" way (75–76). Far from being a logical extension of religious liberty, Williams viewed laws against persecution of the tongue as a violation of it and a threat to toleration itself. Remember: "he that is a Briar" may be "a member of Jesus Christ to morrow"—but if and only if "the Word of the Lord runs *freely*" (95).

Here we come to the most distinctive—and radical—institutional innovation associated with Williams's toleration. *The Bloudy Tenent* called, in fact, for two things: first, the "permission of the most *Paganish, Jewish, Turkish,* or *Antichristian consciences* and *worships*" and, second, "that they are only to be fought against with that sword which is only, in soul matters, able to conquer: to wit, the sword of God's Spirit, the word of God" (3). In other words, evangelistic activities must receive the same "free exercise and enjoyment" as any other form of worship. Williams's objections to the so-called *Humble Proposals* while in London again in 1652 illustrated his determination to put this idea of evangelical liberty into practice outside of Rhode Island. The proposals were a plan for reforming the ecclesiastical structure of the Church of England presented to the Rump Parliament as part of a concerted campaign to discipline "the propagation of the Gospel" after a decade of spiritual anarchy.[89] Among other things, they proposed a system of licensing for preachers through a combined process of civil "approval" and ecclesiastical ordination. Not only did this violate Williams's principled commitment to the separation of church and state; unlike his fellow Congregationalists or "Independents" in Parliament, Williams viewed the propagation of the gospel as a duty of all Christians. Hence he thought that evangelical liberty must be extended beyond professional clerics or a state-supported ministry to ensure the unimpeded witnessing of the true saints—wherever and whenever they appeared.[90]

In his endorsement of "mechanick" preaching, Williams contributed to the erosion of the distinction between clergy and laity initiated by Luther years before.[91] Although his commitment to universal evangelical liberty would be tested in his conflict with the Quakers, unlike Luther, Williams held firm. His own experiences as a "fire-brand" were once again decisive. Civil conversations need not necessarily be polite. Unlike politeness and complaisance, mere civility did not aim to make discourse pleasant by avoiding offense. The expression of disagreement or disapproval in spiritual matters, no matter how civilly done, would always produce some heat. And yet men insisted on running to the magistrate whenever they found "Opinions offensive":

> If the Jews . . . blasphemously call our Christ a Deceiver: Nay, if the *Mahumetans* the *Turkes* . . . if they . . . prefer their cheating *Mahomet* before him, What now? Must we raile, revile, &c. and cry out *Blasphemers, Hereticks?* Must we run to the *Cutlers* shop, the *Armories* and *Magazines* of the Cities of Nations, Must we run to the . . . Senates, and cry, Helpe you men of *Ephesus?*[92]

Williams insisted that despite their civility, the ease with which the Americans took offense or "indignation" was "a great kindling of Warres amongst them," as well (Key, 200–202). While civility required that citizens abstain from gratuitous insulting that might add "Oile or Fuell to the flam[e]," it also required that they engage continually with those with whom they disagreed so that they might become less sensitive to it.[93] A tolerant society must be prepared to tolerate quite a lot of outrage, offense, and discomfort—and to tolerate a lot of incivility, too.

Conclusion

Williams's conclusion that the best way to maintain the *vinculum* of civility in a tolerant society was to liberate men's tongues flew in the face not only of common sense but of the overwhelming weight of tolerationist argument since Erasmus, which had identified *verbal* persecution as among the most insidious forms. Yet whereas others—including theorists of colloquy like Erasmus and Bodin—theorized toleration in elite and largely monocultural Christian contexts in which *concordia* remained a legitimate, if unlikely, aspiration, Williams did not have that luxury. Life in the wilderness demanded that one make one's peace with discord and din. Accordingly, Williams was one of the first to grasp just how radical the change inaugurated by the Reformation had been—and to see that a society bound together by mere civility, rather than concord, might be all the stronger for it.

Williams was not sanguine that ceaseless conversation about salvation would ultimately persuade anyone. Partiality and pride were permanent features of the human condition. "That our selves and all men are apt and prone to differ" and "that either part or partie is most right in his owne eye his Cause Right his Cariage Right, his Argumts Right his Answeres Right" is "no new Thing in all former Ages [or] in all parts of this World."[94] Accordingly, "if Paul, if Jesus Christ, were present here at London, and the question were proposed, what Religion would they approve of—the Papists, Prelatists, Presbyterians, Independents, &c. would each say, Of mine, of mine" (BT, 11). It was because of this inevitable partiality that the standard of mere civility must be defined with reference to the requirements of an ongoing conversation—literally, a "civilizing" discourse—wherein disputants, who entered the conversational fray in order to convert their neighbors, developed patience and indifference to offense instead.

Paradoxically, perhaps, it was Williams's dim view of the possibilities of persuasion that reassured him that this conversation might continue long enough to achieve its secondary, civilizing purpose. We who are as "poore Grasshoppers, hopping and skipping from branch to twig in this vale of tears" would do well not to expect in this world what is possible only in the next.[95] Of course, like most Puritans, Williams believed that the eschaton was fast approaching. It is harder, perhaps, to content oneself with mere civility when one does not believe that the world is ending tomorrow. Even so, it should now be clear why the appeals to Williams by modern civilitarians with which we began this chapter fall short. As his conduct toward the Quakers and the Americans demonstrated, Williams believed mere civility to be compatible with negative judgments, deep disapproval, and disgust. Its virtue lay in the way in which the rules of "respectful behavior" could be observed and maintained even—and especially—in the absence of sincere respect. Men must be willing, like the Americans, to change their clothes once in a while, where the circumstances or customs of the place demanded it. But this change of clothes need not imply any deeper change of mind or heart. Unlike those of conversion, the demands of mere civility were not even skin deep.

For Williams, this insincere and minimalist understanding of civility went hand in hand with the "mere" toleration political theorists like Nussbaum find so wanting. Accordingly, she and others have tried to substitute a much more robust understanding of civility as civic friendship or mutual respect where Williams thought mere civility would do. And yet the very "mereness" of his mere civility was the key to the radical inclusiveness they so admire. In a tolerant society, people must be "suffered to breathe and walke upon the *Deckes* in the ayre of *civill liberty* and *conversation* in the Ship of the *commonwealth*," rather than remain "choaked and smothered" below.[96]

When Williams employed the metaphor of the ship of state he was speaking from the experience of five transatlantic crossings. Like our fellow passengers on a long voyage, the people with whom we share our civil life are largely unchosen. Colonialism and a world made small through exploration only confirmed St. Paul's observation that "we must goe out of the world, in case we may not keep in civill converse with Idolaters" (BT, 116). After being cast out by his fellow colonists, Williams soon found himself once more in the society of men—first of the Americans and thereafter with other dissenters in Providence. The New and Old English policies of persecution, if universalized, would thus lead ultimately to the wholly un-christian conclusion that those with whom one disagrees must "be driven out of the World" (214). While we are stuck in the same boat with people we hate, we had better learn to make the most of it. There is no reason, however, to think that this will make us respect or like each other more. It is usually the opposite.[97]

Williams's achievement in putting his radical theory of toleration into practice in Rhode Island, and with the most unpromising and uncoop-erative of materials, is remarkable. Nevertheless, contemporary observers were justly skeptical that this "livelie experiment" with universal evangelical liberty could succeed.[98] Neighbors complained that "Rogues Island" was a "receptacle for all sorts of riff-raff" and "the sewers (*latrina*) of New En-gland," a reputation for enthusiastic dysfunction that would last well into the nineteenth century.[99] As we shall see, few of Williams's contemporaries would have the stomach for dissent and discord necessary to follow his ex-ample. Thomas Hobbes, the subject of Chapter 3, would have looked at the "brawling continually in Mr Williams medow" and shuddered.[100]

3

"If It Be without Contention"

Hobbes and Civil Silence

For even apart from open contention, the mere act of disagreement is offensive. Not to agree with someone on an issue is tacitly to accuse him of error . . . just as to dissent from him in a large number of points is tantamount to calling him a fool; and this is apparent in the fact that the bitterest wars are between different sects of the same religion and different factions in the same commonwealth, when they clash over doctrines or policy.

—THOMAS HOBBES, *De Cive* (1647)

ON THE SURFACE, Roger Williams—a godly preacher, occasional missionary, and founding member of the state of nature—bears little resemblance to Thomas Hobbes (1588–1679), a man of learning and the new science, famed among other things for irreligion. Both were uncommonly long-lived. Williams died in 1683 at almost 80 and volunteered as a captain in the Rhode Island militia at the age of 73. In that war, the Americans would burn Williams's beloved Providence to the ground, along with most of his precious books and papers. Hobbes was born a "twin with fear" with the Spanish Armada, and he died at the high point of hysteria surrounding the "Popish Plot" hoax at the age of 91.[1] Even so, while war and a state of nature modeled on the New World were the constant preoccupations of his long life and works,[2] he was remarkably successful in his efforts to avoid them personally. As "the first of all that fled" before the Civil War, Hobbes was safely in exile before the outbreak of hostilities. He rode out the war in Paris, serving as a geometry tutor to the royal court in exile, and he returned to London a decade later—but only after the new Commonwealth had been secured.

Nevertheless, Williams and Hobbes both rose from obscurity through educational opportunity to live lives of brilliant paradox that exemplified, in their very different ways, the brave new world of possibilities open to men of ability and ambition in those years of turmoil. Hobbes was born in Malmesbury, the son of a disgraced curate who was excommunicated, among other things, for failing to catechize the young. Sent to Oxford through the combined efforts of a wealthy relative and a beloved teacher, thence into service in an aristocratic household, at the end of his long life Hobbes would enjoy international celebrity as one of the brightest stars in a burgeoning Republic (or, better yet, "Cosmopolis") of Letters. And yet he would escape persecution for his heretical religious and political opinions after the Restoration of his former pupil, Charles II, to the throne only through the protection of his royal and aristocratic patrons. One of the defining paradoxes of Hobbes's life was thus that this man of uncommon genius and independence of mind, celebrated and reviled at home and abroad, spent his life as a servant dependent on men who would never be his equals.

The fact that the evangelical Williams appealed to the concept of *civility* with "obsessive frequency,"[3] while the urbane Hobbes rarely did, may come as a surprise. When the word does appear in the latter's corpus, it is used mainly as a synonym for civilization—as in the progress of science and technology that "distinguisheth the civility of Europe, from the barbarity of the American savages."[4] At other times, it is pejorative. Its lone usage in *Leviathan* denotes a superficially correct form of civil worship consistent with the madness of the "man in Bedlam," who discourses "civilly" enough while claiming to be "God the Father" (L, ii.8.114). *Behemoth* linked civility critically with a ridiculous, aristocratic chivalry of "fine clothes, great feathers," and hypocritical opportunism: "Civility towards men that will not swallow injuries, and injury towards them that will, is the present gallantry" (B, 38). Instances in Hobbes's correspondence carry connotations of generosity, politeness, and more than common courtesy.[5]

Of course, this scant and contradictory textual evidence has not stopped scholars from attributing a full-fledged theory of civility to Hobbes. The noun may appear rarely in his writings, but the adjective *civil* is ubiquitous throughout as a synonym for peaceful—as in the "civil society" contrasted with man's natural "savage" and warlike state—and for the political, as in Hobbes's *scientia civilis*, in contrast with the spiritual and ecclesiastic. Scholars have posited many different Hobbesian "civilities" on this basis. For most, it is the characteristic virtue of "bourgeois morality" subjected, in turn, to successive waves of Romantic, Marxian, and neo-Republican critique;[6] for some, it is a humanist ideal found in early modern handbooks of

civil conversation and courtesy or else a nakedly imperialistic sense of civilizational superiority;[7] still for others, it describes an insurgent secularity
marking the beginning of all "modern" political philosophizing thereafter.[8]

These accounts are helpful, but they can also be misleading. Often, they
read back into Hobbes an eighteenth-century preoccupation with politeness
as the hallmark of civilizational progress over and against the dual "barbarisms" of fanaticism and superstition. Not only does this risk anachronism
by too readily assimilating Hobbes's views to those of a later period,[9] it also
blinds us to the reasons why the concept of civility as a conversational virtue in our sense, and in the sense that preoccupied contemporaries like Williams, is in Hobbes's works conspicuously absent. Still, that Hobbes should
lack a conception of civility as the *vinculum societatis* of a tolerant society
should not be entirely surprising; to offer anything like this, he would have
first had to endorse some degree of toleration. The scholarly consensus has
shifted somewhat since Alan Ryan's recovery of "a more tolerant" Hobbes
thirty years ago; still, one might be forgiven for thinking that his "Erastian" arguments for sovereign supremacy in civil *and* spiritual affairs would
make him an unlikely candidate, at best, for the present inquiry.[10]

In Hobbes we find one of the strongest and most uncompromising expressions of the identification of church and state underlying the early
modern process of confessionalization. Hobbes insisted that "a *commonwealth* [*civitas*] and a *church* [*ecclesia*]" were "exactly the same thing under two different names" (DC, 221), and that the sovereign was thus the
"Supreme Pastor," "Soveraign Prophet," and God's "Vicegerent on Earth"
(L, iii.42.825, 36.678). He was also its chief censor, with the authority to regulate doctrine to ensure its conformity with "Publique Reason"
(ii.18.300). The liberty of conscience claimed by dissenters was thus a
"doctrine repugnant to civil society":

> The Law is the publique Conscience, by which [subjects] hath already
> undertaken to be guided ... in such diversity as there is of private Con-
> sciences, which are but private opinions, the Common-wealth must
> needs be distracted (ii.29.502).

Statements like this would appear to place Hobbes firmly on the side of
persecution against toleration. And yet, as Jeffrey Collins and Mark Goldie
have shown, it was precisely Hobbes's Erastianism, more than any other
feature of *Leviathan*, that offended his early readers and alienated him from
the royalist mainstream.[11] For those committed to *jure divino* episcopacy

(or for that matter, presbytery) in the years after the Long Parliament took the extraordinary step of abolishing bishops in the Church of England, the "essential" distinction between civil and ecclesiastical authority drawn by a radical like Williams would have been far more congenial.[12]

This chapter builds on the recent excellent work by Collins and others to complicate the standard picture of Hobbes as a partisan of coercive uniformity by arguing that the notable omissions in his thought—of a theory of civility on the one hand, and of toleration on the other—are only apparent.[13] Both can be traced to Hobbes's analysis of the difficulties of fundamental disagreement and of the insults, sectarianism, and persecution of the tongue it inspired. In this, the dearth of direct references to civility is more than compensated by his constant preoccupation with "bestial incivility" in any and all forms (B, 125). Like many of his tolerationist contemporaries, Hobbes believed that the question of coexistence under conditions of religious diversity was not about how much *difference* a society could bear, but of how much *disagreement*. How much toleration would be desirable—a little, a lot, or perhaps none at all—depended ultimately on how much disagreement people could bear, before giving up on words and resorting to swords. But whereas Williams insisted on the counterintuitive benefits of open, active, and often evangelical disagreement for toleration, despite its difficulties, Hobbes saw only the dangers. Given "the contrariety of mens Opinions and Manners," he argued in *Leviathan*'s "Review and Conclusion," it is almost "impossible to entertain a constant Civill Amity with all those, with whom the Businesse of the world constrains us to converse." Almost, but not entirely—"for by Education and Discipline they may bee, and are sometimes, reconciled" (L, iii.1132).

When it comes to religion, many readers assume that *Leviathan*'s "Education and Discipline" meant uniformity in an absolute, proto-totalitarian vein. But this chapter will argue that Hobbes's opposition to toleration, as with his indifference to civility, was much more complicated and nuanced than his Erastian arguments suggest. In his attempt to chart his own *via media* between the alternatives of toleration and persecution, he concluded that the sovereign could permit, though not encourage, some degree of diversity in religious association and worship in a commonwealth—but the price of this toleration would always be uncompromising self- and sovereign discipline in speech. In this distinctively Hobbesian vision of a tolerant society as one of "difference without disagreement," secured by the virtues of discretion and complaisance, along with a comprehensive platform of civilitarian legislation, the sovereign could not afford to leave people as they were; he had an essential educative role to play.[14]

Hobbesian difference without disagreement expresses a vision of something like civility in our sense as the indispensible conversational virtue and *vinculum* of tolerant societies. Unlike Williams, however, whose mere civility facilitated active, evangelical disagreement in the public sphere, Hobbes insisted that only a *civil silence* about religious difference would suffice to secure peace by freeing individuals from the unpleasant and inflammatory business of disagreeing at all. In reconciling the inevitable "contrariety" of men's opinions with the "peace and concord" of a commonwealth, this Hobbesian conception of civility called for silence, not harmony. Moreover, its vision of *concordia* maintained a carefully constructed hole where the shared heart should be.

Contumely and Contempt

Hobbes turned to political philosophy only late in life, long after his "discovery" of Euclidian geometry at the tender age of 40.[15] But from the beginning, in his first work of "civil science" the *Elements of Law* (1640), he would single out *contumely* as one of the fundamental problems of social life.[16] In defining this species of incivility, Hobbes was nothing if not thorough. Not only do "all signs which shew to one another of hatred and contempt provoke in the highest degree to quarrel and battle" (EL, 92); *De Cive* (1642/1647) made clear that these included not only "taunting and offensive remarks" but all "deeds, words, facial expression[s] or laughter" that could be so construed (DC, 49). *Leviathan* (1651) insisted that "contumely, in words, or gesture"— including "trifles, as a word, a smile, a different opinion, and any other signe of undervalue"—was so dangerous that it should be considered one of the "principall causes of quarrell" (L, ii.15.234, 13.192).[17]

Hobbes evidently shared his contemporaries' concerns about the wars of words and rampant verbal persecution afflicting English society. Whereas others contented themselves with bemoaning the sorry state of affairs, he brought his unparalleled perspicuity and insight to bear in identifying its causes. Why should such apparently trivial instances of incivility "provoke to fight" (L, ii.15.234)? Understanding this would be an essential first step toward finding a scientific solution.

Throughout his works, Hobbes blamed the destructive effects of insult, real or imagined, on human nature, specifically on men's passion for glory—that "joy" and "exultation of mind" arising "from imagination of a man's own power and ability" (L, ii.6.88).[18] This passion was always relative, because a man's high opinion of himself depended upon his favorable comparison with others and their recognition of the same, in turn: "For every man looketh that his companion should value him, at the same rate he sets upon himselfe." Inevitably disappointed, "upon all signes of contempt, or under-valuing," one "naturally endeavours, as far as he dares . . . to extort a greater value from his contemners, by dommage; and from others, by the example" (L, ii.13.190).

According to Hobbes, then, contempt—meaning simply valuing someone less than he did himself—was a necessary and unavoidable consequence of the human condition, in which every party enters convinced of his superior worth. The harm caused was "Phantasticall" rather than "Corporeall," but lest one think the emphasis placed on it excessive for a materialist like Hobbes, even phantastical "injuries" produced physical effects (L, ii.27.466). Even in dreams, the perception of contempt aroused anger, experienced physiologically as heat (ii.2.32). This, in turn, explained the incendiary effects of incivility. Like any pain or discomfort, individuals experienced insult as evil and conceived a hatred for it, followed by a desire to destroy. "For in those things men hate, they find a continuall, and unavoydable molestation; whereby either a mans patience must be everlasting, or he must be eased by removing the power of that which molesteth him" (ii.27.462).

In addition to the underlying psychology and passions motivating contumely along with one's responses to it, Hobbes showed an almost modern sensitivity to the myriad forms, beyond mere words, that early modern "microaggressions" could take.[19] Not only did overt insults, rude gestures, and the like "provoke to fight"; things as seemingly innocuous as laughter, which Hobbes described in characteristically jaundiced fashion as a "sudden glory arising from [a] conception of some eminency in ourselves, by comparison with the infirmities of others," did too. Hobbes's suspicions extended even to the ostensibly "harmless and inoffensive" conversational diversions of society (L, ii.15.234; cf. EL, 54; DC, 22). As De Cive noted, the vinculum societatis in most social gatherings was malicious gossip and mockery, not the milk of human kindness. "People who are not there are attacked, their words and actions, their whole manner of life is scrutinized, judged, condemned, and exposed to witty scorn; people who are there and talking with others are not spared the same treatment as soon as they leave." It was good policy, therefore, never to be the first to do so (DC, 23).

In such moments, one cannot help but feel that Hobbes was speaking from experience. He and his friends were clearly sensitive to the "uncharitable censure" and "witty scorn" to which he was often subjected, as well as to the rumors circulated by his critics, including the charge that Hobbes was an atheist. (The further rumor that Hobbes fathered an illegitimate daughter divides scholars to this day.)[20] Nevertheless, most scholars have focused on the related issues of glory, contumely, and contempt in Hobbes's thought in the context of the elite discourses of courtesy and civil conversation he would have encountered as secretary and tutor to the aristocratic Cavendish family. Quentin Skinner and Markku Peltonen have stressed the significance of dueling, in particular, as informing Hobbes's insistence on contumely's violent potential.[21] Certainly, for someone convinced that violent death was the *summum malum,* the propensity of "most men . . . to lose their peace and even their lives rather than suffer insult" seemed irrational in the extreme (DC, 49). In *Leviathan,* duels provide a paradigmatic example of "rash speaking" resulting in violence (L, ii.10.142), and as early as 1638 Hobbes had written to his pupil Charles Cavendish, warning him to avoid "all offensive speech" and "harsh language" lest he provoke one.[22]

Hobbes was well aware that differences in their sensitivity to offense might result from men's different upbringings and natural "constitution"; the "vain-glorious," in particular, "are subject to ANGER, as being more prone than others to interpret for CONTEMPT the ordinary liberty of conversation" (L, ii.26.195).[23] Because of this, some scholars have assumed that his analyses of contumely and contempt were intended primarily as a critique of "vainglorious" aristocrats and that Hobbes had the coming bourgeois age firmly in view.[24] Yet, as Arash Abizadeh has pointed out, Hobbes's view of human nature stressed that no man—or woman—was immune to insult.[25] Partiality and pride were natural to men as such, to the "modest" and "vain-glorious" alike. None were immune to the passions of anger and hatred attendant on insult, nor would most men, if any, be sufficiently magnanimous to disdain the offense (DC, 26–27).

Hobbes's analysis of the drama of the drawing room thus pointed beyond the affairs of honor between ambitious aristocrats to illuminate a danger that struck on all levels of society—a danger that the cutting tongues of his contemporaries in religious and political disagreement threatened to unleash on an unprecedented societal scale. That danger would, of course, come to pass. In his retrospective history of England's civil wars, *Behemoth,* Hobbes would emphasize the fact that "a kind of war between the pens of

Parliament and those of the sectaries, and other able men that were with the King" had broken out long before a single sword had been drawn (B, 81). He meant this identification to be more than merely metaphorical: "There was [yet] no blood shed; they shot at one another nothing but paper"; nonetheless, "it were a war before" (109). As evidence, Hobbes noted the widespread circulation of contumelious terms of abuse like "tyrant," "Jesuit," and "Antichristian," which like "heated" dreams conjured up the image of an enemy and a desire to destroy.

Hobbes had little patience for anti-Catholic persecution of the tongue, which he credited with successfully fomenting popular intolerance and hatred against Charles I and his Catholic queen.[26] There was "nothing . . . more hateful to the people; not because [the Roman Religion] was erroneous (which they had neither learning nor judgment enough to examine) but because they had been used to hear[ing] it inveighed against . . . [which] was indeed the most effectual calumny, to alienate the people's affections from him" (B, 60). Much like Erasmus, Hobbes was attuned to the role of technology in the spreading of "paper war" through the pulpits, presses, and other organs of the Stuart public sphere. The popularizing of the conflict, as both sides appealed to "the judgment of the people, to whom, by printing [their petty quarrels] were communicated," had thus been crucial (84). As *Leviathan* had warned, the incendiary effects of uncivil disagreement were exacerbated in groups: "For the Passions of men, which asunder are moderate . . . in Assembly are like many brands, that enflame one another, (especially when they blow one another with Orations) to the setting of the Common-wealth on fire" (L, ii.25.408–410).[27]

The Dangers of Disagreement

If anger and hatred were characteristically aristocratic responses to expressions of contempt, the printing press had evidently lifted the lid on controversy and unleashed everyone's inner aristocrat. On Hobbes's telling, uncivil disagreements characterized by sectarianism, rhetorical "heat," and verbal persecution, such as those that had preceded the outbreak of hostilities in England, constituted a state of war in the bosom of so-called "civil" society. His analysis of contumely led to another, equally worrying conclusion—namely, that expressions of contempt or undervalue were as inevitable as they were destructive. Little wonder then that war, not peace, was man's natural state.

What was to be done? In enumerating the laws of nature—those "Precept[s] or generall Rule[s], found out by Reason" that instruct men to "seek Peace"—Hobbes put the focus squarely on eradicating insult (L, ii.14.198–200). The *Elements* insisted that "it must necessarily be implied as a law of nature, That no man reproach, revile, deride, or any otherwise declare his hatred, contempt, or disesteem of any other" (EL, 92). This conclusion was bolstered by biblical supports in *De Cive* and repeated with an expanded list of the modes of offending declaration—"by deed, word, countenance or gesture"—in *Leviathan* (DC, 62; L, ii.15.234). Indeed, "cursing, Swearing, Reviling, and the like, do not signifie as Speech; but as the actions of a tongue accustomed" (ii.6.94).

Thus far, Hobbes's analysis would seem in keeping with the standard narrative about the rise of toleration as a response to religious violence described in Chapter 1. Waldron, for instance, in investigating toleration and "calumny" in the early modern period dismisses *Leviathan*'s eighth law of nature against contumely as simply a proscription of "fighting words."[28] Yet there was an additional species of contumely on Hobbes's account that was absolutely essential. As he put it in *De Cive*, "even apart from open contention, the mere act of disagreement is offensive"; "not to agree with someone on an issue is tacitly to accuse him of error . . . just as to dissent from him in a large number of points is tantamount to calling him a fool" (DC, 26–27).[29] The Latin makes the point even clearer: "*Etenim non modo contra contendere, sed etiam, hoc ipsum non consentire, odiosum est.*" Here, in the contrast between *contra contendere* (contending or arguing against something) and *non consentire* (simply withholding assent), Hobbes followed Roger Williams in denying the salience of the distinction between the manner and the fact of disagreement in causing offense. *Leviathan* restated the same point, with an emphasis on dissent: "To agree with an opinion, is to Honour; as being a signe of approving his judgment, and wisdome [but] to dissent, is Dishonour; and an upbraiding of errour; and (if . . . in many things) of folly" (L, ii.10.138).

Still it is here, in Hobbes's analysis of the inevitable *disagreeableness* of disagreement that his fundamental departure from Williams's mere civility comes fully into view. Hobbes could not offer a theory of civil disagreement of the kind put forward by Williams for the simple reason that, for Hobbes, "civil disagreement" was a contradiction in terms. The culprits once again were men's natural partiality and pride.[30] Not only was it *difficult* to disagree on fundamental questions without lapsing into contumely or contempt; rather, the fact of disagreement was *itself* an insult, as an assault on equal dignity. Civilizing speech by eradicating contumely would therefore not suffice to solve the problem. If the bare fact of expressing a "different opinion" implied the inherent contempt of low value, any and every disagreement posed a threat to peace (DC, 79).

The Case for Conformity

In *De Cive*, Hobbes presented his analysis of the dangers of disagreement as an explanation for why "the bitterest wars" were often "those between different sects of the same religion" (DC, 26–27). If every difference of opinion—empirical as well as moral—was potentially destructive, it seemed that the abstractness of theology (tainted by Hellenism and "vain philosophy"), the obscurity and interestedness of the authorities, and the height of the stakes made religious disagreements even more so. Differences in worship were especially problematic. When "individuals follow their reason in worshipping God, [they] are so different from each other that they . . . judge each other's worship unseemly and impious; and [do] not accept that the others [are] worshipping God at all" but "heaping scorn upon" Him (183). Any "disesteem" shown in the process was therefore an injury to God's honor as well as man's. Little wonder, then, that "dissension" over ceremonies seemingly so "indifferent" as the "baring the head . . . or taking off one's shoes or bowing; making one's petitions standing, prostrate or on one's knees" (117), nevertheless generated violent disagreement, as Archbishop Laud and Charles I had learned the hard way.

England's troubles—the cause of which, Hobbes would argue consistently, had been sectarian strife, not rival political theories—were thus only the latest example of the devastating effects of uncivil disagreement to which the history of Christendom had borne witness since the conversion of Constantine.[31] In this, Hobbes like Erasmus was well attuned to the ratcheting effect of persecution of the tongue on sectarian competition. He argued that the Hellenistic philosophical sects had pioneered the use of labels like "criminal, sacrilegious, thieving, parricidal . . . (accursed), and the other names which the lowest class of people use when they are aroused almost to fisticuffs" (L Appendix, iii.2.1192). "The Stoics," in particular, "being fiercer men, used to revile those that differed from them, with the most despiteful words they could invent."[32] This sectarian labeling transferred thereafter to religion, and "after heresies had arisen in the Church, the greatest reproach of all was 'heretic'" (iii.2.1192).

Thus, while Hobbes agreed with Williams about the difficulty of distinguishing the manner of disagreement from its substance, he drew the opposite conclusion. To combat contumely alone would be to treat the effect while neglecting the cause. Rather than liberating men's tongues, conscientious sovereigns must attack the problem root and branch by addressing the source of uncivil disagreement itself—namely, the "different opinions" behind it. Hobbes's hostility to "liberty in religion" of the kind called for by radicals like Williams should thus be understood as part and parcel of a wider campaign against incivility. The sovereign had a duty to judge all "Opinions and Doctrines," and to that end "on what occasions, how farre, and what men are to be trusted . . . in speaking to Multitudes of people," as well as those "who shall examine the Doctrines of all bookes before they be published" (L, ii.18.272). Anyone teaching or preaching a doctrine or opinion contrary to published standards "may lawfully be punished"—even if that opinion were true.[33] Once again, his concerns were not limited to religious and political elites. They extended to the ignorant and intolerant "vulgar" who supplied their audiences in the pews and in the broader reading public, as well. There could be no freedom of expression, no liberty of conversation. A conscientious sovereign must limit dissension as far as he was able by governing his subjects' tongues.

For generations of readers, these arguments have cemented Hobbes's reputation for exemplary intolerance. *Leviathan* offered a pioneering and uncompromisingly Erastian reimagining of the eirenic distinction between the "things indifferent" (*adiaphora*) and "fundamentals" (*fundamenta*) of religion. As we saw in Chapter 1, writers like Erasmus and Castellio had drawn on this distinction in order to distinguish between what St. Paul called the "superstruction"—the "hay and stubble" of beliefs and practices—and those essential to salvation. Although Williams had eschewed such arguments, they had been embraced by most seventeenth-century defenders of toleration and comprehension alike.[34] Still, as Jeremy Taylor's latter-day turn to persecution illustrated, latitudinarian arguments could easily run the other way. Hobbes's peculiar latitudinarian "theology of reduction" was a notoriously minimalist version of "meer" Christianity in which all externals were adiaphorous, while "Jesus is the Christ" and obedience to the sovereign were the only fundamentals.[35] On this view, religion—that "*Feare* of power invisible, feigned by the mind, or imagined from tales publiquely allowed" (L, ii.6.86)—was essentially a matter of expressing this inward opinion of "honour" outwardly, through the external worship of reverent speech and deeds (ii.3.560–562). "To speak to another with consideration, to appear before him with decency, and humility, is to Honour him; as signes of fear to offend," as was to "do those things to another, which he [himself] takes for signes of Honour, or which the Law or Custome makes so" (ii.10.136–138).

Like Williams, Hobbes was struck by the apparent arbitrariness of particular modes of honoring across different times, places, and cultures, while at the same time *within* a particular culture the ceremonies of "Civill" worship and "Divine" differed only in their objects.[36] "To fall prostrate before a King, in him that thinks him but a Man, is but Civill Worship; And he that but putteth off his hat in the Church . . . that he thinketh it the House of God, worshippeth with Divine Worship" (L, iii.45.1028). This suggested that the outward forms employed in each were alike "of an indifferent nature," their significance as signs of honor depending on convention—that is, on their being taken as such by spectators to the act (ii.31.572). Only the worshipper's inward beliefs about the object of his attentions mattered. Thus in embracing the latitudinarian distinction between *fundamenta* and *adiaphora* Williams had rejected, Hobbes drew the conclusion Williams feared most—namely, that the conventionality of worship justified the sovereign's intervention therein. Their "indifference" evidently did not stop religious differences from becoming sources of civil strife; hence, it most certainly did not mean that worship should be left to custom or the whims of individual conscience. No one likes to see his neighbor "heaping scorn upon God" (DC, 183).

As we shall see in Chapter 4, Hobbes's extreme version of the intolerant latitudinarian position would be taken up by others, including a young John Locke. This argument for the absolute power of the sovereign in religion proceeded by way of an analogy between the ceremonies of civil worship and divine. The right to regulate the former—including "titles of Honour" and what "Order of place, and dignity, each man shall hold," as well as all other "signes of respect"—was inseparably annexed to sovereignty (L, ii.18.276). It followed that the sovereign's right extended to the external signs employed in worship of either kind, including even the "motion of their tongues" by which men "shew others the knowledge, opinions, conceptions, and passions which are within themselves" (EL, 39). All speech about God, His attributes, and individuals' duties towards Him, whether in the written or spoken word, remained an "externall action" subject to the civil sword. The Hobbesian social contract therefore demanded that one "so speak"—or not—"as (by lawfull Authority) we are commanded" (L, iii.32.578). "Profession with the tongue is but an externall thing, and no more than any other gesture whereby we signifie our obedience [to the sovereign]"—and, through him, to God (iii.42.784).

Although Hobbes sometimes claimed that there were "natural" forms of worship—such as "prayers, thanks, and obedience"—that could not be made otherwise by "the Institution, or Custome of men," like most of the limits he set to sovereign power, this one dissolved upon further inspection. Obedience to the dictates of God's will ("that is, in this case, to the laws of nature") meant obedience to the will of his representative on earth, the sovereign, who would be responsible for defining the controversial categories of "natural" and "arbitrary," as well as "religious" and "spiritual" (L, ii.31.562). The elusiveness of Hobbes's "natural divine worship" as a limit on state-mandated impiety was pointed out by Bishop Bramhall, who noted that this "Hobbian principl[e] . . . in points of religion" meant that "subjects, being commanded by their sovereign, [should] deny Christ."[37]

In his defense, Hobbes readily conceded the charge. It seemed that solving the problem of uncivil disagreements in and about religion required nothing less. To argue for limits to the sovereign's power on the basis of a distinction between "civility" and "spirituality" was similarly specious; "Temporall and Spirituall Government, [were] but two words brought into the world, to make men see double, and mistake their Lawfull Soveraign" (L, iii.39.734). Even if one were called upon to affirm an article one did not believe, there could be no cause for complaint. For all its absoluteness, the sovereign's power could touch only "externals," not the fundamental "internals" of belief. In one masterstroke, Hobbes thus turned the claims of radicals like Williams to liberty of conscience against them: "A private man has alwaies the liberty, (because thought is free,) to beleeve, or not to beleeve, in his heart. . . . But when it comes to confession of that faith, the Private Reason must submit to the Publique" (iii.37.696).

This argument, made famously by Locke in his *Letter Concerning Toleration,* would serve quite a different purpose in *Leviathan,* where Hobbes's concession of an inviolable liberty *in foro interno* emancipated the inward man only to enslave the outward.[38] This "liberty" was in fact the license that the prophet Elisha had granted to Naaman, the Syrian, "who was converted in his heart to the God of Israel" but nevertheless bowed before the idol of Rimmon, "lest he offend his king" (L, iii.42.784–786). Like Naaman, individuals were free to withhold their internal assent to the sovereign's dictates. But when it came to expressing their opinions, they must have faith that God would take the will for the deed and forgive their hypocrisy in the hereafter.

Needless to say, this sop to tender consciences did little to satisfy Hobbes's contemporaries—including many in favor of a comprehensive national church, who agreed with Milton that the uniformity achieved thereby would be but "the forced and outward union of cold, and neutral, and inwardly divided minds" and embraced it nonetheless.[39] For Hobbes, however, that was precisely the point. Like Whitgift and Elizabeth before him, he would not have the sovereign make windows into men's souls. Nevertheless, peace required uniformity—or rather its simulacrum, *conformity*. Whereas Whitgift had surrendered hope for *homonoia* in favor of an outward approximation of *concordia*, Hobbes did him one better. The "multitude" united in speech and deed through obedience to the sovereign will would achieve "more than Consent, or Concord; [but] a reall Unitie of them all" (L, ii.17.260).

Hobbesian Toleration?

Thus far, the argument of this chapter would seem to confirm the traditional picture of an intolerant Hobbes. Although it belonged to the sovereign, in principle, to decide what ecclesiastical arrangements to impose on his subjects—whether episcopacy or even popery—toleration would necessarily mean the existence of different worships and professions in a commonwealth. According to Hobbesian civil science, there was no way to do this without individuals slipping into open and disastrous disagreement upon each. If everyone were allowed to follow "his own opinion, the disputes which [would] arise must inevitably be innumerable and insoluble, and that would be the occasion (*for by their nature men take disagreement as an insult*) first of resentment and then of quarrelling and war; and all society and peace would perish" (DC, 230; my emphasis). It seemed that only religious uniformity would defuse the dangers of disagreement by uniting the multitude and depriving individuals of the opportunity to quarrel about their differences, once and for all.

Or would it? In recent years a growing number of scholars have challenged this interpretation. They note, among other things, that Hobbes's hostility to the liberty of conscience claimed by sectarians like Williams seems to be in tension with the expression of sentiments more commonly associated with toleration in his works. While Hobbes's "indifferentism" was crucial to his case for conformity, other aspects of his thought—including his own unabashed heterodoxy, anticlericalism, and skepticism towards competing truth claims in religion (which he treated always as a matter of opinion rather than knowledge), along with his ecumenical construction of the fundamentals of Christianity, have given readers pause. Hobbes's complex combination of "attitudinal" tolerance, on the one hand, and "institutional" intolerance, on the other, has led Andrew Murphy to classify his position as "tolerant anti-toleration."[40] Other scholars have argued, however, that Hobbes was much less hostile to religious difference than he at first appears, and indeed that he thought at least *some* different opinions in religion could and should be outwardly expressed.[41]

The Hobbes that emerges in these accounts is far from a full-throated defender of free exercise on the model of Williams or Locke. Nevertheless, his contemporary reception seems to support this picture of a "less intolerant," if not necessarily "more tolerant," Hobbes. While critics like Bramhall blanched at his Erastianism and the license of Naaman, other contemporaries embraced them in making their own cases for toleration.[42] The first printed reference to *Leviathan* came only a few weeks later in *The Christian Moderator,* which cited Hobbes on *adiaphora* in its argument for the toleration of English Catholics.[43] As Jeffrey Collins has shown, Hobbes was also taken up by "Magisterial Independents"—that is, Puritan Congregationalists in and out of Parliament who defended the limited toleration of the Cromwellian Protectorate on Erastian grounds.[44] The continued adoption of Hobbesian arguments by avowed tolerationists after the Restoration led eventually to Samuel Parker's complaint about "the Consequences that some men draw from Mr. Hobs's Principles in behalf of Liberty of Conscience."[45]

Even so, for scholarly arguments in favor of a tolerant Hobbes to hold, one must demonstrate that Hobbes *himself* believed it would be possible to sever the outward expression of religious difference from the uncivil disagreements it inspired. The best textual evidence for this comes in Chapter 47 of *Leviathan*, in the so-called "endorsement of Independency."[46] This passage described how Christians who had initially been left at liberty in "their Consciences" were thereafter enslaved by successive waves of self-interested priestly power.[47] But in England, beginning with the Reformation and ending with Parliament's failure to enact a Presbyterian church settlement after the abolition of episcopacy, these "knots" had been successively untied:

And so we are reduced to the Independency of the Primitive Christians to follow Paul, or Cephas, or Apollos, every man as he liketh best: Which, if it be without contention, and without measuring the Doctrine of Christ, by our affection to the Person of his Minister, (the fault which the Apostle reprehended in the Corinthians,) is perhaps the best (L, iii.47.1116).

Richard Tuck has called this "a passionate defense of toleration," while others like Collins and Abizadeh are more measured.[48] Nevertheless, this apparent endorsement of the "Independency of the Primitive Christians" remains the primary source for scholars concerned to defend a more tolerant Hobbes.

Given Hobbes's analysis of the dangers of disagreement, it is tempting to dismiss this passage as an ironic attempt to pander to the ascendant Independent faction in Parliament while conveying his true anti-toleration, anti-Independent opinion. This may well be right, but it would be wrong to diminish the importance of this passage, which still tells us something deep and important about Hobbes's views on toleration—specifically, because of the conditionals he attached to it. Both—"if it be without contention" and "without measuring the Doctrine of Christ, by our affection to the Person of his Minister, (the fault which [Paul] reprehended in the Corinthians,)"—were consistent with his earlier analysis of disagreement as a form of contumely in pinpointing uncivil wars of words between sectarians as the chief obstacle to coexistence. Read in light of his insistence a few pages later in the "Review and Conclusion" that adequate "Education and Discipline" might reconcile the "contrariety" of men's opinions with "civil amity," this passage does indeed suggest that Hobbes envisioned a path by which religious difference and disagreement might be severed after all.

This Hobbesian vision of what I call "difference without disagreement" hints at something altogether more interesting than the simple binary between "intolerant" or "more tolerant" employed by political theorists and historians allows.[49] Whereas before it seemed that peace would require the suppression of any and all religious differences, this reading suggests that Hobbes's understanding of the ethical and institutional arrangements necessary to eliminate contention and sectarian affection under conditions of fundamental diversity were more nuanced. Specifically, it suggests that it might well be possible to tolerate some religious differences in deed (that is, worship and association), so long as the sovereign could impose a compensatory conformity in *speech*. Achieving this would require careful attention not simply to understanding people as they were but also to shaping citizens as they must be through civic education designed to inculcate the necessary Hobbesian virtues.

Civil Silence

One of the chief problems with the many different theories of civility attributed to Hobbes by scholars is that they focus on a term he did not use while ignoring those he did. In particular, they neglect the two kindred conversational virtues to which Hobbes appealed again and again across his works—discretion and complaisance. Here at last, something like civility in our sense, as the characteristic conversational virtue and *vinculum* of tolerant societies, comes into view.

Leviathan defined discretion as a virtue of judgment, "particularly in matters of conversation and business wherein times, places and persons are to be discerned," and of knowing what actions—and especially which words—were appropriate to each. "The secret thoughts of men run over all things, holy, profane, clean, obscene . . . which verball discourse cannot do"—"as if a man, from being tumbled into the dirt, should come and present himselfe before good company." Discretion thus consisted in knowing when to bite one's tongue and keep one's inward thoughts or "private spirit" private. "In profest remissnesse of mind, and familiar company, a man may play"; however, "in a Sermon, or in publique, or before persons unknown, or whom we ought to reverence, there is no Gingling of words" (L, ii.8.108).[50] If discretion had been the characteristic virtue of "the heathen poets," Hobbes argued, *indiscretion* was the English clergy's most lamentable vice. For when the latter "call unseasonably for zeal, there appears a spirit of cruelty; and by the like error, instead of truth, they raise discord . . . and controversy, instead of religion."[51]

In Hobbes's hands, discretion became a virtue of self-restraint regulating the boundary between the inward realm of opinion and the outward realm of speech. As a sensitivity to one's audience and environment and a willingness to conform to the appropriate norms, it bears a faint resemblance to Williams's mere civility. And yet all of the contentious conversational behaviors permitted—nay, encouraged—by Williams were ruled out by Hobbesian discretion. Speaking one's mind regardless and expressing one's

opinions, no matter how controversial, constituted an indiscreet breach of
civility against which a conscientious sovereign must act, especially when it
came to whom "was to be trusted withal, in speaking to multitudes of people." "Petty men," like the Presbyterian preachers described in *Behemoth*,
had "nothing in them that can be beneficial to the public, except their silence" (B, 172). If such indiscreet individuals refused to bite their tongues
and insisted on inflaming their listeners instead, the sovereign had a duty to
intervene. It was "a strange thing, that scholars, obscure men . . . should be
suffered to bring their unnecessary disputes, and together with them their
quarrels, out of the universities into the commonwealth." It was stranger
still "that the state should engage in their parties, and not rather put them
both to silence" (62).

Unlike mere civility, discretion described a kind of civil silence which
consisted first and foremost in knowing what *not* to say and when not to
say it. Still, discretion was not the only conversational virtue extolled by
Hobbes. In *Leviathan*, "COMPLEASANCE" formed the basis of the fifth
law of nature—that "every man strive to accommodate himselfe to the rest":

> [For] there is in mens aptnesse to Society, a diversity of Nature, rising
> from their diversity of Affections; not unlike to that we see in stones
> brought together for building of an Aedifice. For as that stone which
> by the asperity, and irregularity of Figure, takes more room from oth-
> ers, than it selfe fills; and for the hardnesse, cannot be easily made
> plain, and thereby hindereth the building, is by the builders cast away
> as unprofitable, and troublesome: so also, a man. . . . The observers
> of this Law may be called SOCIABLE (the Latines call them *Commo-
> di*); The contrary, Stubborn, Insociable, Froward, [and] Intractable (L,
> ii.15.232).

Hobbes was hardly the only seventeenth-century English writer to praise
complaisance as an essential social virtue. Contemporaries often used it as
a synonym for politeness, but with the further, affirmative sense of making
oneself "agreeable."[52] According to the *Art of Complaisance, or the Meanes to
Oblige in Conversation* (1673), this virtue had two chief parts: "One is a certain decency or sweet behaviour to which we ought to conform our selves as
much as possible," while "the other is an agreeable affability . . . which renders us not onely accessible to all those, who would address themselves to
us, but also makes our society and conversation desirable," so as to "engage
the love and respect of those with whom we converse."[53]

Even its champions would acknowledge, however, that the virtue of complaisance could shade dangerously close to a kindred vice. In her attempt to distinguish it from "flatterie," Madeleine de Scudéry could offer no better definition of the latter than as a kind of "sordid Complaisance."[54] In a 1611 pamphlet entitled *A Discourse against Flatterie,* likely penned by Hobbes's pupil William Cavendish, the offending vice was identified as a form of "dishonest civilitie" and "conformitie being false and fained."[55] Accordingly, many radical dissenters like Locke's friend and Quaker Benjamin Furly denied that there was any distinction—"civility," "complaisance," and "flattery" were alike forms of vicious hypocrisy and idolatrous worship of one's fellow men.[56] While its emphasis on agreeableness may have made complaisance disagreeable to Quaker defenders of conscientious incivility like Furly or hot Protestants like Watson and Williams, this was precisely what attracted Hobbes. His complaisant man would go along to get along in a spirit of easygoing accommodation redolent of the indifferent conformism he advocated in religion.

De Cive made this connection between complaisance—rendered in Latin as *animus civilis* or "civil spirit"—and inauthentic "profession" explicit. Hobbes always chose his words carefully, often employing a word or phrase familiar to contemporaries in order to twist it to his own, radically different ends. *Animus civilis* was no exception. An English-Latin dictionary of 1662 defined this virtue as "an humble mind, a frame of spirit not affecting to domineer over his fellows, gentle," while a textbook of 1721 translated it as a "regard to the Good of the Public."[57] Both definitions drew from classical Latin, in which *civilis animus,* a sister concept to *civilitas,* denoted a virtue of public spiritedness, particularly in the self-restraint and willingness of great men to submit themselves as equals under law.[58] As per usual, Hobbes turned this classical republican virtue on its ear. *De Cive* identified *animus civilis* instead as one of a number of reasons people might affirm or agree to a proposition without believing it to be true: "We may . . . allow a proposition simply as such, perhaps from fear of the laws, and that is to profess or confess by external signs; or from the automatic deference, which men give out of [civil spirit] to those whom they respect" (DC, 237).[59]

"Respecting" others in this case meant "agreeing to agree." Complaisance thus accomplished what even the civil silence of discretion, easily construed as a sullen indication of dissent, could not by insulating individuals from the discomfort of unintended contempt once and for all. Together then, the virtues of discretion and complaisance provided the key to unlocking the conditionals in Hobbes's endorsement of Independency and so supplied the ethical core to "difference without disagreement" as an authentically Hobbesian ideal. The inherent disagreeableness of disagreement meant that coexistence in a tolerant society would demand nothing less than a discreet civil silence or reflexive *agreeableness* from its members on all controversial questions. This perhaps explains why *Leviathan* transformed "civil spirit" from an elite, supererogatory ethic of gentility into a fundamental law of nature applicable to all, thus extending a duty of inauthentic profession beyond one's interactions with the sovereign to those with one's fellow men.

The fifth law of nature presented complaisance as an antidote to diversity and a form of social cement binding individuals together despite their natural "asperity." In this, Hobbes's language deliberately recalled the idea of the *vinculum societatis,* but with a crucial difference. In embracing the hypocritical or dissimulating aspect of complaisance along with discretion,[60] Hobbes proposed not only to silence the social harmony of a tolerant society but to turn the "shared heart" of *concordia* inside out—into a demand for conformity in the external forum, rather than unity in the internal one.

Regulating Civil Worship

As the sum of complaisance and discretion, Hobbes's conception of civility is certainly a far cry from that of Roger Williams. Whereas Williams seemed to think that mere civility was the purview of exemplary individuals with a uniquely high tolerance for controversy, or what was left when the ceaseless grind of evangelical disagreement left the thin-skinned adequately calloused, Hobbes viewed inculcating the necessary conversational virtues as an essential task of civic education.[61] But he also made clear that virtuous education alone would not suffice. Contemporary civilitarians might content themselves with jeremiads against the wars of words afflicting English society, but Hobbes insisted on the importance of discipline—not only self-, but sovereign.[62]

Hobbes's sustained attention to the question of enforcement marks a major departure from moralists like Erasmus or Allestree, who were likewise preoccupied with the government of unruly tongues. Indeed, his institutional solutions to the problem of uncivil disagreement rivaled Williams's in ingenuity—only for Hobbes, civilitarian legislation of all kinds was the key. The seeds of Hobbes's legislative program were planted in the eighth law of nature. Although their morally obligatory status has been the subject of heated scholarly debate for the better part of a century, as "the conditions of society and Peace among men" Hobbes evidently intended a conscientious sovereign to take them as guidelines and punish infractions (L, ii.14.216–218; DC, 21).[63] "For the Lawes of Nature . . . of themselves, without the terrour of some Power, to cause them to be observed, are contrary to our naturall Passions, that carry us to Partiality, Pride, Revenge, and the like" (L, ii.17.254). Unlike animals, men possessed not only a passion for glory but a sharp and critical tongue as well.[64] Accordingly, the eighth law of nature dictated that the sovereign should do his utmost to restrict expressions of hatred, contempt, and dishonor so as to eliminate contumely altogether.

In effect, the deregulation of religion would require the sovereign to shift his attention from *spiritual* worship to *civil*. Individuals beholding others' contrary religious worships might still think them "unseemly and impious" (DC, 183), but they must cede the right of judging offense to the sovereign. This was the only way to avoid the "Emulation, Quarrells, Factions, and at last Warre" arising from the different "values men are naturally apt to set upon themselves; [and] what respect they look for from others" (L, ii.18.276). *Leviathan* went into detail about the specific regulations Hobbes thought this might require. These had to do with "Civill Honour"—that is, the "Magistracy, Offices, Titles; and in some places Coats, and Scutchions painted"—by which the "DIGNITY" or "publique worth of a man, which is the Value set on him by the Common-wealth" was acknowledged (L, ii.10.136–138).[65] Also included were the social rituals of "Civill Worship" by which a subject magnified his sovereign and those of "manners"—that is, the "Decency of behaviour; as how one man should salute another, or how a man should wash his mouth, or pick his teeth before company, and such other points of the Small Moralls" (ii.11.150).[66] He insisted that the sovereign's absolute right to regulate "titles of Honour; and to appoint what Order of place, and dignity, each man shall hold" also, crucially, extended to "what signes of respect, in publique or private meetings, they shall give to one another" (ii.18.276).

Hobbes did not weigh in directly on the laws banning persecution of the tongue popular with his contemporaries. However, the close resemblance between his formulation of the eighth law of nature and the prohibitions against "reproachful" or "reviling" speech adopted in the New World and earlier Tudor injunctions against "contumelious words" like "Papist, Hypocrite and Pharisee" is striking.[67] *Leviathan* did insist that some degree of toughening up against perceived slights would be required and noted that laws against insult, where it "produce[d] no other harme, than the present griefe of him that is reproached," had been "neglected [by] the Greeks, Romans, and other both antient and moderne Common-wealths; supposing the true cause of such griefe to consist, not in the contumely, (which takes no hold upon men conscious of their own vertue,) but in the Pusillanimity of him that is offended by it" (L, ii.27.480).[68] But even if one takes this statement as more than simply an attempt to embarrass England's thin-skinned aspirants to republican virtue, it seems highly unlikely that Hobbes intended it as a genuine endorsement of Grecian lawgiving in the English case.

Hobbes did, however, propose a number of other forms of sovereign discipline directed toward restricting expressions of religious difference and limiting opportunities for individuals to disagree. Some of his policy recommendations, like press censorship, will be familiar; yet others, including the licensing of preachers, have received considerably less scholarly attention.[69] While the civil silencers admired by Bodin in Chapter 1 had focused mainly on doctrines—by banning theological disputations or even discussions of religion *tout court*—Hobbes turned his attention from principles to personnel. As we saw earlier, he blamed England's civil wars on her burgeoning public sphere, which served as a source not only of seditious doctrines but also of the increasingly uncivil disagreements that culminated in a "paper war." But *Leviathan* and *Behemoth* stressed that it was "the preachers"—more so even than the "democratical gentlemen"—who were "the beginning of our trouble" (B, 26, 39; L, iii.46.1097).

Behemoth described how the Presbyterians, in particular, had taken advantage of Charles I's failure to regulate the spoken word by going "abroad preaching in most of the market-towns of England" and thus "came into such credit, that numbers of men used to go forth of their own parishes . . . to hear them preach" (B, 24). In the unfortunate cycle of evangelical competition that ensued, charismatic and enthusiastic styles of preaching had the upper hand. The Presbyterians, "both by the manner"—which "was or seemed to be extempore"—as well as "the matter of their preaching, applied themselves wholly to the winning of the people to a liking of their doctrine and good opinion of their person" (24–25). Consequently, the people came to "despise their own and other preachers," especially ministers of the Church of England who, "instead of sermons did read to the people such homilies as the Church had appointed" and who were denominated "dumb dogs" for their trouble (B, 23–24).

Proponents of a tolerant Hobbes might read this analysis as an implicit argument for liberalization. Had the Anglican Church forborne their persecutory provocations in imposing the Book of Common Prayer on the Scots and if the ministry had been allowed to respond by preaching freely outside of the set form, then their charismatic competitors may well have fared worse. But this was not quite Hobbes's point. The Anglicans' real "disadvantage" was the people's dislike for the prayer book on the basis of what Hobbes saw as its most desirable feature—namely, that it was "a set form, premeditated, that [allowed] men [to] see to what they were to say Amen" (B, 25). Hobbes's criticism of the Presbyterians' "vehemence, which [the people] mistake for zeal," recalls Cotton's criticism of Williams. In his response to John Wallis, himself a Presbyterian as well as Oxford's Savilian Professor of Geometry, Hobbes explained that these sermons found favor because of "their zeal to their own ends, which they mistake for zeal to God's worship"—"I have heard besides divers sermons made by fanatics, young men . . . and found little difference between their sermons and the sermons of such as you, either in respect of wisdom, or eloquence, or vehemence, or applause of common people."[70]

Thus, while Charles and Laud were busy banning disputations within the Church, they had fatally neglected what was going on outside of it. Specifically, they had neglected the abundance of preaching that stemmed "from a liberty that men have, upon every Sunday and oftener, to harangue all the people of a nation at one time, whilst the state is ignorant of what they will say," a policy the likes of which Hobbes noted was not "permitted in all the world out of Christendom, nor therefore any civil wars about religion" (B, 63–64).[71] Peace would thus remain elusive "till preaching be better looked to" by "Christian sovereigns" (144).

But what did this "better looking to" require? Hobbes had outlined his definite notions on this score many years before in *Leviathan*'s longest chapter. Ch. 42, "Of Ecclesiastical Power," described preaching and teaching as "the same thing"—namely, that "act, which a Crier, Herald, or other Officer useth to doe publiquely in Proclaiming of a King" and "what right he cometh [by]" (L, iii.42.776, 790). When the king in question was God, these activities, along with prophecy defined in a characteristically deflationary way as all "speak[ing] to the people in Gods name," contained all public speech about religion (ii.40.746). According to Hobbes, would-be evangelists thus needed to know that the offices of preacher, teacher, and prophet they assumed in addressing themselves to groups of people were thus "ministerial" and "representative" of the sovereign's public voice. They occupied these positions, whether they knew it or not, solely at the sovereign's discretion.[72] While this was clearly intended to undermine the claims of self-styled prophets to divine inspiration, Hobbes insisted that the same held true for all teachers of the people, including in geometry (L, iii.42.790, ii.27.476; cf. ii.23.378). "Better looking to" thus required sovereigns to exercise due diligence over anyone presumptuous enough to occupy one of these positions and so to discipline the organs of public opinion formation—namely, the presses, pulpits, and the universities.[73]

What Hobbes envisioned, in effect, was a system of "civil" ordination and state licensing for preachers and teachers. "Much preaching [was] an inconvenience"; still, "I cannot think that preaching to the people the points of their duty, both to God and man, can be too frequent, so [long as] it be done by grave, discreet, and ancient men" (B, 63–64). Here again the virtues of discretion and complaisance were paramount. The "duly ordained Ecclesiastics" elevated by the existing processes of ecclesiastical ordination had evidently not been selected on the basis of their willingness to preach peace (DC, 233).[74] Yet if all public speakers were ministers of sovereignty, then the sovereign had a duty to exercise his right to approve the same. Even as he criticized the Inquisition's attempts to punish the most secret thoughts of men, "notwithstanding the Conformity of their Speech and Actions," Hobbes argued that it was entirely appropriate for the sovereign, "intending to employ a Minister in the charge of Teaching, [to] enquire of him, if hee bee content to Preach such, and such Doctrines; and in case of refusall, [to] deny him the employment" (L, iii.46.1076).

Force could not compel belief, but it could nevertheless purge the pulpits and the universities of "Divinity-Disputers," "seditious haranguers," and "fanatic" prophets and replace them with discreet preachers instead (B, 144).[75] In this, Hobbes's theory had clear, practical precedents. As Collins notes, the reformed University Visitations committees and "Triers and Ejectors" established under Cromwell accomplished something quite similar.[76] Moreover, these programs had been adapted from the *Humble Proposals*, the very plan for disciplining the "propagation of the Gospel" with which Williams took serious issue in Chapter 2. That Hobbes found these institutional innovations more congenial than Williams can be inferred from his explicit endorsement of the Cromwellian Visitations in *Behemoth*, an affirmation all the more striking in a work written after the Restoration and presented personally to Charles II for approval (B, 148). Given Hobbes's own enthusiasm for sovereign censorship, it is perhaps fitting that permission to publish was denied.

The Affront of Evangelism

Hobbes's analysis of the Presbyterian preachers in *Behemoth* made his hostility to the unrestricted liberty of preaching—or "haranguing"—claimed by men like Roger Williams quite clear. A system of licensing would ensure that only discreet preachers would be put before the people. Taken together, however, Hobbes's proposed reforms went even further. One form of speech especially dear to dissenters needed to be checked. The problem, as he saw it, was that individuals rarely claimed liberty of conscience for their worship alone. Rather, they wanted a "farther liberty of persuading others of their opinions"—which usually entailed accusing them of damnable errors and telling them to convert or suffer the consequences (EL, 154). Evangelism thus represented a kind of "unwanted counsel," and "counsel unwilling heard is a needless offense to him that is not willing to hear it, and offences tend all to the breach of peace" (96).[77]

Once again, Hobbes did not restrict his concerns to the speech of elites. The affront of evangelism implicated not only the appointed preachers and teachers of the people, but everyone. *Leviathan* characterized all missionary activity as a violation of the Golden Rule: "If a man come from the Indies hither, and perswade men here to receive a new Religion . . . [he] may be justly punished for the same, not only because his doctrine is false, but also because he does that which he would not approve in another" (L, ii.27.456).[78] These arguments against evangelism reflect the modern pluralistic intuition that attempts to convert others are inherently disrespectful violations of reciprocity. Yet Hobbes's discomfort with evangelism was not limited to its offensiveness. Evangelical competition also engendered a partisan spirit that heightened the hateful rhetoric between sects (L Appendix, iii.2.1210). As with the mischievous Presbyterians, direct comparisons between evangelists resulted in affection for one and contempt for others. It was only human to feel affection for one's minister.

In his opposition to evangelism, Hobbes was once again speaking the language of post-Reformation eirenicism. While he shared the eirenicists' emphasis on unity however, he rejected as absurd the idea that evangelical persuasion could serve as a means to that end.[79] Attempts to convert others were nothing more than offensive invitations to competition and contention, not mutual understanding. Like other comprehensive theologies, Hobbes's doctrinal minimalism had an intolerant flipside. There could be no "warrant to preach Christ" to anyone who qualified as a Christian on his limited definition, "for no man is a Witnesse to him that already beleeveth, and therefore needs no Witnesse." He joked that missionaries alone were excluded from the license of Naaman: "None, but such as are sent to the conversion of Infidels . . . [with the] warrant to preach Christ come in the flesh . . . [are] obliged to suffer death for that cause" (L, iii.42.788).

Given Hobbes's insistence on disciplining the appointment of preachers and teachers, the fact that he viewed the unregulated "mechanick" preaching and liberty of prophecy defended by Williams and other tolerationists as a nonstarter should not come as a surprise. Even so, his interest in lay preaching is sometimes cited as evidence for the tolerant Hobbes as a willingness to liberalize expression.[80] His point seems to have been, however, that only duly and *civilly* ordained voices should be allowed to preach, in pulpits *or* in universities. As Hobbes told Wallis in 1657, "If the Sogeraign [sic] power give me command (though without the ceremony of imposition of hands) to teach the Doctrine of my *Leviathan* in the Pulpit, why am not I . . . a Minister as well as you, and as publick a person as you are?"[81] In an exchange about the rise of self-proclaimed "prophets" and "prophetesses" during the Civil War in *Behemoth,* the older and wiser interlocutor, A, corrected B's erroneous opinion that such "dreams and prognostications of madmen" were not "of any great disadvantage to the commonwealth" and cited the Roman practice of banishing "fortune-tellers and astrologers" approvingly (B, 187–188).

Conclusion

I began this chapter by reflecting on the paradoxical quality that unites the lives and works of Roger Williams and Thomas Hobbes, despite their many differences. Now it seems that Hobbes, like Williams, also offered a brilliantly counterintuitive vision of a tolerant society that turned the terms and expectations of his contemporaries upside down. Difference without disagreement required complaisant individuals to voice only those things that united them, rather than using their cutting tongues to tear the members of the commonwealth apart. The sovereign, too, must discipline citizens' civil worship and speech so as to realize the virtue of civil silence on a social scale.

Hobbes's peculiar vision of a tolerant society was thus designed to suppress precisely the kind of uncivil and evangelical sectarianism Williams sought to accommodate. The contrast could not be starker. For Williams, civility was important because disagreement was important, and disagreement was important because evangelism was a signal religious freedom and the primary motivational inducement to toleration. Without mere civility, the evangelical and inevitably contentious toleration he desired would be impossible. For Hobbes, by contrast, evangelism was an egregious form of contumely and an inherently offensive activity that had no place in a tolerant society. Hobbes may have shared the tolerationists' rejection of Christian concord as a social and spiritual ideal; nevertheless, he insisted that external conformity might serve as a substitute for internal unity while dampening the din. The resulting vision of a tolerant society was diametrically opposed to Williams's mere civility and discord. Hobbesian civility was not a means to disagreement, but an end to it, its corresponding toleration a hollow simulacrum of *concordia* with the heart and tongue cut out.

Here, one might raise an important objection—namely, that this vision of difference without disagreement stands in considerable tension with what we know about Thomas Hobbes, the man, and his biography, from his self-imposed exile as "the first of all that fled" before the war, to his vociferous public controversies with Wallis, to his brushes with the persecutory fires of *de haeretico comburendo* late in life.[82] At the end of his *Verse Life*, Hobbes claimed that his "life and Writings speak one Congruous Sense."[83] But one when one shifts attention from the prescriptions of his civil science to the "reputation, loyalty, manners, and religion, of Thomas Hobbes" what emerges is a resolutely heterodox, controversial, and hilarious freethinker, one who took it decidedly amiss when others sought to punish him for his indiscretion.

If Williams served as his own model of mere civility, could it be that Hobbes viewed himself as an exemplar of discretion and complaisance? If so, he failed to impress his contemporaries and managed mostly to throw "Hobbist" conformism into disrepute.[84] When Bramhall accused him of "too much indifferency in religion," Hobbes readily admitted that "whatsoever the church of England . . . shall forbid me to say in matter of faith, I shall abstain from saying it . . . [for] I think it unlawful, if the church define [doctrines], for any member of the church to contradict them."[85] When it came to defending *Leviathan* against the charge of heresy, he pled not guilty by reason of the silence of the laws in the extraordinary moment in which the book had been published. The anarchy of civil war meant that there were no "human laws left in force to restrain any man from preaching or writing any doctrine concerning religion that he pleased." Not only was preaching his doctrine then no crime—what added harm could heated rhetoric do "in this heat of the war," wherein "it was impossible to disturb the peace of the state, which then was none"?[86]

By justifying the publication and rhetorical excesses of *Leviathan* as an accurate discernment of the "times, places, and persons" in and for which it was written, Hobbes presented himself as the very soul of discretion. Yet his own sensitivity to offense seemed to cut the other way. Although he loved the "learned conversation" of the intimate social and scientific circles he belonged to in Paris and London, he loved the undue "liberty of conversation" assumed with him by "ignorant" strangers far less.[87] According to Aubrey, Hobbes withstood the "bayt[ing]" of "the witts at Court" with good cheer, "marvelous happy and ready in his replies, and that without rancor." But if "provoked," he could be brutal; "the King would call him the Beare: *Here comes the Beare to be bayted*."[88] This bearishness was on full display in his increasingly contumelious controversy with Wallis, one installment of which ended with a magnificently uncivil metaphor comparing the professor's "railing" to the "stinking wind" of a flatulent horse "too hard girt upon a full belly." Hobbes excused his incivility by citing Wallis's own "insolent, injurious, and clownish words"—effectively pleading his natural right to self-preservation in a state of paper war.[89] After all, his civil science predicted that nothing less than his destruction would placate the wounded pride of his opponents.

Hobbes would not be the first philosopher to fail to live up to his own exacting standards. Perhaps in his own run-ins with the kind of censorship and persecution he happily prescribed for others, he was simply hoisted by his own petard. Or perhaps this is why the prospect of toleration as difference without disagreement so intrigued him. Whether this vision should really count as "tolerant" is another, more difficult question. Hobbes certainly showed a good, latitudinarian indifference in *adiaphora* and may even have been willing to allow individual congregations to follow their consciences therein. And yet his proposed system of sovereign education and discipline was designed to ensure significant uniformity of doctrine regardless. Moreover, while his minimalist rendering of the *fundamenta* of Christianity might encompass, if not satisfy, all self-identified Christians— maybe even Catholics of a sufficiently Erastian bent—non-Christians who could not affirm the tenet "Jesus is the Christ" would necessarily fall outside of the establishment. One might imagine that Hobbes would be sympathetic to the informal toleration extended to the stranger communities of Jews and Muslims in Cromwell's London—and to Judaism especially as a non-proselytizing religion. Still, it is not clear what kind of restrictions he thought should be placed on them and whether their teachers would be subjected to licensing, given the depth of the differences in fundamental doctrines and worship involved.

In this respect, the question of whether Hobbes himself was "intolerant" or "more tolerant" is beside the point. His vision of toleration as difference without disagreement, in which the price of pluralism was the civil silence necessary for men to differ in religion without disagreeing about it, was both. Hobbes did not reject the more expansive forms of toleration put forward by his contemporaries because he was an unreasonable, intolerant bigot but because he knew that other people were. For this very same reason, he insisted that the freedoms of religion and of speech were not simply difficult to reconcile, they were entirely inconsistent:

> To err, to be deceived, or to have a wrong opinion, is not a crime in itself; nor can error become a crime so long as it is confined to a person's heart. . . . But words can be a crime, and can be punished without injury with whatever punishments the legislators wish—indeed, with the ultimate penalty. If blasphemy against the king can be punished by death, much more can blasphemy against God (L Appendix, iii.2.1202).

Moreover, Hobbes appeared open to any and all means of "cutting off" the intolerably uncivil from the conversation of the commonwealth. His sympathy to Protestant martyrs since the time of Luther evidently did not extend to those seditious Presbyterian preachers: "Had it not been much better that [they], which were not perhaps 1000, had been all killed before they had preached? It had been (I confess) a great massacre; but the killing of 100,000 is a greater" (B, 95).

If this is a more tolerant Hobbes, it is hardly one that will satisfy modern liberals, just as difference without disagreement would not have satisfied radical tolerationists like Williams in his own day. And yet while such statements, one hopes, will repulse many modern readers, the concerns underlying them still resonate. Not only do modern lamentations about the destructive effects of uncivil disagreement and contemptuous speech have profound Hobbesian echoes; the increasingly frequent calls for civil silence characteristic of our own tolerant societies—be they commonwealths or universities—closely recall Hobbes's mandate for discreet quiescence and complaisance. Even in America, the occasional inheritor of the schismatic and evangelical toleration defended by Williams, difference without disagreement is not an inapt description of the secular celebration of diversity that converts deep difference into superficial similarity, or the ecumenical (or "indifferentist") tolerance that sees all religions as allies, following different paths to the same God.

In this, one can detect the Hobbesian intuition that our differences in "meer" religion are simply not worth disagreeing about.[90] *De Cive* concluded with another passage from Paul making precisely this point:

> Everyone knows that it is the nature of men to hurl abuse and anathemas at each other when they disagree over questions of power, profit, or intellectual preeminence. It is no wonder therefore when men grow warm in dispute, almost any dogma is said by one or the other to be necessary for entry into the kingdom of heaven . . . to which I now add this one from St. Paul: One who eats should not reject one who does not; one who does not should not criticize one who does. For God has accepted him. One man thinks one day is better than another, another man values all days alike: let each be filled with his own conviction (DC, 147).[91]

No doubt, many modern liberals will share Hobbes's concerns in this passage while concluding, nevertheless, that civil silence and complaisance go too far. We want difference *and* disagreement, so long as we can keep the latter "civil." As we shall see in Chapter 4, the purported father of "liberal toleration" John Locke was motivated by much the same concern.

4

"A Bond of Mutual Charity"

Locke and the Quest for Concord

> We hold it to be an indispensable duty for all Christians to main-
> tain love and charity in the diversity of contrary opinions: by
> which charity we do not mean an empty sound, but an effectual
> forbearance and good-will, carrying men to communion, friend-
> ship and mutual assistance of one of another, in outward as well as
> spiritual things; and by debarring all magistrates from making use
> of their authority, much less their sword (which was put into their
> hands only against evil doers) in matters of faith or worship.
>
> —JOHN LOCKE, "Pacific Christians" (1688)

IN A BOOK ABOUT TOLERATION, one might expect to find John Locke
(1632–1704) at the beginning, rather than the end. While traditional, tri-
umphal narratives about the rise of early modern toleration as the origin of
modern liberalism have been subjected to abundant revision in recent years,
Locke's pride of place—even in revisionist narratives—has been preserved.
No less a revisionist than John Dunn, in a work otherwise dedicated to com-
bating this lasting "Locke obsession" in genealogies of liberalism,[1] has argued
that "the only argument in his entire political philosophy which does seem
to me still to be interesting as a starting point for reflection about any issue
of contemporary political theory is the theme of the *Letters on Toleration*."[2]

Even so, at the heart of an obsession shared across many different disciplines one finds many different Lockes. The historians' Locke is alternative-
ly a political radical, a new scientist, a boring Christian, and a bureaucratic
functionary whose thought was largely reactive to that of his associates,
place, and time. This multitude of Lockes is made possible by the fact that
the historical Locke wore many different hats and seemed to live at least
nine intellectual lives concurrently—as a scholar, a physician, a secretary
and tutor, an economist, a suspected traitor, a philosopher, a civil servant, a
Christian apologist and exegete, and last but certainly not least, a political

theorist. And yet, for the relative abundance of historical and biographical material to which Locke scholars now have access in assessing their subject, the man himself remains decidedly opaque. Famously secretive, one contemporary remarked that "there is not in the world such a master of taciturnity."[3] The upshot of this opacity is that while what Locke had for breakfast on any given morning is not an uninteresting question for historians, the truth behind his many apparent changes of mind and heart on the matter of toleration remains out of reach.

Political theorists can generally agree that *their* Locke is not the historians', and yet a plethora of different Lockes peppers their pages as well, each ready to say whatever "Locke" *should* have said in order to vindicate the author's secret hopes—or fears—about liberalism.[4] Today, it seems the latter is more often the case, especially when it comes to toleration. In recent accounts, Locke stands accused of compounding his greater civilizational sins by transmitting the shortcomings of *tolerantia*—that negative, medieval ideal of permission without approval—to the modern age.[5] According to its critics, the ostensibly "Lockean" emphasis on the irrationality of persecution, the neutrality of a secular state, and individual rights and equal protection entails a corresponding ethical minimalism and *laissez-faire* that places few, if any, demands on individuals within a framework of natural rights. "What one misses above all in Locke's argument," writes Waldron, "is a sense that there is anything morally wrong with intolerance, or a sense of any deep concern for the victims of persecution."[6] By treating toleration primarily as a "vertical" matter of state policy, critics like Waldron argue that Locke neglected, at best, and consciously undermined, at worst, the "horizontal" social and ethical supports needed to sustain inclusion—a fear that the notorious limits of toleration he articulated in *A Letter Concerning Toleration* (1689) would seem to bear out.

In the *Letter*, Locke declared that "the Toleration of those that differ from others in Matters of Religion" was a demand both of revelation and "the genuine Reason of Mankind" (LCT, 11). And yet its subsequent placement of Catholics, atheists, "Turks," and the intolerant beyond the pale meant that Locke's toleration was considerably narrower than Roger Williams's had been (64).[7] While his modern supporters generally seek to downplay or rationalize these exclusionary caveats, Locke's critics can point to centuries of consternation.[8] Joseph Priestley would complain in 1774 about the ease with which "all preceding writers" on religious liberty had "acquiesced in the arguments and limits of Mr Locke," with many availing themselves "of [his] authority for intolerance," while Thomas Jefferson, in celebrating Locke's greatness, lamented the fact that he had "stopped short, [but] we may go on."[9] Even so, English Whigs would appeal to Locke's *Letters* to support their continued opposition to Catholic claims to toleration well into the nineteenth century.[10]

This chapter will demonstrate that whether it is presented as the moral core of liberalism or as a sinister principle of marginalization and oppression, the "Lockean" toleration invoked by political theorists bears little resemblance to that described and defended in Locke's *Letter*, which despite its prominence also comes nowhere near to exhausting his thinking on the subject. In addition to the unpublished *Tracts on Government* (1660, 1662), Locke wrote *An Essay Concerning Toleration* (1667) and three other *Letters* in defense of the original, along with numerous published and unpublished works on related themes.[11] More importantly (and surprisingly) perhaps, Locke did not even *write* the English *Letter*. He wrote the original *Epistola de Tolerantia* in Latin for a European audience in 1685 in response to Louis XIV's revocation of the Edict of Nantes.[12] The English version published in 1689 was an unlicensed and somewhat loose translation by an associate, William Popple, a London merchant and friend of William Penn's inclined to Unitarianism.

When these facts are taken together, the Lockean toleration of which political theorists remain so certain begins to look a bit more complicated. The conventional view depicts Locke as a consummately liberal thinker content to leave individuals to their own devices—and vices—in the private sphere, so long as they respected one another's rights, narrowly construed. While the edges of this picture have been troubled by the occasional Foucauldian analysis, it remains remarkably resilient.[13] This chapter will challenge the conventional view of Locke's toleration on many fronts. Far from being indifferent, Locke was deeply concerned about wars of words and persecution of the tongue as obstacles to the peaceful accommodation of religious difference. Like Williams and Hobbes before him, he feared that the private hatreds and mutual contempt produced by fundamental disagreement would dissolve the *vinculum societatis*. This, in turn, had important implications for the development of his views on toleration.

The word *development* here is key, because Locke—the ostensible architect of "Lockean" toleration—was not always a tolerationist. The *Tracts* called for uniformity, while his 1667 *Essay Concerning Toleration* embraced indulgence and comprehension as complementary policies. Two years later the *Fundamental Constitutions of Carolina* (1669), which Locke had some hand in composing as secretary to the Lords Proprietor of the colony, established liberty of conscience for members of recognized churches (excluding atheists) and banned religious insult outright.[14] It was many years before Locke finally endorsed a radical form of toleration that called not for indulgence outside of a comprehensive Christian establishment, but for the separation of church and state and the repeal (not suspension) of penal laws against dissent. And when he did, he concluded that the widening scope of toleration would require a highly demanding ethos of civility from individuals to maintain the *vinculum* of mutual trust.

Thus, by the time Locke had come around to the "Lockean" view that no one "ought to be excluded from the Civil Rights of the Commonwealth, because of his Religion" (LCT, 58–59)—a view defended almost fifty years earlier by Roger Williams—he was well-versed in the concepts and categories forged over two centuries of debate. These, in turn, left a lasting impression on his approach to religious difference. This chapter will argue that Locke's views changed so significantly over the course of his life in response to his concerns about incivility—concerns much like those at the center of our own crisis of civility today. Throughout, he sought to determine just how much disagreement a tolerant society could bear, how much similarity would be required, and where to draw the line. In his successive attempts to answer these questions, civility was the concept around which all else turned. Following Locke on his journey can thus help the modern student of civility and toleration determine to what extent she is a "Lockean"—and what might be at stake in accepting or rejecting that label.

An Intolerant Hobbist

Locke is often seen as the father—or perhaps the grandfather—of modern liberal toleration.[15] From the perspective of this book, however, he was a junior partner in an enterprise begun centuries before. Born in 1634, Locke was a much younger contemporary of Hobbes and Williams, who when the Civil War began in 1642 were well into middle age. Locke's family were minor gentry with Puritan sympathies, and his father fought on the Parliamentary side. Political patronage and his obvious brilliance won him a place and a scholarship to the prestigious Westminster school at the age of thirteen and then to Oxford five years later.[16]

Hobbes and Williams, too, spent their formative years at university, in Oxford and Cambridge, respectively. Yet whereas both seem to have left as

soon as they were able, Hobbes at least with some bitterness, Locke stayed.[17]
He was elected to a studentship at Christ Church in the early days of the English Commonwealth, a position which was permanent, at least in theory.
With the help of a later royal dispensation exempting him from the requirement that he take holy orders, he would hold that position continuously—
despite the change of regime, long absences from Oxford, and considerable
controversy—until he was finally ejected in 1684 on the (evidently false)
suspicion of his involvement in the "Rye House" plot to assassinate the king.
Thus, in addition to the many other hats he was to wear during his life,
Locke began as an academic, cloistered among the dreaming spires of an
ancient university. It is important to keep this fact in mind in understanding his changing views on toleration—and civility.

It may also come as a surprise to some readers that Locke began his
intellectual career as a Hobbist. By this, I do not mean that he was a
crypto-atheist or "liberal absolutist," as some commentators claim.[18] Rather, I mean that Locke was one of the many bright young men at Oxford in
the 1650s who read *Leviathan* and got excited, inspired by its latitudinarian
arguments about religion, in particular.[19] For men like Locke and his col-
league at Christ Church, Edward Bagshaw, Hobbes's radical reinterpretation of the eirenic distinction between religious *fundamenta* and *adiaphora*
offered the intriguing prospect of a silver bullet, a conceptual distinction
that might, at a stroke, solve all of the religious and political controversies
of their age, once and for all.[20]

The *Tracts* reveal Locke to have been deeply affected by the political upheavals of his youth: "I no sooner perceived myself in the world but I found
myself in a storm, which hath lasted almost hitherto" (FT, 7). Written shortly after the Restoration and unpublished during his lifetime, Locke wrote
the *First Tract* as a direct response to Bagshaw's pamphlet *The Great Question Concerning Things Indifferent in Religious Worship* (1660), which employed a Hobbesian analysis of *adiaphora* to argue that individuals should
be left at liberty in all indifferent religious ceremonies. Locke, by contrast,
took the intolerant latitudinarian line on the basis of an equally Hobbesian
analysis of the sources of civil strife. Peace required that "the supreme magistrate of every nation what way soever created, must necessarily have an
absolute and arbitrary power over all the indifferent actions of his people"
(FT, 6, 9).[21]

Locke, like Hobbes, made his case for the magistrate's authority in religious *adiaphora* by way of an analogy with the ceremonies of civility. Taking

off one's hat to another, whether in a church or on the street, was simply a ritual expression of respect or esteem. The staggering variety of these rituals across history and cultures was testament enough to their indifference: "He that will open his eyes upon any country or age but his own will presently see . . . our rudeness [is] others civility." Indeed, "there is nothing so uncouth or unhandsome to us which doth not somewhere find applause and approbation" (FT, 29–30). This impartial observer would also recognize that the respectful rituals of civil worship were generally imported into religion, and not the other way around. Accordingly, "should the eastern and turbaned nations embrace Christianity, 'twould be as uncomely to them to be bare in public worship of God as to us to be covered" (31–32).

The *Second Tract* illustrated the strength of people's attachments to their culturally contingent norms of worship with the story of a Chinese city, "which after a prolonged siege was driven at last to surrender." Having thrown open the gates, the denizens abandoned themselves, their families, lives, liberty, and property to the enemy:

> But when they were ordered to cut off the plait of hair which, by national custom, they wore on their heads, they took up their arms again and fought fiercely until, to a man, all were killed. . . . Although they were ready to allow their whole civil existence to be reduced to slavery . . . [they] were so unable to allow them even the least interference with their hair, worn according to an ancestral custom, that the slightest of things and one of no significance, a mere excretion of the body, but all but sacrosanct by general esteem and the custom of their race, was easily preferred to life itself and the solid benefits of nature.

Locke did not, however, conclude from this parable that the magistrate had better steer clear of interfering with civil or spiritual *adiaphora*. Rather, he argued that the contingency of customs testified to the fundamental *irrationality* of such attachments, among the English as well as the Chinese. Indeed, "whoever cares to contemplate our own civil commotions will confess that perhaps even among us war has at times been waged by some with equal barbarity and similar bitterness over issues of no greater weight" (ST, 59–60).

For Locke, this irrationality only strengthened the argument against toleration. He illustrated the danger with reference to the customary *bêtes noires* of Reformed Protestant orthodoxy, Anabaptists and Quakers. Were the magistrate to surrender his right to regulate worship, he argued:

I know not how a Quaker should be compelled by hat or leg to pay a due respect to the magistrate or an Anabaptist to pay tithes, who if conscience be sufficient plea for toleration . . . have as much reason not to feel constraint as those who contend so much for or against a surplice, for not putting off the hat grounded upon a command of the Gospel, though misunderstood, is as much an act of religion and matter of conscience to those so persuaded as not wearing a surplice (FT, 22–23).

While Locke would later count at least one Quaker, Benjamin Furly, among his closest friends, in his early years at Oxford he was openly hostile and dismissed them as mad, a malady the budding physician jokingly attributed to their brains overheating due to keeping on their hats.[22]

The Quaker refusal to pay hat honor to their social and political superiors may have seemed funny to the young Locke, but he took its antinomian implications very seriously as evidence that "there is no action so indifferent, which a scrupulous conscience will not . . . make a spiritual concernment." Yet the strength of this conviction did not in any way prove that such civil things as "a courteous saluting, a friendly compellation, a decency of habit according to the fashion of the place, and indeed subjection to the civil magistrate [itself]" should be exempt from regulation (FT, 24). Otherwise, individuals would "all of an instant [become] converts, [so that] conscience and religion shall presently mingle itself with all their actions and be spread over their whole lives to protect them from the reach of the magistrate." Anyone who would claim conscience in these matters sincerely—like the Quakers, who considered "civil respect to a man as impious as if it were divine adoration"—was evidently crazy, and toleration would only encourage them.[23] "If private men's judgments were the moulds wherein laws were to be cast, 'tis a question whether we should have any at all" (FT, 21).

Like Hobbes, the young Locke was highly attuned to the problems that men's natural partiality and pride in their own judgments posed for social life. In an almost Hobbesian display of wit, the *First Tract* complained that "the generality of men, conducted either by chance or advantage, take to . . . their opinions as they do their wives"; "once they have espoused them they think themselves concerned to maintain [them], though for no other reason but because they are theirs." He thus agreed that the Civil War had been a consequence of the increasingly uncivil disagreements unleashed by "the scribbling of the age"; hence, in the late "furies, war, cruelty . . . [and] confusion . . . the pens of Englishmen [bore] as much guilt as their swords" (FT, 5).

According to Locke, this war of words had exacerbated spiritual, social, and political divisions and corroded civil society from within. In this, he was on firm Hobbesian ground. But in expounding on why England, in particular, had succumbed to these forces of partisanship and polarization, he foregrounded the problem of *religious* persecution of the tongue in a way *Leviathan* had not. The English had branded one another with "odious names" like "heretic, idolater, and will-worshipper," and these "disgraceful appellations" had exacerbated sectarian divisions and paved the way for mutual persecution. Locke argued that the demonizing and dehumanizing effects of religious insult were "not unlike the cruelty of the barbarous heathens that covered the Christians with those skins they had taken off from ravenous beasts that under that disguise they might the better bait them" (FT, 30). To make matters worse, the English were also oversensitive to offense and enthusiastic in religion. This left them "ready to conclude God dishonoured upon every small deviation from [their] way of his worship" and "apt to judge every other exercise of religion as an affront to theirs" (42).

In *The Tracts*, Locke cited these dual propensities—that of religious disagreement to lead to mutual condemnation "of both the persons and practices of others" and that of the recipient to take enthusiastic offense and fight for God's honor—as crucial evidence in his argument *against* toleration. Like any good Erastian, he left the policy to be adopted (anything from uniformity to complete religious liberty) to the magistrate's discretion. He even conceded that if only people would "suffer one another to go to heaven everyone his own way," then toleration might well "promote a quieter world" (FT, 41–42). Still, he insisted with the help of another Hobbesian allusion that one "must confess himself a stranger to England that thinks that meats and habits, [or] places and times of worship would not be as sufficient occasion of hatred and quarrels amongst us" as Juvenal's leeks and onions (8).[24] Until such "temper and tenderness were wrought into the hearts of men" as described by the Apostle, their inveterate intolerance and incivility meant that liberty of conscience would "prove only a liberty for *contention, censure* and persecution, and turn us loose to the tyranny of *religious rage*" (7).

In the *Tracts*, one thus finds Locke arguing the *intolerant* Hobbist position more explicitly and forcefully than Hobbes himself ever did. The

position that he would later develop at length in the *Letter*—namely, that
faith was a matter of the sincere "internal persuasion" of the mind—was,
like the license of Naaman, marshaled in the *Tracts* to the opposite end.[25]
Any attempt by the civil magistrate to impose in matters of belief would
serve only "to make enemies rather than proselytes"; and yet, "rigor which
cannot work an internal persuasion may notwithstanding [work] an outward conformity, all that is here required" (FT, 13–14). In exercising his
commission to "take care of the actions of his subjects," the magistrate "may
possibly increase their sin" by making them hypocrites, yet this was evidently a tolerable evil (28).[26]

In calling for conformity, the *Tracts* thus demanded not the bonds
of Erasmian *concordia* through Christian charity and consensus on the
fundamentals of faith, but Milton's "forced and outward union of cold,
and neutral, and inwardly divided minds."[27] Like Hobbesian difference
without disagreement, Locke's argument relied on the assumption that
the magistrate's right to regulate civility was unequivocal. But once this
authority was allowed in civil *adiaphora*, "why should not the magistrate's
stamp" extend to religion and "make one [form] current as well as the
other"? As long as one's inward opinion of esteem for another remained
inviolate, "why should anyone complain his heart and affections . . . were
more taken off from God than his friend, by the circumstantial deter-
minations of the magistrate" (FT, 29–30)? Individuals might remain attached to their peculiar forms of worship; nevertheless, the depth of this
attachment did not make these things any less indifferent or in any way
diminish the sovereign's fundamental right. Toleration would remain a
dangerously self-defeating proposition until the day men surrendered
their unreasonable enthusiasms in religion and gave up the rampant incivility and verbal persecution they inspired.

The Turn to Toleration

It can be difficult to recognize the author of *The Two Treatises* in a work
that begins by boasting that "there is no one can have a greater respect and
veneration for authority than I" (FT, 7). And yet, even in *The Tracts* Locke
acknowledged that toleration would be an attractive policy, if only people
were more *tolerant*—that is, if they could be more reasonable, less contentious, and simply more indifferent to the religious errors of others. In true
Hobbesian fashion, Locke expressed this hope with a Pauline conditional:

"If the believer and unbeliever could be content as Paul advises to live together, and use no other weapons to conquer each other's opinions but
pity and persuasion (1 Cor. 7) . . . [the] doctrine of toleration might . . . at
last bring those glorious days that men have a great while sought after the
wrong way" (41).[28]

If Locke was pessimistic about this possibility when writing the *Tracts*
in 1660–1662, his *Essay Concerning Toleration* (1667) and the *Fundamental Constitutions of Carolina* (1669) reflect a dramatic shift in his outlook.
The reason or reasons for this *volte-face* remain obscure. The failure of the
post-Restoration legislative program meant to impose uniformity through
a restored episcopal church—a contentious combination of comprehension and persecution comprising the Act of Uniformity (1662), the Quaker
Act (1662), the Conventicle Act (1664), and the Five Mile Act (1665)—and
to placate controversy likely contributed. As Scott Sowerby has reminded
us most recently, the primary agent of intolerance after the Restoration was
the Cavalier-dominated Parliament, which enacted these uniformist policies over the objections of Charles II, who had promised "a liberty to tender
consciences"—mainly English Catholics and nonconformists—in the Declaration of Breda (1660). Like his ill-fated brother James, Charles would
try and fail on several occasions to get a royal Declaration of Indulgence
to stick over Parliamentary opposition. Time and again it would founder
in the face of popular antipopery and the (not unfounded) suspicion that
English Catholics would be the chief beneficiaries.[29]

Most scholars appeal to biographical factors in explaining the change.
Locke's first extended absence from Oxford after his arrival in 1652 was
a visit to Brandenburg in 1665, during which he remarked with incredulity that Protestants and Catholics in Cleves "quietly permit one another
to choose their way to heaven; and I cannot observe any quarrels or animosities amongst them on account of religion . . . [or] any secret hatred or
rancor"—a possibility for which his years in academia had evidently not
prepared him.[30] The second came shortly after his return, with Locke's increasing association with Anthony Ashley Cooper, the future Lord Shaftesbury and leader of the radical Whig opposition, first to the Cavaliers in
Parliament, and then increasingly to Charles himself. Locke left Oxford for
London in 1667 in order to join Shaftesbury's household, where he served
as physician and secretary as well as tutor to Ashley's son.[31]

While the precise cause of Locke's "conversion" from uniformity to
toleration remains mysterious, the preceding analysis suggests that the

distance traveled was not so far as commonly supposed.[32] At this stage, the conversion, such as it was, was from intolerant Hobbism to a more tolerant version reflecting a shift in Locke's prudential calculus in light of a growing conviction that religious difference could be severed from uncivil disagreement, after all. Written as a memorandum for Shaftesbury and circulated privately among his associates, *An Essay Concerning Toleration* reversed Locke's claim in the *Tracts* that verbal persecution and sectarian animosities must necessarily accompany any toleration of religious difference. Religious opinions might continue to divide men, but disagreement as such was not the problem: "He that differs in an opinion is only so far at a distance from you, but if you use him ill for that which he believes to be the right he is then at perfect enmity, the one is barely a separation, the other a quarrel." Rather, the determination to "force and compel others to be of my mind, or censure and malign them if they be not" was the issue. And yet this was "not a consequence of this or that form of devotion, but the product of a depraved ambitious human nature [which] makes use of all sorts of religion" (ECT, 128).

Isolating incivility as the catalyst for the devastating cycle of religious hatreds made it possible for Locke to counter the claims of his former allies. Trust, not uniformity, was the true "Bond of Society"; hence, toleration would be possible so long as mutual trust could be preserved.[33] And what better way to win the trust of dissenters from an established church than to grant them the toleration for which they were evidently willing to fight, suffer, and die? As we shall see later when we come to the *Letter,* Locke's emphasis on trust as the *vinculum* of tolerant societies would only grow in later works. In the short term, however, it led him to take a much different line on the tolerability of religious "Enthusiasm" in *An Essay Concerning Toleration* than he had in the *Tracts.* A grant of toleration would unite the "fanatics" and make them "become friends to the state"—although Locke now insisted that the term *fanatic* was itself an unfortunate example of ill usage and should be avoided (ECT, 125).[34]

The prudential importance of toleration in securing sectarian loyalties was not the only significant change from the *Tracts.* While Locke continued to use latitudinarian language, he henceforth rejected "indifference" as the proper standard of magisterial jurisdiction in favor of "injury." Despite its evident contingency, worship was acceptable to God only insofar as it was *sincerely* offered. "However [its ceremonies] may be in their own nature perfectly indifferent," when used in "religious worship nothing is indifferent, for it being the using of those habits, gestures, etc., and no other, which I think acceptable to God" (ECT, 133). To impose or restrict forms of worship over the conscientious objections of citizens would only erode the precious trust upon which society depended by punishing dissenters for their sincerity. Contrary to the long-standing identification of sedition and dissent, *An Essay Concerning Toleration* suggested that dissenters who demonstrated their sincerity by suffering the consequences were generally better and more trustworthy citizens than the orthodox. Hobbesian hypocrisy in spiritual matters, it seemed, was no longer such a tolerable evil (127).

While these are significant departures, the continuities between Locke's early intolerant Hobbism and his arguments in *An Essay Concerning Toleration* are also important.[35] While the latter rejected uniformity in favor of toleration or indulgence, it also endorsed comprehension (or "latitudinism") as the policy best suited to "preven[t]" the "factions, wars, and disturbances in civil societies" to which Christianity gave rise (ECT, 131). "Toleration conduces no otherwise to the settlement of a government than as it makes the majority of *one mind* and encourages virtue in all"; yet this would be accomplished only by "making the terms of church communion as large as may be," the *fundamenta* of your creed "few and large," and your *adiaphorous* worships "few and easy" (132). Supplementary indulgence for non-Christians and fanatics who remained outside the bounds of communion would be necessary in order to "persuade them to lay by their animosity and become friends to the state, though they are no sons of the church." However, the most desirable thing for domestic stability and national security would be, in the end, "to alter their minds and bring them over to your profession" (125–126).

Despite his about-face on the power of the state over spiritual worship, traces of his early Hobbism can also be seen in Locke's continued insistence on the magistrate's right to regulate civil *adiaphora*. The magistrate could still suppress the signs, symbols, and rituals of civility, even in religion, insofar as he judged it necessary for public order. For instance, should any "distinct party" in the commonwealth grow "so numerous as to appear dangerous," the magistrate could "forbid the fashion" by which its members identified one another, including the "wearing of hats or turbans," an "ecclesiastical cowl or any other religious habit" (ECT, 118–119). Like the more famous examples of animal sacrifice and infant baptism in the *Letter,* the magistrate's judgment of public necessity, *not* injury to the rights of another, was the standard for interference. Even the Quakers could be forced to doff and don their hats, should the magistrate judge them "numerous enough to become dangerous to the state" and "the not standing bare" as something worth "level[ing] his severity against" (119).

In advising Shaftesbury in *An Essay Concerning Toleration,* Locke struck a balance similar to that of Hobbes's "difference without disagreement": the greater the liberty granted in religious worship, the more restraint was demanded in civility. His next tolerationist endeavor with Shaftesbury would present a similar trade-off. While Locke continued his medical pursuits— he oversaw the operation to insert what would become known as "Shaftesbury's tap" to drain an abscess on his patron's liver in 1668—and began to write on economics, Shaftesbury was plotting their next venture—this time in America. Locke would act as secretary to the Lords Proprietor of Carolina for seven years, and although the extent of his authorship remains a "vexed issue," he was undoubtedly involved in drafting a constitution for the new colony in 1669.[36] Years later, Locke is reported to have disavowed involvement in an article formally establishing the Anglican Church in the colony. The fact that he did not seek to distance himself from an earlier article proclaiming liberty in "matters of religion" suggests that the latter, at the very least, was not inconsistent with his views.[37]

The Fundamental Constitutions of Carolina introduced religious liberty not only as a political necessity but as an evangelical one, as well. In this, its authors seemed to have had their competitors in Maryland (and perhaps even Rhode Island) in mind:

> Since the natives of that place . . . and those who remove from other parts to plant there, will unavoidably be of different opinions concerning matters of religion, the liberty whereof they will *expect to have allowed them* . . . that civil peace may be maintained amidst the *diversity of opinions,* and our agreement and compact with all men may be duly and faithfully observed . . . and also, that Jews, heathens, and other dissenters from the purity of Christian religion may not be scared and kept at a distance from it, but by having an opportunity of acquainting themselves with the truth and reasonableness of its doctrines, and the peaceableness and inoffensiveness of its professors, may, by *good usage and persuasion* . . . be won over to embrace, and unfeignedly receive the truth: therefore any seven or more persons *agreeing in any religion* shall constitute a church or profession, to which they shall give some name to distinguish it from others.[38]

Apart from its prudential sensitivity, this vision of a tolerant society on the surface seems quite far from that of *An Essay Concerning Toleration* two years earlier. The word *toleration* appeared nowhere in the *Fundamental Constitutions*, and the liberty granted therein was not one of conscience or worship, exactly, but of like-minded individuals "agreeing together" to constitute a church and have it recognized. "The terms of admittance and communion . . . shall be written in a book and therein be subscribed by all the members . . . which book shall be kept in the public register of the precinct where they reside." Worship outside of such a recognized body was not permitted—nor was not belonging to one. Atheists were, as ever, out of luck.[39]

And yet the language of the *Carolina* article reflects a profound sensitivity to uncivil disagreement and sectarianism as obstacles to coexistence familiar from Locke's earlier writings, in particular his reasoning about the dangers of "ill usage" in *An Essay* two years earlier. Its emphasis on maintaining respectful and "inoffensive" speech between the members of different churches—including empowering each newly constituted church to name (i.e., denominate) itself—is particularly suggestive, as is its provision for a special court with "the power to regulate all fashions [and] habits," along with other civil *adiaphora*.[40] Subsequent articles raised the issue of persecution of the tongue directly, such as "no person of any church or profession shall disturb or molest any religious assembly," and finally in an explicit religious insult provision of the kind discussed in Chapter 1: "No person shall use any reproachful, reviling, or abusive language against the religion of any church or profession." Once again, the justifications were both political and evangelical—"that [language] being the certain way of disturbing the public peace, and of hindering the conversion of any to the truth, by engaging them in quarrels and animosities, [and] to the hatred of . . . that profession."[41]

As Chapter 1 demonstrated, this article was hardly unique for its time, and there is no way of knowing whether Locke instigated or even approved it. And yet its presence in the *Fundamental Constitutions* demonstrates, at the very least, that Locke was well aware of attempts to put the tolerant Hobbist combination of religious toleration and the regulation of civility—in the form of anti-insult statutes in particular—into practice long before he would comment directly on William Penn's provision in the "Great Law of Pennsylvania" (1682) over a decade later.

Written in 1686, one year after the composition of the *Epistola*, Locke's unpublished commentary on Penn's *Frame of Government for Pennsylvania* explicitly rejected laws banning persecution of the tongue as a means to civility. Penn's formulation provided that "if any person shall abuse or deride another for his different persuasion and practice in matters of religion, such shall be looked on as a disturber of the peace and punished accordingly."[42] Yet despite its similarity to the *Carolina* article, Locke contended that Penn's law would have the opposite of its intended effect and provide only "a matter of perpetual prosecution and animosity" between citizens instead.[43] Whether Locke's judgment was based on experience is hard to tell; the Hobbesian experiment with difference without disagreement in Carolina was imperfectly tried. The *Fundamental Constitutions* were "frequently revised and just as often ignored" before they were overthrown forty years later.[44]

Regardless, it should now be clear that Locke did not reject such legislation around the same time he was writing the *Epistola* because he was no longer worried about uncivil disagreement or verbal persecution; in fact, as we shall see, his preoccupation with incivility only grew. Yet the *Letter* and its many sequels would eschew Locke's earlier emphasis on the outward realm of civil worship and turn their focus inward, to the beliefs, attitudes, and dispositions of individuals. Locke may have rejected the legal enforcement of civility; however, his understanding of the conversational virtues required in a tolerant society expanded accordingly.

"A Duty of Toleration"

Much transpired in the years between the *Fundamental Constitutions* and Locke's return to the topic of toleration in the *Epistola de Tolerantia* (1685) and the "Notes on the Pennsilvania Laws" (1686). As Shaftesbury fell out of favor in politics, Locke took advantage of the lull to focus on medicine, visit France, and begin work on his new obsession, epistemology. But as the political situation began to degenerate once again in 1678, first with the anti-Catholic hysteria surrounding the bogus "Popish Plot" that led to the judicial murder of over twenty suspected "Jesuits," followed by a failed attempt to exclude Charles II's Catholic brother, James, from the line of succession—both efforts spearheaded by a resurgent Shaftesbury and in which Locke would be implicated—questions of religion and politics came once more to the fore.[45]

By 1685, Shaftesbury was dead and Locke was in exile, suspected of involvement in a plot to assassinate both Stuarts.[46] It is significant that Locke, like Williams and Hobbes before him, wrote his most systematic treatment of toleration after an experience of exile—albeit in the commercial and cosmopolitan cities of the Netherlands and not in the wilds of North America or the refined courts of Paris. He wrote the *Epistola* to a Dutch friend in response to the plight of another set of exiles, the Huguenot *Refugiez* (the origin of the English *refugee*) displaced by persecution following Louis XIV's revocation of the Edict of Nantes on the specious grounds that there were no longer any Protestants in France.[47] Locke's rejection of Penn's law as a matter for "perpetual prosecution and animosity" in 1686 may well have been based on the evident failure of l'Hôpital's provisions against the labels *Huguenot* and *Papiste* in France, rather than on events in Carolina.[48] In any case, the *Epistola* was published anonymously four years later, after the so-called Glorious Revolution unseated James II and made it possible for Locke to come home in 1689. Popple's English translation followed later that same year.

By the time he wrote the *Epistola,* Locke had evidently left much of his earlier Hobbism behind.[49] The personal and political traumas described above coincided with Locke's composition of his as-yet-unpublished "Critical Notes on Stillingfleet" (c. 1681). This rejoinder to the (newly intolerant) latitudinarian bishop's sermon "The Mischief of Separation" reaffirmed Locke's earlier critique of the ambivalence of arguments for toleration like Bagshaw's, but from the opposite direction.[50] As with his earlier conversion, however, tracing the conceptual and logical continuities—and disjunctions—with Locke's earlier works is important for understanding his "mature" views on toleration and civility. It is important, too, to keep the distance between Locke and Popple in mind.

The *Letter* continued the prudential justifications inaugurated in *An Essay Concerning Toleration*: "It is not the Diversity of Opinions, (which cannot be avoided) but the Refusal of Toleration to those that are of different Opinions . . . that has produced all the Bustles and Wars that have been in the Christian World, upon account of Religion." But gone was the quasi-Erastian insistence on the absolute and arbitrary power of the civil magistrate in religious *or* civil *adiaphora*. Far from being of the same nature, Locke now insisted that religious and civil communities—the church and the commonwealth—were "most different." To "confound" them was the essence of persecution (LCT, 60).[51] Contra Hobbes, Locke was now unequivocal: "There is absolutely no such thing, under the Gospel, as a Christian Commonwealth" (42).

Political theorists generally associate *A Letter Concerning Toleration* (1689) with the passage of the famous Act of Toleration by Parliament in the same year. But in fact, the *Epistola* was written for a European audience four years earlier, and Popple's translation was published five months after the Act was passed. Actually "An Act for Exempting their Majestyes Protestant Subjects dissenting from the Church of England from the Penalities of certaine Lawes," the Toleration Act provided a consummate example of indulgence by suspending the enforcement of laws against conventicles and recusancy for some dissenters (e.g., Trinitarian Protestants) but not others (e.g., non-Trinitarians and Catholics). In another letter to Philipp van Limborch, the dedicatee of the original *Epistola*, Locke praised the Act as laying "the foundations . . . of that liberty and peace in which the church of Christ is one day to be established."[52] The Unitarian Popple, by contrast, seems to have been motivated to publish his translation largely by his disappointment with Parliament's efforts.

In his introduction to the *Letter*, Popple explained to readers that the "toleration" called for therein was no mere "Indulgence."[53] Its separation of the standards of civil and spiritual communion explains why. As we saw earlier with Roger Williams, it was this separation between the spiritual community of the church and the civil community of the commonwealth—not the more familiar institutional separation between church and state—that made it possible to sever the categories of "good citizen" and "good man" (or rather, "good Christian") once and for all. Popple may have been more radical than Locke, but the latter also showed himself willing to follow this thought through to its logical conclusion. The *Letter* began by arguing only for the "mutual Toleration" of (Protestant) Christians (LCT, 20), but by the end the full scope of its project was revealed: "Nay if we may openly speak the Truth and as becomes one Man to another; neither *Pagan*, nor *Mahumetan*, nor *Jew*, ought to be excluded from the Civil Rights of the Commonwealth, because of his Religion" (58–59). Locke's toleration demanded that a society not only treat dissenters as well as it did stranger communities of Jews and Muslims but that it treat these non-Christians as well as it did Anglican citizens. Separating civil and spiritual standards in this way meant that one no longer needed to be a Christian—or a communicating member of the Church of England—in order to enjoy the full rights and privileges of an Englishman.

Like Williams before him, in the *Letter* one can see Locke consciously "dismembering" the *corpus Christianum*—the communalist idea of a

Christian society united by a uniform confession and communion—and constructing a *corpus civile* in its place. His definition of a church as "a voluntary Society of Men, joining themselves together of their own accord" recalled the voluntary constitution, or incorporation, of churches described in the *Fundamental Constitutions* (LCT, 15). And yet the examples supplied to elucidate it—namely, "private" societies such as those of "Philosophers for Learning, of Merchants for Commerce" (including "Clubs for Clarret"), "or of men of leisure for mutual Conversation and Discourse," as well as formal corporations "for Trade and Profit"—are important (16, 56). This transformation of the traditional Christian, corporate understanding of membership as concord in and with the body of Christ into one of voluntary membership in a club or business corporation sounds a lot like Williams in *The Bloudy Tenent*, which likened a "company of worshippers" unto "a Body or Colledge of Physitians in a Citie, like unto a Corporation, Society, or Company of East-Indie or Turkie-Merchants, or any other Societie or Company in London" (BT, 73).

The comparison between a church and a commercial corporation is sometimes adduced as evidence that Locke was influenced by Williams. And yet the model foremost in the former's mind seems to have been that of an informal philosophical society—in Locke's Latin, "an association of learned persons to pursue philosophy . . . [or] men of leisure seeking conversation and entertainment."[54] Indeed, the pithy "Clubs for Clarret" line was Popple's, and it is missing from the *Epistola*.[55] Locke's metaphor implies something *less* formal than the legal corporations—such as colleges or businesses—described by Williams, which may "sue and implead each other at Law . . . [and yet the Citie] was before them, and stands absolute and entire when such a Corporation or Societie is taken down" (BT, 73). Williams's analogy suggests something more akin to the registered congregations envisioned in the *Fundamental Constitutions*, while Locke's implies a very different form of association, one based on the mutual pleasure of reasoned and reasonable conversation in the collective pursuit of truth reminiscent of Erasmus's ideal of colloquy. Locke was a member of many such societies in Holland and then again in London. Indeed, his acquaintance with Popple stems from their joint membership in the Dry Club established "for the amicable improvement of mix'd"—and sober—"conversation."[56]

Thus, while in the *Letter* one finds Locke at last endorsing something like the radical form of toleration espoused by Williams and commonly associated with "Lockean" liberalism, the vision of a tolerant society it presented is still different. The most striking feature of Locke's mature toleration writings also marks his greatest departure from Hobbes *and* Williams—namely, his focus on the robust ethical demands that "mutual toleration" would place on individuals. Political theorists often conceive of Lockean toleration as ethically minimal and principally as a regime of church-state separation, limited government, and individual rights. The *Letter,* however, devoted considerable attention to toleration as an interpersonal practice for people dealing with difference in their everyday lives. And in this, Locke insisted, "the narrow Measures of bare Justice"—that is abstaining from injury by not invading others' rights—would not suffice (LCT, 20). As Waldron and others have increasingly pointed out, the "Duty of Toleration" described in the *Letter* placed significant ethical demands both on particular churches and on individuals.[57] "Charity, Bounty, and Liberality" across religious differences, as well as "Equity" and even "Friendship," must "always mutually . . . be observed" (21–23). In particular, individuals must forego all "rough Usage of Word or Action" and maintain always "the softness of Civility and good Usage" in their disputes (19, 23).

The particular elements of this duty, and how Locke would have understood them, have received less attention.[58] Charity's first place position in the Duty of Toleration echoed the organization of the *Letter* itself, which began with an extended reflection on toleration as a duty of charity belonging to all Christians. Modern readers often overlook this opening salvo in favor of the more secular arguments that follow, but Locke put charity first for a reason—namely, to evoke and emulate the eirenic project initiated by Erasmus and Castellio by reinterpreting a concept polemically central to his opponents.[59] Proponents of persecution still followed Augustine in citing Christ's *compelle entrare* to justify the use of "due and moderate" punishments in the correction of spiritual errors.[60] While Castellio had convinced most would-be persecutors of the folly of "cutting off" heretics in order to convert them (with some notable exceptions), Locke had a more difficult task. He had to convince them that the matter was one of principle, not proportion; hence even "moderate" punishments, such as exclusion from public office, special taxes, fines, and imprisonment, were no different in kind than the torture, fire, and gallows employed by the Inquisition.

And so Locke seized on charity. To claim that it was "out of a Principle of Charity . . . and Love to Mens Souls" that "they deprive them of their Estates, maim them with corporal Punishments, starve and torment them in noisome Prisons, and in the end even take away their Lives" simply added insult to injury. "No body, surely, will ever believe that such a Carriage can proceed from Charity, Love, or Good-will" (LCT, 9–10). Rather than a form of loving chastisement toward a wayward brother, to punish another in his body or goods for spiritual errors was not only unjust but counterproductive. If the Gospels were to be believed, "no Man can be a Christian without *Charity*" and "*that Faith which works,* not by Force, but by *Love*" (8). Locke recognized that charity placed positive as well as negative demands on Christians, but, again, this was a selling point. "Mutual toleration" emphatically did not mean that citizens should simply observe a respectful *laissez-faire* in matters of faith but rather that they should engage one another in "charitable Admonitions" and "Arguments" aimed at their neighbor's best interests in this world—and in the next (LCT, 46).

"The Softness of Civility"

Locke's introduction of a vital, evangelical element to toleration was once again in keeping with the *Fundamental Constitutions*.[61] But it also reflected his redefinition of a church as a reasoned and reasonable conversational society, while directing the ethical demands of that dialogue beyond the members of a particular communion. It is in this context that "the softness of Civility" as a conversational virtue came to the fore in the *Letter* as a signal demand of the Duty of Toleration.

As in *An Essay Concerning Toleration,* the *Letter* maintained that incivility and "ill usage," and not religious diversity as such, were to blame for fomenting religious hatreds. "Any one may employ as many Exhortations and Arguments as he pleases, towards the promoting of another man's Salvation"; nevertheless, "nothing is to be done imperiously" (LCT, 46). A tolerant society required more from its members than abstaining from religious insult—namely, "such a Carriage" toward others as *could* be believed to "proceed from Charity, Love, or Good-will" (10). In its close connection with charity, Locke's conception of civility—and the Duty of Toleration as a whole—were evidently more than mere. Still, the *Letter* left its precise contours ambiguous.

Perhaps the fault is Popple's, because the "softness of Civility" is his phrase (23). Elsewhere in the *Epistola,* Locke adhered to the secular and political sense of the civil, as opposed to the spiritual or religious. Yet Popple chose to translate Locke's more pedestrian "humanity and goodwill" to reflect the conversational virtue pertinent to the practice of *disagreement*

the author clearly had in mind.[62] Locke would embrace the conversational sense of civility in his English writings of the same period, so Popple's
choice appears justified and effectively captured the sense of a "human"
standard of behavior distinct from Christianity. But what, exactly, would be
required to keep a disagreement "civil" or "humane" in Locke's sense?

The answer can be found by looking beyond the *Letter* to Locke's own
handbook of civil conduct and conversation, *Some Thoughts Concerning
Education* (1693). Written as a series of letters to a friend advising him on
the rearing of his son, *Some Thoughts* described civility as the "first and
most taking of the social virtues" and a necessary qualification for the "civil
conversation and business" that was a gentleman's life's work (STCE, 47–
48). In this, Locke positioned himself against the early modern manuals of
civil conversation inspired by Castiglione and Erasmus described in Chapter 1. These works taught civility as "good breeding" by focusing on the particulars of civil worship—for instance, how to "put off" one's hat or "make
legs" (110). Yet Locke insisted that this was to confuse the outward forms
of civility for its true substance. His reasoning closely followed the *Tracts'*
latitudinarian analysis of spiritual and civil *adiaphora.* The particular forms
of civility were "as peculiar and different in several countries of the world
as their languages"; true civility could not therefore consist in behavioral
rectitude in "putting off the hat" or "making compliments" (STCE, 65). The
essence of worship was the sincere opinion of esteem, not the culturally
contingent forms in which it was expressed.

This inward turn in Locke's definition from his earlier focus on external
adiaphora is striking.[63] In an unpublished fragment on "Morality" written
around 1677, Locke had defined civility as "nothing but outward expressing of good will and esteem, or at least of no contempt or hatred."[64] Like
Williams's mere civility or Hobbes's complaisant civil silence, this civility was an essentially outward affair consistent with any number of unsavory inward passions. Yet Locke's emphasis on sincerity in *Some Thoughts*
was completely different. The focus on ceremonial rigor was evidently as
wrongheaded in civil worship as it was in spiritual. True civility consisted
not in actions but in inward states—namely, "that general good will and
regard for all people which makes anyone have a care not to show [them]
. . . any contempt, disrespect, or neglect," and rather to "express according
to the fashion and ways of the country a respect and value" (STCE, 107).
The outward civility dominating popular understanding was simply "the
language whereby that internal civility of the mind [was] expressed" (43).

In a suggestive passage reminiscent of Williams's *Key Into the Language of America*, Locke suggested that the best exemplars of civility were not Europeans but "the Indians, whom we call barbarous" and yet "observe much more decency and civility in their discourse and conversation" (112).[65] In civility, as in religion, it was what was on the inside that counted, namely, the "disposition of the mind not to offend others" (107).

Despite his reversal on the nature of civility, Locke's mature writings demonstrate the same sensitivity to the difficulties of disagreement that animated his earlier works. *Some Thoughts* presented the inward nature of civility—"in truth, nothing but a care not to show any slighting or contempt of anyone in conversation" (STCE, 110)—as a necessary consequence of its role in facilitating disagreement. This is clear from Locke's extended discussion of *incivility* and the "faults" from which "[it] commonly has its rise." These closely tracked Hobbes's analysis of the sources of contumely. Locke described "roughness" as an "uncomplaisant" lack of sensitivity and an unwillingness "to accommodate [our]selves" to others, while "contempt" was "a want of due respect discovered either in looks, words, or gesture" that always brought "uneasiness": For "nobody can contentedly bear being slighted." "Censoriousness" was problematic because "men, whatever they are or are not guilty of, would not have their faults displayed"—to themselves or to others. So too with "raillery," which could not help but provoke "uneasiness" and so should be left alone by all but the most talented practitioners. Finally, Locke's analysis of "contradiction" echoed Hobbes in stressing the negative affective dimension of disagreement as such: "All opposition to what another man has said [is] apt to be suspected of censoriousness" and so is "seldom received without some sort of humiliation" (107–108).[66]

In the sense of a native ability to make oneself agreeable, Locke's occasional use of *complaisance* as a synonym for civility makes sense. Unlike Hobbes, however, Locke insisted that treating others civilly did not require one always to agree with them. Nevertheless, disagreement must be undertaken with "due caution and care of circumstances" and "made in the gentlest manner and softest words [that] can be found" (STCE, 108). Here Locke offered the familiar hope of a "civilitarian" solution: it was the "manner of doing it," and not disagreement itself, that was the issue. While not a contradiction in terms, as Hobbes might have it, civil disagreement remained a minefield. Not even the most civilized members of society were immune to the heat of disagreement; the slightest incivility was as tinder to a flame.[67] One should emulate the Americans in "giving one another a

fair and silent hearing till they have quite done and then answering them
calmly without noise or passion" (112). Children must be disabused early
of their "forwardness to interrupt" and to "correct others in their discourses," both of which conveyed "a very great disrespect" that could not "but be
offensive" (140).

The standard of civility described in *Some Thoughts* reflected Locke's
considered judgments about what it would take to render disagreement
peaceful and productive. Even if a war of all against all did not ensue,
should disagreement become *too* disagreeable, mass defection might. For
someone whose preferred model for religious and social arrangements
was a conversational or philosophical society committed to the "opposite
arguings of men of parts" as a means to moral, intellectual, and spiritual
improvement, this would be a devastating result (STCE, 112). One of the
rules for the Dry Club, written by Locke or endorsed by him, provided that
at "any appearance of growing warmth" the particular debate "is fit to be
stopd" so as to preserve the pleasant tone of collegiality and the possibility
of further discourse.[68]

The ideal form of civility as "the most taking of the social virtues" expressed in *Some Thoughts* was formulated aspirationally as the characteristic
virtue of a gentleman whose chief business was civil conversation, whether
in a philosophical club or the everyday intercourses of civil society—if not,
perhaps, in a university. Indeed, one of the forms of incivility singled out
in *Some Thoughts* was "formality" or the scholastic approach characteristic
of a university disputation. This form of disagreement served only to make
one an "opinionated" yet "insignificant wrangler" or, worse, an inveterate
skeptic, priding oneself in "questioning [of] everything and thinking there
is no such thing as truth" but "only victory in disputing." Both failings,
Locke insisted, amounted to the "end of all debate" and were inconsistent
with civil conversation, which demanded a willingness to "yield to plain
reason and the conviction of clear arguments" (STCE, 140–141).[69]

Here Locke's elitism, in comparison with Williams's more inclusive,
"meerly" civil approach is striking. Like the ideal disputants in the philosophic colloquies of Erasmus and Bodin, Locke's universal gentleman
would know how to make himself acceptable to inferiors and superiors
alike at home, as well as "persons of quality" abroad. Moreover, he would
be able to disagree without being disagreeable and so correct others' errors
without offending them. He who "knows how to make those he converses
with easy without debasing himself to low and servile flattery" possessed

"the true art of living in the world" (STCE, 109). If people could be made to love good company, then they might even come to seek out their own correction (45).

In light of this aspiration, what was formerly an external matter of cultural conformity and self-restraint quickly became an internal art of inoffensiveness and an acute sensitivity to the sensitivities of others. This new conception of civility raised obvious problems for enforcement, of which Locke seemed well aware. As the disposition "not to offend," the ultimate standard of civil behavior lay in the judgment of its recipient, who alone could judge whether another's conduct had, in fact, offended. "Mistaken civility" could arise equally from any "excess of ceremony" or the mere "suspicion of flattery [or] dissimulation" (STCE, 109). Like God, men "naturally hate whatever is counterfeit"—especially worship insincerely offered. But here again, Locke stressed the importance of sincerity. Just as the strictest observation of external forms could offend if they seemed "wanting in sincerity," mistakes in civil worship might be forgiven if the heart behind them was true (42–44). It was "no great matter how they put off their hats and make legs"; the key to civil disagreement lay rather in teaching children sincerely "to love and respect other people" (110).

Refastening the *Vinculum*

Locke wrote *Some Thoughts* during the same period as *A Second Letter Concerning Toleration* and *A Third Letter for Toleration* (1690–1692) in defense of Popple's translation. In its aspirational account of civility, he may have had his exasperating critic, the Anglican minister Jonas Proast, in mind. Certainly, Locke's identification of sincerity as the essence of civility therein was connected with his ongoing reflection on the nature and character of a tolerant society, the members of which were no longer bound together by the ties of religious communion.

Yet in importing the demand for sincerity characteristic of spiritual worship into civility, Locke did something neither Hobbes nor Williams had dared. Merely civil behavior or hypocritical conformity would never suffice to civilize men's disagreements. In order to defuse the animosity attendant on fundamental disagreement, one's outward performances had to be seen as a reliable expression of a *sincere* inward esteem. And this, in turn, had important implications for his theory of toleration. The change appears to have been the product of two factors: Locke's reinterpretation of the *vinculum societatis* as a matter of trust, on the one hand, and his increasingly cosmopolitan perspective on the problem of toleration, on the other. When *An Essay Concerning Toleration* had initially proposed trust as the *vinculum* of tolerant societies, Locke's concerns had been primarily domestic, with England's hotter Protestants as the limit case. But as the scope of his toleration expanded, Locke's emphasis on trustworthiness—and his sense of its prerequisites—expanded, as well.

Critics often characterize "Lockean" toleration as a parochial affair preoccupied with minute distinctions between Protestant Christians. Yet the *Letter*'s embrace of a more radical form of toleration went hand in hand with an increasing openness to a much wider range of religious differences.[70] This universalism supplied the force of the so-called "Alpine" argument, which pointed out that the right claimed by proponents of uniformity for a Protestant magistrate in punishing dissent must be granted to a Muslim or Pagan—or, worse yet, a Catholic—as well. "If you will enlarge [your thoughts] a little beyond the confines of England," Locke wrote to Proast, "you will easily imagine that if in Italy, [and] Spain" and "in other parts those severities that are used to keep or force men into national religion" were abolished," "true [i.e., Protestant] religion would be a gainer by it" (SL, 64).

Like all arguments for toleration, Locke's hinged on the idea that society might safely bear quite a lot of religious difference, so long as its members were sufficiently similar in other respects. His increasingly global perspective thus reinforced the selection of trust or *fides*—man's capacity to make and keep promises—as the *vinculum societatis*.[71] Every example of peaceful cohabitation throughout history (whether or not it ascended to the level of "civil society" on his definition) evidenced the ubiquity and universality of trust as the "bond of humanity."[72] Trust*worthiness* thus became Locke's necessary and sufficient condition for toleration. Because men *qua* men (and not *qua* Christians) were capable of trust, one need not fear extending civil membership to people of different cultures or religions—to a "rational Turk or Infidel" as well as to "a sober sensible Heathen" (TL, 239).

As Locke's toleration became more radical and expansive, he also became increasingly concerned with the conditions of trustworthiness. What, exactly, must the members of a tolerant society *share* in order to make their disagreements nonthreatening and so maintain the bonds of trust? In his changing answer to this question, sincerity was crucial. Trust demanded that one ameliorate the hard, Hobbesian distinction between the inward and outward man he had previously endorsed. Instead, one's trustworthiness depended on the harmony between one's inward persuasions and their outward expression; because of this, one should embrace those "who conscientiously, and out of a sincere persuasion, embrace any religion, though different from [one's own], and in a way, I think, mistaken" (SL, 115–116). Civility in disagreement was not a demand of the Duty of Toleration simply because it made edifying conversations more pleasant; rather, as an expression of good faith and sincerity it would continually create and reinforce the *vinculum societatis* of mutual trust *through the very practice of disagreement itself.*

Society could evidently tolerate quite a lot diversity and irrationality in religion, so long as its members were sincerely civil. At the same time, the threat to social life posed by anything that might undermine citizens' trust in one another on suspicion of insincerity was devastating. The *Letter* defined the limits of toleration on this basis. Not only did the magistrate have a duty to protect citizens from the "injurious": "No Opinions contrary to human Society, or those moral Rules which are necessary to the preservation of Civil Society, are to be tolerated" (LCT, 49–50). In other words, certain persons and creeds must be excluded from toleration, regardless of whether or not they were peaceable, because their beliefs placed them under suspicion. For instance, Locke excluded atheists on the grounds that the "Promises, Covenants, and Oaths" that were "the Bonds of Humane Society" were useless without the security of an all-knowing God prepared to punish offenders (52–53).[73] And although a sincere belief in God was a necessary condition for trust, it was not therefore sufficient; for instance, the sincerity of one's Catholic faith did not entitle one to toleration. All of the problematic tenets of Catholicism Locke identified—including that "*Dominion is founded in Grace*" and their alleged loyalties to the "*Mufti of Constantinople*"—were summed up in the principle "*that Faith is not to be kept with Hereticks*" (50–52).

The idea that Catholics were not obliged to keep their promises to "those who differ from them in Religion" cut right to the heart of the issue of sincerity, and it remained a staple of English anti-Catholic propaganda for centuries.[74] For Protestant critics, Catholic persecution from the Inquisition to the French *dragonnades* offered ample evidence of their hypocrisy in claiming toleration for themselves. But in this, Locke suggested, Catholics were not unique. The "intolerant" as such, whether Catholics or Protestants, were guilty of a deadly form of moral subjectivism. How could they be trusted not to engage in persecution as soon as the balance of power shifted in their favor? Lowering the stakes of religious conflict would not be enough. Maintaining the *vinculum* of trust meant that citizens had to *accept* and *affirm*—in Popple's parlance, "own and teach"—the Duty of Toleration toward "all men in matters of meer religion" (LCT, 50–51).

Rethinking "Lockean" Toleration

Trustworthiness may, at first, sound like a fairly minimal condition for inclusion. Yet the limits of Locke's toleration suggest a higher bar. Tolerant societies were in need of stronger stuff than the soft hypocrisy of mere civility or civil silence. One's assurance of another's trustworthiness depended on the sense that his outsides were an accurate reflection of his insides and that, despite their differences, the members of a tolerant society could agree on certain fundamental principles—including the existence of God, the Duty of Toleration, and the Golden Rule, which Locke described as "such a *fundamental* truth for the regulation of human society" that by it alone "one might without difficulty determine all the cases and doubts in social morality."[75] Even if atheists, Catholics, irrational Turks, and the intolerant behaved perfectly peaceably, swearing oaths, abiding by the laws, and honoring their contracts, they would remain hypocrites in principle, which Locke now viewed as an intolerable civil, as well as spiritual, sin.[76]

Despite their superficial similarities, Locke was clearly no Roger Williams. But neither does he seem particularly "Lockean." We are certainly a long way from the traditional picture of ethical minimalism, individual rights, and secular neutrality associated with Lockean toleration by both its defenders and detractors today. As we have seen, the Duty of Toleration was quite ethically demanding, and if the "softness of Civility" was increasingly difficult to distinguish from sincere charity on Locke's account as a "brotherly kindness [in] the diversity of opinions" (SL, 80), this appeared to be intentional. As he put it in "Pacific Christians" (1688), an unpublished draft of rules for a religious society, it was an "indispensable duty for all Christians to maintain love and charity in the diversity of contrary opinions"—that is, not an "empty sound, but an effectual forbearance and good will, carrying men to communion, friendship and mutual assistance one of another, in outward as well as spiritual things."[77]

In the end, Locke's conception of civility as a sincere form of *civil* charity derived from his lifelong attachment to "the opposite arguings of men of parts" as an engine of truth production, on the one hand, and his lingering concerns about the pressures placed by religious disagreement—especially in the face of an ever-receding eschaton—on the *vinculum* of social trust, on the other.[78] To balance religious difference and disagreement successfully under these conditions, not *hating* one's neighbor was not enough. In a 1689 letter to his friend Limborch, Locke proposed the counterintuitive idea that religious liberty could *itself* supply the "bond of mutual charity" without which a tolerant society could not stand: "Men will always differ on religious questions and rival parties will continue to quarrel and wage war on each other unless the establishment of equal liberty for all provides a *bond of mutual charity* by which all may be brought together into one body."[79]

Locke's emphasis on the need for unifying, affective "bonds" in a tolerant society—of mutual charity, trust, and good will—in this passage and elsewhere recalls nothing more than the bonds of church communion shattered by the Reformation. This, again, was intentional. In his letter to Limborch, Locke deliberately invoked the traditional language of post-Reformation eirenicism with its aspirations to *concordia*—the Christian ideal of communion and unity in diversity—but with a twist. In effect, he reimagined toleration not only as a means to, but as *itself* a kind of *concordia*, one meant to reign within the body politic, rather than the voluntary "corporation" of the Church. The toleration defended in the *Letter* and its many sequels was thus something much, much more than *tolerantia*. Instead of a negative ideal of permission without approval, Locke offered a positive vision of a tolerant society as a community bound together by mutual trust, wherein the difficulties of disagreement would be assuaged through true and sincere civility.

Institutionally, the Lockean toleration that emerges in this account is a far cry from the proto-liberal arrangements of disestablishment, equal protection, and individual rights of worship, association, and expression we saw earlier in Williams. Political theorists tend to associate Locke above all with the separation of church and state and settling "the just Bounds that lie between the one and the other" (LCT, 12). But for Locke, this was primarily a *conceptual* distinction, not an institutional one; unlike Williams's evangelical liberty it did not necessarily entail disestablishment. Although Locke apparently objected to an Anglican establishment in Carolina, he appears to have been entirely comfortable with the existence of a state-supported church in England, both politically and personally. Despite his considerable heterodoxy, he remained a communicating member of the Church of

England until his death. And while the *Letter* argued that magistrates had a public duty to "impartially set themselves up against vice," as Christians it insisted that they also had a duty to "make use of Arguments, and thereby draw the Heterodox into the way of Truth, and procure their Salvation" (13–14). Far from counseling neutrality, Locke urged the magistrate to set citizens a good example as one evangelist—albeit one with superior resources—among others.

In this, his theory and practice were consistent. Locke's arguments for toleration were frequently coupled with demands that magistrates turn their attention from punishing dissent to reforming "manners" instead. Here, he once more made common cause with latitudinarian Anglicans like Stillingfleet and Gilbert Burnet.[80] "Equal liberty" in religion was under no circumstances to be mistaken for license or libertinism; by cracking down on vice, Locke argued, the magistrate should cooperate with the church to ensure that citizens divided in their religious opinions would remain safely united through virtuous living. His "Essay on the Poor Law" (1697) argued in favor of public "working schools" where children caught begging might be made to "come constantly to church every Sunday," for due to "their idle and loose way of breeding up, they are as utter strangers both to religion and morality as they are to industry."[81] Locke was even open to state-sponsored evangelism of the kind decried by Williams. As Jack Turner has shown, during his tenure as a member of the Board of Trade (1696–1700) Locke approved and facilitated missionary efforts among the American Indians.[82]

Perhaps it is significant that Locke, the former radical, offered his most sustained and systematic reflections on civility and toleration at a time when he was becoming an established figure—a bureaucrat, no less—within the new regime. Yet even in the *Epistola,* one can see that Locke's early flirtation with comprehension had left a lasting impression on his toleration. As Chapter 1 demonstrated, comprehension promised to accommodate diversity within an established church by lowering the bar to membership through a minimal consensus on the *fundamenta* of Christianity. Like Rawls's idea of an overlapping consensus, the appeal of comprehension for Locke lay in the way it created unity out of diversity by fostering bonds of affection between individuals while acknowledging that their differences of opinion would inevitably persist.[83] Comprehension acknowledged that "thinking Men" would disagree and yet could remain members of the same church, bound together by Christian love and sacramental communion (SL, 80–81).

Although some scholars have dismissed his endorsement of "latitudinism" in 1667 as an attempt to curry favor with Charles II,[84] there is plenty of evidence in the later *Letters* that Locke remained committed to some combination of comprehension and toleration as the best means for achieving civil concord. In an earlier letter to Limborch, he identified *both* as forms of toleration—"The former signifies extension of the boundaries of the Church, with a view to including greater numbers by the removal of part of the ceremonies," while "the latter signifies toleration of those who are either unwilling or unable to unite themselves to the Church of England on the terms offered to them."[85] And when the Latin *Epistola* became available in London in 1689, it was bound and sold with an eirenic tract entitled "A Theological Dissertation on Peace in the Church."[86] Like Erasmus and Castellio, Locke's toleration was also evangelical in key respects. When Proast expressed consternation over the toleration of Jews and Muslims in the *Letter,* Locke replied that "it is our duty to pray every day for their conversion," but it is "hardly to be believed that we pray in earnest if we exclude them from the other ordinary and probable means of conversion; either by driving them from, or persecuting them when they are amongst us" (SL, 62).[87] In this, one can recognize the eirenic hope that affective belonging might serve as a leading line to *homonoia* hereafter.

Conclusion

In associating himself with the cause of eirenic Christianity in the *Letters,* Locke was not unique. As we saw in the first chapter, in seventeenth-century England hopes for Christian reconciliation motivated arguments for and against toleration alike. And yet, in sounding these traditional, eirenic themes, Locke was deploying them for vastly different ends: the realization of a vision of *concordia* as the essence of toleration in a civil society, rather than of communion in the body of the church. This is a far cry from the grudging, forbearant form of *tolerantia* with which Locke is commonly associated. And yet this chapter has argued that the new, positive vision of a tolerant society he developed in the *Epistola* had its roots in fears first articulated in the anti-toleration *Tracts*—fears about the difficulties of disagreement between partial and proud creatures in an inalterably expanded public sphere.

Thus, even as he turned toward toleration and an increasingly inward conception of civility as a sincere form of civil charity, Locke never fully abandoned the Hobbesian concerns animating the *Tracts*. Unlike Hobbes, however, Locke believed that by addressing the manner of disagreement, one could "civilize" it and forestall its negative effects. Absent civility, open religious disagreement under these new conditions would only exacerbate the radical moral dissensus he believed to be natural to mankind.[88] With civility, however, religious disagreements might *themselves* become sources of solidarity through which individuals could come to recognize and appreciate the reasonableness, respectability, and good will of their opponents—but always, necessarily, within limits.

Today, those limits remain the most offensive aspect of Locke's argument for both his critics and defenders alike. Both treat his exceptions—particularly of atheists and Catholics—as an unfortunate consequence of a thin conception of "mere" toleration.[89] And yet this chapter suggests that the exclusionary potential of Locke's toleration derived instead from his conviction that religious diversity would require more than mere *tolerantia* to sustain it and thus from his determination to theorize civility as an ever more demanding ideal. Every citizen need not master the myriad "languages" of civility, nor ascend to the heights of tact, charm, and social grace commanded by the universal gentleman; yet the virtue of civility universalized through the Duty of Toleration was hardly less exacting. In contrast with Williams's mere civility, Locke's civil charity was an unabashedly elite and elitist standard. This suggests that he rejected legislative enforcement of civility in 1686 (in his notes on Penn) not because he had lowered his expectations but because he had raised them.[90] Still, in matters of civility, as in religion, where sincerity was the thing, the best instruction would come from the good examples and public reasoning of universal gentlemen demonstrating the "softness of Civility" in the public sphere.

In his own controversial writings against Proast, Locke positioned himself as just such an (anonymous) exemplar—a reputation his early biographers were eager to cement.[91] He had little time for the separatist scruples and censorious bombast of "fanatics" like Williams. Any "Christian" who would deny that name to others was guilty of schism and of "tear[ing] in pieces the church of Christ" (TL, 239). Instead, the members of Locke's tolerant society, Christian and non-Christian alike, must give up their "implacable enmities" and "diligently endeavor to allay and temper all that Heat and unreasonable averseness of Mind." Once each surrendered his "fiery Zeal for his own Sect," he might recognize that all others were, in fact, as "several paths that are in the same road"—"and lead in the same direction"

(LCT, 24).[92] The *Reasonableness of Christianity* (1695) represented Locke's own attempt at offering a latitudinarian theology meant to achieve the kind of overlapping consensus necessary to foster the bonds of affection between individuals. Perhaps not surprisingly, its Christological and minimalist construction of the fundamentals of Christianity reminded some readers of nothing more than Hobbes's mantra, "Jesus is the Christ."[93]

As we have seen, Locke was not the first, nor the last, proponent of civility to treat himself as an exemplar and wish that other minds were a little bit more like his own. However, his particular determination to define civility ever upward—and inward—belied his lasting suspicion that disagreements about *fundamenta* simply could not be kept civil (or safe) for very long. The Duty of Toleration, in effect, called for a communion and mutual affection between citizens only possible through an agreement more fundamental than the disagreements that divided them, in light of which their differences could be downplayed or dissolved. In the end, the vision of *concordia* in a tolerant society defended by Locke was the authentic, eirenic kind, not the Hobbesian simulacrum. A considerable degree of *homonoia* would be required, after all.

This transformation of Lockean civility into a matter of shared beliefs rather than behaviors explains why Locke's toleration was much less accommodating than Williams's had been. Like the early modern eirenicists and Williams's persecutors in Massachusetts Bay, his positive vision of *concordia* led Locke to conflate the manner of disagreement with the fact. In the end, he readily sacrificed diversity for the sake of peaceful and productive disagreement. As we turn once more to the modern crisis of civility with which this book began, we shall see that Locke's hope—and his sacrifice—remain alive and well today.

Conclusion

The Virtue of Mere Civility

Take away, O ass! those panniers of airy nothingness; and speak, if
you can, three words that have an affinity to common sense; if it
be possible for the tumid pumpkin of your skull to discover for a
moment anything like the reality of intellect.
—JOHN MILTON, *Second Defense of the People of England* (1654)

THIS BOOK BEGAN with the promise that the competing conceptions
of civility put forward by Williams, Hobbes, and Locke might bring
some sorely needed analytical clarity and insight to a contemporary debate
stymied by the endless back and forth between proponents of civility and
its critics. By today's standards, John Locke represents an altogether more
civil and tolerant figure than that fundamentalist schismatic and purvey-
or of religious insult, Roger Williams. In dealing with other faiths, Locke
urged always respect, ecumenical "indifferency," and an open mind; he
condemned private intolerance itself and not just persecution.[1] Though he
ultimately eschewed the legal proscription of religious insult, Locke never
personally indulged in the epithets that came so easily to Williams, who
routinely denied the name of "Christian" to those with whom he disagreed
on points of the profoundest indifference. Reserving the right for sects to
denominate themselves, Locke would not even identify Catholics by name
when discussing the limits of toleration in the *Letter;* instead, he observed a
civil silence and referred to them obliquely, analogizing the pope to the Ottoman mufti—and not to the Antichrist, as Luther and Williams had done.[2]

By contrast, in his intemperate zeal Williams referred to Catholics as "Anti-Christians," accused his fellow New English of "spiritual whoredom," and
described the Americans as worshipping the "Divell" (BT, 92–93; Key, 210).
Yet despite this evangelical shock and awe, he extended toleration to all of
these groups, and to the intolerant, atheists, "rational" as well as "irrational"

144

Turks, and the Quakers besides. In this, the contrast between Locke and Williams could not be starker, and it demonstrates an important fact that both the proponents of civility and their critics too often overlook—namely, that an aversion to intolerance does not entail a commitment to inclusion. Nor, for that matter, does it entail a commitment to toleration—of difference *or* disagreement.

If Williams is the hero of this book, I fear that Locke must be its villain. Given their shared commitment to inclusion as the be-all and end-all of a tolerant society, one might expect partisans on both sides of the popular and scholarly debates about civility discussed in the Introduction to agree.[3] And yet today, while echoes of Hobbes and Locke abound, Williams's voice is conspicuously absent. This is true especially in political theory, where despite the pervasive sense of crisis, discussions of civility have remained oddly moribund since the 1990s. In that decade a wide range of theorists seized upon civility as an essential virtue of intellectual community, civil society, deliberative democracy, and even justice itself.[4] The close connection between civility and toleration as "hallmarks of liberal citizenship" in the face of deep disagreements about the good was—and still is—taken for granted.[5] The precise relationship between these "hallmarks," however, along with the concrete demands they place on individuals and society at large, remains frustratingly fuzzy.

Like their early modern ancestors, its modern proponents are usually much clearer when it comes to what they think civility rules out—whether threats of coercion, insults or other forms of "verbal violence," narrow-mindedness, or "dogmatic" appeals to authority or ideology. While many so-called civilitarians do not support legislation in the form of gag rules or speech codes,[6] others do by arguing that these forms of incivility pose intolerable threats to tolerant societies as such.[7]

When it comes to the particular conceptions of civility put forward by political theorists as the *vinculum,* the early modern resonances grow even more pronounced. For some, civil silence is key. Mark Kingwell describes civility as a kind of "pragmatic not-saying," "sensitivity," and "tact" that manifests in "a willingness *not* to say all the true, or morally excellent, things one could say."[8] Similarly, Bruce Ackerman stresses the importance of "conversational constraints" in dialogue, including bans on *all* assertions of superiority—of oneself or one's conception of the good.[9] (Hobbes's warning in *The Elements of Law* against the contumely of "unwanted counsel" comes immediately to mind.) The idea that conversation could continue in the absence of such self-discipline is "childish," argues Thomas Nagel; it "represents a misunderstanding of the mutually protective function of con-ventions of restraint, which avoid provoking unnecessary conflict."[10] These modern Hobbesians stress the common-sense notion that civil dialogue requires a willingness to mind one's own business, bite one's tongue, and avoid certain topics.[11] Arguments in favor of public reason constraints on democratic deliberation, what John Rawls described in *Political Liberalism* (1996) as a "duty of civility," reflect a similar intuition.[12] Citizens can and will continue to differ in their comprehensive doctrines (within the bounds of "reasonableness"); however, they should not bring up those differences in the course of public disagreement on matters of basic justice or constitu-tional essentials. If "good fences make good neighbors,"[13] then neighborli-ness also demands that we keep hopelessly controversial discussions about fundamental premises off of the agenda.

Hobbes's hope for "difference without disagreement" achieved through virtuous discretion appears to be alive and well.[14] Nevertheless, the pre-dominant spirit in contemporary political theory is that of John Locke. While the civil silencers emphasize the negative dimension of civility as self-restraint, these theorists stress its "affirmative and positive" dimension as the communication of mutual respect.[15] Sarah Buss has pointed to the "expressive function of manners": "By behaving politely, we are, in effect, 'saying' something to one another" and "acknowledg[ing] one another's special dignity."[16] Other theorists employ the language of recognition to de-scribe a similar phenomenon. Following Oakeshott, Richard Boyd defines civility as "the mutual recognition of others as our moral equals,"[17] while Robert Pippin argues that the "daily ritual" of civility acknowledges their "equal status as free agents within a cooperative enterprise."[18]

For these modern Lockeans, conversational civility is integral to the stronger social and civic bonds called for by theorists of political liberal-ism, as well as their republican and communitarian critics. In this, their emphasis on a minimal form of consensus on certain moral and political *fundamenta* as the key to social solidarity and cohesion recalls the low-church latitudinarian approach to toleration in the *Letter*. For some, like Stephen Carter, the Christian resonances of this positive conception of civility as a source of communal solidarity, even charity, are unapologetic. "Civility," he argues, "is the sum of the many sacrifices we are called to make for the sake of living together . . . as a signal of respect for our fel-low citizens, marking them as full equals, both before the law and before

God." Hence, we must "learn anew the virtue of acting with love toward our neighbors . . . [and] the genuine appreciation for each other on which a successful civility must rest."[19]

Even for ostensibly secular liberals like Rawls, however, the language of harmony and social concord used to express their hopes for civility confirms that they, too, envision a tolerant society characterized by something more than *tolerantia*. Rawls's discussion of the difference between a "mere *modus vivendi*" and the "social concord" achieved through overlapping consensus on a political conception of justice in *Political Liberalism* reads like a twentieth-century gloss on Locke's letter to Limborch.[20] Although Rawls links the concord of a "well-ordered society" conceptually and historically to the "gradual acceptance of the principle of toleration" in Europe after centuries of religious warfare,[21] what he describes is something much closer to comprehension: a liberal polity, the stability and harmony of which reflect that "everyone accepts, and *knows that everyone else accepts and publicly endorses,* the very same principles of justice."[22]

In making his own case for conversational civility as essential to the public goods of inclusiveness and "assurance" in *The Harm in Hate Speech*, Waldron appeals to Rawls's definition of a well-ordered society directly.[23] Civil interactions are how we know "that everyone accepts" our equal dignity as an acknowledgement of our status as members of society in good standing.[24] While Waldron justifies laws against hate speech and religious insult on the grounds that such assurance is especially valuable to the most vulnerable, a similar emphasis on civility's affective importance can be found among the civil silencers. In his defense of gag rules, Stephen Holmes insists that, "by tying our tongues about a sensitive question, we can secure forms of cooperation and fellowship otherwise beyond reach." Here, Holmes defends discussion bans on the same grounds that their early modern supporters did; he even cites Bodin's praise for the king of Muscovy as an epigraph.[25]

It seems that many modern civil silencers are, like Waldron, not true Hobbists but proponents of sincere civil charity who are nevertheless willing to deploy Hobbesian means in the pursuit of Lockean ends. While Rawls and Waldron insist that the *fundamenta* on which reasonable comprehensive doctrines converge—with reasonableness being defined as a commitment to fair principles of cooperation—are procedural, not substantive, it is clear that the importance of overlapping consensus for them, as for Locke, is *affective* as well as cognitive. Sincerity in civility thus spells the difference between a modus vivendi and the mutual confidence of a "moral conception

. . . affirmed on moral grounds" without which "citizens could easily fall into bitterness and resentment."[26] Gutmann and Thompson's search for "more reliable criteria for recognizing, or at least good grounds for suspecting, insincerity" is similarly motivated: "Although the principles [of civic magnanimity] refer to the way that opinions are held and expressed, their object is not mainly a matter of style or rhetoric but, rather, of attitude and conduct as manifested in public actions."[27]

Despite small differences in emphasis, all of these theorists take advantage of the conceptual minimalism of civility as nothing out of the ordinary and well within reach. And yet, time and again, they set the deliberative bar quite high, placing constraints not only on the manner in which fundamental disagreements are conducted but also on what kinds of disagreements can take place, where, and with whom.[28] The "attentive listening" requirement of most contemporary theories of civility affords an illustrative example. As Philip Selznick describes it, this requires more than taking turns, but actually recognizing the validity of opposing views and a willingness to revise our own, a quality of "open-mindedness" stressed by deliberative democrats as well.[29] If civility implies a respect for others as "free agents in the pursuit of self-development," yet with whom we disagree on issues spanning the spectrum of seriousness, then that respect should not only afford them the space in which to strive but also extend to the results of that striving—to their "conscientious commitments," too.[30] Once again, the issue is assurance: "Our sense of our own value, as well as our self-confidence, depends on the respect and mutuality shown us by others. . . . [Thus] by publicly affirming the basic liberties, citizens in a well-ordered society express their mutual respect for one another as reasonable and trustworthy, as well as their recognition of the worth all citizens attach to their way of life."[31]

Yet in their robust conceptions of civility, these modern Hobbesians and Lockeans also reproduce the normative problems of their predecessors. The latter, especially, present a demanding ethos of civility as a way to heal the wounds of a dismembered polity, but at the cost of a moralizing emphasis on sincerity and the contemptuous exclusion of anyone unwilling or unable to submit to its rigors.[32] As agonistic critics of public reason and deliberative democracy have long argued, the exclusionary potential of these theories arises from the suggestion that truly civil disagreement can take place only between good faith partners committed to a just social order—that is, those who subscribe to the relevant moral principles *already*.[33] Under the auspices of "civility," these theorists follow their early modern forebears in drawing up a list of *fundamenta* (mutual respect, reciprocity, recognition) and then proposing to "civilize" disagreement by demanding others affirm it—and then complain about their lack of conformable complaisance when they do not.

The problem seems to be that, like Locke, these theorists take an elite, and frankly elitist, standard of civil discourse appropriate to particular formalized and limited conversational contexts—a philosophy seminar, a legislative chamber, the Supreme Court, or an "ideal speech situation"—as paradigmatic for civility, and then apply it to others where the rules of civility are more nebulous. In this rarified and restricted vision of civil conversation in a tolerant society, only sufficiently reasonable and gentlemanly evangelists (such as themselves) can take part.[34] Rather than continuing the conversation, such a robust conception of civility more often serves to banish the wide swath of one's co-citizens that one finds less than reasonable or morally respectable from the conversation. The end result is a Bodinian colloquy in which the key to harmony is the fact that the participants are identical in all respects but one.[35]

I shall return to these criticisms—and theorists' possible responses to them—below. For now, it would seem that bringing historical perspective to bear on contemporary debates simply confirms the contentions, if not the suspicions, of civility's critics who call attention to its power to stigmatize others as backward or barbarous and so preclude their participation in political and social life.

Of course, complaints about civility as a "civilizing discourse" that silences dissent have their own early modern resonances.[36] In recent analyses of the stifling and stultifying tyranny of "bourgeois respectability," one can recognize a more tempered version of the radical Puritan critique of civility as a ploy to persecute righteousness and godly zeal.[37] Randall Kennedy has argued that civility is "just a genteel way to mask the inevitable tensions and antagonisms of democratic society," one that "foster[s] a crippling crybabyism" while marginalizing already marginal voices.[38] Michael Walzer insists that civility is actively hostile to true civic virtue in the form of uncompromising challenges to an unjust status quo.[39] These modern critics, like their early modern counterparts, argue that the "silver alarums" of dissent always appear uncivil to those privileged by existing arrangements. Calling for civility is simply an effective way of indulging one's intolerance of dissent while hiding it from others—and, more importantly, from oneself.

Far from being tantamount to justice, as Kingwell claims, on this view civility serves only to protect existing injustices—status differentials and social hierarchies—while stifling the legitimate, often disruptive demands to destroy them. In her critique of Richard Rorty, Rebecca Comay argues that "exhortations to 'civility' . . . serve above all to legitimate the exclusion of marginal or dissident voices from the conversation [and] the appearance of open pluralistic debate may more often mask the monolithic interests of the dominant power group."[40] According to such critics, calling for civility is not just "strewing flowers on a dead corpse," as the Puritan preacher Thomas Watson once put it, but interfering with the autopsy when a violent pollen allergy was the real cause of death.

It may be tempting to dismiss these criticisms as hypocritical or unrealistic. After all, theorists who deny that civility is a virtue generally rely on the fact that their opponents do not. While they critique them into oblivion, the norms of academic civility make it possible for them to argue and to have their voices heard. Yet the modern revivals of Hobbesian civil silence and Lockean civil charity noted above suggest that while these critics may be wrong about their opponents' motives, they are right about the logic of repression implicit in their theories of civility. There may be important differences between Hobbes's endorsement of discretion to the point of dissimulation and Locke's demand for sincerity in civil as well as spiritual worship; nonetheless, both strategies—suppression, on the one hand, and exclusion, on the other—are on display in contemporary debates. Here, proponents' defense that the consensus demanded by civility is procedural, not substantive, cuts little ice. George Gillespie's adverbial redefinition of heresy and Richard Allestree's accusation of incivility against atheists for their indifference to the "offensiveness" of their discourse to believers both demonstrate how easily the manner of disagreement is reduced to the fact, thereby "cutting off" those one deems as beyond the pale from the conversation—and on ostensibly procedural grounds.[41]

And yet in highlighting the abuses, modern critics—like the early Quakers—often lapse into defenses of incivility that downplay or deny its harms. As Williams, Hobbes, and Locke knew quite well, deep disagreements about the good are inevitably fraught, but the alienation and upset attendant on uncivil disagreement is often a conversation-stopper, a signal for vulnerable or unpopular minorities to retreat, and an invitation for everyone to withdraw to the more enjoyable give-and-take of their own like-minded conversational communities. There is a reason that *agreeable* is a synonym for pleasant. Nevertheless, this retreat only exacerbates the disagreeableness of disagreement when it inevitably occurs, thus strengthening the impression that deliberation is only possible, let alone productive, when limited to those who agree already on the fundamentals. The familiar "chilling" of debate, the ideologizing of differences, and the balkanization and resegregation of tolerant societies evident today is the inevitable result.

If civility describes the conversational virtue that makes it possible to keep disagreements going, no matter how fundamental, it would seem that both sides of the contemporary debate—both the proponents of civility and its critics—are themselves guilty of *incivility*. After all, accusing others of civilizational imperialism or perspectival "privilege" and thus promoting ad hominem from a logical fallacy to a knock-down argument is its own, very effective way of shutting down debate. Because some calls for civility function as self-serving defenses of the status quo, does that mean that all must? The uncharitable interpretation of its proponents' failure to acknowledge their implicit quest for commonality is that accusations of incivility are too useful a tool to bludgeon the downtrodden with to bother explaining what one means. A more charitable reading, however, is that their commitment to toleration and inclusion makes modern proponents of civility understandably hesitant to speak too definitively about what they have in mind.

Rather than engaging with their opponents, civility's critics usually end up substituting their own conception of what kinds of conversation—and conversationalists—are respectable members of a tolerant society and which must be "cut off." Thus, by condemning any and all calls for civility as irredeemably exclusionary, intolerant, and unjust, its modern critics exacerbate the dynamic of exclusion they blame on their opponents. Like the failed Colloquy of Poissy, the discussion falls apart before it can get off the ground. Participants on both sides respond by anathematizing their opponents (as "civilitarians" or "postmodernists") and redouble their commitment to conversing only with those they can be confident will share their views, nursing the hope that "every man who loves his country [holds] in his inmost heart: the suppression of half his compatriots."[42]

It seems that, once again, we are at an impasse. Yet here historical perspective allows us to say much more about the relationship between civility and toleration than we could when we began—and to suggest a possible way forward. In the first place, civility captures an important element of the "horizontal"

aspect of toleration as a social practice and interpersonal relationship between individuals.[43] As such, it describes how the members of a tolerant society should speak to each other and, more importantly, how they should
disagree about the fundamental questions that divide them most deeply. In
addition to its ethical dimension, civility also designates social norms or conversational constraints that exist independently of and external to the virtuous individuals that follow them. It thus relates to toleration as a "vertical"
matter, as well, as one of the social or institutional arrangements structur-
ing the expression of fundamental difference. Whether enforcement of the
norms of civility should be left to self-restraint, social pressure, or legal sanc-
tion will remain a subject of dispute. However, one's answer to this question
will affect one's views on where the limits of toleration lie.[44]

Here the close connection between manners and membership assumed
by seventeenth-century tolerationists and contemporary "civilitarians"
alike is key. As the minimum standard of behavior needed to keep a disagreement going,[45] a call for civility thus necessarily raises a question of
toleration—or rather one question in three parts: (1) how much difference
can we bear, (2) how much must we share in order to make that difference
bearable, and (3) where should we draw the line? Civility attempts to answer the second question implicitly. It says that we must share *this*, at least,
to preserve a sense of community in diversity, whatever "this" the speaker has in mind: a norm of conversation, a consensus on the fundamental
principles of politics or morality, or a vision of social life. In the midst of
a heated argument, a call for civility is thus a call for restraint on the basis
of something *shared*, a common ground or a conversational standard the
speaker believes to be binding on all parties despite their differences—and
whether they recognize it or not.

The inherent, vexing conservatism of civility-talk noted by its critics—
whether in politics, religion, or academia—arises from the difficulty of determining what the *vinculum* between the members of a tolerant society
can, or should, be. As an implicit answer to the second question, a call for
civility suggests that there exists a particular way of doing things that is
good because it is "ours,"[46] while refusing to explain why or where it comes
from—or, for that matter, to acknowledge that the call is itself a solid indication that some of "us" deviate. The importance of having a shared way
of doing things—as a precondition of predictability, mutual expectation,
and trust—is obvious. Without it social life in tolerant societies, especially,
would be impossible. Yet while modern proponents of civility, even as they

"celebrate" diversity, acknowledge the second question, if only implicitly, their critics seem to suggest that it is uncivil even to raise it.

In being able to avoid asking and answering this second question of toleration directly, we enjoy a luxury that the participants in the early modern toleration debates described in previous chapters did not. But because of this, studying their appeals to civility in historical context makes it possible for us to recognize the ineliminable element of repression stressed by civility's modern critics, while also saying something more. As Roger Williams's disagreements with John Eliot and the Quakers illustrate, all civilizing discourses are not created equal. Some may well be indispensable. Williams's great insight, derived from his experience of founding a tolerant society under conditions lacking precisely the stability and "assurance" modern liberals argue is essential for toleration, was that while social life requires common ground, it requires much less than we think. This is because our judgments of in/civility are inevitably *partial*—to ourselves and to our sect.[47]

Recognizing the partiality of our judgments, as Williams well knew, does not free us from the responsibility or necessity of making them. Nevertheless, it does teach us that whatever we do, we must not make the mistake of imposing and enforcing our partial judgments of civility as impartial standards on others. While men like Cotton, Eliot, or even Locke drew the limits of toleration with reference to civility, Williams knew from experience that one always runs up against the limits of what one finds acceptable or offensive long before one exhausts the diversity of peoples, practices, and views. As we ask and answer all three questions of toleration today, we must be careful not to conflate our answers to the second question with our answers to the third. A tolerant society cannot pick and choose its materials and remain tolerant for very long.

Throughout this book, I have sought to show that there is a peculiar virtue—and value—in the understanding of mere civility developed by Roger Williams. Whereas Hobbes and Locke learned about civility in the drawing room, Williams experienced it on the frontier. In his quest for the minimal conditions of social life and umurderous coexistence, his crucial contribution was not a proto-multiculturalist celebration of diversity, but rather the insight that the commonality needed to sustain a tolerant society could be much more minimal and superficial than traditionalist defenders of religion as the *vinculum societatis* supposed.

The conclusion at the heart of his conception of mere civility—that civility and spiritual goodness must be different standards—seems obvious. And yet it was *this* separation between the standards of civil and spiritual belonging, and not the more familiar one between church and state, that represented the real revolution in early modern toleration arguments. It made Williams's plea for toleration on behalf of "Antichristians" and "Pagans" alike possible, as well as Locke's declaration that "neither *Pagan,* nor *Mahumetan,* nor *Jew,* ought to be excluded from the Civil Rights of the Commonwealth" (LCT, 58–59). Of course unlike Locke, Williams did so while knowing he would have to live in close quarters with those Pagans and Antichristians on terms of equal liberty thereafter.

Whereas Hobbesian civil silence sacrificed disagreement for the sake of diversity and Lockean civil charity sacrificed diversity for the sake of productive disagreement, mere civility sought to balance the two. And yet in the contemporary theoretical debates about civility and toleration dominated by Hobbes and Locke's successors, Williams's distinctive voice is nowhere to be found. The reasons for this are not difficult to discover. The radical and inclusive form of toleration that modern readers find most attractive in his works is inextricably linked with the feature that makes them most uncomfortable—namely, the evangelical aspect of mere civility as a conversational virtue consistent with believing others to be damned, as well as *telling* them so. The ridiculous contortions to which his modern-day revivers subject him, especially when it comes to his relationship with the American Indians, reveal the depth of their discomfort with this fact. In nominating Williams as a precursor to Kant and Rawls, Martha Nussbaum not only denies that he ever appealed to his "religious commitments" in making the case for toleration, she also insists against much evidence that it was only "a respectful curiosity about the varieties of humanity" rather than any missionary aspirations that led him to "lodge with them in their filthy, Smoakie holes [and] gaine their Toung."[48]

In their eagerness to revive Williams as a forgotten "First Founder," scholars often present Williams as a stepping-stone to Locke, virtually identical but for the unnecessary and unfortunately long-winded bouts of biblical exegesis.[49] In this, the recent efforts by Nussbaum are no different. As we saw in Chapter 2, both she and James Calvin Davis insist that the civility Williams envisioned as the bond of tolerant societies was unquestionably more than "mere" and intimately bound up with those ideas of "fairness" and "respect" that "continue to be central to the best work in recent political philosophy in the Western tradition."[50] And yet the Williams presented in these accounts is almost unrecognizable, suspiciously stripped of the spiritual exactingness and occasional bigotry that made the unprecedented liberality of his toleration in Rhode Island so striking.

The reasons for this, I suspect, are the same as those that have led political theorists to overlook the obvious genealogical and conceptual relevance of the early modern wars of words described in this book. In their search for civility—what Lawrence Cahoone calls "the thing liberalism forgot"[51]—commentators generally ignore the cesspools of religious insult, anonymous anathemas, and pamphlet outrage that characterized the early modern debates about religious toleration described above in favor of more edifying conversational contexts. While many locate its origins in the civic humanist circles of Renaissance Italy and England,[52] other political theorists and historians pass over the seventeenth century entirely in order to seek civility in the more polite and enlightened eighteenth-century circles of the European Republic of Letters.[53] Even in their broadsides against civility as a civilizing discourse, its critics generally neglect early modern toleration in favor of highlighting civility's aristocratic or bourgeois origins, culminating in the perfection of the distinction between barbarism and civilization in justifications of Western European empire.[54]

By contrast, the seventeenth-century debates explored in the preceding chapters dealt with religious questions and modes of argumentation that the more "Enlightened" participants in the eighteenth-century civil society debates (into which Hobbes and Locke are often subsumed) could agree to be profoundly uncivil.[55] Hence conversational virtues recovered from these contexts do little more than confirm the prejudices shared by modern proponents and critics of civility alike against religious "dogmatism," "enthusiasm," and evangelical "zeal" as fundamentally at odds with inclusion. Modern liberals worry that the theologically intolerant, whose contempt for others' contrary commitments must lend a worryingly fractious heat or the chill of distrust to all social relations, are inevitably uncertain partners in the preservation of liberal institutions. Their postmodern and postcolonial critics, on the other hand, see evangelism as a stalking-horse for empire, and conversion as an instrument of oppression.[56] Despite their many disagreements, partisans on all sides appear motivated by an unspoken agreement with Rousseau: "It is impossible to live in peace with those we regard as damned."[57]

Which of these historical origins a modern commentator will emphasize—whether *civilitas, politesse,* or civilization—usually depends on where
she sits on the question of whether civility is or is not a virtue. And yet all
are notably secularizing stories that depict civility, like toleration, as a matter of waiting for enlightenment or battle fatigue to kick in. Only then can
civil conversation triumph once and for all, and our "civilizing" tendencies
give way to a more progressive stance. Similarly, when commentators refer
to the reemergence of religion as a site of fighting words—and swords—in
the modern world as *la revanche de Dieu,* they suggest that religious fervor is
an atavistic impulse at odds with the brave new political and technological
conditions under which we live.[58] Yet the preceding chapters show that this
combination of technology and sectarian zeal is neither paradoxical nor novel. Our current crisis of civility is simply the most recent efflorescence of an
older phenomenon, one that shaped many of the ideas and institutions that
we, as citizens of modern liberal democracies, take for granted.

Despite the intervening chasms of time and cultural distance, the early
modern wars of words—and often swords—confronting Williams, Hobbes,
and Locke feel eerily familiar. In the expanding, post-Reformation public
sphere, the interminable, anonymous, and increasingly acrimonious pamphlet controversies—like a quickly degenerating comment thread on even
the most sober of Internet blogs—took on lives of their own as incubators of
fantastic forms of contumely, both verbal and visual. John Milton's complaint
about the "tumid pumpkin" of the distinguished classicist Salmasius's skull
or the "Water Poet" John Taylor's scatological illustrations of the "Swarme
of Sectaries and Schismatiques" and the "Rusty, Rayling, Ridiculous, Lying
Libell[er]" (i.e., the Puritan preacher Henry Walker) who defended them as
Satan's issue were products of the same environment.[59] While many writers,
including Hobbes and Locke, boasted of being above the fray, no one was
immune—as the former's comparison of the Savilian Professor of Geometry
at Oxford to a farting horse or the latter's four *Letters on Toleration* and two
Vindications of the *Reasonableness of Christianity* attest.

To modern ears, the insulting denominations or "animal skins"—such as
"Pratlingstants" or "Antichristians—with which persecutory tongues cloaked
their opponents in the seventeenth century can sound harmless and charm-
ingly antiquated. Yet much like today, this exchange of volleys in the war of
words took place under a constant cloud of possible violence. Guy Fawkes
proved that the threat of Catholic terrorism was real enough, and this incident fueled a devastating cycle of "Anti-Popery" that lasted well beyond the

unjust executions of the Popish Plot hysteria and is nevertheless celebrated in England to this day.[60] Nor were Protestant sectarians the "sober and sensible" (to borrow Locke's phrase) mainliners of modern experience. As we saw in earlier chapters, many viewed deliberate acts of social disruption—some even armed rebellion—as sincere demands of conscience. While an earlier generation of Marxist historians sought to turn rebels like Thomas Venner, the leader of a 1661 Fifth Monarchist uprising in London that killed over forty people, into proletarian proto-revolutionaries, recent experience has made it easier to acknowledge them as the righteous holy warriors and spiritual aristocrats they claimed to be.[61]

Early modern thinkers thus faced many of the theoretical and practical challenges characteristic of our contemporary crisis of civility, and they converged on the same question in response: what will keep us together when our fundamental disagreements push us farther and farther apart? In the midst of all the mudslinging, radical defenders of toleration like Williams hit upon the innovative—and, frankly, absurd—notion that the virtue of *civility* might resupply the *vinculum societatis* the warring tongues had cut asunder. It is here, in the chaotic contestations over the meaning of civility as the answer to a seventeenth-century question about religious toleration, that its notoriously manifold connotations converged.

In calling for "a bond of civility" as the key to toleration, Williams was under no illusions that a tolerant society would be a pleasant, harmonious, or particularly peaceful place to be. Yet throughout the Quaker disruptions and the conflicts between the Americans and other settlers over land rights that led to continual "brawling . . . in Mr Williams medow," he strove always to conform his practice to his theory, and to preach what he practiced, in turn.[62] Because of this, Williams not only tolerated the groups he found most abhorrent—Quakers, Catholics, atheists—but granted them the "Soule Freedome" of evangelical liberty besides. In his efforts to build a tolerant society in the wilderness out of these less than ideal materials, Williams confronted the fragility of social order and did not flinch. The bond of civility he imagined was not so thin that it made no demands at all. Certain behaviors were unquestionably grounds for exclusion, as in the case of Richard Chasmore, caught *in flagrante* with his cows. And yet it was thin enough to accommodate a truly radical degree of difference—more radical, certainly, than that which perplexes us today.

Thus, while some commentators may continue to dismiss Williams as "the child of a theological age" and view his radical toleration as "paradoxical," given his religious commitments, I have sought to show that this is exactly wrong.[63] The logic of *inclusion* inherent in his mere civility and evangelical toleration may seem counterintuitive to those who would rather celebrate difference and condemn contempt. Nevertheless, it is no paradox. A more Hobbesian approach that asks people to observe gag rules on contentious topics, or a Lockean request that people sincerely embrace their enemies as friends and brothers, either over- or underreacts to the very real differences between us. In a society committed to the twofold toleration of diversity and disagreement, mere civility offers the modest hope of living together with others, even those whom we find difficult, even impossible, to respect.

This is what makes Williams and his mere civility so interesting and, in the context of our own crisis of civility, I think a model worth reviving. Even so, many readers will not be convinced. For them, the *mereness* of mere civility—not even skin deep!—will remain sufficient grounds for rejection. Prone, as we are, to argument by adjective, political theorists generally employ the modifier *mere*—as in the familiar Rawlsian case of a "mere *modus vivendi*"—in order to indicate that a political, social, or ethical arrangement is falling short and to signal that more and better must be done.[64] As we saw in the Introduction, this is often the case with toleration. For example, Gutmann and Thompson reject "mere toleration" as a "principle of minimal moral content" in favor of an ideal of mutual respect that "demands more"—"a reciprocal positive regard of citizens . . . in the face of irresolvable moral conflict."[65] The same goes for mere civility. While "merely" civil behavior "can be chilly indeed," argues Selznick, "*truly* civil communication [requires] something more": "An effort must be made to truly listen . . . to understand and appreciate what someone else is saying."[66]

It would seem that a big part of the problem with "mere" civility from the standpoint of contemporary political theory is its close connection with "mere" toleration as the descendant of medieval *tolerantia*. As we saw in Chapter 1, the language of concord that runs like a red thread through contemporary political liberalism—in Waldron, as well as Rawls—expresses a Lockean hope for *concordia* that is willing to sacrifice diversity for the sake of harmonious disagreement. Yet Williams recognized, as Locke and his modern inheritors do not, that the tension between difference and disagreement was a permanent problem, one that could only be managed, never solved.

Hence in a tolerant society committed to disagreement as well as difference, discord—and mutual contempt—would be inevitable. As an outward conformity to the norms of civil worship, the virtue of mere civility lay in its ability to coexist with and even communicate our contempt for others' most fundamental commitments while continuing the conversation.

As such, the absence of mere civility from contemporary debates is not surprising. Despite their differences, both civilitarians and their critics can generally agree that contempt is the enemy of the equal dignity and inclusiveness they view as essential to a tolerant society.[67] While the former try to eradicate contempt through their ever more robust conceptions of civility, the latter regard these civilizing discourses as the most insidiously contemptuous of all. Insofar as they valorize disagreement, these agonistic, deliberative, and public reason democrats are alike committed to the idea that it is possible to separate contempt and condemnation, and so to criticize another's beliefs as foolish, mistaken, or even malign without thereby impugning his motives or intelligence.[68] This "perspectival shift" from persons to positions corresponds to the distinction between procedural and substantive consensus invoked by modern Lockeans, or between the manner of disagreement and the fact.[69] Yet as we saw earlier—and as Hobbes and Williams understood quite well—this shift is much easier to make in theory than in practice. Our natural partiality and pride as human beings mean that we invariably judge the rightness of others' reasoning (or the civility of their discourse) with reference to our own. The act of disagreeing *necessarily* calls others' reasoning abilities or "agential capacities" into question for this reason, with contempt an unavoidable result.[70]

While Hobbes and Williams concluded that conversation under such conditions would demand the adoption of Hobbesian strategies of complaisance or civil silence, on the one hand, or making a virtue of merely civil insincerity, on the other, Locke disagreed. In reviving the eirenic ideal of a healthy and harmonious community as one united through bonds of civil charity and undergirded by *homonoia* on the fundamentals of God, hell, and the Golden Rule, Locke departed radically from his predecessors, who had long since accepted some contempt and hypocrisy, civil or spiritual, as inevitable in the face of fundamental difference. As we saw earlier, by equating civil behavior with an expression, then an affirmation, of the moral principles—particularly "mutual respect"—assumed to underlie it, modern supporters of civility like Rawls and Waldron often conflate the cognitive and affective aspects of consensus and so replicate Locke's error. "Civility" becomes on these accounts just another example of our respect or recognition of others' equal dignity, rather than a distinct or distinctive virtue.

In falling victim to this *reductio ad respectum* determined to turn every good thing in social and political life into a form of neo-Kantian respect for persons, civility has suffered the same fate at the hands of political theorists and moral philosophers that the concept of toleration did before it.[71] As a symptom of moral rationalism, this *reductio* elides the plurality of more or less morally praiseworthy motivations—many of which do not ascend to the level of "reasons"—that can underlie a willingness to tolerate others or to treat them civilly. Only here Williams's mere civility offers a much-needed corrective. It reminds us that although such behavior *might* well reflect a sincere respect for persons, in the abstract, and one's interlocutors in particular—it might arise just as easily, and more reliably, from unreflective habits of good breeding, from respect not for others but for God or the social order, from a recognition of another's superior (or inferior) merit, from personal pride or chauvinism, or even from private intolerance and evangelical zeal.[72]

While all of these foundations for civil behavior are consistent with mere civility as preached and practiced by Roger Williams, all are deeply unappealing and problematic from the perspective of contemporary political theory. Certainly, the endorsement of insincerity that makes this plurality of motivations possible shades far too close to hypocrisy for modern Lockean tastes.[73] And yet unlike hypocrisy, mere civility does not aim to deceive. As Williams knew well, it is often a more effective way of communicating our contempt for others *to* them than the most inventive insult. Nevertheless, at the very same time it encourages continued engagement and active disagreement with those we view as hypocrites, "profane persons," and the purveyors of doctrines we deem damnable. Williams's defense of insincerity in civil worship as integral to sincerity and single-minded devotion in religion places him firmly beyond the criticism that communitarians often level at liberalism—namely, that its elevation of civility is predicated on an apathetic or relativistic indifference to the Good that saps the vitality of public life and undermines engagement with one's co-citizens.

At this point, however, the proponent of a more robust kind of conversational virtue might well object. After all, in defining *civility* in terms of sincerity or mutual respect, the aim is generally to offer an aspirational account, not a descriptive one. Lockean civil charity, on this view, represents an ideal for the members of a tolerant society to shoot for in their disagreements, while knowing full well that they will almost always fall short. The exclusionary implications of Locke's ethos (or Erasmus's for that matter) are, on this view, not inherent in the theories themselves, but rather difficulties that arise from putting them into practice—often in ways that their authors never intended.[74]

These are important objections. They suggest that what is at stake in the disagreement between Locke and Williams, as well as their conceptions of civility, is partly a methodological question about how aspirational a political theory should be.[75] Yet when it comes to theorizing civility, the historical debates recounted in this book confirm that aspirations are not simply unrealistic; they are entirely inapposite. Civility emerges as an essential virtue in tolerant societies in response to a practical problem, not a theoretical one. In trying to make sense of others' different opinions, human beings conclude not that these differences are reasonable byproducts of the burdens of judgment but that their opponents are bigoted, ignorant, malicious, even insane. We might hope—and strive—to do otherwise. But rather than conflating this aspiration with civility, political theorists must recognize the latter as the virtue called upon to fill the breach when reality fails to meet our expectations.[76]

In arguing in favor of *mere* civility my point is not that it has nothing to do with respect, sufficiently minimally construed.[77] It is rather that in *equating* civility with mutual respect, theorists necessarily move the discussion to an aspirational realm of ideal theory in which the kinds of problems civility is needed to address *do not even arise*. The result is an impoverishment of our ethical vocabulary, which, in turn, exacerbates the vacuity of our moral and political discourse in confronting the very problems to which we appeal to civility and toleration as solutions. James Calvin Davis's reconstruction of Roger Williams's conception of civility as the duty to "argue our beliefs in the public forum with patience, respect for our opponents, and a commitment to the social kinship that binds us to even the one most different from us" is virtually indistinguishable from the bromides offered in recent years by countless politicians and public intellectuals.[78] What is more surprising—and frustrating—is that the same bromides about mutual respect, fellow feeling, and an open mind reign uninterrupted among political theorists and philosophers, too, scholars we might hope would know better and be able to offer something more precise. It seems reasonable to expect theorists to understand reality, first, before moralizing about how to change it.

Williams's mere civility may be at odds with the aspirational tone of much contemporary theory. Nevertheless, it remains quite demanding. In place of the deeply ethical norms of political community, friendship, and mutual respect espoused by theorists, it calls upon individuals to display the mental toughness necessary to manage and mind the gap between what we would have others think—of us, and in general—and what they actually do. In this, it shifts much of the burden of civil conversation from the speaker to the listener, requiring the latter to cultivate, among other things, insensitivity to others' opinions and an identity separate from that immersed in debate.[79]

In an age of trigger warnings and the identity politics of intersectionality, Williams's call for thicker skins and divided selves can sound deeply unappealing, even aggressive. Critics of civility might remind us that, like all accusations of incivility, such demands fall disproportionately on the disenfranchised and disaffected, thus adding insult to injury while reaffirming their subjection. Here again, the New World chapters of our story would seem to confirm the critics' fears. In celebrating Williams's dealings with the Americans, his modern-day revivers conspicuously omit the ending, which was tragic for both Williams and the Narragansett alike. When at last the Narragansett united with other tribes in a desperate effort to eject the New English, Williams gave up on words and took up arms against them. He would later participate in the sale of American captives into slavery in the Caribbean; and in the midst of one last poignant attempt at parley, his former friends burnt Providence to the ground.[80]

It is not hard to see why Nussbaum and others have been tempted to leave this out. But this civil silence only exacerbates the impasse by refusing to confront the dynamic of repression and exclusion inherent in civility—a dynamic of which Williams was well aware. As a precondition for evangelism, he envisioned mere civility as part and parcel of a literally civilizing—even missionary—discourse. Accordingly, critics might well object that even *mere* civility reflects a hope for homogenization and "cultural genocide" sufficient to discredit it as an approach to difference in the seventeenth century *or* today.[81] They would certainly be right to warn that we must remain attentive to the dark side—and the limits—of civility. And yet the debates described in this book also suggest that we must not be too quick to reduce its meaning to an irredeemably imperialistic or civilizational discourse that is guilty of its own anachronism. Like most things in the early modern period, the concept of civility was contested, and we do a disservice to all of the people involved by underestimating the difficulty of the dilemmas they faced or ignoring their profound disagreements in favor of caricatures of a monolithic "Western" or "Protestant" consensus imposed upon prostrate Americans.

It should go without saying (although it may not) that there are many things more important than mere civility. For Williams, these included justice as well as salvation. Civility provides a middle ground between whatever the social order happens to be and our conscientious objections to it. Here the dual early modern senses of *meer* described in Chapter 2 are worth remembering. Williams's "meer" civility was not only minimal in the sense disdained by contemporary political theory, but also pure, unmixed, and "essentially distinct"—in this case, from the religious or spiritual standards he and Richard Baxter associated with "MEER Christianity."[82] Thus, while there was undoubtedly an emergent sense of secularity in Williams's "meer" civility—as a standard of conduct or virtuous behavior appropriate to this world—that was not the full story. The modifier indicated that, though separate, the standards of civility and spirituality would remain mutually dependent and referential, with the value of the former secondary and *subordinate* to the latter. The "mereness" of Williams's civility was thus relative and relational. Any positive account of its requirements would be open to the objection that they were partial, exclusionary, and unjust, in the same way that any proposed list of *fundamenta,* no matter its latitude, could and would be met with conscientious dissent.

It was thus in the nature of "merely" civil behavior that it eluded definitive articulation as a formal standard that could be applied—and enforced—on others. The standard lay somewhere beneath one's hopes but above one's fears, always out of reach. Nevertheless, Williams was sure that mere civility *was* a virtue, if a separate and subordinate one. If there is a form of egalitarianism implicit therein, it is not the leveling up associated with the democratization of aristocratic dignity popular in contemporary political theory.[83] Rather, Williams's mere civility suggested a leveling down, a resolutely early modern awareness of the low-status equality of the *saeculum* and men's inferiority—their "lowness and filthiness," as he might put it—before God. As such, mere civility said next to nothing about the structure of society or the content of the social norms to which individuals were expected to conform. Even while observing such practices, Williams made his objections to "hat honour," as well as the American practice of exchanging trophies from the dead, perfectly clear.[84] Mere civility was hardly tantamount to an unqualified or uncritical endorsement of the status quo—as we have seen time and again, Williams was endlessly critical of the "publike sins" of the societies in which he lived. Nevertheless, civility did require that, even in sounding one's "silver alarums" against the social order, one doff one's hat to it, so to speak.

It may come as an unwelcome shock to some readers that mere civility is not necessarily a democratic virtue. Unlike the true egalitarians of the period, the Quakers, Williams's demand for "respective behavior" was not a demand for equal dignity—instead, it meant that one's behavior toward others should reflect a deference appropriate to their respective places in a social order that was unquestionably hierarchical. Indeed, his antipathy to the Quakers stemmed in no small part from their insistence that spiritual equality demanded social and political equality, too. He saw their conscientious incivility as an attempt to reform society in accordance with their partial judgments, and thus to make their faulty estimation of the best the enemy of the good. In their anarchic rendering of the view that "all are equal in CHRIST," the Quakers failed to appreciate something that they would learn the hard way in Pennsylvania—namely, that a society depends on hierarchies (political, legal, and social) to function.[85] For Williams, the key thing was rather to distinguish those hierarchies that were just from those that were not, without mistakenly imbuing this world with one's expectations for the next. As he never tired of reminding his opponents, in destroying the wilderness for the sake of the garden, one destroys the garden, too.

There is something resolutely early modern, low but solid, about Williams's conception of civility, in which low expectations in this world went hand in hand with heightened expectations in the hereafter. Mere civility acknowledges that the standard of behavior required to keep a conversation going will always be much lower than that required to reach a resolution. The best sign that the bar has been met is that conversations continue—particularly those critical of the status quo. Against the modern critics who dismiss even *mere* civility as an oppressive code meant to delegitimize dissent and stymie debate, there is another way to view it: as the set of habits of speaking and listening that make passionate debate possible, by allowing us to disagree, and to tolerate the inevitable contempt and disagreeableness involved in doing so—rather than congratulating ourselves on our open minds and sound views, while conversing exclusively with those who already agree with us.

A low standard, loosely applied, combined with a thick-skinned determination to tolerate what we perceive as others' incivility—these were the
essentials of Williams's mere civility. Nevertheless, the growing dissatis-
faction with "mere" toleration among political theorists reflects a Lockean
suspicion that nothing less than the shared hearts and minds of *concordia*
will do. The contrast between Locke and Williams should provide a salutary reminder, however, of the exclusion implicit in this positive ideal, the
breaking down of which—more than Enlightenment or battle fatigue—was
essential to the progress of early modern toleration. Even if one cannot
embrace Roger Williams, all of these early modern authors have a valuable
lesson to teach on this score.

In theorizing civility neither Williams nor Hobbes (nor even Locke) set
out to discover the behavior befitting a republican citizen, an aristocratic
courtier, or an English gentleman. Instead they began by asking and answering a set of questions altogether more mundane: What standard of behavior does coexistence require from ordinary people in this world, before we
shuffle off into the next? How should people, both vulgar and elite, divided
by faith, speak to each other, and how should they disagree—if we can disagree at all? In answering these questions, Williams, Hobbes, and Locke all
sought insights in the polemical swamps and cacophonous wars of words
with which we began. Political theorists would do well to follow their example. If we did, we might see that when it comes to wars of words, religion is
not the problem; people are. While religious questions provide a particularly fraught example, political forms of believing and belonging—including
cosmopolitan ones—have the same effect.[86] Accordingly, Williams, Hobbes,
and Locke all diagnosed partiality and pride as the psychological factors
behind the wars of words *and* the impossibility of imposing an impartial
solution. When encountering those who differ from us, everyone is a little
imperial, and not simply because everyone is his own exemplar of right
reason, but his own exemplar of civility as well.[87] In this, our authors were
no different. Locke may have been the only one to write a manual, yet each
considered himself a paragon of his chosen conception.

Even if one rejects Williams's mere civility, along with the Hobbesian and
Lockean alternatives, as intolerant or repressive, it is important to remember that all of these positions arose out of a serious and sustained engagement with a truth that modern commentators too often seem determined to
overlook. It is a difficult thing, indeed, to love and respect those with whom
one disagrees. Just as men naturally recoil from the heat of disagreement,

they are also inclined to prefer friendship with the like-minded "with whom [they] can be at ease," for no one "love[s] to be uneasie [and] under constant rebukes" (STCE, 37). The affective bonds of social life are difficult to maintain in the absence of a consensus on certain fundamentals. *Pace* Obama, disagreement *as such* is disagreeable. This is what merely human beings are like.

What is often left out by both sides of the civility debate today is the messy real world of unmurderous coexistence between individuals divided on the fundamentals and mutually disdainful of others' contrary commitments. While Plato's "divine bonds" of true opinion remain elusive, the alternative to holding each other contemptuously at arm's length is not the full embrace of friends and brothers. It is Hobbes's society of scrupulously silent tongue-biters constantly tempted to lash out and push each other overboard. Still, modern liberal democracies are dedicated to the proposition that perpetual talking about the things that divide us most deeply will bring us closer. If civility is to be more than a pious wish for concord, it must address the difficult work of negotiating and navigating this deep disagreement. And if it is to have a meaning distinct from a shared vision of public life predicated on a fundamental consensus, it must accommodate the feelings of disrespect, disaffection, and contempt to which these disagreements inevitably give rise. In theorizing civility it thus behooves us to pay attention to the worst in human nature, while remaining suspicious of the best.

While civil charity and civil silence will remain lofty and attractive ideals, Williams's example illustrates that maintaining even mere civility in the face of prolonged disagreement on the fundamentals can be a difficult undertaking. And yet, as we navigate our own wars of words, it remains an eminently worthy aspiration.

Epilogue

Free Speech Fundamentalism

CIVILITY CAME TO THE FOREFRONT of debates about toleration in early modern England and America in response to concerns about heated and hateful disagreement that still resonate. Yet then, as now, appealing to "civility" simply as the key to peaceful and productive disagreement was not enough. Although most early modern tolerationists could agree that civility was, on the whole, a good and necessary thing, at the same time they disagreed profoundly not only about what it entailed, but how it should be enforced. Should a tolerant society give free reign to verbal persecution? Or should it bridle its members' intolerant tongues through law? As we saw in the Introduction, these questions continue to perplex citizens of liberal democracies today, especially when it comes to hate speech and religious insult.

While most political theorists reject attempts to legislate civility, Jeremy Waldron notes that in most modern liberal democracies the answer to the second question has been an emphatic yes.[1] In its commitment to tolerating the uncivil speech of its citizens, however extreme, the United States remains an outlier. While defamation, libel, obscenity, and so-called fighting words are generally excluded from First Amendment protection, speech that is simply offensive or insulting is not. James Whitman notes the preeminent scholar of American torts, William Lloyd Prosser's "charming American huffiness" in explaining why individuals cannot be held liable for "mere insult":

> Our manners, and with them our law, have not yet progressed to the point where we are able to afford a remedy in the form of tort damages for all intended mental disturbance . . . [or] every trivial indignity. There is no occasion for the law to intervene with balm for wounded

feelings in every case where a flood of billingsgate is loosed in an argument. . . . The plaintiff must necessarily be expected and required to
be hardened to a certain amount of rough language, and to acts that
are definitely inconsiderate and unkind. There is still, in this country
at least, such a thing as liberty to express an unflattering opinion of
another, however wounding it may be to the other's feelings.[2]

For Prosser, like Roger Williams, a crucial component of American civility
was hardening oneself to rough language, surrendering wounded feelings,
and simply toughening up. However, as Waldron rightly notes, before the
advent of modern First Amendment jurisprudence in the early twentieth
century, Americans were quite open to restricting uncivil speech on the
local, state, and federal levels.[3] Despite their refusal to embrace the laws
against "hate propaganda" or "group defamation" adopted elsewhere, growing concerns that calls for free speech can serve as specious cover for racial
and sectarian hatreds have been accompanied by an increasing openness
to such legislation in the United States today, especially among the young.[4]

Even as the peculiar American permissiveness toward incivility has come
under increasing attack in recent years, few of its critics or supporters have
thought to ask where it comes from. Societies with histories of hereditary
aristocracy have long treated personal honor as a legally protectable interest;
hence, in countries like France or Germany, as Whitman notes, "the regulation of hate speech is only one aspect of a more complex cultural pattern of
the maintenance of respectful interpersonal relations."[5] Americans, by contrast, have long shown a cultural—and sometimes principled egalitarian—
deafness to the issues of honor, dignity, and insult at stake in debates about
hate speech to which Europeans have historically been much more sensitive.[6]

Waldron attributes Americans' characteristic deafness to the harms in
hate speech to their "First Amendment Faith"—the idiosyncratic view that
the freedoms of religion and of speech, as well as association, are equally sacred and entirely consistent.[7] Even in the midst of the current civility crisis,
many Americans take umbrage at the suggestion that these freedoms might
be in tension. When it comes to our free speech "fundamentalism," we appear to be quite sensitive to perceived insults against this First Amendment
Faith.[8] As an explanation of that faith, however, citing the First Amendment
simply begs the question. Why should Americans assume that religious
freedom and free speech go hand in hand, when in most places and times
they emphatically have not? Other liberal democracies may pay lip service

to this connection, yet they routinely restrict citizens' speech in the name of tolerance. Why should America be exceptional?

Given political theorists' persistent appeals to early modern toleration in attempts to understand and indict the liberal tradition, a more sophisticated understanding of this history when it comes to questions of regulating civility would serve us well. As we saw in the chapters on Williams, Hobbes, and Locke, all of these figures were interested not only in institutional questions about church-state relations or individual rights but with the ethical obligations associated with toleration, as well. Understanding the limits they thought a tolerant society should place on the expression of religious difference might thus help theorists to move past the unhelpful dichotomy between toleration, on the one hand, and persecution, on the other, to which we remain beholden, especially when it comes to issues like religious insult.

Viewing toleration as our early modern authors did—as a matter of particular policies addressed to particular problems—is especially helpful in an age where everyone claims to be against "intolerance" or "incivility" and yet sees each in entirely different places. Not only did Locke and other seventeenth-century writers consider the policies of comprehension and indulgence alike under the rubric of "toleration," they generally saw the separation of church and state as compatible with more or less latitudinarian forms of national establishment. This is worth pointing out, because despite the persistent tendency among political theorists to treat *toleration, religious freedom,* and *liberty of conscience* as synonyms—and to equate all of them with disestablishment—established churches remain common in Europe to this day.[9] Moreover, as we saw in Chapter 1, while religious insult statutes were linked with toleration in places like Maryland, Pennsylvania, and Carolina, elsewhere they were used to suppress dissent in the service of religious uniformity. In both cases, however, they were motivated by concerns about the contingent and intrinsic harms of persecution of the tongue familiar today.

The persistent scholarly neglect of early modern religious insult statutes is particularly unfortunate. For modern defenders of a First Amendment Faith, the fact that the relationship between religious freedom and free speech in the seventeenth century was far from straightforward and, moreover, that key figures in the Anglo-American liberal pantheon took the problem of religious insult seriously enough to consider laws against it as a corollary of toleration should be worrying. No one will be surprised to know that Hobbes embraced laws against contumely, at least in theory—although they may be surprised to learn that he was at all ambivalent in noting that the "Grecians" had done without.[10] Rather, what should surprise us is that, given the emphasis that they placed on civility in establishing the limits of a tolerant society, both Williams and Locke ultimately rejected the laws one might have expected them to endorse.

Their different reasons for doing so—like their competing conceptions of civility—are instructive. While Williams defended unrestricted evangelical liberty as essential to free exercise, Locke's about-face on the issue of religious insult legislation was not inspired by the kind of natural rights defense of free expression a casual reader of the *Second Treatise of Government* might expect. Instead, Locke's unpublished comments on the "Pennsilvania Laws" suggested that the 1682 Great Law against "reproachful" and "reviling" language in religion—despite its striking similarity to the *Fundamental Constitutions of Carolina* (1669)—would be "a matter of perpetual prosecution and animosity."[11]

So why did Locke change his mind? Perhaps a lingering antipathy to Quakers was the cause—or an awareness of the deterioration of relations between Catholics and Protestants in France, despite the ban introduced by l'Hôpital on the injurious names of "*Lutheriens, Huguenots,* [and] *papistes.*"[12] Although his notes on Penn are cursory, Locke implied there that laws against uncivil speech in and about religion were essentially counterproductive. Similarly, in a memorandum against the proposed renewal of the Licensing Act in 1695, Locke stressed the difficulty of legal definition for contested terms like "Christian religion" or "offensive books" and so pressed for "an absolute liberty for printing of everything that is lawful to speak."[13] The argument in both cases seems to have been that restrictions on "offensive" speech encouraged an individual to act as judge in his own case concerning the degree or nature of the offense and then tempted him with the use of the civil sword in punishing the offender. A tolerant society in which different "persuasions" existed side by side would inevitably be home to many hot tempers, bruised egos, and hurt feelings. Legal limits on religious insult would be impossible to apply impartially and would necessarily invite abuse.

Rather than indulging these feelings by seeking revenge at dawn or in the courts, Locke would argue that tender consciences needed to toughen up. Life's "many inconveniences," he wrote in *Some Thoughts Concerning Education,* "require we should not be too sensible of every little hurt"; children should thus be trained in "manly steadiness" so as to equip them for the "war-fare of life" (STCE, 84, 87–88). Here Locke sounds a lot like Roger Williams. And yet, although he would also justify toleration on evangelical grounds, the universal evangelical liberty demanded by Williams was simply not on Locke's agenda. Rather, the most plausible explanation for the shift in his position between the *Fundamental Constitutions of Carolina* (1669) and the "Pennsilvania Laws" (1686)—like that between *The Tracts* (1660–1662) and "An Essay on Toleration" (1687)—is that it reflected yet another shift in Locke's prudential calculation as to the effects of such a policy on peace and public order. Williams's rejection of religious insult laws, by contrast, was a matter of principle. For Christians who took their charitable duty to preach and proclaim the Gospel—loudly—seriously, any scheme for toleration that infringed upon that liberty was unworthy of the name.[14]

Rhode Island's policy of disestablishment as the only adequate "wall of separation" between church and state is undoubtedly more famous. But as Chapter 2 demonstrated, it was Williams's commitment to *liberating* men's tongues in and about religion that represented the "livelie" experiment's most radical feature.[15] Most modern liberals—inspired by an earlier tradi-tion of Whig historiography—assume that free expression as an individual right was part of toleration from the beginning and that it found its way into liberalism that way. And yet historically, the toleration of religious dif-ference has more often been accompanied by restrictions on evangelism than not. For example, the so-called millet system in the Ottoman Empire was predicated on forbidding conversion from Islam or between recog-nized religious minorities. While conversion *to* Islam was permitted and occasionally encouraged, Western Christian missionaries were restricted to evangelizing among Eastern Orthodox populations.[16] Many societies, including many liberal democracies, have thus agreed with Hobbes and Locke that toleration requires restraint (whether self- or sovereign) on per-secution of the tongue, as well as restrictions on proselytism as a violation of the negative religious freedom of others. Even today, while *Cantwell vs. Connecticut* (1940)—in which a Jehovah's Witness evangelized two Catho-lics in the street by playing a record detailing the whoredoms of "Antichris-tianity"—is a landmark free speech decision in the United States, Jehovah's Witnesses and other sectarian evangelicals have been on the receiving end of loss after loss in the European Court of Human Rights.[17]

Just as Locke was not a defender of the "Lockean" toleration of individual rights to free exercise, association, and expression, he and most other early modern defenders of toleration viewed radical Protestants' attachment to enthusiastic evangelism as an obstacle to coexistence, not an inducement. Ironically, Williams's nemeses the Quakers were the key exception. Their founder, George Fox, declared that the liberty of conscience demanded "universal liberty for what people soever":

> Let them speak their minds. . . . And let him be Jew, or Papist, or Turk, or Heathen, or Protestant, or what soever, or such as worship sun or moon or sticks and stones, let them have liberty where every one may bring forth his strength, and have free liberty to speak forth his mind and judgment.[18]

In proposing a law against religious insult in Pennsylvania, William Penn seems to have violated the movement's founders' founding principle. Roger Williams could not have said it better.

Americans tend to regard themselves as uniquely Lockean among the world's liberal democratic peoples. But if even Locke was not a Lockean when it came to free speech and toleration, neither, it seems, are we. I would not credit Roger Williams as the inspiration for the First Amendment, much less the "creation of the American soul," as some scholars have done.[19] Still, I would argue that the American polity's unique and seemingly paradoxical combination of complete religious disestablishment and a singularly God-intoxicated public sphere can be traced, in part, to the early presence and energy of competing strands of evangelical Protestantism in British America, of which Williams was one, extreme example.[20]

On this view, the characteristic liberal institutional combination of disestablishment and individual freedoms of worship, expression, and association begins to look less and less secular and more and more like a form of *established* disestablishmentarian congregationalism. Still, the suggestion that when it comes to free speech even secular Americans are really Williams-style evangelicals may make many modern readers uncomfortable. Certainly, the deep discomfort Hobbes and Locke felt when it came to what we call "in-your-face" proselytism is shared today by many of their modern inheritors.[21] For these proponents of civil silence or civil charity—most of whom proclaim a commitment to free expression—the secular, prudential arguments against religious insult laws offered by the real John Locke will likely sound more appealing.

Perhaps they are sufficient. But they still concede a tension between toleration and free speech at odds with the First Amendment Faith espoused by many Americans. What if, for instance, the prudential calculus shifts? Defenders of free speech can cite studies showing that laws banning religious insult are counterproductive,[22] but their opponents can always cite the latest massacre. Moreover, instrumental justifications of free speech and the marketplace of ideas as engines of truth production are open to the very strong objection that they are simply false. The "free trade in ideas" has, after all, produced some notoriously bad ones.[23]

Though they may sound quite alien, Williams's evangelical arguments in favor of unlicensed preaching as a complement to disestablishment and an essential element of free exercise have the advantage of making a strong case for a connection between religious freedom and free speech that is more than just prudential. This unapologetically evangelical form of toleration will seem foreign to many modern liberals. Nonetheless, one can recognize in it an ingenious solution to the problem of uncivil religious disagreement—one that has fundamentally shaped the institutional and intellectual context in which we live.

Of course, I have not written this book because I think that Williams should be of exclusively genealogical interest for understanding America's peculiarly evangelical democracy. I have written it because, both as a mode and a motivation of conversational engagement, evangelism seems uniquely well suited to explain—and to *sustain*—a commitment to on-going, active, and often heated disagreement in the public sphere. Often these are disagreements in which, if we were the truly civil, open-minded, and deliberative public reasoners envisioned by political theorists, we would not engage at all. Familiarity with those from whom we differ in politics, as in religion, is as likely to breed contempt as its opposite. Given this, surely there is something to be said for the view that the true test of tolerance is whether we allow others to speak freely and, more importantly, to win converts to their cause.

In this respect, there are important analogies between early modern concerns about how to cope with what Locke called the "fiery zeal for one's own sect" and the concerns about political partisanship and polarization that dominate our own debates. Indeed, the term "evangelism" captures quite well much of what democratic citizens actually *do* in the public sphere.

Commentators routinely employ the metaphor of conversion when describing political changes of mind and heart, and partisans witness for their beliefs and anathematize their opponents much like early modern sectarians did. Everyone seems vastly more certain of the righteousness of their political opinions—and their opponents' errors—than they have any right to be. When disagreements begin to look more like proselytizing than public reasoning, a truly evangelical commitment to competing for converts, rather than preaching to the converted, might well be a good thing.

As we saw in the Conclusion, robust conceptions of civility often end up exacerbating the problems they purport to solve by imposing partial judgments as to what counts as "uncivil" on others. The same holds true for laws against hate speech and religious insult, with significant costs to free expression besides. Whether we adopt them or not, we will have to acknowledge that some speech will continue to offend and harm. And if we continue to insist on the unrestricted expression of fundamental disagreement, despite its disagreeableness, we must have a strong faith in the more than merely prudential good that will come of it—a faith not unlike that which enabled Williams to tolerate his equally evangelical opponents, under considerable provocation and pressure.

Justifying the status quo is rarely easy. It seems that many academics and public intellectuals would rather rely on the inertia of strong institutional commitments to academic freedom, free expression, and civility while critiquing them into oblivion—only to complain, then, when we find ourselves hoisted by our own petards. In a world of deep diversity, in an age of increasing religious and political polarization, Williams's evangelical insights into the dynamics of believing and belonging seem more salient than ever. As we contemplate our ideological opponents, we would do well to remember: "He that is a Briar, that is, a Jew, a Turke, a Pagan, [or] an Anti-christian to day, may be *(when the Word of the Lord runs freely)* a member of Jesus Christ to morrow."

Notes

References

Acknowledgments

Index

NOTES

Introduction

1. In 2008, the new chairman of the National Endowment for the Humanities, Jim Leach, embarked on a 50 State Civility Tour in order to warn that civility was "breaking down" in America, with citizens "becoming disrespectful of their leaders, other faith systems and each other." Jim Leach, "Civility in a Fractured Society," *Denver Post,* August 5, 2010, http://www.denverpost.com/recommended/ci_15677293. President Obama, too, made civility a constant theme throughout his presidency. In a speech after a shooting in Tucson, Arizona, that killed six and seriously injured thirteen others, including US Representative Gabrielle Giffords, Obama insisted that Americans must learn to be "better in our private lives, to be better friends and neighbors," starting with observing "more civility in our public discourse." Barack Obama, "Remarks by the President at a Memorial Service of the Victims of the Shooting in Tucson, Arizona," January 12, 2011, https://www.whitehouse.gov/the-press-office/2011/01/12/remarks-president-barack-obama-memorial-service-victims-shooting-tucson. These remarks came after commentators linked the tragedy to the "eliminationist rhetoric" and "uncivil" tenor of political disagreement in an election year. See, for example, Paul Krugman, "Climate of Hate," *New York Times,* January 9, 2011, http://www.nytimes.com/2011/01/10/opinion/10krugman.html.

2. See, for example, Robert D. Putnam, *Bowling Alone* (New York: Simon and Schuster, 2001); and Stephen L. Carter, *Civility* (New York: Harper Perennial, 1999).

3. Although it may be possible to "disagree" with a person or proposition internally, I will use the term *disagreement* throughout this book to refer to the outward expression and exchange of differing opinions with others. This is akin to, but more expansive than, minimalist definitions of *deliberation* as the "reasoned exchange of arguments for or against something," because offering

reasons and arguments for one's opinions is not required. See Hélène Lande-more, "On Minimal Deliberation, Partisan Activism, and Teaching People How to Disagree," *Critical Review* 25, no. 2 (June 1, 2013): 211.

4. Exhibit A is often US Representative Joe Wilson's breach of decorum during a presidential address to Congress in 2009, in which he shouted, "You lie!" See for example Susan Herbst, *Rude Democracy: Civility and Incivility in American Politics* (Philadelphia: Temple University Press, 2010), 2; J. Cherie Strachan and Michael R. Wolf, "Political Civility," *PS: Political Science & Politics* 45, no. 3 (July 2012): 401; and Diana C. Mutz, *In-Your-Face Politics: The Consequences of Uncivil Media* (Princeton, NJ: Princeton University Press, 2015), 4. Given that Congress is an elite deliberative forum with well-defined rules of order and decorum, however, this is not a particularly good illustration of the al-leged "crisis" of civility in the broader public sphere, in which the norms of civility are more nebulous.

5. Since the global controversy over the Danish cartoons depicting the Prophet Muhammad in 2005, Europe has seen a spate of high-profile prosecutions against politicians and private citizens for religious insult—that is, speech that calls for "a person or group of persons to be subjected to hatred, discrimina-tion, or violence on the grounds of their religion." See Resolution 1510, "Free-dom of Expression and Respect for Religious Beliefs" (2006), and Resolution 1805, "Blasphemy, Religious Insults, and Hate Speech against Persons on Grounds of Their Religion" (2007), Parliamentary Assembly of the Council of Europe. As Jeremy Waldron notes, similar statutes have been adopted beyond Europe, including Canada and New Zealand. Jeremy Waldron, *The Harm in Hate Speech* (Cambridge, MA: Harvard University Press, 2012), 8.

6. There are many, but two prominent examples are the National Institute for Civil Discourse at the University of Arizona, which was founded as a "non-partisan center for advocacy, research, and policy," with former presidents George H. W. Bush and Bill Clinton as honorary chairmen, and the Center for Civil Discourse at the University of Massachusetts-Boston, which "advances the voices of reason and civility in our society . . . [in] the search for reasoned political discourse and common ground in our public institutions." See http://www.nicd.arizona.edu and http://scholarworks.umb.edu/ccd/.

7. These demands came to international attention in late 2015 with much-reported protests at Yale, Princeton, and Oxford in which students accused administrators of failing to address systemic discrimination within their academic institutions. Coined in the 1970s to describe covert racism in ad-vertising, psychologists define microaggressions as "verbal, behavioral, or environmental indignities, whether intentional or unintentional, that com-municate hostile derogatory or negative . . . slights and insults." Derald Wing Sue, *Microaggressions in Everyday Life: Race, Gender, and Sexual Orientation*

(Hoboken, NJ: John Wiley & Sons, 2010), 29. By contrast, the term *safe space* originated in LBGTQ activism to designate an official place on campus "where anyone can relax and be fully self-expressed without fear of being made to feel uncomfortable, unwelcome, or unsafe on account of biological sex, race/ethnicity, sexual orientation, gender identity or expression, cultural background, age, or physical or mental ability; a place where the rules guard each person's self-respect and dignity and strongly encourage everyone to respect others." See "Glossary," *Advocates for Youth: Rights, Respect, Responsibility,* www.advocatesforyouth.org.

8. Mari J. Matsuda, *Words That Wound: Critical Race Theory, Assaultive Speech, and the First Amendment* (Boulder, CO: Westview Press, 1993).

9. The common psychological effects involved in "fundamental" disagreements across political and religious lines are treated in Jonathan Haidt, *The Righteous Mind: Why Good People Are Divided by Politics and Religion* (New York: Pantheon Books, 2012). Haidt focuses on moral psychology and the way in which religious and political commitments "bind and blind" individuals into groups. Ascriptive identities of race, ethnicity, or gender are not obviously subject to the same dynamics. Yet one of the key effects of the identity politics of "intersectionality" is that ascriptive identities become ideologized and experienced as morally fundamental over time. To exaggerate only slightly, if every difference of opinion—whether about criminal or social justice, literature or culture—can be traced to systemic oppression or institutionalized "privilege," every disagreement is potentially of fundamental importance in defining oneself and one's opponents.

10. Bill Bishop and Robert G. Cushing, *The Big Sort: Why the Clustering of Like-Minded America Is Tearing Us Apart* (Boston: Mariner Books, 2009). The same trend is visible in media consumption patterns. See the Pew Research Center report, "Political Polarization in the American Public," June 2014, http://www.people-press.org/files/2014/06/6-12-2014-Political-Polarization-Release.pdf. On this view, recent pushes for racially segregated safe spaces on campuses can be seen as having less to do with ethnic than with ideological purity. Like their parents, students prefer the company of those who identify as of the same race, not because they *look* alike, but because they can be supposed to *think* alike in some fundamental way, having experienced the same systemic oppressions.

11. Often the anecdotes are fictional, as in the opening vignettes of Carter, *Civility,* 3; and Waldron, *The Harm in Hate Speech,* 1. The vastness of the generalizations offered by scholars of civility is usually inversely proportional to the data available. For attempts to trace the trend empirically, see the symposium on "Political Civility," *Political Science & Politics* 45 (2012): 401–434; and Mutz, *In-Your-Face Politics,* 3–5. Mutz sidesteps the longitudinal problem in favor of assessing in/civility's effects on democratic deliberation, with mixed results.

12. See Daniel M. Shea and Alex Sproveri, "The Rise and Fall of Nasty Politics in America," *PS: Political Science & Politics* 45, no. 3 (July 2012): 416–421. Shea and Sproveri note that their data "do not provide direct evidence that nasty rhetoric was used at any point in American history . . . [but] we cannot imagine why [the authors included in their content analysis] would use such terms if it were not true" (420). This suggests some lack of imagination.

13. See Herbst, *Rude Democracy*, chap. 1; and Mary P. Ryan, *Civic Wars: Democracy and Public Life in the American City during the Nineteenth Century* (Berkeley: University of California Press, 1997).

14. "A civil society demands from each of us good will and respect, fair dealing and forgiveness." George W. Bush, "Inaugural Address," January 20, 2001, https://georgewbush-whitehouse.archives.gov/news/inaugural-address.html.

15. Michael J. Sandel, "The Problem with Civility," in *The Public Philosophy: Essays on Morality in Politics* (Cambridge, MA: Harvard University Press, 2005), 54–55.

16. See Louis Sandy Maisel, "The Negative Consequences of Uncivil Political Discourse," *PS: Political Science & Politics* 45 (2012): 405–411.

17. Michael J. Sandel, *Liberalism and the Limits of Justice* (Cambridge: Cambridge University Press, 1998), xv; and Waldron, *The Harm in Hate Speech*.

18. Jacob T. Levy, *Rationalism, Pluralism, and Freedom* (Oxford: Oxford University Press, 2014), 34–35. Here, Levy follows earlier arguments made by Lon Fuller.

19. For instance, Georgetown University's Code of Student Conduct prohibits "incivility," defined as any "behavior, either through language or actions, which disrespects another individual." See http://studentconduct.georgetown. edu/code-of-student-conduct. For more examples, see the Foundation for Individual Rights in Education's report, "Spotlight on Speech Codes 2015," https://www.thefire.org/spotlight-speech-codes-2015.
    In 2014, the University of Illinois at Urbana-Champaign justified its decision to fire a new professor on the basis of his online comments as a violation of civility: "What we cannot and will not tolerate . . . are personal and disrespectful words or actions that demean and abuse either viewpoints themselves or those who express them. . . . Differing points of view [must be] discussed in and outside the classroom in a . . . civil, thoughtful and mutually respectful manner." Chancellor Phyllis M. Wise, "The Principles on Which We Stand," August 22, 2014, https://illinois.edu/blog/view/1109/115906. The professor, Steven Salaita, successfully sued the Uuniversity, but he was not reinstated.

20. This understanding of civility as a matter of rule-based formality provides the connection between Waldron's arguments about hate speech and his more recent writings, e.g., Jeremy Waldron, "Civility and Formality," in *Civility, Legality, and Justice in America*, ed. Austin Sarat (Cambridge: Cambridge University Press, 2014), 46–68.

21. Mutz points to the advent of "in-your-face" cable news, while Herbst identifies the immediacy and intimacy of the Internet as the key to the shift in our experience of disagreement. Mutz, *In-Your-Face Politics,* chap. 1; Herbst, *Rude Democracy,* 5.

22. Plato, "Euthyphro," in *Four Texts on Socrates,* ed. and trans. T. G. West and G. S. West (Ithaca, NY: Cornell University Press, 1998), 7b–d.

23. See Markku Peltonen, *Rhetoric, Politics and Popularity in Pre-Revolutionary England* (Cambridge: Cambridge University Press, 2013), 67. Peltonen points to Cicero's *De Oratore* and Quintilian's *Institutio Oratoria* as examples.

24. Romila Thapar, trans., "A Translation of the Edicts of Asoka," in *Asoka and the Decline of the Mauryas* (Delhi: Oxford University Press, 1997).

25. Brad S. Gregory, *The Unintended Reformation: How a Religious Revolution Secularized Society* (Cambridge, MA: Harvard University Press, 2015).

26. I discuss these dynamics at length in Chapter 1. In seventeenth-century England, "tender consciences" was a catchall term for nonconformists and dissenters from the Anglican Church who appealed to liberty of conscience.

27. "[R]eligious worship ought to be given to God alone, yet civil worship may, and ought to be given unto creatures: this is a duty from Inferiors to their Superiors, from Children to their Parents, from Servants to their Masters, from subject to Kings and Magistrates; these Gods must have civil worship . . . thus when Joseph came into the presence of Jacob his father, it is said that he *bowed himself with his face to the earth;* this was civil worship." From a sermon by the Rev. Benjamin Needler, included in *The Morning-Exercise against Popery. Or, the Principal Errors of the Church of Rome Detected and Confuted,* ed. N. Vincent (London, 1675), 462. As we shall see in Chapter 1, an important eirenic and "latitudinarian" strand within early modern toleration arguments focused on distinguishing "things indifferent" or *adiaphora* from the *fundamenta* or "fundamentals" of faith as a way of achieving *concordia* among Christians. Analogizing religious worship to the conventional and indifferent rituals of "civil worship" was a key move in these arguments.

28. This neologism has been attributed to Benjamin DeMott, "Seduced by Civility: Political Manners and the Crisis of Democratic Values," *The Nation,* December 9, 1996.

29. Quoted in Benjamin J. Kaplan, *Calvinists and Libertines: Confession and Community in Utrecht, 1578–1620* (Oxford: Clarendon Press, 1995), ch. 7.

30. Jean Bodin, *The Six Bookes of a Common-weale,* trans. R. Knolles (London, 1606), iv.7.536.

31. We shall discuss the examples of Maryland, Carolina, and Pennsylvania in Chapter 1 and the exceptional case of Rhode Island in Chapter 2.

32. While the continued exclusion of English Catholics from toleration and civic equality has long been a source of difficulty for Whig historians, the role

played by groups like the Quakers and American "Pagans" in establishing the limits of early modern toleration, both in theory and practice, has not received adequate attention. For a good overview of the former, see Mark Goldie and Richard Popkin, "Scepticism, Priestcraft, and Toleration," in *The Cambridge History of Eighteenth-Century Political Thought,* ed. Mark Goldie and Robert Wokler (Cambridge: Cambridge University Press, 2006).

33. Waldron, *The Harm in Hate Speech,* 207.

34. Ibid., 12.

35. I will delve more deeply into this complicated word history in Chapter 1.

36. For a good overview, see Peter Burke, Brian Harrison, and Paul Slack, eds., *Civil Histories: Essays Presented to Sir Keith Thomas* (Oxford: Oxford University Press, 2000).

37. Étienne Balibar, *Violence and Civility: On the Limits of Political Philosophy,* trans. G. M. Goshgarian (New York: Columbia University Press, 2015). Although, as Balibar notes, some theorists understand civility and other ostensibly noncoercive norms as "the worst kind of violence" (141). Arguments against hate speech in feminist and critical race theory rely on a similar claim about "assaultive" speech. See, for example, Rae Langton, "Beyond Belief: Pragmatics in Hate Speech and Pornography," in *Speech and Harm,* ed. Ishani Maitra and Mary Kate McGowan (Oxford: Oxford University Press, 2012), 72–93; Matsuda, *Words That Wound.*

38. Philip Pettit treats civility and civic virtue as synonyms; both involve "not just the internalization of public values and the disciplining of personal desires ... [but also] identification with larger groups, even with the polity as a whole." Philip Pettit, *Republicanism: A Theory of Freedom and Government* (Oxford: Oxford University Press, 1999), 281.

39. In debates about "civil society" in the 1990s, civility was treated as the consummate virtue of "free" societies with vibrant voluntary associations, in contrast with the former Communist countries of the Eastern Bloc. See, for example, Robert W. Hefner, ed., *Democratic Civility: The History and Cross Cultural Possibility of a Modern Political Ideal* (New Brunswick, NJ: Transaction Publishers, 1998). Edward Shils and Robert Putnam made civility synonymous with civic virtue and self-restraint through which citizens of liberal democracies tempered the pursuit of self- with sensitivity to the common interest. Edward Shils, *The Virtue of Civility: Selected Essays on Liberalism, Tradition, and Civil Society* (Indianapolis, IN: Liberty Fund, 1997); Putnam, *Bowling Alone.* The "civic" and "bourgeois" senses of civility are sometimes positioned as opposites—as in Michael Walzer, "Civility and Civic Virtue in Contemporary America," *Social Research* 41, no. 4 (1974): 593–611; and J. G. A. Pocock, "Virtues, Rights, and Manners: A Model for Historians of Political Thought," *Political Theory* 9, no. 3 (1981): 353–368—but they are also often conflated.

40. Mark Kingwell, *A Civil Tongue: Justice, Dialogue, and the Politics of Pluralism* (University Park: Pennsylvania State University Press), 15. The prime example here is John Rawls's introduction of a "duty of civility" in public reasoning in *Political Liberalism.* I will discuss this along with other appeals to civility in theories of deliberative democracy in the Conclusion.

41. This is itself a suggestive phrase. It derives from the historical "Pale" in Ireland, which served to divide the "civil" and civilized Anglicized Protestants from the barbarian Irish Catholics beyond.

42. Elias's magisterial two-volume work, *The Civilizing Process* (1939), and Freud's *Civilization and Its Discontents* (1930) have set the agenda for generations of social and cultural historians concerned to expose this dark side of civility. See Norbert Elias, *The Civilizing Process* (Oxford: Blackwell, 1969); and Sigmund Freud, *Civilization and Its Discontents* (London: Penguin, 2004).

43. Samuel Johnson, "Civility," in *A Dictionary of the English Language* (London: W. Strahan, 1755), 382. See, for example, John Kasson, *Rudeness and Civility: Manners in Nineteenth-Century Urban America* (New York: Hill and Wang, 1991); DeMott, "Seduced by Civility"; Nina Eliasoph, *Avoiding Politics: How Americans Produce Apathy in Everyday Life* (Cambridge: Cambridge University Press, 1998); Thomas L. Dumm, *A Politics of the Ordinary* (New York: New York University Press, 1999); Randall Kennedy, "The State of the Debate: The Case against Civility," *The American Prospect,* December 19, 1998; Christine T. Sistare, ed., *Civility and Its Discontents: Civic Virtue, Toleration, and Cultural Fragmentation* (Lawrence: University Press of Kansas, 2004); Austin Sarat, ed., *Civility, Legality, and Justice in America* (Cambridge: Cambridge University Press, 2014); and Linda Zerilli and Leti Volpp's contributions to Sarat, *Civility, Legality, and the Limits of Justice.*

44. James Tully, *Strange Multiplicity: Constitutionalism in an Age of Diversity* (Cambridge: Cambridge University Press, 1995).

45. Ring Lardner, *The Young Immigrunts* (Indianapolis, IN: Bobbs-Merrill, 1920), 78.

46. I wade into the "more tolerant" Hobbes debate revived by Alan Ryan in Chapter 3. See Alan Ryan, "Hobbes, Toleration and the Inner Life," in *The Nature Of Political Theory*, eds. David Miller and Larry Siedentop, (Oxford: Clarendon Press, 1983) and "A More Tolerant Hobbes?" in *Justifying Toleration: Conceptual and Historical Perspectives,* ed. Susan Mendus (Cambridge: Cambridge University Press, 1988), 37–59.

47. See also Teresa M. Bejan, "Difference without Disagreement: Rethinking Hobbes on 'Independency' and Toleration," *Review of Politics* 78: 1-25.

48. John Rawls, *Political Liberalism* (New York: Columbia University Press, 1996), 444–445, 465. Generally speaking, appeals to civility in contemporary theory include (sometimes several) aspects of the following: an overlapping

consensus on fundamental moral principles; mutual respect for persons, occasionally extending to their comprehensive doctrines (so long as they are "reasonable"); an attitude of open-mindedness, self-criticism, and humility about our own commitments; an affirmation of the intrinsic worth of diversity as such, regardless of its "reasonableness"; and good will toward our fellow citizens as partners in a shared enterprise. See, for example, Carter, *Civility;* Amy Gutmann and Dennis Thompson, *Democracy and Disagreement* (Cambridge, MA: Belknap, 1996); Cheshire Calhoun, "The Virtue of Civility," *Philosophy & Public Affairs* 29 (2000): 251–275; Leroy S. Rouner, ed., *Civility* (Notre Dame, IN: University of Notre Dame Press, 2000); Martha Nussbaum, *Liberty of Conscience: In Defense of America's Tradition of Religious Equality* (New York: Basic Books, 2008) and *The New Religious Intolerance: Overcoming the Politics of Fear in an Anxious Age* (Cambridge: Belknap Press, 2012); and Waldron, "Civility and Formality." I will consider these arguments and the uses to which civility has been put in contemporary political theory in the Conclusion.

49. Andrew Murphy, *Conscience and Community: Revisiting Toleration and Religious Dissent in Early Modern England and America* (University Park: Pennsylvania State University Press), ix. Other works by political theorists that employ a similar approach and from which I have learned a great deal include Pettit, *Republicanism;* Jeremy Waldron, *God, Locke, and Equality* (Cambridge: Cambridge University Press, 2002); Bryan Garsten, *Saving Persuasion: A Defense of Rhetoric and Judgment* (Cambridge, MA: Harvard University Press, 2006); Rainer Forst, *Toleration in Conflict: Past and Present* (Cambridge: Cambridge University Press, 2013); and Levy, *Rationalism, Pluralism, and Freedom.*

50. Rawls, *Political Liberalism,* xxiv. Notable exceptions here are Gary Remer, *Humanism and the Rhetoric of Toleration* (University Park: Pennsylvania State University Press, 1996); and Gregory, *The Unintended Reformation.* While Waldron's *The Harm in Hate Speech* appeals to "Enlightenment Philosophes" like Locke, Bayle, and Voltaire as offering early modern justifications for modern hate speech laws, he misses the full scope of their concerns. As I argue in Chapter 4, he also misrepresents Locke's views on religious insult in important respects.

51. Waldron, *The Harm in Hate Speech,* 29.

52. Stanley Fish, *There's No Such Thing as Free Speech, and It's a Good Thing Too* (Oxford: Oxford University Press, 1994), 125, 136-137.

53. See, for example, Ronald Beiner, *Civil Religion: A Dialogue in the History of Political Philosophy* (Cambridge: Cambridge University Press, 2011); and Jeffrey Collins, *The Allegiance of Thomas Hobbes* (Oxford: Oxford University Press, 2005). Hobbes drew the distinction between "civil" and "divine" worship in *Leviathan,* but he was picking up on a long tradition of biblical interpretation. For instance, the distinction was essential to interpretations of Acts 10:35 in

which Cornelius fell down at the feet of Peter. Early modern commentators were at pains to distinguish this "civil worship" from the "divine worship" owed to God.

54. Romance languages lack this distinction, although the German terms *Toleranz* and *Duldung*, respectively, carry a similar positive and negative valence.

55. See Michael Walzer, *On Toleration* (New Haven, CT: Yale University Press, 1999), xi; and Andrew Murphy, "Tolerance, Toleration, and the Liberal Tradition," *Polity* 29 (1997): 593–623. In this book, I will be concerned primarily with "toleration" as a practice both of states and of individuals. For the horizontal/vertical distinction, see Forst, *Toleration in Conflict*, 6; and Melissa Williams and Jeremy Waldron's Introduction to Williams and Waldron, eds., *Toleration and Its Limits* (New York: New York University Press, 2008), 1–27.

56. On *tolerantia*, see István Bejczy, "*Tolerantia*: A Medieval Concept," *Journal of the History of Ideas* 58 (1997): 365–384.

57. Thomas Paine, *Political Writings* (Cambridge: Cambridge University Press, 1995), 102.

58. "Dulden heisst beleidigen." Quoted in Rainer Forst, "Toleration, Justice, and Reason," in *The Culture of Toleration in Diverse Societies*, ed. Catriona McKinnon and Dario Castiglione (Manchester: Manchester University Press, 2003), 83n10.

59. Wendy Brown, *Regulating Aversion: Tolerance in the Age of Identity and Empire* (Princeton, NJ: Princeton University Press, 2008).

60. Nussbaum, *Liberty of Conscience*, 24; Amy Gutmann and Dennis Thompson, "Moral Conflict and Political Consensus," *Ethics* 101 (1990): 65, 76. Rainer Forst has also sought to distinguish between a repressive "permission conception" of toleration, in which the tolerated remains in a state of precarious dependence, and a superior "respect conception" rooted in reciprocity and mutual justification, and characterized by a shared commitment to equal dignity. Forst, "Toleration, Justice, and Reason," and *Toleration in Conflict*. For other examples, see David Heyd, "Is Toleration a Political Virtue?" in *Toleration and Its Limits*; Anna Galeotti, *Toleration as Recognition* (Cambridge: Cambridge University Press, 2002); and Thomas Scanlon, "The Difficulty of Tolerance," in *Toleration: An Elusive Virtue*, ed. D. Heyd (Princeton, NJ: Princeton University Press, 1996), 226–239.

61. Similar concerns inspired the turn to "recognition" in the 1990s by Charles Taylor and others. See Charles Taylor, *Multiculturalism and "The Politics of Recognition,"* ed. Amy Gutmann (Princeton, NJ: Princeton University Press, 1992).

62. For versions of this argument, see John Gray, "Pluralism and Toleration in Contemporary Political Philosophy," *Political Studies* 48 (2000): 323–333; and Jakob De Roover and S. N. Balagangadhara, "John Locke, Christian Liberty, and the Predicament of Liberal Toleration," *Political Theory* 36 (2008):

523–549. For recent restatements of the "Protestantization" critique in arguments about the limits of liberalism in approaching religious insult, see Talal Asad and Saba Mahmood's contributions to Talal Asad, Judith Butler, and Saba Mahmood, eds., *Is Critique Secular?: Blasphemy, Injury, and Free Speech* (Berkeley, CA: Doreen B. Townsend Center for the Humanities, 2009). For some pushback, see Andrew March, "Speech and the Sacred: Does the Defense of Free Speech Rest on a Mistake about Religion?" *Political Theory* 40 (2012): 319–346.

63. Martha Nussbaum, *Liberty of Conscience;* Alan Ryan, "A More Tolerant Hobbes?"; Richard Tuck, "Hobbes and Locke on Toleration," in *Thomas Hobbes and Political Theory,* ed. Mary Dietz (Lawrence: University of Kansas Press, 1990), 153–171; Edwin Curley, "Hobbes and the Cause of Religious Toleration," in *The Cambridge Companion to Hobbes's* Leviathan, ed. Patricia Springborg (Cambridge: Cambridge University Press, 2007), 309–336.

64. For the idea of history of political thought-as-exorcism, see Quentin Skinner, "Introduction: Seeing Things Their Way," in *Visions of Politics,* vol. 1, *Regarding Method* (Cambridge: Cambridge University Press, 2002), 6.

65. Michael W. McConnell, "America's First 'Hate Speech' Regulation," *Constitutional Comment* 9 (1992): 17-23.

66. As the late Istvan Hont put it, "History cannot be expected to solve the core analytical puzzles of political or economic theory. But it has its hour when the long-expected solutions . . . fail to materialize. History is the tool of skeptics. It helps us ask better questions. More precisely, it can help us avoid repeating some questions again and again, running in circles unproductively." Quoted in Levy, *Rationalism, Pluralism, and Freedom,* 85.

1. "Persecution of the Tongue"

1. Diana Mutz and other scholars seeking to investigate political civility empirically have stressed this dimension; civility describes "the rules that allow people of diverse views to smooth over differences and promote social harmony," or those that "sustain social harmony and allow people who disagree with one another to maintain ongoing relationships." Diana C. Mutz, *In-Your-Face Politics: The Consequences of Uncivil Media* (Princeton, NJ: Princeton University Press, 2015), 7; J. Cherie Strachan and Michael R. Wolf, "Political Civility," *PS: Political Science & Politics* 45, no. 3 (July 2012): 402.

2. John Rawls, *Political Liberalism* (New York: Columbia University Press, 1996), 485.

3. Quoted in Jeremy Waldron, *The Harm in Hate Speech* (Cambridge, MA: Harvard University Press, 2012), 216. The passage comes from Bayle's *Philosophical Commentary.* Pierre Bayle, *A philosophical commentary on these words of the Gospel,*

Luke 14.23: 'Compel Them to Come in, that My house may be full,' ed. John Kilcullen and Chandran Kukathas (Indianapolis, IN: Liberty Fund, 2005), 144.

4. Plato, *Statesman,* trans. J. B. Skemp (London: Routledge, 1961), 309c–d.

5. Plato, *Republic,* trans. G. M. A. Grube (Indianapolis, IN: Hackett, 1992), 432a.

6. Aristotle, *Politics,* trans. Sir Ernest Barker (Oxford: Clarendon Press, 1946), 1263b35.

7. "Concord, then, seems to be political friendship [*politike philia*], as indeed it is commonly said to be.... Now such concord is found among good men; for they are in accord both in themselves and with one another, being, so to say, of one mind [*homonoia*]" (*Politics,* 1267a37–43). Contrast this with Waldron's opening contention in *Law and Disagreement* that disagreement is the fundamental fact about modern democratic societies, hence the need for fair procedures to resolve it. Jeremy Waldron, *Law and Disagreement* (Oxford: Clarendon, 1999), 3–4. This emphasis on like-mindedness as essential to political friendship has been curiously downplayed by contemporary neo-Aristotelians.

8. "It was hardly even an 'idea' for the most part—just a happening—the sort of thing that happens when no choice is left and there is no hope of further struggle being worth while." Herbert Butterfield, "Toleration in Early Modern Times," *Journal of the History of Ideas* 38, no. 4 (1977): 573–584, 573. This battle fatigue narrative was itself a revisionist response to an older Whig triumphalist narrative of inevitable Enlightenment pioneered by Macaulay, who wrote that "the history of our country during the last hundred and sixty years is eminently the history of physical, or moral and of intellectual improvement." Thomas Babington Macaulay, *The History of England from the Ascension of James the Second,* (Philadelphia: E.H. Butler & Co., 1856), 1.1. For a recent retelling of this narrative of early modern toleration as the harbinger of liberal modernity, see Perez Zagorin, *How the Idea of Religious Toleration Came to the West* (Princeton, NJ: Princeton University Press, 2003). Both narratives have been challenged by recent historiography. For an excellent overview, see Jeffrey Collins, "Redeeming the Enlightenment: New Histories of Religious Toleration," *The Journal of Modern History* 81 (2009): 607–636.

9. I owe this phrase to John Dunn.

10. Waldron presents this as a debate internal to early modernity, contrasting a Hobbesian approach to religious insult and toleration with the more truly tolerant visions of Locke, Bayle, and Voltaire. Waldron, *The Harm in Hate Speech,* 231.

11. See, for example, Alexandra Walsham, *Charitable Hatred: Tolerance and Intolerance in England, 1500–1700* (Manchester: Manchester University Press, 2006); John Marshall, *John Locke, Toleration and Early Enlightenment Culture* (Cambridge: Cambridge University Press, 2006); Benjamin J. Kaplan, *Divided By Faith: Religious Conflict and the Practice of Toleration in Early Modern*

Europe (Cambridge, MA: Belknap Press of Harvard University Press, 2007); and Stuart Schwartz, *All Can Be Saved: Religious Tolerance and Salvation in the Iberian Atlantic World* (New Haven, CT: Yale University Press, 2008).

12. Waldron, *Harm in Hate Speech*, 104. Waldron links his argument about hate speech as a violation of the public good of "assurance" to Rawls's account of a "well-ordered society" in *Political Liberalism* as one in which "everyone accepts, and knows that everyone else accepts, the very same principles of justice" (Rawls, *Political Liberalism*, 35). See Waldron, *Harm in Hate Speech*, 65–69.

13. Erasmus, "The Tongue," in *The Collected Works of Erasmus*, ed. Elaine Fantham and Erika Rummell, trans. Elaine Fantham (Toronto: University of Toronto Press, 1989), 29.364, 349. Erasmus links slander or calumny (Latin *calumnia*) with the Greek *diabole*, thus highlighting its satanic provenance (341).

14. Ibid., 349.

15. Martin Luther, "The Freedom of a Christian," in *Three Treatises*, trans. W. A. Lambert, rev. Harold J. Grimm (Minneapolis, MN: Fortress Press, 1970), 311–312

16. From Martin Luther, *Wider den Meuchler zu Dresden* (1531), quoted in Antónia Szabari, "The Scandal of Religion: Luther and Public Speech in the Reformation," in *Political Theologies: Public Religions in a Post-Secular World,* ed. Hent de Vries and Lawrence E. Sullivan (New York: Fordham University Press, 2006), 130.

17. Martin Luther, "An Argument in Defense of All the Articles of Dr Martin Luther Wrongly Condemned in the Roman Bull" (1520), in *The Works of Martin Luther* (Albany, NY: Books for the Ages, 1997), 3.42.

18. *Decet Romanum Pontificem* (1521), in *A Reformation Reader,* ed. Denis R. Janz (Minneapolis, MN: Fortress Press, 2008), 384.

19. This is what William Perkins (1607) would later call the "Art of Prophecying," defined as any "publike and solemne speech of the Prophet [i.e., the Minister of the Word], pertaining to the worship of God and to the salvation of our neighbor"; "Every Prophet is partly the voyce of God, to wit, in preaching: and partly the voyce of the people, in the act of praying." William Perkins, "The Art of Prophecying," in *The Works of that Famous and Worthy Minister of Christ in the University of Cambridge, M. William Perkins* (London: John Leggatt, 1631), 2.646.

20. Letter to Spalatin (c. February 16, 1520). Quoted in Lyndal Roper, *Martin Luther: Renegade and Prophet* (London: Bodley Head, 2016), 154.

21. Martin Luther, "Preface to the New Testament," in *The Reformation Writings of Martin Luther,* trans. and ed. Bertram Lee-Woolf (London: Lutterworth Press, 1956 [1534]), 2.278.

22. One historian described the arrival of Quakers in Massachusetts as follows: "Their spirit was a frenzy, for which the only proper place was Bedlam. . . . There

was no official dignity that they did not revile; no sense of social decorum that they did not outrage. One of the women stripped herself naked and walked through the aisles of a crowded meeting-house and another through the town of Salem. . . . The first comers of the sect to Massachusetts may justly be called 'avowed firebrands,' not intending permanent settlement, but with the deliberate design of antagonizing the religious and civil institution of the colony, a design formed and entered upon in a thoroughly quarrelsome spirit." Sanford Cobb, *The Rise of Religious Liberty in America* (New York: Macmillan, 1902), 214–216.

23. The term meant "rebaptizer" and was possibly coined by the Swiss reformer Ulrich Zwingli.

24. For a good discussion see Kaplan, *Divided By Faith,* chaps. 1 and 4.

25. Similarly, it matters that martyrology became big business for publishers, most famously in England with Foxe's *Actes and Monuments* (and after the Council of Trent, a revised and expanded Roman martyrology followed suit). Michael P. Carroll, *Veiled Threats: The Logic of Popular Catholicism in Italy* (Baltimore: Johns Hopkins University Press, 1996), 217.

26. Brad S. Gregory, *The Unintended Reformation: How a Religious Revolution Secularized Society* (Cambridge, MA: Harvard University Press, 2015).

27. Sebastian Castellio, *Concerning Heretics,* ed. Roland Bainton (New York: Octagon Books, 1965 [1554]), 212.

28. For the importance of labeling in the construction of sectarian identities, see Peter Burke, *The Art of Conversation* (Ithaca, NY: Cornell University Press, 1993), chap. 3.

29. Jeremiah 9:8; 2 Corinthians 12:20 (KJV of 1611, orthography updated).

30. James 3:1–18 KJV.

31. Erasmus, "The Tongue," 367.

32. Ibid., 364–365.

33. John Whitgift, *The Works of John Whitgift* (Cambridge: Cambridge University Press, 1852), 3.320.

34. See Lawrence Stone, *The Causes of the English Revolution 1529–1642* (New York: Routledge, 2002); and Peter Lake and Steve Pincus, "Re-Thinking the Public Sphere, in Early Modern England" *Journal of British Studies* 45, no. 2 (2006).

35. William Walwyn, "Gold Tried in the Fire," in *The English Levellers,* ed. Andrew Sharp (Cambridge: Cambridge University Press, 1998), 80.

36. Thomas Watson, "Discourses Upon Christ's Sermon on the Mount" in *Discourses upon Important and Interesting Subjects: Being the Select Works of Thomas Watson* (Edinburgh, 1829), 2.350-351.

37. Quoted in Joseph Lecler, *Toleration and the Reformation* (New York: Association Press, 1960), 2.45.

38. Erasmus, *The Complaint of Peace,* trans. Thomas Paynell (Chicago: Open Court, 1917), 27.

39. L'Hôpital is generally treated as a paradigmatically *politique* thinker open to toleration on prudential grounds, but Lecler emphasizes the eirenic aspects of his thought as well. Lecler, *Toleration and the Reformation,* 2.45–46.

40. The "celestial bodies . . . move and ever have moved, without clashing, and in perfect harmony" (Erasmus, *Complaint of Peace,* 3). This was Plato's preferred metaphor, which was taken up subsequently by the Stoics. See, for example, Cicero's *Dream of Scipio* in Book 6 of *De re publica.*

41. Erasmus, *Complaint,* 26.

42. Kaplan, *Divided by Faith,* 72.

43. Paul 12:3–5 KJV.

44. Erasmus, *Complaint,* 22, 25.

45. Ibid., 12.

46. Erasmus, "The Tongue," 259–260.

47. Jerome, *Epistle on the Galatians* [*Epistolem ad Galatas*] 3, cited in St. Thomas Aquinas, *Summa Theologiae,* in *Aquinas: Political Writings,* trans. and ed. R. W. Dyson (Cambridge: Cambridge University Press, 2002), 275.

48. Aquinas cites Jerome in arguing that the rites of unbelievers, including Jews, could be tolerated, but heretics could not: "For it is a much more grievous thing to corrupt the faith which gives life to the soul than to forge money, which supports temporal life . . . [but] on the side of the Church, however, there is mercy, which seeks the conversion of those who err; and so she condemns not at once, but 'after the first and second admonition', as the Apostle directs. After that, if the heretic is found to be pertinacious still, the Church no longer hoping for his conversion, looks to the salvation of others by separating him from the Church through the sentence of excommunication; and, further, she hands him over to the secular tribunal to be removed from the world by death." Thomas Aquinas, *Aquinas: Political Writings,* trans. and ed. R. W. Dyson (Cambridge University Press, 2002), 275.

49. Mark Goldie, "The Theory of Religious Intolerance in Restoration England," in *From Persecution to Toleration: The Glorious Revolution and Religion in England,* ed. Ole Peter Grell, Jonathan I. Israel, and Nicholas Tyacke (Oxford: Oxford University Press, 1991), 331–368.

50. Augustine of Hippo, "On the Correction of the Donatists," trans. Rev. Marcus Dods, in *The Works of Aurelius Augustine* (Edinburgh: Murray and Green, 1872), 3.482.

51. "For there is but one bread which is the sacrament of unity . . . [and] the Catholic Church alone is the body of Christ. . . . Outside this body, the Holy Spirit giveth life to no one, seeing that . . . he is not a partaker of the divine love who is the enemy of unity." Augustine, "Correction of the Donatists," 519.

52. Ibid., 512.

53. "What then is the function of brotherly love? Does it, because it fears the shortlived fires of the furnace for a few, therefore abandon all to the eternal fires of hell?" Ibid., 491.

54. Luke 14:23 KJV: "And the lord said unto the servant, Go out into the highways and hedges, and compel them to come in, that my house may be filled." Augustine established the doctrine of *compelle entrare* in the course of his controversy with Donatus: "Because it was right that when the Church had been strengthened, both in power and in extent, men should be compelled to come in to the feast of everlasting salvation.... Wherefore, if you were walking peaceably, absent from this feast of everlasting salvation and of the holy unity of the Church, we should find you, as it were, in the highways; ... The sheep which is compelled is driven whither it would not wish to go, but after it has entered, it feeds of its own accord in the pastures to which it was brought.." Letter 173, trans. J. G. Cunningham, in *Nicene and Post-Nicene Fathers,* ed. Philip Schaff, vol. 1 (Buffalo, NY: Christian Literature Publishing Co., 1887). According to Mark Goldie, Augustine's usage "rang down the centuries, becoming the canonical citation in the history of persecution" (Goldie, "Religious Intolerance," 338). Bayle's *Philosophical Commentary* took this biblical passage as its target.

55. Goldie, "Religious Intolerance."

56. John Calvin, quoted in Sebastian Castellio, "Reply to Calvin," in *Concerning Heretics,* 272.

57. Castellio, *Concerning Heretics,* 271, 277.

58. See, for example, Edwin Curley, "Sebastian Castellio's Erasmian Liberalism," *Philosophical Topics* 31 (2003): 47–73; Gary Remer, *Humanism and the Rhetoric of Toleration* (University Park: Pennsylvania State University Press, 1996); and Zagorin, *How the Idea of Religious Toleration Came to the West,* 97.

59. Bernard J. Verkamp, *The Indifferent Mean: Adiaphorism in the English Reformation to 1554* (Athens: Ohio University Press, 1977), 20–25.

60. Ibid., 23–24. As Erasmus explained in the *Enchiridion* (1501): "I do not disapprove in any way of the external ceremonies of Christians ... but to worship Christ through visible things for the sake of visible things ... to be complacent in oneself and condemn others on this basis ... this would be to desert the law of the gospel, which is spiritual, and to sink into a kind of Judaism." Desiderius Erasmus, *Enchiridion Militis Christiani,* ed. John W. O'Malley (Toronto: University of Toronto Press, 1988), 73–74. This "handbook for a Christian knight" was first published in English in 1531.

61. Desiderius Erasmus, "Letter to Jean de Carondelet, 5 January 1523," in *The Correspondence of Erasmus: Letters 1252 to 1355,* ed. Sir Roger Aubrey Baskerville Mynors (Toronto: University of Toronto Press, 1989), 250–252.

62. Quoted in Mark Goldie and Richard Popkin, "Scepticism, Priestcraft, and Toleration," in *The Cambridge History of Eighteenth-Century Political Thought,* ed. M. Goldie and R. Wokler (Cambridge: Cambridge University Press, 2006), 100–101. Other influential eirenic proponents of comprehension include George Cassander and Hugo Grotius. In his unpublished manuscript *Meletius* (1611), Grotius emphasized the dynamics of partisanship and sectarian attachments serving to enflame religious disagreements as a key obstacle to toleration. Hugo Grotius, *Meletius,* ed. and trans. G. H. M. Posthumus Meyjes (New York: E.J. Brill, 1988), 103.

63. Kaplan, *Divided by Faith,* 132–133.

64. Castellio, *Concerning Heretics,* 132–133.

65. Ibid., 133.

66. I explore this significance at length in Teresa M. Bejan, "Evangelical Toleration," *Journal of Politics* 77 (2015): 1103–1114.

67. István Bejczy, "*Tolerantia:* A Medieval Concept," *Journal of the History of Ideas* 58, no. 3 (1997): 365–384.

68. For a good example of this distinction, see Aquinas, *Summa Theologiae,* 267–278.

69. Castellio, *Concerning Heretics,* 269.

70. Nevertheless, Erasmus acknowledged execution as an appropriate punishment for cases of extreme and unrepentant heresy. Castellio, by contrast, favored a high level of spiritual autonomy given his own doubts about certain orthodoxies.

71. Erasmus, "The Tongue," 365.

72. Remer, *Humanism and the Rhetoric of Toleration.* See also Lecler, *Toleration and the Reformation.*

73. Remer, *Humanism and the Rhetoric of Toleration,* chap. 1.

74. Quoted in Lecler, *Toleration and the Reformation.* 1.237-238.

75. Lecler, *Toleration and the Reformation,* 1.226.

76. Additional colloquies were held at Worms, Regensburg, and Leipzig. Lecler, *Toleration and the Reformation,* 1.228–235. Also see Nadia Urbinati, "Half-Toleration: Concordia and the Limits of Dialogue," in *Boundaries of Toleration,* ed. Alfred Stepan and Charles Taylor (New York: Columbia University Press, 2014), 130–170.

77. Quoted in Lecler, *Toleration and the Reformation,* 1.231.

78. Ibid., 2.59.

79. Ibid., 2.63.

80. John Coffey counts eleven Protestant national creeds issued in the years between 1536 and 1575. Coffey, "A Ticklish Business: Defining Heresy and Orthodoxy in the Puritan Revolution," in *Heresy, Literature, and Politics in Early Modern English Culture*, ed. David Loewenstein (Cambridge: Cambridge University Press, 2006), 113.

81. Richard Baxter, *Reliquiae Baxterianae: or, Mr Richard Baxter's Narrative of the Most Memorable Passages of his Life and Times*, ed. Matthew Sylvester (London, 1696), 2.198. See also Coffey, "A Ticklish Business," 126.

82. See E. Gordon Rupp and Philip S. Watson, eds., *Luther and Erasmus: Free Will and Salvation* (Louisville, KY: John Knox Press, 1969).

83. Desiderius Erasmus, "Hyperaspistes," in *Collected Works of Erasmus: Controversies* (Toronto: University of Toronto Press, 1999), 246.

84. Castellio, *Concerning Heretics*, 133. Erasmus also observed that "If the Turk is to be driven from the necks of the people, these holy men claim that they have neither soldiers nor money . . . but to slay their brother with slander or pierce their neighbors with a stab of the tongue is seen as violating no obligation" (Erasmus, "The Tongue," 350). See Murad Idris, "Alternative Political Theologies: Erasmus on Peace, Speech, and Necessity," *Theory and Event* 17, no. 4 (2014).

85. Quoted in Lecler, *Toleration and the Reformation*, 238. See also Remer, *Humanism and the Rhetoric of Toleration*, 104.

86. Remer and Lecler discuss many different examples. Erasmus himself published a number of different colloquies, including "An Examination Concerning Faith," which depicted a conversation between a Catholic and a Lutheran who discover in the course of their discussion that the two differ only in *adiaphora*—a happy ending in stark contrast to Erasmus's real-life colloquy with Luther. Remer, *Humanism and the Rhetoric of Toleration*, 64. Witzel himself published *Drei Gesprechbuechlein von der Religionssachen* (1539), a popular colloquy in German that described a conversation between five speakers, "Teuto, a strict Lutheran, Ausonius, an uncompromising Catholic; Core, a moderate Lutheran; Orthodoxus, a moderate Catholic and Witzel's mouthpiece; and Palaemon, the referee whose part consist in declaring that Orthodoxus is right" (Lecler, *Toleration and the Reformation*, 1.239).

87. Jean Bodin, *Colloquium of the Seven about Secrets of the Sublime* (University Park: Pennsylvania State University Press, 2010), 4. What Bodin means his readers to conclude from the dialogue remains a subject of dispute. The participants depart "having embraced each other in mutual love. Henceforth, they nourished their piety in remarkable harmony and their integrity of life in common pursuits and intimacy. However, afterwards they held no more conversation about religions, although each one defended his own religion with the supreme

sanctity of his own life" (471). Some scholars read this encomium to civil silence as an indictment of colloquy, while others including Remer and Marion
Leathers Kuntz read it as an endorsement of toleration in contrast with Bodin's
limited embrace of uniformity in *The Six Bookes of the Republique*. See Gary
Remer, "Dialogues of Toleration: Erasmus and Bodin," *The Review of Politics*
56, no. 2 (March 1994): 305–336; and Marion Leathers Kuntz, "The Concept of
Toleration in the *Colloquium Heptaplomeres* of Jean Bodin," in *Beyond the Persecuting Society: Religious Toleration before the Enlightenment*, ed. John C. Laursen
and Cary J. Nederman (Philadelphia: University of Pennsylvania Press, 1998),
125–144. I think that scholars exaggerate the shift in Bodin's position between
these works because they have lost sight of *concordia* as an end pursued through
coercive uniformity *and* toleration, often in combination.

88. Archbishop John Whitgift, "The Defence of the Answer to the Admonition,"
in *The Works of John Whitgift* (Cambridge: Cambridge University Press, 1852),
2.62.

89. The growth in the volume of printed material was enormous. Lake and Pincus
note that "whereas the Elizabethan Bond of Association in the 1580s generated dozens of signatures in individual counties, that number pales in comparison to the hundreds of thousands of people that signed the 1696 Bond of
Association in Lancashire alone" (Lake and Pincus, "Re-Thinking the Public
Sphere," 279). See also Stone, *Causes of the English Revolution*, 96.

90. John Milton, *Paradise Lost* (Oxford: Oxford University Press, 2005), 59.

91. For the most part, the progress of toleration in seventeenth-century England consisted in exempting dissenters from legal penalties through "in-
dulgences" that could proceed by royal prerogative as well as parliamentary statute. Charles II and James II both issued Declarations of Indulgence
during their reigns, and the famed 1689 Toleration Act in England, the turning point for so many Whig historians, was actually entitled "An Act for Exempting their Majestyes Protestant Subjects dissenting from the Church of
England from the Penalties of certaine Lawes." It purposely excluded Catholics and non-Trinitarian Protestants and did not mention the word *toleration* at all.

92. Christopher Fowler, quoted in Blair Worden, "Toleration and the Cromwellian
Protectorate," in *Persecution and Toleration*, ed. W. J. Sheils (Oxford: Blackwell,
1984), 200.

93. The multiplicity of sects corroding the concord of Christendom was catalogued
vividly and unsympathetically by the heresiographer Thomas Edwards in his
aptly (and exhaustingly) titled pamphlet *Gangraena, Or a Catalogue and Discovery of many of the Errours, Heresies, Blasphemies and pernicious Practices of
the Sectaries of this time, vented and acted in England these four last years, As also
a particular Narration of divers Stories, Remarkable passages, Letters, an Extract*

of many Letters, all concerning the present Sects, together with some Observations upon, and Corollaries from all the fore-named Premises (London, 1646).

94. Jeremy Taylor, *A Discourse on the Liberty of Prophesying* (London: R. Royston, 1647), 39, 3, 9–10. "And yet such is the iniquity of men, that they suck in opinions as wild Asses doe the wind, without distinguishing the wholesome from the corrupted ayre, and then live upon it a venture, and when all their confidence is built upon zeale and mistake, yet therefore because they are zealous and mistaken, they are impatient of contradiction" (18).

95. Ibid., 9–10.

96. Ibid., 22.

97. Ibid., 13.

98. Ibid., 184.

99. Ibid., 14.

100. Ibid., 33, 22.

101. Ibid., 12.

102. Ibid., 3, 29.

103. See, for example, the Tudor tracts collected in N. Vienne-Guerrin, ed., *The Unruly Tongue in Early Modern England: Three Treatises* (Madison, NJ: Fairleigh Dickinson University Press, 2012). See also Marshall, *John Locke, Toleration, and Early Enlightenment Culture*, 299.

104. Richard Allestree, *The Government of the Tongue* (At the Theatre in Oxford, 1667), 10–11. Allestree's most famous work, *The Whole Duty of Man*, came in for criticism by Hobbes in *Behemoth*. Thomas Hobbes, *Behemoth, or the Long Parliament*, ed. S. Holmes (Chicago: University of Chicago Press, 1990 [1681]), 47–53.

105. Allestree, *Government of the Tongue*, 54, 57–58.

106. Ibid., 47.

107. Ibid., 81.

108. Ibid., 46.

109. For Allestree, this meant that atheists in particular must observe a civil silence because of the offense their discourse would cause to believers: "To those indeed who have a zeal for their Faith, there can be no Discourse so intolerable, so disobliging: it turns conversation into skirmishing, and perpetual disputes . . . and sure, those who do acknowledge a Divine Power cannot contentedly sit by to hear him blasphemed." Ibid., 37–38.

110. Ibid., 209, 108.

111. Norbert Elias, *The Civilizing Process: The History of Manners* (Oxford: Blackwell, 1969), 1.54. Erasmus's treatise was translated into English in 1532 and issued as a catechism for children in 1534.

112. See, for instance, Anna Bryson, *From Courtesy to Civility: Changing Codes of Conduct in Early Modern England* (Oxford: Oxford University Press, 1997);

Burke, *The Art of Conversation;* C. Dallett Hemphill, *Bowing to Necessities: A History of Manners in America, 1620–1860* (Oxford: Oxford University Press, 2002); and Markku Peltonen, *The Duel in Early Modern England: Civility, Politeness and Honour* (Cambridge: Cambridge University Press, 2006).

113. Bryson, *From Courtesy to Civility,* 282. Bryson notes against Pocock and other scholars of civic republicanism that the distinction between civility and "civic" virtue in their accounts is anachronistic and misplaced. Ibid., 60–61, cf. J. G. A. Pocock, "Virtues, Rights, and Manners," in *Virtue, Commerce, and History* (Cambridge: Cambridge University Press, 1985), 40–41. See also Markku Peltonen, who has pointed to the persistence of dueling as evidence that seventeenth-century England remained a highly competitive and honor-obsessed society (Peltonen, *The Duel in Early Modern England,* 68).

114. As William Sherlock explained: "Civil Worship is confined to the Inhabitants of this World, and is thereby distinguished from religious Worship; so the Different Degrees of Civil Honour, though the External Signs and Expressions of it are the same, are distinguished by the visible presence of the Object to which it is paid; for when a man bows or uncovers his head, we know what kind of Honour it is, by considering the Relation or the Quality, of the Person to whom it is paid, whether he be a Father, a Prince, or a wise and good man." William Sherlock, *An Answer to a Discourse Intituled Papists Protesting against Protestant-popery* (1686), 39–40.

115. Thomas Starkey, quoted in Bryson, *From Courtesy to Civility,* 50.

116. Anthony Pagden notes that the transformation of the Americans into "barbarians" was largely the work of the neo-Scholastic theologians of Salamanca, who criticized "barbaric" Spanish conquests in contrast them with the truly "civil" Christians on linguistic, cultural, and religious grounds. Anthony Pagden, *The Fall of Natural Man: The American Indian and the Origins of Comparative Ethnology* (Cambridge: Cambridge University Press, 1986). See also Jill Lepore, *The Name of War: King Philip's War and the Origins of American Identity* (New York: Vintage, 1999).

117. One of the highpoints of Elias's narrative is the introduction of the fork in medieval Europe as "the embodiment of a specific standard [of propriety] . . . and level of revulsion" (Elias, *The History of Manners,* 68–69, 127). The fork had been introduced earlier in Byzantium, and Elias tells the story of the Grecian princess on a visit to the Venetian Doge who fell under suspicion due to the strangeness of the practice. Becker also has a good fork story: the controversy over Veronese's painting of the Last Supper arose in part because of its depiction of an Apostle using a fork. Veronese was forced to retitle it *Feast at the House of Levi* by the Inquisition because of this anticommunal affect. Marvin B. Becker, *Civility and Society in Western Europe 1300–1600* (Bloomington: Indiana University Press, 1988), 2.

118. An entire chapter (Section 13) of Taylor's *Liberty of Prophesying* was devoted to describing the "deportment to be used towards persons disagreeing."

119. Erasmus, "The Tongue," 364. One imagines that Erasmus would have been less favorable to Solon's law demanding citizens take sides in partisan disputes.

120. Not only could the argument that dissent from the English church-state amounted to treason justify a plethora of speech controls, it also accounts for the persistence of religious tests for office well into the nineteenth century. Religious tests for Catholics were not removed until the passage of the Roman Catholic Relief Act in 1829.

121. Taylor, *Liberty of Prophesying*, 18.

122. Ibid., 22.

123. Burke, *Art of Conversation*, 107–108.

124. Jean Bodin, *The Six Bookes of a Common-weale*, trans. R. Knolles (London, 1606), iv.7.536. The participants in Bodin's *Colloquium Heptaplomeres* extol the virtues of such bans before embarking on their own discussion of the "secrets of the sublime," including the truth of religion. Remer reads this as evidence that Bodin is reversing his earlier judgment (Remer, *Humanism and the Rhetoric of Toleration*, chap. 5). Yet given the conclusion of the dialogue discussed above, Bodin's point seems more hermetic and elitist—bans are necessary for the vulgar, but even philosophic elites recognize the virtues of civil silence.

125. L. J. Reeve, *Charles I and the Road to Personal Rule* (Cambridge: Cambridge University Press, 2003), 63.

126. See Lawrence Klein, "Coffeehouse Civility, 1660–1714: An Aspect of Post-Courtly Culture in England," *Huntington Library Quarterly* 59: 39.

127. William Aglionby, *The Present State of the United Provinces of the Low Countries* (London, 1671), 227–228. Quoted in Benjamin J. Kaplan, *Calvinists and Libertines: Confession and Community in Utrecht, 1578–1620* (Oxford: Clarendon Press, 1995), 280.

128. Lecler, *Toleration and the Reformation*, 46, 53.

129. Walsham, *Charitable Hatred*, 127–128.

130. John Yates, *Ibis Ad Caesarem. Or A Submissive Appearance before Caesar in Answer to Mr Mountagues Appeale, in the Points of Arminianisme and Popery, Maintained and Defended by Him, against the Doctrine of the Church of England* (London, 1626), 3.40. Also quoted in Walsham, *Charitable Hatred*, 128.

131. Alexandra Walsham, *Church Papists: Catholicism, Conformity and Confessional Polemic in Early Modern England* (Woodbridge: The Boydell Press, 1999), 111, and *Charitable Hatred*, 127–128.

132. Donald S. Lutz, ed., *Colonial Origins of the American Constitution: A Documentary History* (Indianapolis, IN: Liberty Fund, 1998), 271. See also Michael W. McConnell, "America's First 'Hate Speech' Regulation," *Constitutional Comment* 9 (1992): 17–23.

133. William Penn, "The Great Law of Pennsylvania," in *Church and State in the Modern Age: A Documentary History,* ed. J. F. Maclear (Oxford: Oxford University Press, 1995 [1682]), 52–53.

134. Locke, "The Fundamental Constitutions of Carolina," in *Locke: Political Essays,* ed. Mark Goldie (Cambridge: Cambridge University Press, 1990), 179.

135. For the difference, see Andrew Murphy, "Tolerance, Toleration, and the Liberal Tradition," *Polity* 29, no. 4 (July 1, 1997): 593–623.

136. Scott Sowerby, *Making Toleration: The Repealers and the Glorious Revolution* (Cambridge, MA: Harvard University Press, 2013).

137. Quoted in ibid., 41. The king went on to argue that if "there should be a law made that all black men should be imprisoned, twold be unreasonable and we had as little reason to quarell with other men for being of different opinions as for being of different complexions." James was supported in his program by many dissenters, one of whom wrote that he "looked forward to the day when 'to go under several different Denominations, shall be no more a Reproach to them, than it is for citizens to be free of several Companies'" (66).

138. Watson, *Discourses upon Important and Interesting Subjects,* 29, 230, 235–236.

139. Ibid., 236.

140. Burke, *Art of Conversation,* 25.

141. Benjamin Furly (a radical Quaker and friend of Locke's in Rotterdam), quoted in Peltonen, *The Duel in Early Modern England,* 224. We shall return to the Quaker critique of civility in Chapter 2.

142. Both quoted in Coffey, "A Ticklish Business," 116 (my emphasis). Here we catch a glimpse of what Ethan Shagan has called the "rule of moderation" in which the ideal of moderation functioned in religious controversies as an early modern ideology of control. Ethan H. Shagan, *The Rule of Moderation: Violence, Religion and the Politics of Restraint in Early Modern England* (Cambridge: Cambridge University Press, 2011).

143. In this respect, it is notable that the only person ever convicted under the Maryland Toleration Act before its repeal in 1654 was a Catholic, William Lewis, fined for "interfering by opprobrious reproaches with two Protestants" (quoted in McConnell, "America's First 'Hate Speech' Regulation," 18). McConnell takes this as an "encouraging sign, since most colonial officials at the time were Catholics," but the subsequent persecution of Catholics in Maryland suggests not.

2. "Silver Alarums"

1. See John Coffey, "Puritanism and Liberty Revisited," *The Historical Journal* 41 (1998): 985, and *Persecution and Toleration in England, 1558–1689* (London: Longman, 2000), 207–208; Jon Parkin, "Toleration," in *The Oxford Handbook*

of British Philosophy in the Seventeenth Century, ed. Peter R. Anstey (Oxford: Oxford University Press, 2013); and Perez Zagorin, *How the Idea of Religious Toleration Came to the West* (Princeton, NJ: Princeton University Press, 2003), 196–208.

2. For more on the relationship between Williams and Jefferson and the "wall of separation" in his 1802 "Letter to the Danbury Baptists," see John M. Barry, *Roger Williams and the Creation of the American Soul* (New York: Viking Press, 2012); Daniel Dreisbach, *Thomas Jefferson and the Wall of Separation between Church and State* (New York: New York University Press, 2002); Benjamin J. Hertzberg, "Religion's Influence on the Wall of Separation: Insights from Roger Williams, James Burgh, and Thomas Jefferson," *Sigma* 23 (2005), 1-21; and Alan E. Johnson, *The First American Founder: Roger Williams and Freedom of Conscience* (Pittsburgh, PA: Philosophia, 2013).

   Attributing the origins of the phrase to Williams may itself be a mistake. Waldron insists that the first use was by Richard Hooker, in his *Laws of Ecclesiastical Polity,* published in 1594: "Out of the difference betweene the *Church* and the *Commonwealth* . . . the walles of separation between these two, must for ever be upheld." Richard Hooker, *Of the Laws of Ecclesiastical Polity* (Cambridge, MA: Harvard University Press, 1981), 8.320. And yet Book 8 of Hooker's *Laws* in which the phrase appears was itself first published posthumously in 1648—five years after Williams's *Mr Cotton's Letter Lately Printed* (1644). Like the other posthumous chapters, Book 8 was not written by Hooker but compiled from pieces and notes written before his death. John Spenser, who was granted access to the last three books of *The Laws* and was later sued for corrupting the text, insisted that he had only "perfected" them, but this was—and is—contested. See the "Textual Introduction" to the edition cited above. The editors of that edition side with Spenser, but needless to say, the occurrence of the phrase in both texts is suspicious, especially given Williams's notoriety at the time Spenser was engaged in his project of "perfection." I am grateful to Emma Planinc for drawing my attention to the discrepancy.

3. For a recent popular biography see Barry, *American Soul.* See also Martha Nussbaum, "The First Founder: The American Revolution of Roger Williams," *New Republic,* September 10, 2008, and *Liberty of Conscience: In Defense of America's Tradition of Religious Equality* (New York: Basic Books, 2008), 47; Teresa M. Bejan, "'The Bond of Civility': Roger Williams on Toleration and Its Limits," *History of European Ideas* 37 (2011): 607–626, and "Evangelical Toleration," *The Journal of Politics* 77, no. 4 (2015): 1103–1114; and Rainer Forst, *Toleration in Conflict* (Cambridge: Cambridge University Press, 2013), chap. 5, §15.

4. Charter of Rhode Island and Providence Plantations, July 15, 1663. *The Avalon Project: Documents in Law, History and Diplomacy,* Yale Law School:

http://avalon.law.yale.edu/17th_century/ri04.asp. On the "livelie exper-
iment," see Teresa M. Bejan, "'When the Word of the Lord Runs Freely':
Roger Williams and Evangelical Toleration," and Evan Haefeli, "How Special
Was Rhode Island?: The Global Context of the 1663 Charter," in *The Lively
Experiment: Religious Toleration in American from Roger Williams to the Pres-
ent*, ed. Chris Beneke and Christopher S. Grenda (London: Rowman and
Littlefield, 2015).

5. Nussbaum, *Liberty of Conscience*, 57.
6. See Jonathan Beecher Field, "A Key for the Gate: Roger Williams, Parliament,
   and Providence," *The New England Quarterly* 80 (2007): 353–382; Jessica R.
   Stern, "A *Key* into *The Bloudy Tenent of Persecution*: Roger Williams, the Pequot War, and the Origins of Toleration in America," *Early American Studies*
   9 (2011): 576–616; and Teresa M. Bejan, "When the Word of the Lord Runs
   Freely."
7. Nussbaum, *Liberty of Conscience*, 52.
8. James Calvin Davis, *On Religious Liberty* (Cambridge, MA: Harvard University Press, 2008), 36, *The Moral Theology of Roger Williams: Christian Conviction and Public Ethics* (Louisville, KY: Westminster John Knox Press, 2004),
   51, and "A Return to Civility," *Journal of Church and State* 43, no. 4 (2001):
   689–706, 690, 705. See also Davis, *In Defense of Civility: How Religion Can
   Unite America on Seven Moral Issues That Divide Us* (Louisville, KY: Westminster John Knox Press, 2010).
9. For more speculation, see Barry, *American Soul*, 45. Williams's shorthand was
   indecipherable for centuries, but in 2012 researchers at Brown University—
   led by an undergraduate math major—managed to "crack the code" and de-
   cipher a previously unreadable and unpublished treatise by Williams. Written in the margins of another book sometime between 1679 and his death in
   1683, the tract was entitled "A Brief Reply to a Short Book Written by John
   Eliot" and was a refutation of Eliot's "An Answer to John Norcot against Infant
   Baptism." Both essays are published in Linford Fisher, J. Stanley Lemons, and
   Lucas Mason-Brown, eds., *Decoding Roger Williams: The Lost Essay of Rhode
   Island's Founding Father* (Houston, TX: Baylor University Press, 2013).
10. See also Roger Williams, *The Correspondence of Roger Williams*, ed. G. LaFan-
    tasie, 2 vols. (Hanover, NH: Brown University Press, 1988), 2.664. This would
    have been an extraordinary achievement for the time. Although we know little
    about his early life in England, many of these conversations—as well as his
    knowledge of Dutch and his mastery of shorthand—would have stemmed
    from his upbringing as the son of a merchant in the cosmopolitan and com-
    mercial city of London. The manuscript recently deciphered by research-
    ers at Brown contains his painstaking shorthand notes on Peter Heylyn's
    1652 book *Cosmographie*, which purported to offer a complete geographic,

demographic, and cultural description of the known world (Fisher, Lemons, and Mason-Brown, *Decoding Roger Williams,* 8–9).

11. Barry, *American Soul,* 6, and Part 1 ("The Law"); Nussbaum, *Liberty of Conscience,* 53, 80. Nussbaum goes so far as to claim that Williams "nowhere alludes to [his religious] beliefs in arguing for liberty of conscience—nor should he, since it is his considered position that political principles should not be based on sectarian religious views of any sort" (Nussbaum, *Liberty of Conscience,* 43). For a brief exchange between Nussbaum, David Little, and Kent Greenawalt on this issue, see "'Liberty of Conscience': An Exchange," *New York Review of Books* (May 2008), www.nybooks.com/articles/archives/2008/jun/12/liberty-of-conscience-an-exchange.

12. As the historian William Lamont once noted: "Williams, as a good Calvinist, accepted that mankind was divided into wheat and tares . . . nor did he shrink from the prospect of the destruction of those tares. The good Book of Revelation offered this mouth-watering prospect of revenge. . . . [This inspires] a renewed impatience with the 'alchemistic tricks' perpetrated by historians who have domesticated Williams into a gentle liberalism." William Lamont, "Pamphleteering, Protestant Consensus and the English Revolution," *Freedom and the English Revolution: Essays in History and Literature,* ed. R. C. Richardson and G. M. Ridden (Manchester: Manchester University Press, 1986), 81–82.

13. Murphy, "Tolerance, Toleration, and the Liberal Tradition," 610–615.

14. Edwin S. Gaustad, *Roger Williams* (Oxford: Oxford University Press, 2005), 20.

15. See "The Road to Banishment," in Williams, *Correspondence,* 1.6.

16. Quoted in Williams, *Correspondence,* 1.9–11 fn.

17. Roger Williams, *The Hireling Ministry None of Christ's* (1652), in *The Complete Writings of Roger Williams* (New York: Russell & Russell, 1963), 7.168–169.

18. Roger Williams, "Mr Cotton's letter lately printed, examined and answered" (1644), in *The Complete Writings of Roger Williams* (New York: Russell & Russell, 1963), 1.321.

19. Quoted in Field, "A Key for the Gate," 376. For the significance of the timeline of *Bloudy Tenent,* also see Field, "A Key for the Gate."

20. During this second visit, Williams published a sequel to *The Bloudy Tenent* entitled *The Bloody Tenent yet more Bloody: by Mr. Cotton's Endeavor to wash it white in the Blood of the Lamb; of whose precious Blood, spilt in the Bloud of his Servants; and of the Blood of Millions spilt in former and later Wars for Conscience sake, that most Bloody Tenent of Persecution for Cause of Conscience, upon a second Tryal is found more apparently and more notoriously guilty, &c.* (1652).

21. Nussbaum, *Liberty of Conscience,* 28.

22. Roger Williams, "The Examiner Defended in a Fair and Sober answer to the Two and Twenty Questions which Lately Examined the Author of 'Zeal

Examined'" (1652), in *The Complete Writings of Roger Williams* (New York: Russell & Russell, 1963), 7.263.

23. George Gillespie, "To the Christian and Courteous Reader," in *Wholesome Severity Reconciled with Christian Liberty* (London, 1644).

24. In his edition of Williams's writings, J. C. Davis, ed., *On Religious Liberty: Selections from the Works of Roger Williams* (Cambridge, MA: Harvard University Press, 2008), 264.

25. John Cotton, *A Reply to Mr Williams his examination; and answers to the letters sent to him by John Cotton* (London, 1647), 4; Williams, "Mr Cotton's letter," 324–325.

26. Williams, "Mr Cotton's Letter," 392.

27. Ibid., 335.

28. "mere," adj. OED (2015); see, for example, Richard Hooker: "Our God is one, or rather verie Onenesses, and mere vnitie" (*Of the Laws of Ecclesiastical Politie,* 1594).

29. John Milton, "Digression," in his "History of Britain," *Complete Prose Works,* ed. French Fogle and Max Patrick (New Haven, CT: Yale University Press, 1971), 5:442–444, 450, and "Of Education," in *Complete Prose Works,* ed. Ernest Sirluck (New Haven, CT: Yale University Press, 1959), 2:377–379, 381. See the illuminating discussion in Steve Pincus, "Neither Machiavellian Moment nor Possessive Individualism: Commercial Society and the Defenders of the English Commonwealth," *The American Historical Review* 103 (1998): 705–736.

30. See Alan Simpson, "How Democratic Was Roger Williams?" *The William and Mary Quarterly* 13 (1956): 53–67.

31. Roger Williams, "Christenings Make Not Christians" (1645), in *The Complete Writings of Roger Williams* (New York: Russell & Russell, 1963), 7.35.

32. Gillespie, *Wholesome Severity,* 3.

33. Williams, "Mr Cotton's Letter," 319.

34. Ibid., 326. Despite claims to the contrary, their policy of refusing to allow "many worthy persons . . . to live in the same Common-wealth together with them, if they set up any other church and Worship then what themselves practise[d]" revealed the frame of their churches to be "implicitly National" (394).

35. The increasing English mania for oaths of allegiance in the seventeenth century was an attempt to establish an alternative *vinculum* of mutual trust in the midst of social, political, and religious conflict. As one observer, William Castell, put it in 1642: "There are few towns, castles, Cities, [or] governments that are not bound by oath . . . by oaths the lives and states of all men are tryed, and the whole religious world governed." William Castell, *The Jesuits Undermining Parliament and Protestants with their Foolish Phancy of a Toleration* (London, 1642), 3–4. But as the title of Castell's pamphlet indicates, the necessity of

oaths to a stable social order was usually adduced—including by Locke—as an argument against the toleration of Catholics and atheists, and they were used to ferret out radical Protestants like the Quakers as well. An English statute passed in 1662 declared that anyone who "disdained or denied the legality of solemn binding statements of this kind thereby identified him or herself as a Quaker" as a matter of law. Alexandra Walsham, *Charitable Hatred: Tolerance and Intolerance in England, 1500–1700* (Manchester: Manchester University Press, 2006), 62.

36. Jack L. Davis, "Roger Williams among the Narragansett Indians," *The New England Quarterly* 43 (1970): 600.

37. For some treatments of contemporary usage, see Jill Lepore, *The Name of War: King Philip's War and the Origins of American Identity* (New York: Vintage, 1999). See also John Canup, *Out of the Wilderness: The Emergence of an American Identity in Colonial New England* (Middletown, CT: Wesleyan University Press, 2009); Timothy Fitzgerald, *Discourse on Civility and Barbarity: A Critical History of Religion and Related Categories* (Oxford: Oxford University Press, 2007); and Bernard Sheehan, *Savagism and Civility: Indians and Englishmen in Colonial Virginia* (Cambridge: Cambridge University Press, 1980).

38. Williams, *Hireling Ministry,* 168.

39. Nussbaum, *Liberty of Conscience,* 36, as well as Canup, *Out of the Wilderness,* 125–133; Francis Jennings, *The Invasion of America: Indians, Colonialism, and the Cant of Conquest* (Chapel Hill: University of North Carolina Press, 1975); and Edmund S. Morgan, *Roger Williams: The Church and the State* (New York: Harcourt, 1967), 126–127. But see George Tinker, *Missionary Conquest: The Gospel and Native American Cultural Genocide* (Minneapolis, MN: Augsburg Press, 1993), 24.

40. See Richard W. Cogley, *John Eliot's Mission to the Indians before King Philip's War* (Cambridge, MA: Harvard University Press, 1999), 49, 167–168. Eliot's work was instrumental in the founding of the Society for the Propagation of the Gospel in 1649. The governor of the SPG, the chemist Robert Boyle, took particular interest in Eliot's efforts to translate the New Testament (a project of which Williams was highly critical): "Wee are glad to heare of the progress of [the] Gospell . . . tending to the glory of God & [the] spirituall good of those poore naked Sonnes of Adam." Robert Boyle, "Letter to the Commissioners of the United Colonies on Indian Civilization, March 7, 1664," *Yale Indian Papers Project,* ed. P. Grant-Costa et al., http://jake.library.yale.edu:8080/neips/data/html/1664.03.07.00/1664.03.07.00.html.

41. John Eliot, "The Glorious Progress of the Gospel amongst the Indians in New England," in *The Eliot Tracts: With Letters from John Eliot to Thomas Thorowgood and Richard Baxter,* ed. Michael P. Clark (Westport, CT: Praeger, 2003), 158; Thomas Flint and Simon Willard, "The Cleare Sunshine of the Gospell,

breaking forth upon the Indians of New-England," in *The Eliot Tracts,* 114–115. For more detail, see Roy Harvey Pearce, "The 'Ruines of Mankind': The Indian and the Puritan Mind," *Journal of the History of Ideas* 13 (1952): 200–217, 212.

42. Eliot, "Glorious Progress," 159.

43. Williams, "Letter to the Town of Providence 15 Jan. 1681/2," in *Correspondence,* 2.774.

44. The Chasmore case also testifies to the fragility of order in Williams's fledgling colony. For background, see LaFantasie, "The Richard Chasmore Case, Summer 1656–1657," in Williams, *Correspondence,* 2.464–470.

45. "The Letter of Mr. Eliot to T. S. [Thomas Shephard] concerning the late work of God among the Indians, 'The Cleare Sun-shine of the Gospell,'" in *The Eliot Tracts,* 124.

46. Williams, "Letter to John Winthrop, c. 9 Sep. 1637," in *Correspondence,* 1.117.

47. Williams, "Letter to the General Court of Massachusetts Bay, 7 May 1668," in *Correspondence,* 2.577, "Letter to the General Court of Massachusetts Bay, 12 May 1656," in *Correspondence,* 2.451, and "Letter to [General Court of Commissioners of Providence plantations?], 25 Aug. 1658," in *Correspondence,* 2.489.

48. Williams concluded: "They are a Melancholy people, & judg themselves, (By the former Sachim & these English) oppressed, & wronged: you may knock out their braines, & yet not make them peaceably to surrender; even as some oxen will die before they will rise; yet with patience, & gentle meanes will rise, & draw, & does good service." Williams, "Letter from Roger Williams to Robert Carr, March 1, 1666," *Yale Indian Papers Project,* http://jake.library.yale.edu:8080/neips/data/html/1666.03.01.00/1666.03.01.00.html. These complaints about the Americans postdate the Pequot War significantly, the event that Jessica Stern has identified as a turning point for Williams, after which she suggests that he became much more appreciative of Indian culture. Stern, "A *Key* into *The Bloudy Tenent.*"

49. Nussbaum, *Liberty of Conscience,* 52; Davis, *Moral Theology,* 51.

50. Nussbaum mistakenly assumes that "antichristian" was a reference to atheists, rather than followers of the papal Antichrist (Nussbaum, "The First Founder"). It is often claimed that Williams proposed to tolerate atheists, although he never mentioned them explicitly. One contemporary critic of *The Bloudy Tenent* ventriloquized its author thus: "Dear Brother Atheist, you are a godly pious hereticke, and have no God but your conscience; and doe not for feare of your conscience believe that there is a God, and I dare not rebuke you, but be going on in your Divinity; I have as little infallible assurance there is a God, as you have there is no God, and neither you nor I are to be punished for our consciences" (Samuel Rutherford, quoted in John Coffey, *Persecution*

and Toleration, 34). Williams's failure to *exclude* atheists explicitly was itself significant and placed him at the edge of the radical fringe.

51. Richard Mather, *Church-Government and Church-Covenant Discussed* (London, 1643), 83 (my emphasis).

52. "Mr Cotton's Letter," 362.

53. Ibid., 347 (my emphasis).

54. Nussbaum, *Liberty of Conscience,* 54. See also Perry Miller, *Roger Williams: His Contribution to the American Tradition* (Indianapolis, IN: Bobbs-Merrill, 1953), 49–52.

55. The Massachusetts Bay charter also cited evangelizing the Americans as "the principall Ende of this Plantacion." "The Charter of Massachusetts Bay—1629," *The Avalon Project,* Yale Law School, http://avalon.law.yale.edu/17th_century/mass03.asp.

56. Williams, *Hireling Ministry,* 168–169. After he renounced his ministry, Williams continued to preach informally. His final surviving letter reports his efforts to solicit Eliot's help in publishing his sermons. Williams, "To Governor Simon Bradstreet, 6 May 1682," in *Correspondence,* 2.777.

57. Nussbaum, *Liberty of Conscience,* 47; Williams, "Letter to an Assembly of Commissioners, 17 Nov. 1677," in *Correspondence,* 2.750.

58. Williams, "Letter to Mrs. Anne Sadleir, ca. Winter 1652/53," in *Correspondence,* 1.375. See also *Christenings,* 38.

59. Acts 17:10–12 KJV (KJV of 1611, orthography updated).

60. Williams, *Hireling Ministry,* 151.

61. Williams, "Letter to Mrs. Anne Sadleir," in *Correspondence,* 1.376.

62. "From Mrs. Anne Sadleir, ca. Winter 1652/53," in *Correspondence,* 1.377. Sadleir also took issue with his recommendation of Milton's *Eikonoklastes,* a response to Charles I's *Eikon Basilike*—"For Meltons book that you desire I should read if I be not mistaken, that is he that has wrot a book of the lawfulness of devorce, and if report sais true he had at that time two or thre wives living. This perhaps were good doctrine in new England, but it is most abominable in old England. For his book that he wrot against the late King that you would have me read, you should have taken notice of gods judgment upon [him] who stroke him with blindness. . . . God has began his Judgment upon him here, his punishment will be here after in hell" (378–379).

63. Williams, "A Brief Reply to a Short Book," 104.

64. Williams, "Christenings," 40.

65. Canup describes this as a process of "mutual acculturation." Canup, *Out of the Wilderness,* 144.

66. I have omitted the Narragansett translation.

67. The *Key* also reports a dialogue overheard between the Narragansett sachim, Miantonomo, and a "Qunnihiticut Indian," who complained that Williams's

teachings about the afterlife contradicted what "our fathers have told us, that our soules goes to the Southwest." "[W]hen did he (naming my selfe) see a soule goes to Heaven or Hell? The Sachim . . . replied[:] He hath books and writings, and one which God himselfe made, concerning mens soules, and therefore may well know more than wee that have none, but take all upon trust from our forefathers" (*Key,* 220). For a more detailed treatment of Williams's evangelical toleration among the Americans, see Bejan, "'When the Word of the Lord Runs Freely.'"

68. "Mr Cotton's Letter," 370.

69. Williams, "Letter to the General Court of Massachusetts Bay, 5 Oct. 1654," in *Correspondence,* 2.409–410.

70. Unsurprisingly, Williams goes unmentioned in Gary Remer's account of dialogue as the forefront of tolerant early modernity in *Humanism and the Rhetoric of Toleration* (University Park: Pennsylvania State University Press, 1996). And yet *The Bloudy Tenent* and its sequel were written in the form of dialogues between "Truth" and "Peace" and were decidedly harmonious and consensual affairs.

71. Canup, *Out of the Wilderness,* 129.

72. Four Quakers were publicly executed (Marmaduke Stephenson, William Robinson, Mary Dryer, and William Ledra) in Massachusetts, and many more were imprisoned or had their death sentences reduced to public flogging and ostracism. For more on the Quaker executions, see Carla Gardina Pestana, *Quakers and Baptists in Colonial Massachusetts* (Cambridge: Cambridge University Press, 1991), and "The Quaker Executions as Myth and History," *The Journal of American History* 80, no. 2 (1993): 441–469.

73. Walsham, *Charitable Hatred,* 47.

74. Cotton Mather, *Magnalia Christi Americana,* ed. T. Robbins, 2 vols. (Hartford, 1853), 2.522

75. The Quakers denied this, although the most "egregious" of them, William Edmundson, confessed that "if the Lord God did stir up any of his Daughters to be a Sign of the nakedness of others he believe it to be a great Cross to a Modest womans Spirit, but the Lord must be obeyed" (*George Fox,* 310).

76. This concern with verbal persecution was long-standing. In an early letter to Winthrop, Williams had announced that it would ever be his "endeavour to pacifie and allay where I meete with rigid and censorious spirits who not only blame your actions but doome your persons: and indeede it was one of the first grounds of my dislike of John Smith . . . and especially of his wife viz: their judging of your Persons as divills &c." Williams, "Letter to John Winthrop, 16 April 1638," in *Correspondence,* 1.149.

77. Williams, "To John Throckmorton, ca. 23 July 1672," in *Correspondence,* 2.664, and *George Fox,* 6.

78. Williams, "Letter to John Throckmorton, ca. 23 July 1672," in *Correspondence*, 2.662–663, 666, 656. When his opponents pointed out that the title *George Fox Digg'd Out His Burrowes* implied "scorn and derision," Williams defended himself by "protesting before the Lord, that I had no such thought." Ibid., 53.

79. Williams, "Letter to Governor John Winthrop, ca. 14 June 1638," in *Correspondence*, 1.164–165. Cotton Mather declared that Williams was "a Haberdasher of small Questions against the Power." Quoted in *Correspondence*, 1.167fn13.

80. Williams, "Letter to John Whipple, 24 August 1669," in *Correspondence*, 2.602–604. Williams criticized Whipple for neglecting this maxim and disrupting town meetings by "Continually and Voluntarily thrust[ing]" himself in "amongst Your Adversaries, though you declaime agnst their Persons, Meetings and practices, and You to them be as wellcome as Water into a Ship."

81. Williams, "Letter to the Town of Providence, ca. Jan. 1654/5," in *Correspondence*, 2.423–424. This discussion was addressed to Quakers who refused to join the militia in the latest conflict with local tribes. Williams thought that there were at least two civil duties against which one could never claim conscience—taxes and military service. See Timothy Hall, *Separating Church and State: Rogers Williams and Religious Liberty* (Champaign: University of Illinois Press, 1998), 107. As we shall see in Chapter 3 and the Conclusion, Williams would volunteer to serve as a captain of the militia himself during King Philip's War.

82. For a deft treatment of this issue, see Hall, *Separating Church and State*, 99–111.

83. Williams, "Letter to the Town of Providence, 31 Aug. 1648," in *Correspondence*, 1.238.

84. *George Fox*, 39.

85. Quoted in "Samuel Gorton in Providence, 1640/41," in *Correspondence*, 1.211.

86. Williams, "Letter to Governor John Leverett, 11 Oct. 1675," in *Correspondence*, 2.704.

87. Williams, "Town of Providence to the Governor and council of Rhode Island, 31 August 1668," in *Correspondence*, 2.580–581, and "Christenings," 39. In *Hireling Ministry*, he said of the "Second sort" of offensive opinions (i.e., "opinions of Incivility") "doubtlesse the opinions as well as practices are the proper Object of the civill sword" (180).

88. *Key*, 210; *Bloudy Tenent*, 92–93; "Mr Cotton's Letter," 412.

89. As we shall see in Chapter 3, something quite like this system was adopted as part of the Cromwellian church settlement. See Jeffrey Collins, *The Allegiance of Thomas Hobbes* (Oxford: Oxford University Press, 2005), 167–168, and "The Church Settlement of Oliver Cromwell," *History* 83 (2002): 18–40.

90. According to Clark Gilpin, "Williams's interpretation . . . implied that the witnesses required complete freedom to speak and write as their consciences

directed them. Only if they were left unfettered by the state could the witnesses carry out their eschatological task of razing the popish additions to Christ's holy temple." W. Clark Gilpin, *The Millenarian Piety of Roger Williams* (Chicago: University of Chicago Press, 1979), 84.

91. Cotton, *Reply to Mr Williams,* 36.

92. Williams, *Hireling Ministry,* 179–180.

93. Williams, "Letter to the Town of Providence, 31 Aug. 1648," in *Correspondence,* 1.238.

94. Ibid.

95. Williams, "Letter to John Winthrop Jr., 1648," in *Correspondence,* 1.257. For the seminal treatment of Williams's millenarianism, see Gilpin, *Millenarian Piety.*

96. Williams, *Bloudy Tenent,* 204, and "Letter to the Town of Providence, ca. Jan. 1654/5," in *Correspondence,* 2.424.

97. Williams's reliance on ship metaphors resembles James Tully's vision of multicultural constitutionalism, except that Tully assumes that this ship of state will, over time, become a happy and "harmonious" community of differences. See James Tully, *Strange Multiplicity: Constitutionalism in an Age of Diversity* (Cambridge: Cambridge University Press, 1995), 28.

98. Quoted in Vernon Parrington, *Main Currents in American Thought: The Colonial Mind, 1620–1800* (Norman: University of Oklahoma Press, 1987), 73.

99. *Documents of the Senate of the State of New York* (Albany: New York State Legislature, 1902), 14.400. Rhode Island refused to send a delegation to the Constitutional Convention and failed to ratify the new federal Constitution until 1790, well after the adoption of the First Amendment.

100. Quoted in Williams, "Samuel Gorton in Providence," in *Correspondence,* 1.211.

3. "If It Be without Contention"

1. For more on the "Popish Plot" and its significance for Lockean toleration, see Chapter 4.

2. Patricia Springborg, "Hobbes, Donne and the Virginia Company: *Terra Nullius* and 'The Bulimia of Dominium,'" *History of Political Thought* 36, no. 1 (January 1, 2015): 113–164.

3. Martha Nussbaum, *Liberty of Conscience: In Defense of America's Tradition of Religious Equality* (New York: Basic Books, 2008), 42.

4. As in Hobbes's "The Answer of Mr. Hobbes to Sir William Davenant's Preface before *Gondibert,*" in *The English Works of Thomas Hobbes,* ed. William Molesworth (London: Bohn, 1840), 4.449–450.

5. See Hobbes's letter to Josiah Pullen (n. 193, February 1673) in response to his request for a copy of Hobbes's *Opera Philosophica* for his alma mater, Magdalen Hall (now Hertford College), Oxford. "You know how much they have been decryed by Dr Wallis & others of the greatest sway in the Vniversity; and therfore to offer them to any Colledge or Hall had been a greater signe of humility . . . than I have yet attained to. For your owne civility in approving them I give you many thanks." In *The Correspondence of Thomas Hobbes,* ed. Noel Malcolm (Oxford: Oxford University Press, 1994), 2.729.

6. Michael Oakeshott's account of Hobbes as the preeminent theorist of "civil association" has been influential in this regard. Michael Oakeshott, *Hobbes on Civil Association* (Indianapolis, IN: Liberty Fund, 1975). See also Étienne Balibar, *Violence and Civility: On the Limits of Political Philosophy,* trans. G. M. Goshgarian (New York: Columbia University Press, 2015), chap. 2; Richard Boyd, *Uncivil Society: The Perils of Pluralism and the Making of Modern Liberalism* (New York: Lexington Books, 2004), chap. 2; Stephen Daniel, "Civility and Sociability: Hobbes on Man and Citizen," *Journal of the History of Philosophy* 18 (1980), 209–215; Pat Moloney, "Hobbes, Savagery, and International Anarchy," *American Political Science Review* 105 (2011): 189–204; Markku Peltonen, *The Duel in Early Modern England: Civility, Politeness and Honour* (Cambridge: Cambridge University Press, 2006), 170–171; and Steven B. Smith, *Political Philosophy* (New Haven, CT: Yale University Press, 2013), 161–164.

7. For the former, see Quentin Skinner, "Hobbes and the Social Control of Unsociability," in *The Oxford Handbook of Hobbes,* ed. A. P. Martinich and Kinch Hoekstra (Oxford: Oxford University Press, 2013). For the latter, see J. S. Maloy, "The First Machiavellian Moment in America," *American Journal of Political Science* 55 (2011): 450–462; and Srinivas Avamarudan, "Hobbes and America," in *The Postcolonial Enlightenment: Eighteenth-Century Colonialism and Postcolonial Theory,* ed. Daniel Carey and Lynn Festa (Oxford: Oxford University Press, 2009).

8. Leo Strauss, *The Political Philosophy of Hobbes, Its Basis and Genesis* (Chicago: University of Chicago Press, 1952).

9. Civility in the sense in which I am interested here—as a conversational virtue particularly pertinent in the practice of disagreement—is related to the ideas of bourgeois sociability, peaceableness, politeness, and secularity identified by scholars, but reducing it to these neglects some of the most unique and interesting features of Hobbes's account. See also Anna Bryson, *From Courtesy to Civility: Changing Codes of Conduct in Early Modern England* (Oxford: Oxford University Press, 1997); and Keith Thomas, "The Social Origins of Hobbes's Political Thought," in *Hobbes Studies,* ed. K. C. Brown (Oxford: Blackwell Press, 1965): 185–236.

10. Alan Ryan, "A More Tolerant Hobbes?" in *Justifying Toleration: Conceptual and Historical Perspectives*, ed. Susan Mendus (Cambridge: Cambridge University Press, 1988): 37–59. *Erastianism*, the theological position that the civil authorities should be supreme in religion as well as politics, was named after the sixteenth-century theologian Thomas Erastus.

11. See Jeffrey Collins, *The Allegiance of Thomas Hobbes* (Oxford: Oxford University Press, 2005); and Mark Goldie, "The Reception of Hobbes," in *The Cambridge History of Political Thought 1450–1700*, ed. J. H. Burns (Cambridge: Cambridge University Press, 1991): 589–615.

12. Goldie, "The Reception of Hobbes," 610–613.

13. See Collins's *Allegiance of Thomas Hobbes*, as well as Arash Abizadeh, "Publicity, Privacy, and Religious Toleration in Hobbes' *Leviathan*," *Modern Intellectual History* 10, no. 2 (August 1, 2013): 261–291; Jon Parkin, *Taming the Leviathan: The Reception of the Political and Religious Ideas of Thomas Hobbes in England, 1640–1700* (Cambridge: Cambridge University Press, 2007); Eric Nelson, *The Hebrew Republic: Jewish Sources and the Transformation of European Political Thought* (Cambridge, MA: Harvard University Press, 2010), chap. 3; Richard Tuck, "Hobbes and Locke on Toleration," in *Thomas Hobbes and Political Theory*, ed. Mary Dietz (Lawrence: University Press of Kansas, 1990), 153–171; and Noel Malcolm, *Aspects of Hobbes* (Oxford: Clarendon Press, 2002). It also builds on the arguments made in Teresa M. Bejan, "Difference without Disagreement: Rethinking Hobbes on 'Independency' and Toleration," *The Review of Politics* 78, no. 1 (2016): 1–25.

14. Crucially, Hobbesian education was not a matter of eradicating, but reorienting, men's passions. In emphasizing the transformative and educational side of Hobbes's political project, I follow David Johnston, *The Rhetoric of Leviathan: Thomas Hobbes and the Politics of Cultural Transformation* (Princeton, NJ: Princeton University Press, 1986); S. A. Lloyd, *Ideals as Interests in Hobbes's Leviathan: The Power of Mind over Matter* (Cambridge: Cambridge University Press, 1992); Quentin Skinner, *Reason and Rhetoric in the Philosophy of Hobbes* (Cambridge: Cambridge University Press, 1996); and Mark E. Button, *Contract, Culture, and Citizenship: Transformative Liberalism from Hobbes to Rawls* (University Park: Pennsylvania State University Press, 2010). See also Teresa M. Bejan, "Teaching the *Leviathan*," *Oxford Review of Education* 36 (2010): 607–626.

15. John Aubrey, "Thomas Hobbes," in *Aubrey's Brief Lives*, ed. O. L. Dick (Boston: Godine, 1996), 150.

16. For an account of Hobbes's mature "civil science" as the knowledge of causes and consequences, see Quentin Skinner, "Hobbes's Changing Conception of Civil Science," in *Visions of Politics*, vol. 3 (Cambridge: Cambridge University Press, 2002), 66–86.

17. There are many changes—conceptual, philosophical, and aesthetic—over the course of Hobbes's writings, but his analysis of contumely as a source of conflict is remarkably consistent. See Arash Abizadeh, "Hobbes on the Causes of War: A Disagreement Theory," *American Political Science Review* 105 (2011): 298–315; and Gabriella Slomp, "Hobbes on Glory and Civil Strife," in *The Cambridge Companion to Hobbes's* Leviathan, ed. Patricia Springborg (Cambridge: Cambridge University Press, 2007). As for religion, Richard Tuck argues for a seismic shift between *De Cive* and *Leviathan,* from principled Episcopacy to Independency and toleration. Richard Tuck, "Warrender's *De Cive*," *Political Studies* 33 (1985): 313. However, Lodi Nauta and Jeffrey Collins have argued persuasively for continuity underlying any changes in presentation or argumentation due to the shifting political contexts. See Collins, *The Allegiance of Thomas Hobbes;* and Nauta, "Hobbes on Religion and the Church between the *Elements of Law* and *Leviathan*: A dramatic change of direction?" *Journal of the History of Ideas* 63 (2002): 577–598.

18. For the central importance of glory to Hobbes's political theory, see Abizadeh, "Hobbes on the Causes of War"; Julie Cooper, "Vainglory, Modesty, and Political Agency in the Political Theory of Thomas Hobbes," *Review of Politics* 72 (2010), 241–269; Strauss, *The Political Philosophy of Hobbes;* Slomp, "Hobbes on Glory and Civil Strife"; and Richard Tuck, "The Utopianism of *Leviathan*," in *Leviathan after 350 Years,* ed. Tom Sorrell and Luc Foisneau (Oxford: Oxford University Press, 2004).

19. For more on microaggressions, see the Introduction. I am grateful to Clifton Mark for discussions on this point.

20. Hobbes, "Considerations upon the reputation, loyalty, manners, & religion of Thomas Hobbes of Malmesbury written by himself, by way of letter to a learned person," in *The English Works of Thomas Hobbes,* 4.433. Aubrey rebuts several rumors in his "Brief Life," including the charge that Hobbes was afraid of the dark. As for the illegitimate daughter, this claim has been accepted most recently by A. P. Martinich in *Hobbes* (London: Routledge, 2005), 8. Others, including Noel Malcolm, are more skeptical. See "A Visit with Noel Malcolm," *The Leviathan Index* (April 15, 2009), https://leviathanindex09.wordpress.com/2009/04/15/a-visit-with-noel-malcolm/.

21. See Skinner, "Hobbes and the Social Control of Unsociability"; and Peltonen, *The Duel in Early Modern England,* 171.

22. The letter (n. 28) from Hobbes to his pupil in Paris is a wonderful example of tutelary chastisement: "First therefore I must humbly beseech you to avoyd all offensiue speech, not only open reviling but also that Satyricall way of nipping that some use. The effect of it is the cooling of the affection of your servants, & [the] prouoking of the hatred of your equals. So that he which useth harsh languadge whether downright or obliquely shall be sure to haue many haters,

& he that hath so, it will be a wonder if he haue not many iust occasions of Duell . . . neither words uttered in heate of Anger, nor [the] wordes of youths unknowne in the world, or not knowne for Vertue are of scandall sufficient to ground an honourable duell on" (*Correspondence,* 2.52–53).

23. On this point, see Strauss, *The Political Philosophy of Hobbes;* Slomp, "Hobbes on Glory and Civil Strife; and Skinner, "Hobbes and the Social Control of Unsociability."

24. For the latter, see Strauss, *The Political Philosophy of Hobbes;* and C. B. Macpherson, *The Political Theory of Possessive Individualism.*

25. Abizadeh, "Hobbes on the Causes of War," 196–197, 202.

26. For instance, Hobbes defended the pope against the "Anti-Christ" charge in his response to Cardinal Bellarmine (L, iii.42.874-876). The relationship between Hobbes and Catholicism is more complicated than is generally supposed. Much of his anti-Catholic rhetoric is allegorical and aimed at the Episcopalian and Presbyterian divines who claimed *jure divino* authority. Moreover, *Leviathan* makes the scandalous suggestion that "Christian Kings" may "if they please . . . commit the government of their Subjects in matters of Religion to the Pope" so long as they insist that "the Pope is in that point Subordinate to them" (iii.42.866). Collins stresses Hobbes's affinity for the Gallican strain of English Catholicism exemplified by the Blackloists, led by his friend Thomas White, aka "Blacklo" (*The Allegiance of Thomas Hobbes,* 90–91).

27. See also Boyd, *Uncivil Society,* chap. 2. The growing literature on Hobbes's critique of rhetoric has largely ignored this issue of contumely. See Bryan Garsten, *Saving Persuasion: A Defense of Rhetoric and Judgment* (Cambridge, MA: Harvard University Press, 2006); Johnston, *The Rhetoric of Leviathan;* Victoria Kahn, *Rhetoric, Prudence and Skepticism in the Renaissance* (Ithaca, NY: Cornell University Press, 1985); and Skinner, *Reason and Rhetoric.*

28. Jeremy Waldron, *The Harm in Hate Speech* (Cambridge, MA: Harvard University Press, 2012), 232.

29. The word *mere* is introduced in Michael Silverthorne's translation.

30. See Abizadeh, "Hobbes on the Causes of War."

31. *Behemoth* argued that between the Presbyterians, Archbishop Laud, and popular anti-Popery there was plenty of blame to go around. In defending *Leviathan* in the 1668 Appendix, Hobbes glossed his argument as follows: "The cause of the civil war which was being waged at that time . . . was nothing other than the quarreling, first between the Roman Church and the Anglican, and then within the Anglican Church between the Episcopalian pastors and Presbyterian pastors, about theological issues" (L Appendix, iii.3.1226).

32. Thomas Hobbes, "An Historical Narration concerning Heresy, and the Punishment thereof," in *The English Works of Thomas Hobbes,* 4.388.

33. Hobbes's example was Galileo, although his objection to the Inquisition was that only civil, and not ecclesiastical, authorities should have the authority to punish individuals for their opinions: "For disobedience may lawfully be punished in them, that against the Laws teach even true Philosophy. Is it because they tend to disorder in Government, as countenancing Rebellion, or Sedition? Then let them be silenced, and the Teachers punished" (L, ii.46.1102).

34. For example, Edward Bagshaw (whom we will encounter again in Chapter 4) argued that the essential indifference of worship meant that individuals should have "latitude" to follow their consciences therein. For Hobbes's influence on Bagshaw, see Collins, *The Allegiance of Thomas Hobbes*, 238–239. After the Restoration, latitudinarian Anglicans like Stillingfleet (author of *Irenicum* [1659/1662]) in favor of comprehension were also accused of "Hobbism" by their critics. Goldie, "The Reception of Hobbes," 612–613. See also John Marshall, "The Ecclesiology of the Latitude-men, 1660–1698: Stillingfleet, Tillotson, and 'Hobbism,'" *The Journal of Ecclesiastical History* 36, no. 3 (1985): 407–427.

35. See Hans R. Guggisberg, "The Defence of Religious Toleration and Religious Liberty in Early Modern Europe," *History of European Ideas* 4 (1983): 35–50.

36. For Montaigne's influence on this point, see Quentin Skinner, "Hobbes on Rhetoric and the Construction of Morality," in *Visions of Politics*, 3.121, 133–134.

37. For this charge and Hobbes's reply, see Hobbes, "An Answer to Bishop Bramhall's Book, called 'The Catching of the Leviathan,'" in *The English Works of Thomas Hobbes*, ed. Molesworth (London: Bohn, 1840), 4.289–291, 360–361.

38. Jeremy Waldron has identified this as Locke's most important argument in favor of toleration. However, as we shall see in Chapter 4, Locke made the same point in his early anti-toleration *Tracts*. See Waldron, "Locke: Toleration and the Rationality of Persecution," in *Justifying Toleration: Conceptual and Historical Approaches*, ed. Susan Mendus (Cambridge: Cambridge University Press, 1988), 61–86.

39. John Milton, *Areopagitica: A Speech of Mr. John Milton for the liberty of unlicensed printing to the Parliament of England* [1644] (Cambridge: Cambridge University Press, 1981), 50. Grotius complained that he could not "approve" of Hobbes's view in *De Cive* that "it is the duty of each private individual to follow the official religion of his country . . . if not with internal assent, then at least with outward observance." Quoted in Noel Malcolm, "Hobbes and the European Republic of Letters," in *Aspects of Hobbes*, 472–473.

For Milton's part, such "rigid external formality" was "gross conforming stupidity, a stark congealment of 'wood and hay and stubble' forced and frozen together . . . more to the sudden degenerating of a church than many subdichotomies of petty schism" (*Areopagitica*, 60). Their mutual friend John Aubrey reports that Milton "did not like [Hobbes] at all, but he would acknowledge him to be a man of great parts, and a learned man." John Aubrey, "John Milton," in *Aubrey's Brief Lives*, 203.

40. Andrew Murphy, "Tolerance, Toleration, and the Liberal Tradition," *Polity* 29: 610–615.

41. For arguments that Hobbes saw a tolerant society characterized by significant freedom of thought and (some) expression as desirable, see Edwin Curley, "Hobbes and the Cause of Religious Toleration," in *The Cambridge Companion to Hobbes's* Leviathan, ed. Patricia Springborg (Cambridge: Cambridge University Press, 2007); Malcolm, *Aspects of Hobbes;* and J. Judd Owen, "The Tolerant *Leviathan:* Hobbes and the Paradox of Liberalism," *Polity* 37, no. 1 (2005): 120–148.

42. Goldie, "The Reception of Hobbes," 611, 613.

43. "Thus in my judgment doth that learned Protestant absolutely clear the Papists of idolatry." Quoted in Goldie, "The Reception of Hobbes," 613–614. See also Collins, *The Allegiance of Thomas Hobbes,* 139, 179–180.

44. While Whig historians have tended to link Independents as such with the tolerationist cause, as Jeffrey Collins, Andrew Murphy, and Blair Worden have stressed, this is a mistake—radical tolerationists like Williams felt very strongly that in preserving a national establishment, Cromwell did not go far enough. For the true and largely unintended extent of toleration during the Cromwellian Protectorate, see Collins, *The Allegiance of Thomas Hobbes,* 102, 170–171; Murphy, *Conscience and Community: Revisiting Toleration and Religious Dissent in Early Modern England and America* (University Park: Pennsylvania State University Press, 2001), chap. 3; and Worden, "Toleration and the Cromwellian Protectorate," in *Persecution and Toleration,* ed. W. J. Shiels (Oxford: Blackwell, 1984): 207, 210.

45. Quoted in Tuck, "Hobbes and Locke on Toleration," 167. Parker would be accused of Hobbism, in turn, for his *Discourse of Ecclesiastical Politie* (1670) by no less an authority than Locke, who complained: "That the magistrate should restrain seditious doctrines who denies, but because he may, then has he power over all other doctrines to forbid or impose . . . how far is this short of Mr. Hobbes's doctrine?" John Locke, "On Samuel Parker" (c. 1669–1670), in *Locke: Political Essays,* ed. Mark Goldie (Cambridge: Cambridge University Press, 1990), 211.

46. For an in-depth analysis of this passage in light of the historical significance of "Independency" and its implications for the tolerant Hobbes, see Bejan, "Difference without Disagreement."

47. Hobbes, *Leviathan,* iii.47.1114.

48. Tuck, "Hobbes and Locke on Toleration," 163. See Abizadeh, "Publicity, Privacy, and Religious Toleration"; and Collins, *The Allegiance of Thomas Hobbes*, 102–103. For some pushback against tolerationist readings of this passage, see Johann Sommerville, "Hobbes and Independency,". *Rivista di storia della filosofia* 21 (2004).

49. See Bejan, "Difference without Disagreement," 5.

50. Hobbes's distinction here between speech "in a Sermon, or in publique" supports Abizadeh's contention that he envisioned some forms of speaking in front of an audience—"in the sight of the Multitude" (ibid., iii.31.564)—as "private." However, it also shows that the sovereign had a role in regulating even "private" preaching for the sake of discretion, a point which Abizadeh denies and to which I will return below. See Abizadeh, "Publicity, Privacy, and Religious Toleration."

51. Hobbes, "Preface before Gondibert," in *The English Works of Thomas Hobbes*, 4.448.

52. Peltonen, *The Duel in Early Modern England*, 154.

53. S.C, *The Art of Complaisance, or the Meanes to Oblige in Conversation* (London: John Starkey, 1673), 5, 31.

54. Madeleine De Scudéry, *Conversations upon many subjects*, trans. Ferrand Spence (London, 1683), 164.

55. William Cavendish, *A Discourse against Flatterie* (1611), 4. For the disputed question of authorship, see Arlene Saxonhouse, "Hobbes and the *Horae Subsecivae*," in *Three Discourses*, eds. N. Reynolds and A. Saxonhouse (Chicago: University of Chicago Press, 1996), 8; and Skinner, *Visions of Politics*, iii.45.

56. B[enjamin] F[urly], *The Worlds Honour Detected, And, for the unprofitableness thereof, rejected* (London, 1663), throughout, but see especially 22–23, 50–51.

57. Christopher Wase, *Dictionarium Minus: A Compendious Dictionary, English-Latin and Latin-English* (London, 1662); John Clarke, *An Introduction to the Making of Latin* (London: A. Bettesworth, 1721).

58. Tacitus used the phrase to describe a virtuous comportment in contrast with the Emperor Tiberius's failure to maintain the people's faith: "The title of 'father of his country,' which the people had so often thrust on him, Tiberius refused. . . . He did not thereby create a belief in his patriotism [*fidem civilis animi*]." Cornelius Tacitus, *The Annals* (c. 109 CE), in *The Complete Works of Tacitus*, trans. Alfred John Church, William Jackson Brodribb, and Sara Bryant (New York: Random House, 1942), 1.72. It occurs frequently in Suetonius's *The Lives of Twelve Caesars*. He writes in *Divus Julius*: "He bore with great moderation a virulent libel written against him by Aulus Caecinna, and the abusive lampoons of Pitholaiis, most highly reflecting on his reputation [*ciuili animo*]" (75.5); in *Divus Claudius*: "In him the civil and military virtues

were equally displayed [*fuisse autem creditor non minus gloriosi quam ciuilis animi*]" (1.4); and in *Divus Domitianus:* "From his earliest years Domitian was anything but courteous [*ab iuuenta minime ciuilis animi*], of a forward, assuming disposition, and extravagant both in his words and actions" (12.3). C. Suetonius Tranquillus, *The Lives of Twelve Caesars* (121 CE), trans. Alexander Thompson (Philadelphia: Gebbie and Co., 1889). I am grateful to John Oksanish and Emma Planinc for their insights on this point.

59. Hobbes, *De Cive*, 237. Silverthorne translates the phrase *animus civilis* in this sentence as *politeness*.

60. For an argument along similar lines, see Samantha Frost, "Faking It: Hobbes's Thinking-Bodies and the Ethics of Dissimulation," *Political Theory* 29 (2001): 30–57.

61. Mary Dietz, "Hobbes's Subject as Citizen," in *Thomas Hobbes and Political Theory,* ed. Mary Dietz (Lawrence: University Press of Kansas, 1990), 91–92, 96. Julie Cooper has drawn attention to Hobbes's reinterpretation of the Christian virtues of modesty and humility as a curricular priority. Cooper, "Vainglory, Modesty, and Political Agency," 243.

62. In what follows, I depart from Skinner's suggestion that Hobbes saw incivility exclusively as an ethical issue. Quentin Skinner, "Hobbes and the Social Control of Unsociability."

63. This was the fundamental issue in the debate over Hobbes's theory of obligation and the so-called Taylor-Warrender thesis. For a helpful overview, see K. C. Brown, *Hobbes Studies* (Oxford: Blackwell Press, 1965).

64. Compare Hobbes's list of the differences between mankind and genuinely social animals in *De Cive* and *Leviathan* (DC, 71; L, ii.17.260).

65. As Cooper has emphasized, Hobbes's insistence that the "Fountain" of all civil honors was "the Person of the Common-wealth" and "the Will of the Soveraigne" sought to undermine the traditional claims of the aristocracy to independent authority and status. To that end, Hobbes cited "Mr. Selden's most excellent treatise" *Titles of Honour* (1614), which emphasized the historical contingency and diminution of these "offices of honour . . . into mere titles" since the Norman Conquest, approvingly. Cooper, "Vainglory, Modesty, and Political Agency," 258–263.

66. Collins argues that Hobbes actually coined the phrase "civill worship" in his translation of Thucydides as a synonym for civil religion in describing the "Religious worship of the Gentiles" (*The Allegiance of Thomas Hobbes,* 47). He also suggests that Hobbes referred to the idolatrous worship of the Greeks and Romans in *Leviathan* the same way (46 n. 210). I cannot find that Hobbes uses the phrase thus in the pages Collins cites (L, iii.45.1036–1040), although it does occur in Hobbes's distinction between the worship of a King's person with the idolatrous worship of his stool (iii.45.1032–1034). This is then

connected with the civil religion of the gentiles in the *Opera Latina*: "And Christ is called the *character* of the hypostasis of God. Nor did the gentile idolaters themselves always show a concern for resemblance in their idols, but worshipped them, not as similar, but as representative" (1033).

67. Alexandra Walsham, *Charitable Hatred: Tolerance and Intolerance in England, 1500–1700* (Manchester: Manchester University Press, 2006), 127–128.

68. The OL returns to the matter of dueling: "[F]rom a fellow-citizen, which words, however, are not punished by any law that has been made . . . the commonwealth wishes public words, that is, the laws, to matter more to the citizens than the words of a private man; it has neglected to lay down a punishment for such words, because the commonwealth regards those who cannot tolerate even words as the softest of all men" (L, ii.27.464–467).

69. See Bejan, "Difference without Disagreement."

70. Hobbes, "Considerations," 430–431.

71. He continued: "I confess, that for aught I have observed in history . . . [the] heathens were not at all behind us in point of virtue and moral duties, notwithstanding that we have had much more preaching, and they none at all" (B, 63).

72. "Seeing, then, in every Christian Common-wealth, the Civill Soveraign is the Supreme Pastor . . . it followeth also, that it is from the Civill Soveraign, that all other Pastors derive their right of Teaching, Preaching, and other functions" (L, iii.42.852). It followed that the sovereign could perform all of the functions of the clergy—including administering the sacraments (iii.42.856).

73. For the particulars of Hobbes's proposed reforms to the curriculum, see Bejan, "Teaching the *Leviathan*." Although Wallis mocked his arrogance for replacing Aristotle with *Leviathan*, Hobbes defended his "self-praise": "Where did those ministers learn their seditious doctrine, and to preach it, but there? Where therefore should preachers learn to teach loyalty, but there? And if your principles produced civil war, must not the contrary principles . . . produce peace? And consequently his book as far as it handles civil doctrine deserves to be taught there" (Hobbes, "Considerations," 438).

74. Tuck puts considerable weight on Hobbes's use of this phrase in *De Cive* to argue for reading that work as a conventional defense of Anglican episcopacy in contrast with *Leviathan*'s "defense" of toleration. Richard Tuck, Introduction to *De Cive*, xl. For a more skeptical reading, see Collins, *The Allegiance of Thomas Hobbes*, 66–68; Nauta, "Hobbes on Religion and the Church," 592; and Johann Sommerville, "Leviathan and Its Anglican Context," in *The Cambridge Companion to Hobbes's* Leviathan, ed. Patricia Springborg (Cambridge: Cambridge University Press, 2007), 369–370.

75. This emphasis on the need for "discreet" preachers echoed his assertion in *Leviathan* that only the "correctives of discreet Masters," such "as are fit to take

away their Venime," could make the reading of classical authors safe under a monarchy (L, ii.29.508).

76. Collins, *The Allegiance of Thomas Hobbes,* 167–168. For more on the implications of these institutions for Hobbes's views on "Independency," see Bejan, "Difference without Disagreement."

77. Ibid., 96. The introduction to his translation of Thucydides made a similar point: "It is hard for any man to love that counsel which maketh him love himself the less. And it holdeth much more in a multitude, than in one man." Thomas Hobbes, "The History of the Grecian War, written by Thucydides," in *The English Works of Thomas Hobbes,* 8.xvi.

78. Hobbes, *Leviathan,* iii.27.456. Hobbes was not above invoking the evangelical precept to embarrass his opponents. "If I find my selfe amongst the Idolators of America, shall I that am a Christian, though not in Orders, think it a sin to preach Jesus Christ . . . or when I have preached, shall not I answer their doubts, and expound the Scriptures to them; that is, shall I not Teach? . . . to deny these Functions to those, to whom the Civill Soveraigne hath not denyed them, is a taking away of a lawfull Liberty, which is contrary to the Doctrine of Civill Government." Although in this passage Hobbes appears to argue for a natural liberty to evangelize among one's countrymen as among the "Idolators of America," his point is once again that the civil sovereign, not the clergy, is the proper source of ordination. Ibid., iii.46.1098.

79. Thus, we come to the limits of what Curley calls Hobbes's "Erasmian liberalism." Edwin Curley, "Hobbes and the Cause of Religious Toleration," 309–334, 314.

80. Richard Tuck, "Hobbes on Education," in *Philosophers on Education: New Historical Perspectives,* ed. Amelie Oksenberg Rorty (London: Routledge, 1998), 147–155.

81. Thomas Hobbes, "Markes of the Absurd Geometry, Rural Language, Scottish Church Politicks, and Barbarisms of John Wallis," in *The English Works of Thomas Hobbes,* 3.17–19.

82. Hobbes, "Considerations," 414. Tuck draws the tolerationist conclusion that Hobbes favored the abolition of all heresy laws—and presumably those proscribing blasphemy and other kinds of religious "scandal"—on the basis of his later writings on heresy ("Hobbes and Locke on Toleration," 160). But there is a significant difference between saying that he (and his *Leviathan*) should not be prosecuted for heresy and saying that no one else should. As Hobbes's discussion of Galileo demonstrated, his objection to inquisitions had to do with *who* was doing the silencing—i.e., "Ecclesiastiques"—rather than any injustice inherent in the undertaking (L, iii.46.1102).

83. Thomas Hobbes, "The Verse Life," in *Elements,* 264.

84. Contemporary reflections reported years later have Hobbes "making a 'shew of Religion' in the Cavendish chapel out of 'meer compliance to the Orders

of the Family." His evident pride in his willingness to conform to whatever was commanded of him means one should take Aubrey's assertion "that he was a Christian 'tis clear, for he received the sacrament of Dr. [John] Pierson, and in his confession to Dr. John Cosins at . . . his (as he thought) death-bed, declared that he liked the Religion of the Church of England best of all other" with more than a few grains of salt. Both quoted in Collins, *The Allegiance of Thomas Hobbes,* 245

85. Hobbes, "An Answer," 366–367.

86. Hobbes, "An Historical Narration," 407. The state of nature in religion initiated by the abolition of episcopacy persisted well into the Commonwealth period; thus, "when I wrote my *Leviathan* . . . I may safely say there was no lawful church in England, that could have maintained me in, or prohibited me from writing anything . . . and though there was preaching, such as it was, yet no common prayer" (Hobbes, "An Answer," 355).

87. Hobbes, "Considerations," 439.

88. Aubrey, "Thomas Hobbes," 152–153.

89. "Mr Hobbes has been always far from provoking any man, though when he is provoked, you find his pen as sharp as yours." Hobbes, "Considerations," 440, 439.

90. See Mark Knights, "'Meer Religion' and the 'Church–State' of Restoration England: The Impact and Ideology of James II's Declarations of Indulgence," in *A Nation Transformed: England after the Restoration,* ed. Alan Houston and Steve Pincus (Cambridge: Cambridge University Press, 2001).

91. The quotation is from Romans 14:3, 6.

4. "A Bond of Mutual Charity"

1. John Christian Laursen and Cary J. Nederman, *Beyond the Persecuting Society* (Philadelphia: University of Pennsylvania Press, 1998), 2–4.

2. John Dunn, *The Political Thought of John Locke* (Cambridge: Cambridge University Press, 1969), xi.

3. John Fell, the master of Christ Church college at Oxford during much of Locke's time there, quoted in Fox Bourne, *The Life of John Locke* (London: H.S. King & co., 1876), 1.484.

4. For Locke's dubious relationship to liberalism, see Duncan Bell, "What Is Liberalism?" *Political Theory* 42, no. 6 (2014): 682–715.

5. For the civilizational/imperial charge, see Uday Singh Mehta, *Liberalism and Empire* (Chicago: University of Chicago Press, 1999). See also Duncan Bell, "The Dream Machine: On Liberalism and Empire," in *Reordering the World: Essays on Liberalism and Empire* (Princeton, NJ: Princeton University Press, 2016). For the extension of the civilizational critique to Lockean toleration,

see Wendy Brown, *Regulating Aversion: Tolerance in the Age of Identity and Empire* (Princeton, NJ: Princeton University Press, 2008); John Dunn, "The Claim to Freedom of Conscience: Freedom of Speech, Freedom of Thought, Freedom of Worship?" in *The History of Political Thought and Other Essays* (Cambridge: Cambridge University Press, 1996), 100–120; John Gray, "Pluralism and Toleration in Contemporary Political Philosophy," *Political Studies* 48 (2000): 323–333; Jakob De Roover and S. N. Balagangadhara, "John Locke, Christian Liberty, and the Predicament of Liberal Toleration," *Political Theory* 36 (2008): 523–549; and Matthew Scherer, *Beyond Church and State: Democracy, Secularism and Conversion* (Cambridge: Cambridge University Press, 2013).

6. Jeremy Waldron, "Locke: Toleration and the Rationality of Persecution," in *Justifying Toleration: Conceptual and Historical Perspectives,* ed. Susan Mendus (Cambridge: Cambridge University Press, 1988): 61–86, 85. See also Ingrid Creppell, "Locke on Toleration: The Transformation of Constraint," *Political Theory* 24 (1996): 200–240; and Kirstie McClure, "Difference, Diversity, and the Limits of Toleration," *Political Theory* 18 (1990): 361–391.

7. Here I follow John Marshall in taking Locke's reference to the subjects of "the *Mufti* of *Constantinople,* who himself is entirely obedient to the *Ottoman* Emperor" as sincere and not simply as a veiled reference to Catholics—although it was certainly that, as well (*Letter Concerning Toleration,* 52). John Marshall, *John Locke: Resistance, Religion and Responsibility* (Cambridge: Cambridge University Press, 1994).

8. For the most recent criticism, see Rainer Forst, *Toleration in Conflict* (Cambridge: Cambridge University Press, 2013). The recent push to redeem Locke either exculpates him from the sin of intolerance—for example, in Jeremy Waldron, *God, Locke and Equality* (Cambridge: Cambridge University Press, 2002), 221–223; ignores the caveats—for example, in Anthony Wilhelm, "Good Fences and Good Neighbors: John Locke's Positive Doctrine of Toleration," *Political Research Quarterly* 52 (1999): 145–166; or justifies them—for example, in Richard Dees, *Trust and Toleration* (New York: Routledge Press, 2004), 109–110.

9. Quoted in Joseph Priestley, *Political Writings,* ed. Peter Miller (Cambridge: Cambridge University Press, 1993), xxvi–xxvii; and Annabel Patterson, *Early Modern Liberalism* (Cambridge: Cambridge University Press, 1997), 239–240, respectively.

10. See John Marshall, *John Locke, Toleration and Early Enlightenment Culture* (Cambridge: Cambridge University Press, 2006), 690.

11. For example, his unpublished "Critical Notes upon Edward Stillingfleet's Mischief and Unreasonableness of Separation" (1681); *The Reasonableness of Christianity* (1695) and its two *Vindications* (1695); and Locke's final

completed work, *An Essay for the Understanding of St. Paul's Epistles* (and its accompanying *Paraphrases*), published posthumously in 1707. The fourth and final *Letter* was left unfinished at his death in 1704. In addition to these texts, one might argue that all of Locke's major works were informed by his considerations on religious and moral disagreement, including *An Essay Concerning Human Understanding* (1690), the *Two Treatises of Government* (1689), and *Some Thoughts Concerning Education* (1693).

12. See Mark Goldie's Introduction to *A Letter Concerning Toleration*. Locke dedicated and sent the *Epistola* to his friend Philipp van Limborch, who arranged for its publication in 1689. The tradition of treating the English *Letter* as an authentic Lockean production stems from Locke's defense of the English text in the later *Letters*.

13. For examples of the Foucauldian reading that stresses the disciplinary processes and sublimated violence inherent in Locke's political theory, see James Tully, "Governing Conduct," in *Conscience and Casuistry in Early Modern Europe, Ideas in Context,* ed. Edmund Leites (Cambridge: Cambridge University Press, 1988), 12–71; and Uday Singh Mehta, *The Anxiety of Freedom: Imagination and Individuality in Locke's Political Thought* (Ithaca, NY: Cornell University Press, 1992). But see also Creppell, "Locke on Toleration," 200–240.

14. For discussion of the extent of Locke's authorship, see David Armitage, "John Locke, Carolina, and the *Two Treatises of Government,*" *Political Theory* 32 (2004): 602–627; Vicki Hsueh, "Giving Orders: Theory and Practice in the *Fundamental Constitutions of Carolina,*" *Journal of the History of Ideas* 63 (2002): 425–446; J. R. Milton, "John Locke and the *Fundamental Constitutions of Carolina,*" *Locke Newsletter* 21 (1990): 111–133; and Jack Turner, "John Locke, Christian Mission, and Colonial America," *Modern Intellectual History* 8, no. 2 (2011): 267–297.

15. The traditional genealogy runs from Locke to Kant and Mill, then Rawls.

16. John Dunn, *Locke* (Oxford: Oxford University Press, 2003), 1–5.

17. Hobbes complained about his years at Oxford in his short autobiography. See Thomas Hobbes, "The Prose Life," in *The Elements of Law, Natural and Politic: Human Nature and De Corpore Politico,* ed. J. C. A. Gaskin (Oxford: Oxford University Press, 2008), 245–254. There is no indication that Williams shared his friend Milton's legendary bitterness about his time at Christ's College, where he was routinely mocked as "The Lady of Christ's."

18. See, for example, Robert P. Kraynak, "John Locke: From Absolutism to Toleration," *American Political Science Review* 74 (1980): 53–69; Mark Lilla, *The Stillborn God: Religion, Politics, and the Modern West* (New York: Alfred A. Knopf, 2007); McClure, "Difference, Diversity, and the Limits of Toleration"; Leo Strauss, *Natural Right and History* (Chicago: University of Chicago Press, 1965); and Michael Zuckert, *Launching Liberalism: On Lockean Political*

Philosophy (Lawrence: University Press of Kansas, 2002). The determined insistence of many Straussians aside, not everyone clever in the seventeenth century was an atheist.

19. For this context, see Jeffrey Collins, *The Allegiance of Thomas Hobbes* (Oxford: Oxford University Press, 2005), 238–239.

20. A much earlier and different version of the argument of this chapter appears as Teresa M. Bejan, "John Locke on Toleration, (In)civility, and the Quest for Concord," *History of Political Thought* 37, no. 3 (2016).

21. The claim of Locke's early Hobbism is not now so fashionable as it once was; still, *The Tracts* remain Exhibit A. See, for example, Kraynak,"From Absolutism to Toleration," 37.

22. Locke, *The Correspondence of John Locke,* ed. E. S. De Beer (Oxford: Clarendon Press, 1976–1982), 1.41. He also excused the mistreatment of several Quakers at the hands of Oxford undergraduates: "If such people (who cannot in their carrage and raptures be thought any other than madd . . .) fall into the hands of young men . . . what can be expected but some usage?" (*Correspondence,* 1.84).

23. Locke maintained consistently that religious enthusiasm was a form of madness. See "Enthusiasm" (1682), in *A Letter Concerning Toleration,* 177–180, and Douglas John Casson, *Liberating Judgment: Fanatics, Skeptics, and John Locke's Politics of Probability* (Princeton, NJ: Princeton University Press, 2011).

24. Hobbes invoked the same anecdote in Chapter 12, "Of Religion," of *Leviathan* in his discussion of "The absurd opinions of Gentilisme" (L, ii.12.172).

25. On the relative importance of this point for Locke's later arguments for toleration compare Jeremy Waldron, "Locke: Toleration, and the Rationality of Persecution," in *Justifying Toleration: Conceptual and Historical Approaches,* ed. Susan Mendus (Cambridge: Cambridge University Press, 1988); and Paul Bou-Habib, "Locke, Sincerity, and the Rationality of Persecution," *Political Studies* 51 (2003): 611–626; with Timothy Stanton, "Locke and the Politics and Theology of Toleration," *Political Studies* 54 (2006): 84–102; and Alex Tuckness, "Rethinking the Intolerant Locke," *American Journal of Political Science* 46 (2002): 288–298.

26. In this, Locke sided with Cotton, who had insisted against Williams, "better hypocrites than profane persons," for "hypocrites give God his due in an outward form at least." Quoted in Andrew Murphy, *Conscience and Community: Revisiting Toleration and Religious Dissent in Early Modern England and America* (University Park: Pennsylvania State University Press, 2001), 157.

27. John Milton, *Areopagitica: A Speech of Mr. John Milton for the liberty of unlicensed printing to the Parliament of England* (Cambridge, Cambridge University Press, 1981 [1644]), 50.

28. Compare with Hobbes's appeals to Romans and Corinthians.

29. See Scott Sowerby, *Making Toleration: The Repealers and the Glorious Revolution* (Cambridge, MA: Harvard University Press, 2013).

30. Locke, *Correspondence*, 1.228.

31. Richard Ashcraft, *Revolutionary Politics and Locke's* Two Treatises of Government (Princeton, NJ: Princeton University Press, 1986), 88.

32. Mark Goldie, Introduction to Locke, *A Letter Concerning Toleration*, xxi. Since their publication in 1967, much has been made of Locke's curious "conservatism" in the *Tracts*. See Philip Abrams, Introduction to *John Locke: Two Tracts on Government*, ed. Philip Abrams (Cambridge: Cambridge University Press, 1967); and David Wootton, Introduction to *Locke: Political Writings* (Indianapolis, IN: Hackett, 1993). But see also Richard Ashcraft, who argues that dismissing the *Tracts* as "conservative" downplays the "significant development [that] took place in Locke's thinking about toleration" and is insensitive "to the *political* aspects of his development on this issue." Ashcraft, *Revolutionary Politics*, 88n51.

33. John Locke, "Essays on the Law of Nature (1663–1664)," in *Locke: Political Essays*, 132.

34. A decade later, he would expand upon the theme, arguing that "if [religious enthusiasts] are perfect innocents, only a little crazed, why cannot they be let alone, since, though perhaps their brains are a little out of order, their hands work well enough." Locke, "Toleration and Error" (1676), in *A Letter Concerning Toleration and Other Writings*, 170.

35. Kraynak, "Locke: From Absolutism to Toleration"; McClure, "Difference, Diversity, and the Limits of Toleration"; and Eric Nelson, *The Hebrew Republic: Jewish Sources and the Transformation of European Political Thought* (Cambridge, MA: Harvard University Press, 2010), 135–137, among others, also highlight the continuities.

36. See Mark Goldie's introductory note in *Locke: Political Essays*, 160.

37. See Goldie's account in *A Letter Concerning Toleration*, 146n8.

38. John Locke, "The Fundamental Constitutions of Carolina," in *Locke: Political Essays*, 178 (my emphasis).

39. Ibid., 178–179.

40. Ibid., 171.

41. Ibid., 178–179.

42. William Penn, "The Great Law of Pennsylvania," *Church and State in the Modern Age: A Documentary History*, ed. J. F. Maclear (Oxford: Oxford University Press, 1995 [1682]), 52–53.

43. John Locke, "Notes on the Pennsilvania Laws" (1686), MS f.9, fols 33–41. Partially reprinted in *A Letter Concerning Toleration*, 183. While Waldron's recent reconstruction of a Lockean argument in favor of laws against religious insult on this basis is not implausible, it is nevertheless mistaken. Jeremy Waldron,

The Harm in Hate Speech (Cambridge, MA: Harvard University Press, 2012), 213 and 273 n. 20. For a more in-depth argument about where Waldron goes wrong, see Bejan, "John Locke on Toleration."

44. Armitage, "John Locke, Carolina, and the *Two Treatises*," 607. The religious insult provision was still on the books as of 1698 but disappeared thereafter. Partition between North and South Carolina followed in 1729. See the "Fundamental Constitutions of Carolina, April 11, 1698," in *The Colonial and State Records of North Carolina* (Raleigh, NC: Carolina Charter Tercentenary Commission, 1963–), 8.857.

45. For the best and most comprehensive account of this period from the perspective of Locke's views on toleration, including his participation in Shaftesbury's campaign against "Popery," see Marshall, *John Locke, Toleration, and Early Enlightenment Culture.*

46. For a full account stressing Locke's radical *bona fides,* see Ashcraft, *Revolutionary Politics,* chap. 8.

47. Joseph Bergin, *The Politics of Religion in Early Modern France* (New Haven, CT: Yale University Press, 2014), chap. 11.

48. See Chapter 1.

49. Assertions of continuity between the *Letter* and *The Tracts,* especially, by Kraynak, "John Locke: From Absolutism to Toleration"; and McClure, "Difference, Diversity, and the Limits of Toleration," are far too strong.

50. See Marshall, *Early Enlightenment Culture,* 24–25, 30–31. Edward Stillingfleet was the bishop of Worcester and previously the author of *Irenicum* (1659/1662), an eirenic tract urging comprehension. See Chapter 3 for the possible Hobbesian influence on Stillingfleet and other latitudinarian Anglicans after the Restoration.

51. In an unpublished note of 1676, Locke wrote that in order "to settle the peace of places where there are different opinions in religion, two things are to be perfectly distinguished: religion and government," each with its own "officers" ("magistrates and ministers") and these with their separate jurisdictions (the state and the church), rules, and discipline. This argument echoed Williams's earlier claims that "civility" and "spirituality" were of an altogether different "sphere and nature." John Locke, "Toleration B," in *Locke: Political Essays,* 246–248.

52. Locke, *Correspondence,* 3.633.

53. William Popple. "To the Reader," in Locke, *Letter Concerning Toleration,* 4.

54. John Locke, "Epistola de Tolerantia," trans. Michael Silverthorne, in *Locke on Toleration,* ed. Richard Vernon (Cambridge: Cambridge University Press, 2010), 10.

55. Mark Goldie, "Notes on the Texts," in Locke, *A Letter Concerning Toleration,* 20. For a good discussion of the difficulties presented by theories of voluntary

church membership for birthright citizenship, see Holly Brewer, *By Birth or Consent: Children, Law and the Anglo-American Revolution in Authority* (Chapel Hill: University of North Carolina Press, 2007).

56. Marshall, *John Locke, Toleration, and Early Enlightenment Culture,* 514–515. It is perhaps significant that Locke's touchstone of mutual enjoyment in the collective pursuit of truth through dialogue and reasoned inquiry was not a university.

57. Waldron, *The Harm in Hate Speech,* 212–213. See also Wilhelm, "Good Fences and Good Neighbors," 145–166; and Bejan, "John Locke, (In)civility, and the Quest for Concord."

58. Charity is an exception, but most scholars explore it in the context of Locke's thoughts on property, not the ethical demands of toleration. See, for instance, Robert Lamb and Benjamin Thompson, "The Meaning of Charity in Locke's Political Thought," *European Journal of Political Theory* 8, no. 2 (April 1, 2009): 229–252; and Steven Forde, "The Charitable John Locke," *The Review of Politics* 71, no. 3 (2009): 428–458.

59. See Marshall, *Early Enlightenment Culture,* 656–657; and Mark Goldie, "The Theory of Religious Intolerance in Restoration England," in *From Persecution to Toleration: The Glorious Revolution and Religion in England,* ed. Ole Peter Grell, Jonathan I. Israel and Nicholas Tyacke (Oxford: Oxford University Press, 2011).

60. Goldie, "Theory of Intolerance," 335–338. Mark Knights notes that after the Restoration, prudential defenses of uniformity that emphasized its secular political and economic advantages grew increasingly prominent. See Mark Knights, "'Meer Religion' and the 'Church-State' of Restoration England: The Impact and Ideology of James II's Declarations of Indulgence," in *A Nation Transformed: England after the Restoration,* ed. Alan Houston and Steve Pincus (Cambridge: Cambridge University Press, 2001).

61. For a more complete account of the evangelical aspects of Lockean toleration, see Teresa M. Bejan, "Evangelical Toleration," *The Journal of Politics* 77, no. 4 (2015): 1103–1114.

62. See Silverthorne's translation: "Put[ing] effort into refuting the errors in fashion . . . is the only real way to spread the truth, to combine the weight of reason and argument with humanity and goodwill." Locke, "Epistola de Tolerantia," in *Locke on Toleration,* 15.

63. For an in-depth account of the evolution of Locke's views, see Bejan, "John Locke, (In)civility, and the Quest for Concord," sec. IV.

64. Locke, "Morality" (c. 1677–1678), in *Political Essays,* 269.

65. As was noted in Chapter 2, despite their shared connection through the Masham family and Otes, scholarly attempts to prove a direct influence of Williams on Locke have come up empty. This passage has been overlooked,

and I think it presents the best textual evidence that Locke may have read Williams, albeit the *Key* or "Christenings Make Not Christians," not *The Bloudy Tenent.* Of course, moralizing comparisons between "barbaric" Europeans and "civilized" Americans were a long-standing trope, and Locke could have had many different sources. For Locke's interest in the American Indians, see James Farr, "Locke, 'Some Americans,' and the Discourse on 'Carolina,'" *Locke Studies* 9 (2009): 19–96; and Turner, "John Locke, Christian Mission."

66. Raillery was to become the favored method of social criticism for Locke's own pupil, the future Third Earl of Shaftesbury.

67. To illustrate the dangers, Locke offered his own account of drama in the drawing room: the story of two "ladies of quality" who had fallen "into a dispute and [grown] so eager in it, that in the heat of their controversy" they had "got up close to one another in the middle of the room . . . as fiercely as two gamecocks in the pit," oblivious to the amusement of their onlookers (STCE, 112).

68. Marshall, *Early Enlightenment Culture,* 519. Similarly, Locke would criticize the disputatiousness of pamphlet controversies as better ended than prolonged. This is a bit rich coming from someone who was writing a *fourth* letter on toleration at the time of his death.

69. In *Of the Conduct of the Understanding,* Locke insisted that the pursuit of truth, alone and in conversation with others, required that a man "not be in love with any opinion" and instead endeavor an "equal indifferency for all truth." He acknowledged, however, that these characteristics were hard to achieve, contradicted as they were by nature and custom. "The world is apt to cast great blame on those who have an indifferency for opinions, especially in religion." John Locke, "Of the Conduct of the Understanding," in *Some Thoughts Concerning Education and Of the Conduct of the Understanding,* 185–186.

70. This may have been a product of Locke's increasingly cosmopolitan circumstances, as well as his compulsive reading of travel literature. See Ann Talbot, *'The Great Ocean of Knowledge': The Influence of Travel Literature on the Work of John Locke* (London: Brill Publishing, 2010).

71. John Dunn has described trust in Locke's thought as "the key practical capacity which made it possible for human beings to live with one another on tolerable terms at all." John Dunn, "Trust," in *The History of Political Theory and Other Essays,* 93. For an account of this development from the aspect of Locke's interest in economic and monetary theory, see Stefan Eich, "The Currency of Justice: Moments of Monetary Politics," Ph.D. dissertation (Yale University, 2016).

72. Locke, *Essays on the Law of Nature* (1663–1664), in *Political Essays,* 104. See also John Locke, *The Two Treatises of Government,* ed. P. Laslett (Cambridge: Cambridge University Press, 1988), 385.

73. According to Locke, belief in a deity—specifically, of "a God who sees men in the dark, has in his hand rewards and punishments, and has power enough to call to account the proudest offender"—was the foundation of all morality. John Locke, *An Essay Concerning Human Understanding,* in *The Works of John Locke,* 1.37. Rainer Forst calls the antinomian implications of atheism "Locke's Fear" and cites it as the reason that Lockean toleration must fall short of the full-fledged respect for "shared principles" found in the work of his contemporary, Pierre Bayle. See Forst, *Toleration in Conflict,* 427.

74. As evidence, supporters cited the papal practice of excommunicating monarchs and absolving their subjects of obedience, as well as the perfidy of the Council of Constance in reneging on their promise of safe conduct to Jan Hus. See Mark Goldie and Richard Popkin, "Scepticism, Priestcraft, and Toleration," in *The Cambridge History of Eighteenth-Century Political Thought,* ed. M. Goldie and R. Wokler (Cambridge: Cambridge University Press, 2006), 97.

75. Locke, *On the Conduct of the Understanding,* 223 (my emphasis). See also Locke, "Of Ethic in General" (c. 1686–1688?), *Political Essays,* 303, and *Some Thoughts,* 117–118.

76. Locke's disagreement with Williams on the tolerability of atheists and Catholics was due almost entirely to the importance he assigned to oaths as a means of conferring "express" consent and as an expression of trust as the bond of civil society. Oaths of allegiance were not simply a speculative conclusion of Locke's political theory of a social "compact" but a pressing practical question in England after the Restoration and the Glorious Revolution. Waldron and others have tried to exculpate Locke of intolerance toward Catholics on the grounds that those who could prove their civil allegiances would qualify. But in fact, Locke took the willingness of Catholics, including Hobbes's Blackloist associates, to swear an oath of an allegiance as a further sign of their hypocrisy. (I owe this insight to ongoing research by Jeffrey Collins.) And indeed, English anti-Catholicism was fueled less by fear of another Armada than by the suspicion that it was only a matter of time before a suspect "Jesuit" terrorist network recruited another Guy Fawkes—as the Popish Plot hysteria demonstrated.

77. Locke, "Pacific Christians," in *Political Essays,* 305.

78. Locke was influenced by his correspondence with Isaac Newton on this point. Nabil I. Matar, "John Locke and the Jews," *Journal of Ecclesiastical History* 44 (1993): 57–62.

79. Locke, *Correspondence,* 3.689 (my emphasis).

80. As Bishop of Salisbury, Burnet was a key instigator in the pastoral efforts into which low church Anglicans channeled their energies after the passage of the Act of Toleration in 1689. Locke would cite Burnet's *Pastoral Care* approvingly as a guide to the proper manner of "Visiting at home, conferring and instructing, and admonishing Men there" (SL, 94–95).

81. Locke, "Essay on the Poor Law" (1697), in *Political Essays*, 191–192.

82. See Turner, "John Locke, Christian Mission"; and Mark Goldie, "John Locke, Jonas Proast, and Religious Toleration: 1688-1692," in *The Church of England: c. 1689-c. 1833*, eds. J. Walsh, C. Haydon, and S. Taylor (Cambridge: Cambridge University Press, 1993), 143-171.

83. We might also compare Locke's "incurable Weakness and Difference of Mens Understandings" to Rawls's notion of the "burdens of judgment." John Rawls, *Political Liberalism* (New York: Columbia University Press, 1996), 54–58.

84. For a detailed defense of this claim in context, see J. R. Milton and Philip Milton's Introduction to *An Essay Concerning Toleration and Other Writings on Law and Politics* (Oxford: Oxford University Press, 2010).

85. Locke, *Correspondence*, 3.584.

86. Goldie, "John Locke, Jonas Proast, and Religious Toleration," 162.

87. For more on Locke's "reasonable evangelism," see Bejan, "Evangelical Toleration," sec. IV.

88. For an overview of Locke's views in comparison with those of his pupil, the third Earl of Shaftesbury, see Daniel Carey, *Locke, Shaftesbury, and Hutcheson: Contesting Diversity in the Enlightenment and Beyond* (Cambridge: Cambridge University Press, 2006).

89. For "mere toleration," see the Introduction.

90. We shall return to the question of Locke's rejection of religious insult laws in the Epilogue.

91. Damaris Masham observed that Locke exhibited "not only the Civility of a well-educated Person, but even all the Politeness that can be desired," and his early biographer Pierre Coste declared him to be "one of the politest men" who was "as agreeable for his obliging and civil behavior, as admirable for the profoundness and delicacy of his Genius" (both quoted in Marshall, *Early Enlightenment Culture*, 515–516).

92. Locke, *Letter Concerning Toleration*, 24. But Goldie notes that Popple omits this eirenic addendum from the *Epistola* in his translation.

93. In his *Second Vindication of The Reasonableness of Christianity*, Locke claimed ignorance. "For I tell him, I borrowed it only from the writers of the four Gospels and the Acts; and did not know those words, he quoted out of the *Leviathan*, were there, or any thing like them." John Locke, *Second Vindication of the Reasonableness of Christianity*, in *The Works of John Locke* (London, 1824), 6.420. This was not the first time that Locke would defend himself against the charge of Hobbism by claiming an implausible unfamiliarity with that text. In response to Stillingfleet's attack on *An Essay Concerning Human Understanding*, he replied: "For it is with such candid and kind insinuations as these, that you bring in both Hobbes and Spinosa into your discourse . . . neither of those authors . . . having, as it seems, any other business here, but by their names

skillfully to give that character to my book"; but "I am not so well read in Hobbes or Spinosa, as to be able to say what were their opinions in this matter. But possibly there be those, who will think your lordship's authority of more use to them in the case than those justly decried names." John Locke, "Reply to the Bishop of Worcester's Answer to His Second Letter," in *The Works of John Locke* (London: Rivington, 1824), 3.471, 477.

John Dunn describes Hobbism as "a spectre" that haunted Locke throughout his life and quotes Isaac Newton's letter of apology for taking him "for a Hobbist" after reading the *Essay*. Quoted in Dunn, *The Political Thought of John Locke*, 81.

Conclusion

1. John Locke, *Of the Conduct of the Understanding*, in *Some Thoughts Concerning Education and Of the Conduct of the Understanding*, ed. Ruth Grant and Nathan Tarcov (Indianapolis IN: Hackett, 1996), 185–186.
2. Waldron takes this discretion as a sign that Locke wanted to tolerate Catholics, as explicitly excluding them would not have been controversial in England. Jeremy Waldron, *God, Locke, and Equality* (Cambridge: Cambridge University Press, 2002), 221. But see Chapter 4.
3. See Waldron, *The Harm in Hate Speech* (Cambridge, MA: Harvard University Press, 2012), which identifies "inclusiveness" as a defining "public good" in tolerant societies (4).
4. See Richard Rorty, "Science as Solidarity," in *The Rhetoric of the Human Sciences*, ed. J. S. Nelson, A. Megill, and D. N. McCloskey (Madison: University of Wisconsin Press, 1987), 38–52; John Rawls, *Political Liberalism* (New York: Columbia University Press, 1996); and Mark Kingwell, *A Civil Tongue: Justice, Dialogue, and the Politics of Pluralism* (University Park: Pennsylvania State University Press, 2007), respectively.
5. Mark Button, "'A Monkish Kind of Virtue?' For and against Humility," *Political Theory* 33 (2005), 858–859. The pairing is ubiquitous in popular and scholarly accounts. See, for example, James Bohman, "Reflexive Toleration in a Deliberative Democracy," in *The Culture of Toleration in Diverse Societies*, ed. Catriona McKinnon and Dario Castiglione (Manchester: University of Manchester Press, 2003), 111–131; Wendy Brown, *Regulating Aversion: Tolerance in the Age of Identity and Empire* (Princeton, NJ: Princeton University Press, 2008), 11; Lawrence Cahoone, "Civic Meetings, Cultural Meanings," in *Civility*, ed. Leroy S. Rouner (Notre Dame, IN: University of Notre Dame Press, 2000), 40–64; Cheshire Calhoun, "The Virtue of Civility," *Philosophy & Public Affairs* 29, no. 3 (2000), 251–275; Edwin J. Delattre, "Civility and the Limits of the Tolerable," in *Civility*, ed. Leroy S. Rouner (Notre

Dame, IN: University of Notre Dame Press, 2000), 151–167; Clifford Orwin, "Citizenship and Civility as Components of Liberal Democracy," in *Civility and Citizenship in Liberal Democratic Societies*, ed. Edward C. Banfield (St. Paul, MN: Paragon House, 1992), 75–94, and "Civility," in *Endangered Virtues* (Hoover Institution online essay series), ed. Peter Berkowitz (Stanford, CA: Stanford University, 2011), http://www.hoover.org/research/civility; Robert B. Pippin, "The Ethical Status of Civility," in *Civility*, ed. Leroy S. Rouner (Notre Dame, IN: University of Notre Dame Press, 2000), 103–117; Philip Selznick, *The Moral Commonwealth: Social Theory and the Promise of Community* (Berkeley: University of California Press, 1994), chap. 14; Glenn Tinder, *Tolerance and Community* (Columbia: University of Missouri Press, 1995); Michael Walzer, "Civility and Civic Virtue in Contemporary America," *Social Research* 41 (1974): 593–611; and Melissa Williams and Jeremy Waldron, eds., Introduction to *Toleration and Its Limits* (New York: New York University Press, 2008), 7.

6. For this expansive sense of legislation, see the discussion of Jacob Levy and Lon Fuller in the Introduction.

7. Waldron, *The Harm in Hate Speech.*

8. Kingwell, *A Civil Tongue*, 89, 226, 44.

9. Bruce Ackerman, "Why Dialogue?" *The Journal of Philosophy* 86 (1989), 17–18, and *Social Justice and the Liberal State* (New Haven, CT: Yale University Press, 1981), 44. Although Ackerman does not use the language of civility to describe this requirement, others do. See, for example, the first four essays in Christine T. Sistare, ed., *Civility and Its Discontents: Civic Virtue, Toleration, and Cultural Fragmentation* (Lawrence: University Press of Kansas, 2004).

10. Thomas Nagel, "Concealment and Exposure," *Philosophy & Public Affairs* 27, no. 1 (1998): 3–30, 8.

11. See also Thomas Nagel, "Personal Rights and Public Space," *Philosophy & Public Affairs* 24, no. 2 (1995): 83–107; and Orwin, "Civility."

12. Rawls, *Political Liberalism*, 444–445.

13. As Clifford Orwin puts it: "Liberal democracy builds fences, and civility respects and maintains them" (Orwin, "Civility," 2).

14. Most deliberative democrats, like Rawls, conceive of public reason as an ethical and social, but not a legal, requirement. Gutmann and Thompson reject the imposition of external constraints aimed at neutrality of the kind imagined by Ackerman, while likewise emphasizing the importance of self-restraint: "People who disagree (but wish to continue talking) need not prescind from publicly professing beliefs that others reject" but they must observe "an economy of moral disagreement [that] minimizes rejection of the position we oppose." Amy Gutmann and Dennis Thompson, "Moral Conflict and Political Consensus," *Ethics* 101, no. 1 (1990): 81–82n. Calhoun suggests that Rawls's

turn to civility in *Political Liberalism* was directly influenced by Gutmann and Thompson's work on "civic magnanimity" and mutual respect ("Virtue of Civility," 256n).

15. Pippin, "The Ethical Status of Civility," 115.
16. Sarah Buss, "Appearing Respectful: The Moral Significance of Manners," *Ethics* 109 (1999): 795–826, 796, 801. See also Calhoun, "Virtue of Civility," 255; and Amy Gutmann and Dennis Thompson, *Democracy and Disagreement* (Cambridge, MA: Harvard University Press, 1996), 78.
17. Richard Boyd, *Uncivil Society: The Perils of Pluralism and the Making of Modern Liberalism* (New York: Lexington Books, 2004), 266, 46n.
18. Pippin, "The Ethical Status of Civility," 111–113.
19. Stephen L. Carter, *Civility* (New York: Harper Perennial, 1999), 11, 18.
20. Rawls, *Political Liberalism,* 147–148.
21. Ibid., 154. See also Chapter 1.
22. Ibid., 201 (my emphasis).
23. Waldron, *Harm in Hate Speech,* 69 and chap. 4.
24. Jeremy Waldron, "Civility and Formality," in *Civility, Legality, and Justice in America,* ed. Austin Sarat (Cambridge: Cambridge University Press, 2014), 46–68. This idea of the assurance conveyed through observing the norms of civil interaction is what ties Waldron's arguments about hate speech and those about civility in this essay together. "The guarantee of dignity is what enables a person to walk down the street without fear of insult or humiliation . . . and to proceed with an implicit assurance of being able to interact with others without being treated as a pariah." Waldron, *Harm in Hate Speech,* 220.
25. Stephen Holmes, "Gag Rules and the Politics of Omission," in *Passions and Constraint* (Chicago: University of Chicago Press, 1995), 202.
26. Rawls, *Political Liberalism,* lvii, 485. By moral grounds, he means "conceptions of society and of citizens as persons, as well as principles of justice and an account of political virtues through which those principles are embodied. . . . An overlapping consensus, therefore, is not merely a consensus on accepting certain authorities, or on complying with certain institutional arrangements, founded on a convergence of self- or group interests" (147). As Ronald Beiner notes, the demand is ultimately for sincerity: "Rawls's idea is that liberals must not be hypocrites. If they require religionists of various stripes to subordinate their larger conceptions of life (of what is required for salvation, of the meaning of death, of the Creator's purpose in fashioning the universe). . . to the imperatives of shared civic coexistence, then secular liberals are obliged to bracket their own visions of life in deference to the same imperatives." Ronald Beiner, *Political Philosophy: What It Is and Why It Matters* (Cambridge: Cambridge University Press, 2014), 206.
27. Gutmann and Thompson, "Moral Conflict and Political Consensus," 78.

28. One wonders how many of the theorists who enjoin their fellow citizens to be reasonable, open-minded, and willing to revise their views would be capable of attaining this level of conversational virtue themselves. And if they did, what such truly civil citizens would disagree *about,* given that they agree already on the importance of respecting each other's autonomy and of the value diversity, is unclear.

29. Gutmann and Thompson's mutually respectful citizens are "morally committed" yet "self-reflective about their commitments" and "open to the possibility of changing their minds" (Gutmann and Thompson, *Democracy and Disagreement,* 79). See also Tinder's discussion of "communality" in *Tolerance and Community;* Mortimer Sellers, "Ideals of Public Discourse," and Emily R. Gill, "Civic Education and the Liberal State," in *Civility and Its Discontents;* and Gutmann and Thompson, "Moral Conflict and Political Consensus," 88. Similarly, for Kingwell civility requires a "suspension of judgment" about our moral differences (Kingwell, *A Civil Tongue,* 42–43). Button thinks this extra element of "openness" is not implicit in the liberal virtues of civility or tolerance and so advocates "civic humility" as a crucial supplement to enable the right kind of conversation between co-citizens in a pluralistic society ("A Monkish Sort of Virtue," 858–859).

30. Martha Nussbaum, *Liberty of Conscience: In Defense of America's Tradition of Religious Equality* (New York: Basic Books, 2008), 37.

31. Rawls, *Political Liberalism,* 319.

32. I owe this very helpful formulation to Alison McQueen.

33. See Stanley Fish, "Mission Impossible: Settling the Just Bounds between Church and State," *Columbia Law Review* 97 (1997): 2255–2333.

34. See also the account of John Locke's "reasonable evangelism" in Teresa M. Bejan, "Evangelical Toleration," *The Journal of Politics* 77 (October 2015): 1103–1114.

35. Jean Bodin, *Colloquium of the Seven about Secrets of the Sublime,* trans. Marion Leathers Kuntz (University Park: Pennsylvania State University Press, 2010). See also Chapter 1.

36. Brown, *Regulating Aversion,* chaps. 1, 7. See also William E. Connolly, "The New Cult of Civilizational Superiority," *Theory and Event* 2, no. 4 (1998).

37. Iris Marion Young, *Justice and the Politics of Difference* (Princeton, NJ: Princeton University Press, 2011), 137. Thomas L. Dumm invokes Young in his own criticisms of civility in *A Politics of the Ordinary* (New York: New York University Press, 1999), 101–102.

38. Randall Kennedy, "The State of the Debate: The Case against Civility," *The American Prospect,* December 19, 2001, http://prospect.org/article/state-debate-case-against-civility. "The civility movement is deeply at odds with what an invigorated liberalism requires . . . a willingness to fight loudly,

openly, militantly, even rudely for policies and values that will increase freedom, equality, and happiness in America and around the world."

39. Walzer, "Civility and Civic Virtue," 604. See also James Schmidt, "Is Civility a Virtue?" in *Civility*, ed. Leroy S. Rouner (Notre Dame, IN: University of Notre Dame Press, 2000), 17–39.

40. Rebecca Comay, "Interrupting the Conversation: Notes on Rorty," *Telos* 69 (1986): 119–130, 121.

41. Richard Allestree, *The Government of the Tongue* (Oxford, 1667), 37–38. "To those indeed who have a zeal for their Faith, there can be no Discourse so intolerable, so disobliging [as atheistical discourse]: it turns conversation into skirmishing, and perpetual disputes . . . those who do acknowledge a Divine Power cannot contentedly sit by to hear him blasphemed." For Gillespie, see Chapter 1.

42. Emil Cioran, "Letter to a Faraway Friend," in *History and Utopia,* trans. Richard Howard (Chicago: University of Chicago Press, 1987), 4. Of course, those excluded from a conversation as "uncivil" do not disappear. They continue to talk among themselves, usually to discover that they find conversing with the like-minded much more agreeable, as well. This "silo effect" has been much decried in relation to contemporary media and political polarization: "Societies in which Internet users retreat to silos of like-minded people encourage polarization, and *in extremis,* political violence. This could account for the contemporary resurgence of the far-right and of radical Islam." Andrew White, *Digital Media and Society: Transforming Economics, Politics and Social Practices* (New York: Palgrave Macmillan Press, 2014), 57. See also the recent Pew Research Center report "Political Polarization and Media Habits," October 21, 2014, http://www.journalism.org/2014/10/21/political-polarization-media-habits/.

43. For the horizontal/vertical distinction, see Rainer Forst, *Toleration in Conflict* (Cambridge: Cambridge University Press, 2013), 6; and Williams and Waldron, Introduction to *Toleration and Its Limits,* 1–27.

44. For the important distinction between the limit between the un/acceptable and the in/tolerable in theories of toleration (as the limit between moral disapproval and interference), see Forst, *Toleration in Conflict,* chap. 1.

45. Simone Chambers describes this as "minimal civility." Simone Chambers, "An Ethics of Public Political Deliberation," in *Transformations of Democracy: Crisis, Protest, Legitimation,* eds. Robin Celikales, Regina Kreide, and Tilo Wensche (London: Rowman & Littlefield, 127-146).

46. Richard Rorty makes this explicit: "Civility is not a method, it is simply a virtue. The reasons why we invite the moronic psychopath to address the court before being sentenced is not that we hope for better explanations than expert psychiatric testimony has offered. We do so because he is, after all, one of us." Richard Rorty, "Method, Social Science, and Social Hope," in *The Consequences of Pragmatism* (Minneapolis: University of Minnesota Press, 1982), 191–210.

47. See John Rawls, *A Theory of Justice* (Cambridge, MA: Harvard University Press, 1971), 190–194. According to Rawls, the condition of endemic insecurity faced by Williams would have been one wherein he would have been under no obligation to tolerate the intolerant—or, indeed, in which he would have had a duty *not* to tolerate them.

48. Nussbaum, *Liberty of Conscience,* 46–47; Williams, "Letter to an Assembly of Commissioners, 17 Nov. 1677," in *The Correspondence of Roger Williams,* ed. G. LaFantasie, 2 vols. (Hanover, NH: Brown University Press, 1988), 2.750.

49. As Edwin S. Gaustad writes, "Locke, in echoing and often clarifying the sentiments of Roger Williams, became the chief channel of those once unsettling ideas concerning religious liberty." Edwin S. Gaustad, *Roger Williams* (Oxford: Oxford University Press, 2005), 117. See also LeRoy Moore, "Roger Williams and the Historians," *Church History* 32 (1963): 432–451, 443. This tendency is exacerbated by the decision to replace all of the biblical quotations in the *Bloudy Tenent* with ellipses in modern editions. For a recent example, see James Calvin Davis, *On Religious Liberty: Selections from the Work of Roger Williams* (Cambridge, MA: Harvard University Press, 2008).

50. Nussbaum, *Liberty of Conscience,* 37. Davis credits Williams with the definition of civility as a duty that demands "the cultivation . . . [of] mutual respect," "social solidarity," and recognition of our status as "equal moral agents." James Calvin Davis, "A Return to Civility," *Journal of Church and State* 43, no. 4 (2001): 690, 705, and *The Moral Theology of Roger Williams: Christian Conviction and Public Ethics* (Louisville, KY: Westminster John Knox Press, 2004), 44–45, 50, 99.

51. Cahoone, "Civic Meetings, Cultural Meanings," in *Civility,* ed. Leroy S. Rouner (Notre Dame, IN: University of Notre Dame Press, 2000), 40–41.

52. For example, see Ernest Barker, *Traditions of Civility* (Cambridge: Cambridge University Press, 1948); Marvin B. Becker, *Civility and Society in Western Europe, 1300–1600* (Bloomington: Indiana University Press, 1988); Peter Burke, *The Art of Conversation* (Ithaca, NY: Cornell University Press, 1993); and Philip Pettit, *Republicanism: A Theory of Freedom and Government* (Oxford: Oxford University Press, 1999).

53. Habermas has argued for the emergence of a "bourgeois public sphere" in which practices of rational critical discourse in Western Europe were developed and institutionalized in the seventeenth and eighteenth centuries, and many historians of political thought have embraced this paradigm. Jürgen Habermas, *The Structural Transformation of the Public Sphere: An Inquiry into a Category of Bourgeois Society,* trans. Thomas McCarthy (Boston: MIT Press, 1991). See for example, Lawrence Klein, *Shaftesbury and the Culture of Politeness: Moral Discourse and Cultural Politics in Early Eighteenth-Century England* (Cambridge: Cambridge University Press, 2004), 13–14; and John

Marshall, *John Locke, Toleration and Early Enlightenment Culture* (Cambridge: Cambridge University Press, 2006), chap. 16.

54. See Chapter 1.

55. Historians of political thought often point to Locke's pupil the third Earl of Shaftesbury, Edmund Burke, or the authors associated with the Scottish Enlightenment, all of whom explored the moral significance of the "softening" of manners they linked with the progress of commercial sociability and civilization. On Shaftsbury, see Klein, *Shaftsbury and the Culture of Politeness,* "Shaftesbury, Politeness, and the Politics of Religion," in *Political Discourse in Early Modern Britain,* ed. Nicholas Phillipson and Quentin Skinner (Cambridge: Cambridge University Press, 1993), 283–302, and "Liberty, Manners, and Politeness in Early Eighteenth-Century England," *The Historical Journal* 32 (1989), 583–605. On Burke: Jacob T. Levy, "Multicultural Manners," in *The Plural States of Recognition,* ed. Michael Seymour (London: Palgrave Press, 2010), 61–77; and J. G. A. Pocock, "The Varieties of Whiggism from Exclusion to Reform: A History of Ideology and Discourse," in *Virtue, Commerce and History* (Cambridge: Cambridge University Press, 1985), 215–310. On the Scottish Enlightenment: Albert O. Hirschmann, *The Passions and the Interests: Political Arguments for Capitalism before Its Triumph* (Princeton, NJ: Princeton University Press, 1997); Mark Kingwell, *A Civil Tongue* and "Politics and Polite Society in the Scottish Enlightenment," *Historical Reflections* 19, no. 3 (1993): 363–387; Boyd, *Uncivil Society,* chap. 3; and J. G. A. Pocock, "Virtues, Rights, and Manners," in *Virtue, Commerce, and History,* 37–50, and "Cambridge Paradigms and Scotch Philosophers: A Study of the Relations between the Civic Humanist and the Civil Jurisprudential Interpretation of Eighteenth-Century Social Thought," in *Wealth and Virtue,* ed. Istvan Hont and Michael Ignatieff (Cambridge: Cambridge University Press, 1983), 235–252.

56. Saba Mahmood, *Religious Difference in a Secular Age: A Minority Report* (Princeton, NJ: Princeton University Press, 2015); Matthew Scherer, *Beyond Church and State: Democracy, Secularism, and Conversion* (Cambridge: Cambridge University Press, 2013).

57. Jean-Jacques Rousseau, *Rousseau: The Social Contract and Other Later Political Writings,* ed. and trans. Victor Gourevitch (Cambridge: Cambridge University Press, 1997), iv.8.34. Rousseau was himself working out what he took to be the implications of Hobbes and Locke's social contract theories for the constitution of a tolerant society.

58. Gilles Kepel, *Revenge of God: The Resurgence of Islam, Christianity and Judaism in the Modern World* (University Park: Pennsylvania State University Press, 1994), 2.

59. John Milton, "The Second Defence of the People of England," in *The Prose Works of John Milton* (London: Bohn, 1848), 242. John Taylor was a Thames

waterman famous for his insouciant verse and social commentary—as well as an excellent example of the democratization of print. John Taylor, *A Swarme of Sectaries, and Schismatiques* [pamphlet with woodcut], 1641 (British Museum, no. 251), and *A Reply as True as Steele, To a Rusty, Rayling, Ridiculous, Lying Libell* [tract with woodcut], 1641 (British Museum, no. 252). As the charming accompanying couplet to *A Reply* explained: "The Divell is hard bound and did hardly straine, To shit a Libeller a knave in graine." For many more examples, see Helen Pierce, *Unseemly Pictures: Graphic Satire and Politics in Early Modern England* (New Haven, CT: Yale University Press, 2008).

60. The Anti-Christian terrorist is still burnt in effigy every November 5th. It is difficult to imagine a similar tradition taking root in the United Kingdom in response to Islamic terrorism today.

61. See Christopher Hill, *The World Turned Upside Down* (New York: Penguin Books, 1972); and Michael Walzer, *Revolution of the Saints: A Study in the Origins of Revolutionary Politics* (Cambridge, MA: Harvard University Press, 1965).

62. Quoted in Roger Williams, "Samuel Gorton in Providence," *Correspondence*, 1.211.

63. Emil Oberholzer, quoted in John M. Barry, *Roger Williams and the Creation of the American Soul* (New York: Viking Press, 2012), 389–390; Forst, *Toleration in Conflict*, 420.

64. Rawls, *Political Liberalism*, 147–148.

65. Gutmann and Thompson, "Moral Conflict and Political Consensus," 65, 76.

66. Selznick, *The Moral Commonwealth*, 391–392 (my emphasis).

67. Ibid., 392.

68. Stephen Darwall's distinction between "appraisal" and "recognition" respect is often invoked to argue that we can respect or recognize others as our moral equals without respecting (i.e., positively appraising or affirming) their beliefs. Stephen L. Darwall, "Two Kinds of Respect," *Ethics* 88 (1977): 36–49. For an example see Waldron, "Civility and Formality." For a response to Waldron, see Teresa M. Bejan and Bryan Garsten, "The Difficult Work of Liberal Civility," in *Civility, Legality, and Justice in America,* ed. Austin Sarat (Cambridge: Cambridge University Press, 2014), 15–45.

69. David Heyd, ed., Introduction to *Toleration: An Elusive Virtue* (Princeton, NJ: Princeton University Press, 1996). See also T. M. Scanlon, "The Difficulty of Tolerance," in the same volume.

70. Ian Carter, "Respect and the Basis of Equality," *Ethics* 121, no. 3 (2011): 538–571, 551.

71. For example, Nussbaum has declared her preference for the term respect over tolerance, because the latter "seems too grudging and weak." Nussbaum, *Liberty of Conscience,* 24. For criticism of this "profound moralizing tendency"

in recent accounts of toleration, see Federico Zuolo, "Frontiers of Toleration and Respect: Non-Moral Approaches and Inter-Group Relations," *European Journal of Political Theory* 12 (2013): 219.

The language of status and of dignity ubiquitous in contemporary discussions of civility is clearly indebted to Kant: "The respect which I bear others or which another can claim . . . is the acknowledgement of the dignity *(dignitas)* of another man, i.e. a worth which has no price, no equivalent for which the object of valuation *(aestimii)* could be exchanged." Immanuel Kant, "The Metaphysics of Morals, Part II: The Metaphysical Principles of Virtue," trans. James W. Ellington, in *Ethical Philosophy* (Indianapolis, IN: Hackett, 1983), 127. However, the relationship of neo-Kantian appeals to civility and Kant himself is vexed. As Sarah Buss explains, "There are passages in which Kant suggests that in order to acknowledge a person's dignity it is not enough to accommodate our ends to hers. . . . [But] at the same time, Kant seems to reject my interpretation of the relation between morals and manners insofar as he claims that 'I am not bound to venerate others (regarded merely as men), i.e. to show them positive reverence. The only respect which I am bound to by nature is that for the law generally *(revere legem)*' *(Metaphysics,* 133)." Buss, "Appearing Respectful," 797n.

72. This point about the plurality of possible motives for toleration has been made very well by Andrew Sabl in his response to David Heyd. After all, "few have a full-blown Kantian or similar theory of moral agency to ground whatever toleration they may practice." Sabl cites twelve possible foundations for practicing toleration in addition to moral-philosophical "mutual respect." Andrew Sabl, "'Virtuous to Himself': Pluralistic Democracy and the Toleration of Tolerations," in *Toleration and Its Limits,* ed. Melissa Williams and Jeremy Waldron (New York: New York University Press, 2008), 225–226. Michael Walzer also stresses the plural routes to tolerance but limits himself to four: resigned acceptance or battle fatigue, benign indifference, moral stoicism, and openness. Michael Walzer, *On Toleration* (New Haven, CT: Yale University Press, 1999), 10–11. Note that "evangelism" makes the list neither for Sabl nor Walzer. See Bejan, "Evangelical Toleration."

73. Judith Shklar argues that "liberal democracy cannot afford public sincerity [because] honesties that humiliate and a stiff-necked refusal to compromise would ruin democratic civility in a polite society in which people have many serious differences of belief and interest." Judith Shklar, *Ordinary Vices* (Cambridge, MA: Harvard University Press, 1984), 78. But her point, much like Nagel's defense of benign dissimulation, is rather to endorse civil silence and rule out the evangelical ends to which Williams believed mere civility should be put. Nagel stresses, like Williams, that the insincerity demanded by mere civility is not hypocrisy as such, for the simple reason that our social deceptions

are not generally intended to deceive: "Since everyone participates in such practices, they aren't, or shouldn't be, deceptive." Thomas Nagel, "Concealment and Exposure," 9–10.

74. Unlike Hobbes, Locke never made his true and inward civility into the basis of a law of nature. Similarly, Rawls was careful in restricting the application of the duty of civility as a moral, not a legal duty, and one limited to public political deliberation about matters of basic justice and constitutional essentials. Rawls, *Political Liberalism,* 445.

75. I am grateful to one of the Press's anonymous reviewers for pushing me on this point.

76. In this, civility is what Andrew Sabl describes as a "core" as opposed to an "ideal virtue"—that is, one "needed for liberal democracy to literally survive" rather than one "needed for it to do maximally well—i.e. achieve certain values prized by the theorist in question, but not necessarily by other[s]." Theorists of civility, as Sabl notes of other liberal virtue theorists, generally do not do a very good job of making this distinction. Andrew Sabl, "Virtue for Pluralists," *Journal of Moral Philosophy* 2, no. 2 (2005): 207–235, 211. Similarly, in her account of "minimal civility," Chambers describes it as "a baseline and not an ideal . . . defined through its breach, not its fulfillment." Chambers, "An Ethics of Public Political Deliberation."

77. Although it may fall within the letter, as an example of Darwall's "recognition respect" (see supra n. 68), it clearly violates the spirit of mutual respect most theorists have in mind. As Richard C. Sinopoli puts it: "What would it mean . . . to respect someone while thinking their life goals worthless or deleterious to their own good or that of others? . . . [T]o respect actual persons cannot merely be to respect the abstract natures of their personhood but to respect particular identities and senses of self" and, by implication, the ends they choose to pursue. Sinopoli, "Thick-Skinned Liberalism: Redefining Civility," *American Political Science Review* 89, no. 3 (1995): 615. Even if the modern understanding of respect is capacious enough to accommodate William's merely civil behavior, describing it as "mutual" in form is still misleading. Mere civility can be rooted in a conception of reciprocity, but it need not be other-directed. Our civil behavior may have nothing to do with respect for others, but rather respect for one's self, one's God, or for the social order.

78. Davis, "A Return to Civility," 690, 705.

79. Compare Williams's comments on the Americans, otherwise exemplars of civility, and their overhastiness in taking offense, which "indignation" he believed to be "a great kindling of Warres amongst them." Roger Williams, *A Key into the Language of America,* 200–202. In this, his mere civility resembles Sinopoli's "thick-skinned liberalism" or Sabl's "virtues of pretending" as a requirement of pluralistic politics. Sinopoli, "Thick-Skinned Liberalism,"

612–620; Sabl, "Virtue for Pluralists." See also Bryan Garsten, "'Always Watching Ourselves': Benjamin Constant on the Distinctive Character of Modern Enthusiasms," in *The Oxford Handbook of Rhetoric and Political Theory* (Oxford: Oxford University Press, forthcoming).

80. Jill Lepore, *The Name of the War: King Philip's War and the Origins of American Identity* (New York: Vintage, 1999), 120–121. It appears that one captive became a servant in Williams's household.

81. George E. Tinker, *Missionary Conquest: The Gospel and Native American Cultural Genocide* (Minneapolis, MN: Augsburg Press, 1993), 27–28.

82. For Baxter, see Chapter 1.

83. Jeremy Waldron, *Dignity, Rank, and Rights,* ed. Meir Dan-Cohen (Oxford: Oxford University Press, 2012).

84. See Chapter 2.

85. Williams, "Letter to the Town of Providence, ca. Jan. 1654/5," in *Correspondence*, 2.424. For more on the Quakers and the Keithian schism in early Pennsylvania, and its relationship to Penn's policies, see Andrew Murphy, *Conscience and Community: Revisiting Toleration and Religious Dissent in Early Modern England and America* (University Park: Pennsylvania State University Press, 2001), chap. 5.

86. Never mind that religious differences in seventeenth-century England *were* political, and vice versa. In England in the 1620s, the "rival conspiracy theories," comprehended under the labels of "Puritan" and "Arminian" flung back and forth both evidenced and facilitated the polarization of English society—and the very real political consequences and radical upheavals to come. Peter Lake, "Anti-Popery: The Structure of a Prejudice," in *Conflict in Early Stuart England,* ed. Richard Cust and Ann Hughes (London: Longman, 1989), 91–92. Other dichotomies—"Roundheads" vs. "rattle-heads," for instance—also featured. Similar fears would grow around the effects of the labels "Whig" and "Tory" in the late seventeenth and early eighteenth centuries.

87. "And when men that think themselves wiser than all the others, clamour and demand right Reason for judge; yet seek no more, but that things should be determined, by no other mens reason but their own, it is as intolerable in the society of men, as it is in play after trump is turned, to use for trump on every occasion, that suite whereof they have most in their hand" (L, ii.5.66).

Epilogue

1. Jeremy Waldron, *The Harm in Hate Speech* (Cambridge: Harvard University Press, 2012), chap. 1.

2. Quoted in James Q. Whitman, "Enforcing Civility and Respect: Three Societies," *The Yale Law Journal* 109: 1279–1398.

3. Waldron, *Hate Speech,* 12.

4. A 2015 Pew survey found that 40 percent of Americans ages eighteen to thirty-four supported the censoring of speech offensive to minorities. Pew Research Center, "Global Support for Principle of Free Expression, but Opposition to Some Forms of Speech" (November 2015), http://www.pewglobal.org/2015/11/18/global-support-for-principle-of-free-expression-but-opposition-to-some-forms-of-speech/.

5. Whitman, "Civility and Respect," 1282. "To say that America has absolutely no law of civility is to say too much. But to say that in general America has no law of civility—especially as compared with a country like Germany—is to make the right generalization" (1384).

6. Ibid., 1373.

7. It is worth noting that the First Amendment does not mention toleration at all. The full text reads: "Congress shall make no law respecting an establishment of religion, or prohibiting the free exercise thereof; or abridging the freedom of speech, or of the press; or the right of the people peaceably to assemble, and to petition the Government for a redress of grievances." For two good historical overviews of the drafting of the Establishment clause that disagree on its contemporary implications, see Noah Feldman, "The Intellectual Origins of the Establishment Clause," *New York University Law Review* 77 (2002): 346–428; and Vincent Phillip Muñoz, "The Original Meaning of the Establishment Clause and the Impossibility of Its Incorporation," *Journal of Constitutional Law* 8 (2006): 585–639.

8. Stanley Fish, *There's No Such Thing as Free Speech, and It's a Good Thing, Too* (Oxford: Oxford University Press, 1994), 137.

9. Rawls uses all of these terms interchangeably in both *A Theory of Justice* (Cambridge, MA: Harvard University Press, 1971) and *Political Liberalism* (New York: Columbia University Press, 1996).

10. Thomas Hobbes, *Leviathan,* ed. Noel Malcolm, 3 vols. (Oxford: Oxford University Press, 2012), ii.27.480.

11. John Locke, "Notes on the Pennsilvania Laws" (1686), MS f.9, fols. 33–41. Fragment reprinted in *A Letter Concerning Toleration and Other Writings,* ed. Mark Goldie (Indianapolis, IN: Liberty Fund, 2010), 182.

12. Quoted in Emily Butterworth, *The Unbridled Tongue: Babble and Gossip in Renaissance France* (Oxford: Oxford University Press, 2016), 108. For a possible colonial rivalry between Locke and Penn, see Richard Tuck, *The Rights of War and Peace: Political Thought and the International Order from Grotius to Kant* (Oxford: Oxford University Press, 2000), 177–178.

13. John Locke, "Liberty of the Press" (1694–1695), in *Locke: Political Essays,* ed. Mark Goldie (Cambridge: Cambridge University Press, 1990), 329, 331.

14. See Teresa M. Bejan, "'When the Word of the Lord Runs Freely': Roger Williams and Evangelical Toleration," in *The Lively Experiment: Religious Toleration in America from Roger Williams to the Present*, ed. Chris Beneke and Christopher S. Grenda (London: Rowman & Littlefield, 2015).

15. Although he did allow restrictions on seditious and libelous speech, as did other contemporary advocates for toleration like Milton (*Areopagitica: A Speech of Mr. John Milton for the liberty of unlicensed printing to the Parliament of England*, 1644), unlike Milton, Williams denied the magistrate's right to punish blasphemy as a violation of the first table of the Decalogue.

16. Saba Mahmood, *Religious Difference in a Secular Age: A Minority Report* (Princeton, NJ: Princeton University Press, 2015), 37–38, 43–46.

17. A similar aversion to "ostentatious" religious signs lies behind the opposition to headscarves in France and Turkey. Teresa M. Bejan, "Evangelical Toleration," *The Journal of Politics* 77, no. 4 (2015): 1112.

18. Quoted in W. Clark Gilpin, *The Millenarian Piety of Roger Williams* (Chicago: University of Chicago Press, 1979), 55.

19. John M. Barry, *Roger Williams and the Creation of the American Soul* (New York: Viking Press, 2002). See also John Coffey, "Puritanism and Liberty Revisited," *The Historical Journal* 41 (1998), 961-985 and *Persecution and Toleration in England, 1558–1689* (London: Longman, 2000). Note as well the exchange between John Barry and Gordon Wood in the *New York Review of Books*: John Barry, "Roger Williams on His Own," October 25, 2012, a response to Gordon S. Wood, "Radical, Pure, Roger Williams," May 10, 2012.

20. As for his influence on what came after, perhaps Perry Miller puts it best: "Just as some great experience in the youth of a person is ever afterward a determinant of his personality, so the American character has been molded by the fact that in the first years of colonization there arose this prophet of religious liberty." Perry Miller, *Roger Williams: His Contribution to the American Tradition* (Indianapolis, IN: Bobbs-Merrill, 1953), 254.

21. Miss Manners identifies proselytism "of the sort . . . known as in-your-face" as a clear species of incivility because it violates the valuable taboo against bringing up controversial matters—like sex, religion, and politics—at the dinner table and "by extension any social setting." Judith Martin, *Miss Manners Rescues Civilization: From Sexual Harassment, Frivolous Lawsuits, Dissing and Other Lapses of Civility* (New York: Crown, 1996) 366, 393–394.

22. As a spokesman for the State Department did in the wake of the "Innocence of Muslims" controversy in 2012. Daniel Baer, "Remarks," *Live at State: Freedom of Expression* (September 27, 2012), http://m.state.gov/md198332.htm.

23. See Oliver Wendell Holmes Jr.'s dissent in *Abrams v. United States*, 250 U.S. 616, 630 (1919).

REFERENCES

Abizadeh, Arash. 2011. "Hobbes on the Causes of War: A Disagreement Theory." *American Political Science Review* 105: 298–315.

Abizadeh, Arash. 2013. "Publicity, Privacy, and Religious Toleration in Hobbes's *Leviathan.*" *Modern Intellectual History* 10, no. 2: 261–291.

Abrams, Philip, ed. 1967. *John Locke: Two Tracts on Government.* Cambridge: Cambridge University Press.

Ackerman, Bruce. 1981. *Social Justice and the Liberal State.* New Haven, CT: Yale University Press.

Ackerman, Bruce. 1989. "Why Dialogue?" *The Journal of Philosophy* 86: 5–22.

Aglionby, William. 1671. *The Present State of the United Provinces of the Low Countries.* London.

Allestree, Richard. 1667. *The Government of the Tongue.* Oxford: At the Theatre in Oxford.

Aquinas, Thomas. 2002. *Aquinas: Political Writings*, ed. and trans. R. W. Dyson. Cambridge: Cambridge University Press.

Aristotle. 1946. *Politics,* trans. Sir Ernest Barker. Oxford: Clarendon Press.

Armitage, David. 2004. "John Locke, Carolina, and the *Two Treatises of Government.*" *Political Theory* 32: 602–627.

Asad, Talal, Judith Butler, and Saba Mahmood, eds. 2009. *Is Critique Secular? Blasphemy, Injury, and Free Speech.* Berkeley, CA: Doreen B. Townsend Center for the Humanities.

Ashcraft, Richard. 1986. *Revolutionary Politics and Locke's* Two Treatises of Government. Princeton, NJ: Princeton University Press.

Aubrey, John. 1996 [1669–1696]. *Aubrey's Brief Lives,* ed. O. L. Dick. Boston: Godine.

Augustine. 1872 [417]. "On the Correction of the Donatists." In *The Works of Aurelius Augustine,* ed. and trans. Marcus Dods, vol. 3. Edinburgh: Murray and Green.

Augustine. 1887 [416]. Letter 173 ("Letter to Donatus"), trans. J. G. Cunningham. In *Nicene and Post-Nicene Fathers*, ed. Philip Schaff, vol. 1. Buffalo, NY: Christian Literature Publishing.

Avamarudan, Srinivas. 2009. "Hobbes and America." In *The Postcolonial Enlightenment: Eighteenth-Century Colonialism and Postcolonial Theory*, ed. Daniel Carey and Lynn Festa. Oxford: Oxford University Press, 37–70.

Balibar, Étienne. 2015. *Violence and Civility: On the Limits of Political Philosophy*, trans. G. M. Goshgarian. New York: Columbia University Press.

Banfield, Edward C., ed. 1992. *Civility and Citizenship in Liberal Democratic Societies*. St. Paul, MN: Paragon House.

Barker, Ernest. 1948. *Traditions of Civility*. Cambridge: Cambridge University Press.

Barry, John M. 2012. *Roger Williams and the Creation of the American Soul*. New York: Viking Press.

Baxter, Richard. 1696. *Reliquiae Baxterianae: or, Mr Richard Baxter's Narrative of the Most Memorable Passages of his Life and Times*, ed. Matthew Sylvester, 2 vols. London.

Bayle, Pierre. 2005 [1686]. *A Philosophical Commentary on These Words of the Gospel, Luke 14.23: 'Compel Them to Come in, that My House May Be Full,'* ed. John Kilcullen and Chandran Kukathas. Indianapolis, IN: Liberty Fund.

Becker, Marvin B. 1988. *Civility and Society in Western Europe, 1300–1600*. Bloomington: Indiana University Press.

Beiner, Ronald. 2011. *Civil Religion: A Dialogue in the History of Political Philosophy*. Cambridge: Cambridge University Press.

Beiner, Ronald. 2014. *Political Philosophy: What It Is and Why It Matters*. Cambridge: Cambridge University Press.

Bejan, Teresa M. 2010. "Teaching the *Leviathan*: Thomas Hobbes on Education." *Oxford Review of Education* 36: 607–626.

Bejan, Teresa M. 2011. "'The Bond of Civility': Roger Williams on Toleration and Its Limits," *History of European Ideas* 37: 607–626.

Bejan, Teresa M. 2015. "Evangelical Toleration." *The Journal of Politics* 77, no. 4: 1103–1114.

Bejan, Teresa M. 2016. "Difference without Disagreement: Rethinking Hobbes on 'Independency' and Toleration." *The Review of Politics* 78, no. 1: 1–25.

Bejan, Teresa M. 2016. "John Locke on Toleration, (In)civility, and the Quest for Concord." *History of Political Thought* 37 no. 3: 556–587.

Bejan, Teresa M., and Bryan Garsten. 2014. "The Difficult Work of Liberal Civility." In *Civility, Legality, and Justice in America*, ed. Austin Sarat. Cambridge: Cambridge University Press, 15–45.

Bejczy, István. 1997. "*Tolerantia*: A Medieval Concept." *Journal of the History of Ideas* 58, no. 3: 365–384.

Bell, Duncan. 2014. "What Is Liberalism?" *Political Theory* 42, no. 6: 682–715.

Bell, Duncan. 2016. "The Dream Machine: On Liberalism and Empire." In *Reordering the World: Essays on Liberalism and Empire*. Princeton, NJ: Princeton University Press.

Beneke, Chris, and Christopher S. Grenda, eds. 2015. *The Lively Experiment: Religious Toleration in America from Roger Williams to the Present*. London: Rowman and Littlefield.

Bergin, Joseph. 2014. *The Politics of Religion in Early Modern France*. New Haven, CT: Yale University Press.

Bishop, Bill, and Robert G. Cushing. 2009. *The Big Sort: Why the Clustering of Like-Minded America Is Tearing Us Apart*. Boston: Mariner Books.

Bodin, Jean. 1606. *The Six Bookes of a Common-weale*, trans. R. Knolles. London.

Bodin, Jean. 2010. *Colloquium of the Seven about Secrets of the Sublime*, trans. Marion Leathers Kuntz. University Park: Pennsylvania State University Press.

Bohman, James. 2003. "Reflexive Toleration in a Deliberative Democracy." In *The Culture of Toleration in Diverse Societies*, ed. Catriona McKinnon and Dario Castiglione. Manchester: University of Manchester Press, 111–131.

Bou-Habib, Paul. 2003. "Locke, Sincerity, and the Rationality of Persecution." *Political Studies* 51: 611–626.

Bourne, H. R. Fox. 1876. *The Life of John Locke*, 2 vols. London: H.S. King & Co.

Boyd, Richard. 2004. *Uncivil Society: The Perils of Pluralism and the Making of Modern Liberalism*. New York: Lexington Books.

Brewer, Holly. 2007. *By Birth or Consent: Children, Law and the Anglo-American Revolution in Authority*. Chapel Hill: University of North Carolina Press.

Brown, K.C., ed. 1965. *Hobbes Studies*. Oxford: Blackwell Press.

Brown, Wendy. 2008. *Regulating Aversion: Tolerance in the Age of Identity and Empire*. Princeton, NJ: Princeton University Press.

Bryson, Anna. 1997. *From Courtesy to Civility: Changing Codes of Conduct in Early Modern England*. Oxford: Oxford University Press.

Burke, Peter. 1993. *The Art of Conversation*. Ithaca, NY: Cornell University Press.

Burke, Peter, Brian Harrison, and Paul Slack, eds. 2000. *Civil Histories: Essays Presented to Sir Keith Thomas*. Oxford: Oxford University Press.

Buss, Sarah. 1999. "Appearing Respectful: The Moral Significance of Manners." *Ethics* 109: 795–826.

Butterfield, Herbert. 1977. "Toleration in Early Modern Times." *Journal of the History of Ideas* 38, no. 4: 573–584.

Butterworth, Emily. 2016. *The Unbridled Tongue: Babble and Gossip in Renaissance France*. Oxford: Oxford University Press.

Button, Mark. 2005. "'A Monkish Kind of Virtue?' For and against Humility." *Political Theory* 33: 840–868.

Button, Mark. 2010. *Contract, Culture, and Citizenship: Transformative Liberalism from Hobbes to Rawls*. University Park: Pennsylvania State University Press.

C., S. 1673. *The Art of Complaisance, or the Meanes to Oblige in Civil Conversation.* London: John Starkey.

Calhoun, Cheshire. 2000. "The Virtue of Civility." *Philosophy & Public Affairs* 29, no. 3: 251–275.

Canup, John. 2009. *Out of the Wilderness: The Emergence of an American Identity in Colonial New England.* Middletown, CT: Wesleyan University Press.

Carey, Daniel. 2006. *Locke, Shaftesbury, and Hutcheson: Contesting Diversity in the Enlightenment and Beyond.* Cambridge: Cambridge University Press.

Carroll, Michael P. 1996. *Veiled Threats: The Logic of Popular Catholicism in Italy.* Baltimore: Johns Hopkins University Press.

Carter, Ian. 2011. "Respect and the Basis of Equality." *Ethics* 121, no. 3: 538–571.

Carter, Stephen L. 1999. *Civility.* New York: Harper Perennial.

Casson, Douglas John. 2011. *Liberating Judgment: Fanatics, Skeptics, and John Locke's Politics of Probability.* Princeton, NJ: Princeton University Press.

Castell, William. 1642. *The Jesuits Undermining Parliament and Protestants with their Foolish Phancy of a Toleration.* London.

Castellio, Sebastian. 1965 [1554]. *Concerning Heretics,* ed. Roland Bainton. New York: Octagon Books.

Chambers, Simone. 2015. "An Ethics of Public Political Deliberation." In *Transformations of Democracy: Crisis, Protest, Legitimation,* eds. Robin Celikales, Regina Kreide, and Tilo Wensche. London: Rowman & Littlefield, 127-146.

Cioran, Emil. 1987. *History and Utopia,* trans. Richard Howard. Chicago: University of Chicago Press.

Clarke, John. 1721. *An Introduction to the Making of Latin.* London: A. Bettesworth.

Cobb, Sanford. 1902. *The Rise of Religious Liberty in America.* New York: Macmillan.

Coffey, John. 1998. "Puritanism and Liberty Revisited." *The Historical Journal* 41: 961–985.

Coffey, John. 2000. *Persecution and Toleration in England, 1558–1689.* London: Longman.

Coffey, John. 2006. "A Ticklish Business: Defining Heresy and Orthodoxy in the Puritan Revolution." In *Heresy, Literature, and Politics in Early Modern English Culture,* ed. David Loewenstein. Cambridge: Cambridge University Press, 108–136.

Cogley, Richard W. 1999. *John Eliot's Mission to the Indians before King Philip's War.* Cambridge, MA: Harvard University Press.

Collins, Jeffrey. 2002. "The Church Settlement of Oliver Cromwell," *History* 83: 18–40.

Collins, Jeffrey. 2005. *The Allegiance of Thomas Hobbes.* Oxford: Oxford University Press.

Collins, Jeffrey. 2009. "Redeeming the Enlightenment: New Histories of Religious Toleration." *The Journal of Modern History* 81: 607–636.

Comay, Rebecca. 1986. "Interrupting the Conversation: Notes on Rorty." *Telos* 69: 119–130.

Connolly, William E. 1998. "The New Cult of Civilizational Superiority." *Theory and Event* 2, no. 4.

Cooper, Julie. 2010. "Vainglory, Modesty, and Political Agency in the Political Theory of Thomas Hobbes." *Review of Politics* 72: 241–269.

Cotton, John. 1647. *A Reply to Mr Williams his examination; and answers to the letters sent to him by John Cotton.* London.

Creppell, Ingrid. 1996. "Locke on Toleration: The Transformation of Constraint." *Political Theory* 24: 200–240.

Curley, Edwin. 2003. "Sebastian Castellio's Erasmian Liberalism." *Philosophical Topics* 31: 47–73.

Curley, Edwin. 2007. "Hobbes and the Cause of Religious Toleration." In *The Cambridge Companion to Hobbes's* Leviathan, ed. Patricia Springborg. Cambridge: Cambridge University Press, 309–336.

Daniel, Stephen. 1980. "Civility and Sociability: Hobbes on Man and Citizen." *Journal of the History of Philosophy* 18: 209–215.

Darwall, Stephen L. 1977. "Two Kinds of Respect." *Ethics* 88: 36–49.

Davis, Jack L. 1970. "Roger Williams among the Narragansett Indians." *The New England Quarterly* 43: 593–604.

Davis, James Calvin. 2001. "A Return to Civility." *Journal of Church and State* 43, no. 4: 689–706.

Davis, James Calvin. 2004. *The Moral Theology of Roger Williams: Christian Conviction and Public Ethics.* Louisville, KY: Westminster John Knox Press.

Davis, James Calvin. 2008. *On Religious Liberty: Selections from the Works of Roger Williams.* Cambridge, MA: Harvard University Press.

Davis, James Calvin. 2010. *In Defense of Civility: How Religion Can Unite America on Seven Moral Issues That Divide Us.* Louisville, KY: Westminster John Knox Press.

Dees, Richard. 2004. *Trust and Toleration.* New York: Routledge Press.

DeMott, Benjamin. 1996. "Seduced by Civility: Political Manners and the Crisis of Democratic Values." *The Nation* (December 9), 11–19.

De Roover, Jakob, and S. N. Balagangadhara. 2008. "John Locke, Christian Liberty, and the Predicament of Liberal Toleration." *Political Theory* 36: 523–549.

Dietz, Mary, ed. 1990. *Thomas Hobbes and Political Theory.* Lawrence: University Press of Kansas.

Dreisbach, Daniel. 2002. *Thomas Jefferson and the Wall of Separation between Church and State.* New York: New York University Press.

Dumm, Thomas L. 1999. *A Politics of the Ordinary.* New York: New York University Press.

Dunn, John. 1969. *The Political Thought of John Locke.* Cambridge: Cambridge University Press.

Dunn, John. 1996. *The History of Political Theory and Other Essays.* Cambridge: Cambridge University Press.

Dunn, John. 2003. *Locke.* Oxford: Oxford University Press.

Edwards, Thomas. 1646. *Gangraena, Or a Catalogue and Discovery of many of the Errours, Heresies, Blasphemies and pernicious Practices of the Sectaries of this time, vented and acted in England these four last years, As also a particular Narration of divers Stories, Remarkable passages, Letters, an Extract of many Letters, all concerning the present Sects, together with some Observations upon, and Corollaries from all the fore-named Premises.* London.

Elias, Norbert. 1969. *The Civilizing Process: The History of Manners.* Oxford: Blackwell.

Eliasoph, Nina. 1998. *Avoiding Politics: How Americans Produce Apathy in Everyday Life.* Cambridge: Cambridge University Press.

Eliot, John. 2003. *The Eliot Tracts: With Letters from John Eliot to Thomas Thorowgood and Richard Baxter,* ed. Michael P. Clark. Westport, CT: Praeger Publishers.

Erasmus, Desiderius. 1917 [1521]. *The Complaint of Peace,* trans. Thomas Paynell. Chicago: Open Court.

Erasmus, Desiderius. 1989. *The Correspondence of Erasmus: Letters 1252 to 1355,* ed. Sir Roger Aubrey Baskerville Mynors. Toronto: University of Toronto Press.

Erasmus, Desiderius. 1988 [1501]. *Enchiridion Militis Christiani.* In *The Collected Works of Erasmus: Spiritualia,* ed. John W. O'Malley, vol. 66. Toronto: University of Toronto Press.

Erasmus, Desiderius. 1989. "The Tongue." In *The Collected Works of Erasmus,* ed. Elaine Fantham and Erika Rummell, vol. 29. Toronto: University of Toronto Press.

Erasmus, Desiderius. 1999. *Collected Works of Erasmus: Controversies.* Toronto: University of Toronto Press.

Farr, James. 2009. "Locke, 'Some Americans,' and the Discourse on 'Carolina.'" *Locke Studies* 9: 19–96.

Feldman, Noah. 2002. "The Intellectual Origins of the Establishment Clause." *New York University Law Review* 77: 346–428.

Field, Jonathan Beecher. 2007. "A Key for the Gate: Roger Williams, Parliament, and Providence." *The New England Quarterly* 80: 353–382.

Fish, Stanley. 1994. *There's No Such Thing as Free Speech, and It's a Good Thing Too.* Oxford: Oxford University Press.

Fish, Stanley. 1997. "Mission Impossible: Settling the Just Bounds between Church and State." *Columbia Law Review* 97: 2255–2333.

Fisher, Linford, J. Stanley Lemons, and Lucas Mason-Brown, eds. 2013. *Decoding Roger Williams: The Lost Essay of Rhode Island's Founding Father.* Houston, TX: Baylor University Press.

Fitzgerald, Timothy. 2007. *Discourse on Civility and Barbarity: A Critical History of Religion and Related Categories.* Oxford: Oxford University Press.

Forde, Steven. 2009. "The Charitable John Locke." *The Review of Politics* 71, no. 3: 428–458.

Forst, Rainer. 2003. "Toleration, Justice, and Reason." In *The Culture of Toleration in Diverse Societies,* ed. Catriona McKinnon and Dario Castiglione. Manchester: Manchester University Press, 71–85.

Forst, Rainer. 2013. *Toleration in Conflict: Past and Present.* Cambridge: Cambridge University Press.

Freud, Sigmund. 2004. *Civilization and Its Discontents.* London: Penguin.

Frost, Samantha. 2001. "Faking It: Hobbes's Thinking-Bodies and the Ethics of Dissimulation," *Political Theory* 29: 30–57.

F[urley], B[enjamin]. 1663. *The Worlds Honour Detected, and, for the Unprofitableness thereof, Rejected.* London.

Galeotti, Anna. 2002. *Toleration as Recognition.* Cambridge: Cambridge University Press.

Garsten, Bryan. 2006. *Saving Persuasion: A Defense of Rhetoric and Judgment.* Cambridge, MA: Harvard University Press.

Garsten, Bryan. Forthcoming. "'Always Watching Ourselves': Benjamin Constant on the Distinctive Character of Modern Enthusiasms." In *The Oxford Handbook of Rhetoric and Political Theory.* Oxford: Oxford University Press.

Gaustad, Edwin S. 2005. *Roger Williams.* Oxford: Oxford University Press.

Gillespie, George. 1644. *Wholesome Severity Reconciled with Christian Liberty.* London.

Gilpin, W. Clark. 1979. *The Millenarian Piety of Roger Williams.* Chicago: University of Chicago Press.

Goldie, Mark. 1991. "The Reception of Hobbes." In *The Cambridge History of Political Thought 1450–1700,* ed. J. H. Burns. Cambridge: Cambridge University Press, 589–615.

Goldie, Mark. 1991. "The Theory of Religious Intolerance in Restoration England." In *From Persecution to Toleration: The Glorious Revolution and Religion in England,* ed. Ole Peter Grell, Jonathan I. Israel, and Nicholas Tyacke. Oxford: Oxford University Press, 331–368.

Goldie, Mark. 1993. "John Locke, Jonas Proast, and Religious Toleration: 1688-1692." In *The Church of England: c. 1689-c. 1833,* eds. J. Walsh, C. Haydon, and S. Taylor. Cambridge: Cambridge University Press, 143-171.

Goldie, Mark, and Richard Popkin. 2006. "Scepticism, Priestcraft, and Toleration." In *The Cambridge History of Eighteenth-Century Political Thought,* ed. Mark Goldie and Robert Wokler. Cambridge: Cambridge University Press, 79–109.

Gray, John. 2000. "Pluralism and Toleration in Contemporary Political Philosophy." *Political Studies* 48: 323–333.

Gregory, Brad S. 2015. *The Unintended Reformation: How A Religious Revolution Secularized Society.* Cambridge, MA: Harvard University Press.

Grotius, Hugo. 1988 [1611]. *Meletius,* ed. and trans. G. H. M. Posthumus Meyjes. New York: E.J. Brill.

Guggisberg, Hans R. 1983. "The Defence of Religious Toleration and Religious Liberty in Early Modern Europe." *History of European Ideas* 4: 35–50.

Gutmann, Amy, and Dennis Thompson. 1990. "Moral Conflict and Political Consensus." *Ethics* 101: 64–88.

Gutmann, Amy, and Dennis Thompson. 1996. *Democracy and Disagreement.* Cambridge, MA: Belknap Press of Harvard University Press.

Habermas, Jürgen. 1991. *The Structural Transformation of the Public Sphere: An Inquiry into a Category of Bourgeois Society,* trans. Thomas McCarthy. Boston: MIT Press.

Haidt, Jonathan. 2012. *The Righteous Mind: Why Good People Are Divided by Politics and Religion.* New York: Pantheon Books.

Hall, Timothy. 1998. *Separating Church and State: Rogers Williams and Religious Liberty.* Champaign: University of Illinois Press.

Hefner, Robert W., ed. 1998. *Democratic Civility: The History and Cross-Cultural Possibility of a Modern Political Ideal.* New Brunswick, NJ: Transaction Publishers.

Hemphill, C. Dallett. 2002. *Bowing to Necessities: A History of Manners in America, 1620–1860.* Oxford: Oxford University Press.

Herbst, Susan. 2010. *Rude Democracy: Civility and Incivility in American Politics.* Philadelphia: Temple University Press.

Hertzberg, Benjamin J. 2005. "Religion's Influence on the Wall of Separation: Insights from Roger Williams, James Burgh, and Thomas Jefferson," *Sigma* 23: 1-21.

Heyd, David, ed. 1996. *Toleration: An Elusive Virtue.* Princeton, NJ: Princeton University Press.

Hill, Christopher. 1972. *The World Turned Upside Down.* New York: Penguin Books.

Hirschmann, Albert O. 1997. *The Passions and the Interests: Political Arguments for Capitalism before Its Triumph.* Princeton, NJ: Princeton University Press.

Hobbes, Thomas. 1840. *The English Works of Thomas Hobbes,* ed. William Molesworth, 8 vols. London: Bohn.

Hobbes, Thomas. 1990 [1681]. *Behemoth, or the Long Parliament,* ed. S. Holmes. Chicago: University of Chicago Press.

Hobbes, Thomas. 1994. *The Correspondence of Thomas Hobbes,* ed. Noel Malcolm. Oxford: Oxford University Press.

Hobbes, Thomas. 1994 [1651]. *Leviathan* (with select variants from the Latin Edition of 1668), ed. Edwin Curley. Indianapolis, IN: Hackett.

Hobbes, Thomas. 1998 [1642]. *De Cive* [On the citizen], ed. Richard Tuck and trans. Michael Silverthorne. Cambridge: Cambridge University Press.

Hobbes, Thomas. 2008 [1640]. *The Elements of Law, Natural and Politic: Human Nature and De Corpore Politico,* ed. J. C. A. Gaskin. Oxford: Oxford University Press.

Hobbes, Thomas. 2012 [1651]. *Leviathan,* ed. Noel Malcolm, 3 vols. Oxford: Oxford University Press.

Holmes, Stephen. 1995. "Gag Rules and the Politics of Omission." In *Passions and Constraint.* Chicago: University of Chicago Press, 202–235.

Hooker, Richard. 1981 [1594]. *Of the Laws of Ecclesiastical Polity.* Cambridge, MA: Harvard University Press.

Hsueh, Vicki. 2002. "Giving Orders: Theory and Practice in the *Fundamental Constitutions of Carolina.*" *Journal of the History of Ideas* 63: 425–446.

Idris, Murad. 2014. "Alternative Political Theologies: Erasmus on Peace, Speech, and Necessity." *Theory and Event* 17, no. 4.

Janz, Denis R., ed. 2008. *A Reformation Reader.* Minneapolis, MN: Fortress Press.

Jennings, Francis. 1975. *The Invasion of America: Indians, Colonialism, and the Cant of Conquest.* Chapel Hill: University of North Carolina Press.

Johnson, Alan E. 2015. *The First American Founder: Roger Williams and Freedom of Conscience.* Pittsburgh, PA: Philosophia.

Johnson, Samuel. 1755. *A Dictionary of the English Language,* 2 vols. London: W. Strahan.

Johnston, David. 1986. *The Rhetoric of Leviathan: Thomas Hobbes and the Politics of Cultural Transformation.* Princeton, NJ: Princeton University Press.

Kahn, Victoria. 1985. *Rhetoric, Prudence and Skepticism in the Renaissance.* Ithaca, NY: Cornell University Press.

Kant, Immanuel. 1983 [1797]. "The Metaphysics of Morals, Part II: The Metaphysical Principles of Virtue." In *Ethical Philosophy*, trans. James W. Ellington. Indianapolis, IN: Hackett.

Kaplan, Benjamin. 1995. *Calvinists and Libertines: Confession and Community in Utrecht, 1578–1620.* Oxford: Clarendon Press.

Kaplan, Benjamin. 2007. *Divided By Faith: Religious Conflict and the Practice of Toleration in Early Modern Europe.* Cambridge, MA: Belknap Press of Harvard University Press.

Kasson, John. 1991. *Rudeness and Civility: Manners in Nineteenth-Century Urban America.* New York: Hill and Wang.

Kennedy, Randall. 1998. "The State of the Debate: The Case against Civility." *The American Prospect* 41 (December 19), 84–90.

Kepel, Gilles. 1994. *The Revenge of God: The Resurgence of Islam, Christianity and Judaism in the Modern World.* University Park: Pennsylvania State University Press.

Kingwell, Mark. 1993. "Politics and Polite Society in the Scottish Enlightenment." *Historical Reflections* 19, no. 3: 363–387.

Kingwell, Mark. 2007. *A Civil Tongue: Justice, Dialogue, and the Politics of Pluralism.* University Park: Pennsylvania State University Press.

Klein, Lawrence. 1989. "Liberty, Manners, and Politeness in Early Eighteenth-Century England." *The Historical Journal* 32: 583–605.

Klein, Lawrence. 1993. "Shaftesbury, Politeness, and the Politics of Religion." In *Political Discourse in Early Modern Britain,* ed. Nicholas Phillipson and Quentin Skinner. Cambridge: Cambridge University Press, 283–302.

Klein, Lawrence. 1996. "Coffeehouse Civility, 1660–1714: An Aspect of Post-Courtly Culture in England." *Huntington Library Quarterly* 59: 30–51.

Klein, Lawrence. 2004. *Shaftesbury and the Culture of Politeness: Moral Discourse and Cultural Politics in Early Eighteenth-Century England.* Cambridge: Cambridge University Press.

Knights, Mark. 2001. "'Meer Religion' and the 'Church-State' of Restoration England: The Impact and Ideology of James II's Declarations of Indulgence." In *A Nation Transformed: England after the Restoration,* ed. Alan Houston and Steve Pincus. Cambridge: Cambridge University Press.

Kraynak, Robert. 1980. "John Locke: From Absolutism to Toleration." *American Political Science Review* 74: 53–69.

Kuntz, Marion Leathers. 1998. "The Concept of Toleration in the *Colloquium Heptaplomeres* of Jean Bodin." In *Beyond the Persecuting Society: Religious Toleration before the Enlightenment,* eds. John C. Laursen and Cary J. Nederman. Philadelphia: University of Pennsylvania Press, 125–144.

Lake, Peter. 1998. "Anti-Popery: The Structure of a Prejudice." In *Conflict in Early Stuart England,* ed. Richard Cust and Ann Hughes. London: Longman, 72–106.

Lake, Peter, and Steve Pincus. 2006. "Re-Thinking the Public Sphere in Early Modern England." *Journal of British Studies* 45, no. 2: 270–292.

Lamb, Robert and Benjamin Thompson. 2009. "The Meaning of Charity in Locke's Political Thought," *European Journal of Political Theory* 8, no. 2: 229–252.

Lamont, William. 1986. "Pamphleteering, Protestant Consensus and the English Revolution." In *Freedom and the English Revolution: Essays in History and Literature,* ed. R. C. Richardson and G. M. Ridden. Manchester: Manchester University Press.

Landemore, Hélène. 2013. "On Minimal Deliberation, Partisan Activism, and Teaching People How to Disagree." *Critical Review* 25: 210–225.

Langton, Rae. 2012. "Beyond Belief: Pragmatics in Hate Speech and Pornography." In *Speech and Harm,* ed. I. Maitra and M. McGowan. Oxford: Oxford University Press, 72–93.

Lardner, Ring. 1920. *The Young Immigrunts.* Indianapolis, IN: Bobbs-Merrill.

Laursen, John Christian, and Cary J. Nederman. 1998. *Beyond the Persecuting Society.* Philadelphia: University of Pennsylvania Press.

Lepore, Jill. 1999. *The Name of War: King Philip's War and the Origins of American Identity.* New York: Vintage.

Levy, Jacob T. 2010. "Multicultural Manners." In *The Plural States of Recognition,* ed. Michael Seymour. London: Palgrave Press, 61–77.

Levy, Jacob T. 2014. *Rationalism, Pluralism, and Freedom.* Oxford: Oxford University Press.

Lilla, Mark. 2007. *The Stillborn God: Religion, Politics, and the Modern West.* New York: Alfred A. Knopf.

Lloyd, S.A. 1992. *Ideals as Interests in Hobbes's Leviathan: The Power of Mind over Matter.* Cambridge: Cambridge University Press.

Locke, John. 1824. "Reply to the Bishop of Worcester's Answer to His Second Letter." In *The Works of John Locke,* vol. 3. London: Rivington.

Locke, John. 1824. "A Second Letter Concerning Toleration" [1690] and "A Third Letter for Toleration" [1692]. In *The Works of John Locke,* vol. 5. London: Rivington.

Locke, John. 1824 [1695]. "A Second Vindication of the *Reasonableness of Christianity.*" In *The Works of John Locke,* vol. 6. London: Rivington.

Locke, John. 1976–1982. *The Correspondence of John Locke,* ed. E. S. De Beer. Oxford: Clarendon Press.

Locke, John. 1988 [1689]. *The Two Treatises of Government,* ed. P. Laslett. Cambridge: Cambridge University Press.

Locke, John. 1990. *Locke: Political Essays,* ed. Mark Goldie. Cambridge: Cambridge University Press.

Locke, John. 1996. *Some Thoughts Concerning Education and Of the Conduct of the Understanding,* ed. Ruth Grant and Nathan Tarcov. Indianapolis, IN: Hackett.

Locke, John. 2010. *Locke on Toleration,* ed. Richard Vernon and trans. Michael Silverthorne. Cambridge: Cambridge University Press.

Locke, John. 2010. "A Letter Concerning Toleration" [1689] and "An Essay Concerning Toleration" [1667]. In *A Letter Concerning Toleration and Other Writings,* ed. Mark Goldie. Indianapolis, IN: Liberty Fund.

Luther, Martin. 1956 [1534]. *The Reformation Writings of Martin Luther,* ed. and trans. Bertram Lee-Woolf. London: Lutterworth Press.

Luther, Martin. 1970. *Three Treatises,* trans. W. A. Lambert. Minneapolis, MN: Fortress Press.

Luther, Martin. 1997 [1520]. "An Argument in Defense of All the Articles of Dr Martin Luther Wrongly Condemned in the Roman Bull." In *The Works of Martin Luther*, vol. 3 (Albany, NY: Books for the Ages).

Lutz, Donald S., ed. 1998. *Colonial Origins of the American Constitution: A Documentary History.* Indianapolis, IN: Liberty Fund.

Macaulay, Thomas Babington. 1856. *The History of England from the Ascension of James the Second,* vol. 1. Philadelphia: E.H. Butler & Co.

Macpherson, C. B. 1962. *The Political Theory of Possessive Individualism: Hobbes to Locke.* Oxford: Clarendon Press.

Mahmood, Saba. 2015. *Religious Difference in a Secular Age: A Minority Report.* Princeton, NJ: Princeton University Press.

Maisel, Louis Sandy. 2012. "The Negative Consequences of Uncivil Political Discourse." *PS: Political Science & Politics* 45: 405–411.

Malcolm, Noel. 2002. *Aspects of Hobbes.* Oxford: Clarendon Press.

Maloy, J. S. 2011. "The First Machiavellian Moment in America." *American Journal of Political Science* 55: 450–462.

March, Andrew. 2012. "Speech and the Sacred: Does the Defense of Free Speech Rest on a Mistake about Religion?" *Political Theory* 40: 319–346.

Marshall, John. 1985. "The Ecclesiology of the Latitude-men, 1660–1689: Stillingfleet, Tillotson, and 'Hobbism.'" *Journal of Ecclesiological History* 36, no. 3: 407–427.

Marshall, John. 1994. *John Locke: Resistance, Religion and Responsibility.* Cambridge: Cambridge University Press.

Marshall, John. 2006. *John Locke, Toleration, and Early Enlightenment Culture.* Cambridge: Cambridge University Press.

Martin, Judith. 1996. *Miss Manners Rescues Civilization: From Sexual Harassment, Frivolous Lawsuits, Dissing and Other Lapses of Civility.* New York: Crown.

Martinich, A. P. 2005. *Hobbes.* London: Routledge.

Matar, Nabil I. 1993. "John Locke and the Jews." *Journal of Ecclesiastical History* 44: 57–62.

Mather, Cotton. 1853. *Magnalia Christi Americana,* ed. T. Robbins, 2 vols. Hartford.

Mather, Richard. 1643. *Church-Government and Church-Covenant Discussed.* London.

Matsuda, Mari J. 1993. *Words That Wound: Critical Race Theory, Assaultive Speech, and the First Amendment.* Boulder, CO: Westview Press.

McClure, Kirstie. 1990. "Difference, Diversity, and the Limits of Toleration." *Political Theory* 18: 361–391.

McConnell, Michael W. 1992. "America's First 'Hate Speech' Regulation." *Constitutional Comment* 9: 17–23.

Mehta, Uday Singh. 1992. *The Anxiety of Freedom: Imagination and Individuality in Locke's Political Thought.* Ithaca, NY: Cornell University Press.

Mehta, Uday Singh. 1999. *Liberalism and Empire.* Chicago: University of Chicago Press.

Miller, Perry. 1953. *Roger Williams: His Contribution to the American Tradition.* Indianapolis, IN: Bobbs-Merrill.

Milton, J. R. 1990. "John Locke and the *Fundamental Constitutions of Carolina.*" *Locke Newsletter* 21: 111–133.

Milton, J. R., and Milton, Philip. 2010. Introduction to *An Essay Concerning Toleration and Other Writings on Law and Politics,* by John Locke. Oxford: Oxford University Press.

Milton, John. 1848 [1654]. "The Second Defence of the People of England." In *The Prose Works of John Milton.* London: Bohn.

Milton, John. 1959 [1643]. "Of Education." In *Complete Prose Works,* ed. Ernest Sirluck, vol. 2. New Haven, CT: Yale University Press.

Milton, John. 1971 [1670]. *History of Britain.* In *Complete Prose Works,* ed. French Fogle and Max Patrick, vol. 5. New Haven, CT: Yale University Press.

Milton, John. 1981 [1644]. *Areopagitica: A Speech of Mr. John Milton for the liberty of unlicensed printing to the Parliament of England.* Cambridge: Cambridge University Press.

Milton, John. 2005 [1667]. *Paradise Lost.* Oxford: Oxford University Press.

Moloney, Pat. 2011. "Hobbes, Savagery, and International Anarchy." *American Political Science Review* 105: 189–204.

Moore, LeRoy. 1963. "Roger Williams and the Historians." *Church History* 32: 432–451.

Morgan, Edmund S. 1967. *Roger Williams: The Church and the State.* New York: Harcourt.

Muñoz, Vincent P. 2006. "The Original Meaning of the Establishment Clause and the Impossibility of Its Incorporation." *Journal of Constitutional Law* 8: 585–639.

Murphy, Andrew. 1997. "Tolerance, Toleration, and the Liberal Tradition." *Polity* 29, no. 4: 593–623.

Murphy, Andrew. 2001. *Conscience and Community: Revisiting Toleration and Religious Dissent in Early Modern England and America.* University Park: Pennsylvania State University Press.

Mutz, Diana. *In-Your-Face Politics: The Consequences of Uncivil Media.* Princeton, NJ: Princeton University Press, 2015.

Nagel, Thomas. 1995. "Personal Rights and Public Space," *Philosophy & Public Affairs* 24, no. 2: 83–107.

Nagel, Thomas. 1998. "Concealment and Exposure," *Philosophy & Public Affairs* 27, no. 1: 3–30.

Nauta, Lodi. 2002. "Hobbes on Religion and the Church between the *Elements of Law* and *Leviathan:* A Dramatic Change of Direction?" *Journal of the History of Ideas* 63: 577–598.

Nelson, Eric. 2010. *The Hebrew Republic: Jewish Sources and the Transformation of European Political Thought.* Cambridge, MA: Harvard University Press.

Nussbaum, Martha. 2008. "The First Founder: The American Revolution of Roger Williams." *New Republic* (September 10), https://newrepublic.com/article/61558/the-first-founder.

Nussbaum, Martha. 2008. *Liberty of Conscience: In Defense of America's Tradition of Religious Equality.* New York: Basic Books.

Nussbaum, Martha. 2012. *The New Religious Intolerance: Overcoming the Politics of Fear in an Anxious Age.* Cambridge: Belknap Press of Harvard University Press.

Oakeshott, Michael. 1975. *Hobbes on Civil Association.* Indianapolis, IN: Liberty Fund.

Orwin, Clifford. 2011. "Civility," in *Endangered Virtues*, ed. P. Berkowitz. Stanford, CA: Stanford University. http://www.hoover.org/research/civility.

Owen, J. Judd. 2005. "The Tolerant *Leviathan:* Hobbes and the Paradox of Liberalism." *Polity* 37, no. 1: 120–148.

Pagden, Anthony. 1986. *The Fall of Natural Man: The American Indian and the Origins of Comparative Ethnology.* Cambridge: Cambridge University Press.

Paine, Thomas. 1995. *Political Writings.* Cambridge: Cambridge University Press.

Parkin, Jon. 2007. *Taming the Leviathan: The Reception of the Political and Religious Ideas of Thomas Hobbes in England, 1640–1700.* Cambridge: Cambridge University Press.

Parkin, Jon. 2013. "Toleration." In *The Oxford Handbook of British Philosophy in the Seventeenth Century,* ed. Peter R. Anstey. Oxford: Oxford University Press.

Parrington, Vernon. 1987. *Main Currents in American Thought: The Colonial Mind, 1620–1800.* Norman: University of Oklahoma Press.

Patterson, Annabel. 1997. *Early Modern Liberalism.* Cambridge: Cambridge University Press.

Pearce, Roy Harvey. 1952. "The 'Ruines of Mankind': The Indian and the Puritan Mind." *Journal of the History of Ideas* 13: 200–217.

Peltonen, Markku. 2006. *The Duel in Early Modern England: Civility, Politeness and Honour.* Cambridge: Cambridge University Press.

Peltonen, Markku. 2013. *Rhetoric, Politics and Popularity in Pre-Revolutionary England.* Cambridge: Cambridge University Press.

Penn, William. 1995 [1682]. "The Great Law of Pennsylvania." In *Church and State in the Modern Age: A Documentary History,* ed. J. F. Maclear. Oxford: Oxford University Press.

Perkins, William. 1631. "The Art of Prophecying." In *The Works of that Famous and Worthy Minister of Christ in the University of Cambridge, M. William Perkins.* London: John Leggatt.

Pestana, Carla Gardina. 1991. *Quakers and Baptists in Colonial Massachusetts.* Cambridge: Cambridge University Press.

Pestana, Carla Gardina. 1993. "The Quaker Executions as Myth and History." *The Journal of American History* 80, no. 2: 441–469.

Pettit, Philip. 1999. *Republicanism: A Theory of Freedom and Government.* Oxford: Oxford University Press.

Pierce, Helen. 2008. *Unseemly Pictures: Graphic Satire and Politics in Early Modern England.* New Haven, CT: Yale University Press.

Pincus, Steve. 1998. "Neither Machiavellian Moment nor Possessive Individualism: Commercial Society and the Defenders of the English Commonwealth." *The American Historical Review* 103: 705–736.

Plato. 1961. *The Statesman,* trans. J. B. Skemp. London: Routledge.

Plato. 1992. *Republic,* trans. G. M. A. Grube. Indianapolis, IN: Hackett.

Plato. 1998. "Euthyphro." In *Four Texts on Socrates,* ed. T. G. West and G. S. West. Ithaca, NY: Cornell University Press.

Pocock, J.G.A. 1981. "Virtues, Rights, and Manners: A Model for Historians of Political Thought," *Political Theory* 9, no. 3: 353–368

Pocock, J. G. A. 1983. "Cambridge Paradigms and Scotch Philosophers: A Study of the Relations between the Civic Humanist and the Civil Jurisprudential Interpretation of Eighteenth-Century Social Thought." In *Wealth and Virtue,* ed. Istvan Hont and Michael Ignatieff. Cambridge: Cambridge University Press, 235–252.

Pocock, J. G. A. 1985. *Virtue, Commerce, and History.* Cambridge: Cambridge University Press.

Priestley, Joseph. 1993. *Political Writings,* ed. Peter Miller. Cambridge: Cambridge University Press.

Putnam, Robert. 2001. *Bowling Alone: The Collapse and Revival of American Community.* New York: Simon and Schuster.

Rawls, John. 1971. *A Theory of Justice.* Cambridge, MA: Harvard University Press.

Rawls, John. 1996. *Political Liberalism.* New York: Columbia University Press.

Reeve, L. J. 2003. *Charles I and the Road to Personal Rule.* Cambridge: Cambridge University Press.

Remer, Gary. 1994. "Dialogues of Toleration: Erasmus and Bodin," *The Review of Politics* 56, no. 2: 305–336.

Remer, Gary. 1996. *Humanism and the Rhetoric of Toleration.* University Park: Pennsylvania State University Press.

Reynolds, Noel and Arlene Saxonhouse. 1996. *Thomas Hobbes: Three Discourses.* Chicago: University of Chicago Press.

Roover, Jakob De, and S. N. Balagangadhara. 2008. "John Locke, Christian Liberty, and the Predicament of Liberal Toleration." *Political Theory* 36: 523–549.

Roper, Lyndal. 2016. *Martin Luther: Renegade and Prophet.* London: Bodley Head.

Rorty, Richard. 1983. "Method, Social Science, and Social Hope." *The Conse-quences of Pragmatism.* Minneapolis: University of Minnesota Press. 191–210.

Rorty, Richard. 1987. "Science as Solidarity." *The Rhetoric of the Human Sciences,* ed. J. S. Nelson, A. Megill, and D. N. McCloskey. Madison: University of Wisconsin Press, 38–52.

Rouner, Leroy, ed. 2000. *Civility.* Notre Dame, IN: University of Notre Dame Press.

Rousseau, Jean-Jacques. 1997. *Rousseau: The Social Contract and Other Later Political Writings,* ed. and trans. Victor Gourevitch. Cambridge: Cambridge University Press.

Rupp, E. Gordon, and Philip S. Watson, eds. 1969. *Luther and Erasmus: Free Will and Salvation.* Louisville, KY: Westminster John Knox Press.

Ryan, Alan. 1983. "Hobbes, Toleration and the Inner Life." In *The Nature of Political Theory*, ed. D. Miller and L. Siedentop. Princeton, NJ: Princeton University Press, 197–218.

Ryan, Alan. 1988. "A More Tolerant Hobbes?" In *Justifying Toleration: Conceptual and Historical Perspectives,* ed. Susan Mendus. Cambridge: Cambridge University Press, 37–59.

Ryan, Mary P. 1997. *Civic Wars: Democracy and Public Life in the American City during the Nineteenth Century.* Berkeley: University of California Press.

Sabl, Andrew. 2005. "Virtue for Pluralists." *Journal of Moral Philosophy* 2, no. 2: 207–235.

Sandel, Michael. 1998. *Liberalism and the Limits of Justice.* Cambridge: Cambridge University Press.

Sandel, Michael. 2005. "The Problem with Civility." In *The Public Philosophy: Essays on Morality in Politics.* Cambridge, MA: Harvard University Press.

Sarat, Austin, ed. 2014. *Civility, Legality, and Justice in America.* Cambridge: Cambridge University Press.

Scanlon, Thomas. 1996. "The Difficulty of Tolerance." In *Toleration: An Elusive Virtue,* ed. David Heyd. Princeton, NJ: Princeton University Press, 226–239.

Scherer, Matthew. 2013. *Beyond Church and State: Democracy, Secularism, and Conversion.* Cambridge: Cambridge University Press.

Schwartz, Stuart. 2008. *All Can Be Saved: Religious Tolerance and Salvation in the Iberian Atlantic World.* New Haven, CT: Yale University Press.

Scudéry, Madeleine de. 1683. *Conversations upon many subjects,* trans. Ferrand Spence. London.

Selznick, Philip. 1994. *The Moral Commonwealth: Social Theory and the Promise of Community.* Berkeley: University of California Press.

Shagan, Ethan H. 2011. *The Rule of Moderation: Violence, Religion and the Politics of Restraint in Early Modern England.* Cambridge: Cambridge University Press.

Sharp, Andrew, ed. 1998. *The English Levellers.* Cambridge: Cambridge University Press.

Shea, Daniel M., and Alex Sproveri. 2012. "The Rise and Fall of Nasty Politics in America." *PS: Political Science & Politics* 45: 416–421.

Sheehan, Bernard. 1980. *Savagism and Civility: Indians and Englishmen in Colonial Virginia.* Cambridge: Cambridge University Press.

Shils, Edward. 1997. *The Virtue of Civility: Selected Essays on Liberalism, Tradition, and Civil Society.* Indianapolis, IN: Liberty Fund.

Shklar, Judith. 1984. *Ordinary Vices.* Cambridge, MA: Harvard University Press.

Simpson, Alan. 1956. "How Democratic Was Roger Williams?" *The William and Mary Quarterly* 13: 53–67.

Sinopoli, Richard. 1995. "Thick-Skinned Liberalism: Redefining Civility." *American Political Science Review* 89, no. 3: 612–620.

Sistare, Christine T., ed. 2004. *Civility and Its Discontents: Civic Virtue, Toleration, and Cultural Fragmentation.* Lawrence: University Press of Kansas.

Skinner, Quentin. 1996. *Reason and Rhetoric in the Philosophy of Hobbes.* Cambridge: Cambridge University Press.

Skinner, Quentin. 2002. *Visions of Politics.* 3 vols. Cambridge: Cambridge University Press.

Skinner, Quentin. 2013. "Hobbes and the Social Control of Unsociability." In *The Oxford Handbook of Thomas Hobbes,* ed. A. P. Martinich and Kinch Hoekstra. Oxford: Oxford University Press.

Slomp, Gabriella. 2007. "Hobbes on Glory and Civil Strife." In *The Cambridge Companion to Hobbes's* Leviathan, ed. Patricia Springborg. Cambridge: Cambridge University Press, 181–198.

Smith, Steven B. 2013. *Political Philosophy.* New Haven, CT: Yale University Press.

Sommerville, Johann. 2004. "Hobbes and Independency." *Rivista di storia della filosofia* 21: 155–173.

Sommerville, Johann. 2007. "Leviathan and its Anglican Context." In *The Cambridge Companion to Hobbes's* Leviathan, ed. Patricia Springborg. Cambridge: Cambridge University Press, 358–374.

Sowerby, Scott. 2013. *Making Toleration: The Repealers and the Glorious Revolution.* Cambridge, MA: Harvard University Press.

Springborg, Patricia. 2015. "Hobbes, Donne and the Virginia Company: *Terra Nullius* and 'The Bulimia of Dominium.'" *History of Political Thought* 36, no. 1: 113–164.

Stanton, Timothy. 2006. "Locke and the Politics and Theology of Toleration." *Political Studies* 54: 84–102.

Stern, Jessica R. 2011. "A *Key* into *The Bloudy Tenent of Persecution:* Roger Williams, the Pequot War, and the Origins of Toleration in America." *Early American Studies* 9: 576–616.

Stone, Lawrence. 2002. *The Causes of the English Revolution 1529–1642.* New York: Routledge.

Strachan, J. Cherie, and Michael R. Wolf. 2012. "Political Civility." *PS: Political Science & Politics* 45, no. 3: 401–404.

Strauss, Leo. 1952. *The Political Philosophy of Hobbes, Its Basis and Genesis*. Chicago: University of Chicago Press.

Strauss, Leo. 1965. *Natural Right and History*. Chicago: University of Chicago Press.

Sue, Derald Wing. 2010. *Microaggressions in Everyday Life: Race, Gender, and Sexual Orientation*. Hoboken, NJ: John Wiley & Sons.

Suetonius. 1889 [c. 121 CE]. *The Lives of the Twelve Caesars*, trans. Alexander Thompson. Philadelphia: Gebbie and Co.

Szabari, Antónia. 2006. "The Scandal of Religion: Luther and Public Speech in the Reformation." In *Political Theologies: Public Religions in a Post-Secular World*, ed. Hent de Vries and Lawrence E. Sullivan. New York: Fordham University Press, 122–136.

Tacitus. 1942 [c. 109 CE]. *The Annals*. In *The Complete Works of Tacitus*, eds. Alfred John Church, William Jackson Brodribb, and Sara Bryant, vol. 1. New York: Random House.

Talbot, Ann. 2010. *'The Great Ocean of Knowledge': The Influence of Travel Literature on the Work of John Locke*. London: Brill Publishing.

Taylor, Charles. 1992. *Multiculturalism and "The Politics of Recognition,"* ed. Amy Gutmann. Princeton, NJ: Princeton University Press.

Taylor, Jeremy. 1647. *A Discourse on the Liberty of Prophesying*. London: R. Royston.

Thapar, Romila, trans. 1997. *Asoka and the Decline of the Mauryas*. Delhi: Oxford University Press.

Tinder, Glenn. 1995. *Tolerance and Community*. Columbia: University of Missouri Press.

Tinker, George E. 1993. *Missionary Conquest: The Gospel and Native American Cultural Genocide*. Minneapolis, MN: Augsburg Press.

Tuck, Richard. 1985. "Warrender's *De Cive*." *Political Studies* 33: 308–315.

Tuck, Richard. 1990. "Hobbes and Locke on Toleration." In *Thomas Hobbes and Political Theory*, ed. Mary Dietz. Lawrence: University Press of Kansas, 153–171.

Tuck, Richard. 2000. *The Rights of War and Peace: Political Thought and the International Order from Grotius to Kant*. Oxford: Oxford University Press.

Tuck, Richard. 2004. "The Utopianism of Leviathan." In *Leviathan after 350 Years*, ed. Tom Sorrell and Luc Foisneau. Oxford: Oxford University Press.

Tuckness, Alex. 2002. "Rethinking the Intolerant Locke." *American Journal of Political Science* 46: 288–298.

Tully, James. 1988. "Governing Conduct." In *Conscience and Casuistry in Early Modern Europe*, ed. Edmund Leites. Cambridge: Cambridge University Press, 12–71.

Tully, James. 1995. *Strange Multiplicity: Constitutionalism in an Age of Diversity.* Cambridge: Cambridge University Press.

Turner, Jack. 2011. "John Locke, Christian Mission, and Colonial America." *Modern Intellectual History* 8, no. 2: 267–297.

Urbinati, Nadia. 2014. "Half-Toleration: Concordia and the Limits of Dialogue." In *Boundaries of Toleration,* ed. Alfred Stepan and Charles Taylor. New York: Columbia University Press, 130–169.

Verkamp, Bernard J. 1977. *The Indifferent Mean: Adiaphorism in the English Reformation to 1554.* Athens: Ohio University Press.

Vienne-Guerrin, N., ed. 2012. *The Unruly Tongue in Early Modern England: Three Treatises.* Madison, NJ: Fairleigh Dickinson University Press.

Vincent, Nathaniel. 1675. *The Morning-Exercise against Popery. Or, the Principal Errors of the Church of Rome Detected and Confuted.* London.

Waldron, Jeremy. 1988. "Locke: Toleration and the Rationality of Persecution." In *Justifying Toleration: Conceptual and Historical Approaches,* ed. Susan Mendus. Cambridge: Cambridge University Press, 61–86.

Waldron, Jeremy. 1999. *Law and Disagreement.* Oxford: Clarendon Press.

Waldron, Jeremy. 2002. *God, Locke and Equality.* Cambridge: Cambridge University Press.

Waldron, Jeremy. 2012. *Dignity, Rank, and Rights,* ed. Meir Dan-Cohen. Oxford: Oxford University Press.

Waldron, Jeremy. 2012. *The Harm in Hate Speech.* Cambridge, MA: Harvard University Press.

Walsham, Alexandra. 1999. *Church Papists: Catholicism, Conformity and Confessional Polemic in Early Modern England.* Woodbridge: The Boydell Press.

Walsham, Alexandra. 2006. *Charitable Hatred: Tolerance and Intolerance in England, 1500–1700.* Manchester: Manchester University Press.

Walzer, Michael. 1965. *The Revolution of the Saints: A Study in the Origins of Revolutionary Politics.* Cambridge, MA: Harvard University Press.

Walzer, Michael. 1974. "Civility and Civic Virtue in Contemporary America." *Social Research* 41: 593–611.

Walzer, Michael. 1999. *On Toleration.* New Haven, CT: Yale University Press.

Wase, Christopher. 1662. *Dictionarium Minus: A Compendious Dictionary, English-Latin and Latin-English.* London.

Watson, Thomas. 1829. *Discourses upon Important and Interesting Subjects: Being the Select Works of Thomas Watson.* 2 vols. Edinburgh.

White, Andrew. 2014. *Digital Media and Society: Transforming Economics, Politics and Social Practices.* New York: Palgrave Macmillan Press.

Whitgift, John. 1852. *The Works of John Whitgift.* Cambridge: Cambridge University Press.

Whitman, James Q. 1999. "Enforcing Civility and Respect: Three Societies." *The Yale Law Journal* 109: 1279–1398.

Wilhelm, Anthony. 1999. "Good Fences and Good Neighbors: John Locke's Positive Doctrine of Toleration." *Political Research Quarterly* 52: 145–166.

Williams, Melissa, and Jeremy Waldron, eds. 2008. *Toleration and Its Limits*. New York: New York University Press.

Williams, Roger. 1963 [1644]. *The Bloody Tenent of Persecution for Cause of Conscience*. In *The Complete Writings of Roger Williams*, vol. 3. New York: Russell & Russell.

Williams, Roger. 1963 [1652]. *The Bloody Tenent Yet More Bloody*. In *The Complete Writings of Roger Williams*, vol. 4. New York: Russell & Russell.

Williams, Roger. 1963 [1645]. "Christenings Make Not Christians." In *The Complete Writings of Roger Williams*, vol. 7. New York: Russell & Russell.

Williams, Roger. 1963 [1676]. *George Fox Digg'd Out His Burrowes*. In *The Complete Writings of Roger Williams*, vol. 5. New York: Russell & Russell.

Williams, Roger. 1963 [1652]. "The Examiner Defended in a Fair and Sober answer to the Two and Twenty Questions which Lately Examined the Author of 'Zeal Examined.'" In *The Complete Writings of Roger Williams*, vol. 7. New York: Russell & Russell.

Williams, Roger. 1963 [1652]. *The Hireling Ministry None of Christ's*. In *The Complete Writings of Roger Williams*, vol. 7. New York: Russell & Russell.

Williams, Roger. 1963 [1643]. *A Key into the Language of America*. In *The Complete Writings of Roger Williams*, ed. Perry Miller, vol. 1. New York: Russell & Russell.

Williams, Roger. 1963 [1644]. "Mr Cotton's letter lately printed, examined and answered." In *The Complete Writings of Roger Williams*, vol. 1. New York: Russell & Russell.

Williams, Roger. 1988. *The Correspondence of Roger Williams*, ed. G. LaFantasie, 2 vols. Hanover, NH: Brown University Press.

Wootton, David. 1993. "Introduction." In *Locke: Political Writings*. Indianapolis, IN: Hackett.

Worden, Blair. 1984. "Toleration and the Cromwellian Protectorate." In *Persecution and Toleration*, ed. W. J. Sheils. Oxford: Blackwell.

Yates, John. 1626. *Ibis Ad Caesarem. Or A Submissive Appearance before Caesar in Answer to Mr Mountagues Appeale, in the Points of Arminianisme and Popery, Maintained and Defended by Him, against the Doctrine of the Church of England*. London.

Young, Iris Marion. 2011. *Justice and the Politics of Difference*. Princeton, NJ: Princeton University Press.

Zagorin, Perez. 2003. *How the Idea of Religious Toleration Came to the West*. Princeton, NJ: Princeton University Press.

Zuckert, Michael. 2002. *Launching Liberalism: On Lockean Political Philosophy.* Lawrence: University Press of Kansas.

Zuolo, Federico. 2013. "Frontiers of Toleration and Respect: Non-Moral Approaches and Inter-Group Relations." *European Journal of Political Theory* 12: 219–222.

ACKNOWLEDGMENTS

I have incurred many debts in writing this book. First and foremost, I am grateful to my advisors at Yale—Bryan Garsten, Steven Smith, Karuna Mantena, and Jim Whitman. My greatest debt is to my teacher and friend, Bryan Garsten, who has been a constant source of guidance, support, and inspiration. I am also lucky to have had wonderful mentors and colleagues outside of Yale, without whom this book would not have been possible. Upon arriving in Cambridge in 2006 from the University of Chicago, where I had been taught to ask only fundamental questions and read only fundamental texts, I had a vague notion that the history of political thought might be worth studying and that Cambridge might not be a bad place to start. In the course of that year, I had the remarkable good fortune to be taught by Quentin Skinner, Mark Goldie, John Dunn, and Annabel Brett; I could have asked for no better introduction. I am grateful to these scholars for setting me on this path and for their continued support. To Quentin, I owe a special debt for giving me the chance to become first a student, then a scholar, of Hobbes (who himself was a student of Rabelais, not Descartes). This I can never repay.

I have benefited immensely from conversations with colleagues at Yale, Columbia, the University of Toronto, and now Oxford. I am particularly indebted to a number of brilliant scholars and perspicacious critics who have been generous with their comments, cautions, and insights throughout: Eric Adler, Aisha Ahmad, Catherine Arnold, Ronald Beiner, Chris Beneke, Jane Calvert, Joseph Carens, Simone Chambers, Aurelian Craiutu, Jeffrey Collins, Meredith Edwards-Libling, Stefan Eich, Linford Fisher, Shawn Fraistat, Phil Gorski, Christopher Grenda, Evan Haefeli, Ben Hertzberg, Kinch Hoekstra, Murad Idris, Calvert Jones, Daniel Lee, Andrew March, Clifton

Mark, Ruth Marshall, David Mayhew, Andrew Murphy, Jennifer Nedelsky, Eric Nelson, John Oksanish, James O'Leary, Jon Parkin, Philip Pettit, Steve Pincus, Laura Rabinowitz, Oliver Roeder, Lyndal Roper, Alan Ryan, Andrew Sabl, Taylor Seymour, Ezra Siller, Nathan Tarcov, Megan Wachspress, Jeremy Waldron, Melissa Williams, Rebecca Woods, Paul Yowell, and Michael Zuckert. I must also thank my wonderful research assistants: Claire Sabel, Megan Dias, Megan Spurrell, and Taylor Putnam. A special thanks is due to the indomitable Emma Planinc, without whom this book's regeneration would have been impossible, and to John Kulka, Michael Aronson, and Harvard University Press. I am also greatly indebted to the Press's two anonymous reviewers, who provided extensive and invaluable feedback.

The research was generously funded at different stages by the Connaught New Researcher Award Program and the Departments of Political Science at the University of Toronto and the University of Toronto Mississauga; the Fox International Fellowship program, the Department of Political Science, and the MacMillan Center at Yale University; the Humane Studies Fellowship and the Institute for Humane Studies; the Society of Fellows in the Humanities at Columbia University; and Sidney Sussex College, Cambridge. Audiences at Yale, Oxford, Cambridge, Columbia, EHESS, Harvard, Oxford, Princeton, UC-Davis, and the University of Toronto, and at the APSA, MPSA, SPSA, and NPSA annual meetings also provided helpful feedback. Chapters 2, 3, and 4 significantly expand upon arguments I have made elsewhere. I have cited these earlier arguments and publications appropriately throughout.

Finally, I owe everything and more to my family—to their love and support, to their intelligence and ambition, and always, especially, to their humor. For my parents, Mary and Adrian, to whom I dedicate this baggy beast, my Behemoth, it is still but the smallest token of my boundless gratitude. If I err herein, it is because like Locke, I am short-sighted: "We see but in part, and we know but in part, and therefore it is no wonder we conclude not right from our partial views."

INDEX